WHAT OTHERS ARE SAYING ABOUT
PREPAREDNESS PRINCIPLES

"Between the covers of this book are some excellent guidelines and ideas written in a fresh new style by Barbara Salsbury. She points out the steps that families can take that will provide them with the knowledge and security needed in times of stress. Preparedness on the family level is of much value to local and state emergency management."

—*A. Deon Harris, director of emergency services, graduate of the National Emergency Training Center, president of Regional 1 United States Civil Defense Council*

"Common sense alone is not enough, as Barbara Salsbury points out. Preparedness at any level requires knowledge and skills. *Preparedness Principles* captures a reader's interest from the start. It is clear that Barbara has lived the principles she writes about. She has studied and tested the information she shares. Her wisdom is laid out in a concise and practical way, and her information about preparedness can be applied and customized to any situation.

"This book outlines clearly how to prepare before disasters hit. Her step-by-step process covers all aspects of preparedness, from surviving small disasters at home to surviving major natural disasters. Furthermore, she provides information that allows readers to live providently, test concepts, and try principles before anything happens.

"This informative book should be in every home as a study guide to increase knowledge, build skills, and bring peace and assurance that all possible preparation and training is completed before the real tests of life come. And come they will.

"Barbara's years of experience in this field, her wealth of knowledge from her research, testing, writing, and lecturing form a solid foundation for this informative book. Her experiences with people from multicultural backgrounds and with TV and radio appearances come through as the book focuses on key fundamental principles and leads readers along from basics to more complex topics.

"Barbara is well known and respected as a leader in the field of preparedness. She has masterfully taken a serious topic, given it life and light, and transformed it to an understandable format. She is more than expert; she is a master teacher and trainer whose wisdom and experience need to be studied and applied.

"Reading this book and applying its preparedness principles may save you and your loved ones. Now is the time to prepare."

—*Helena A. Hannonen, Ph.D., professor of management, Saint Mary's College of California*

PREPAREDNESS PRINCIPLES

PREPAREDNESS PRINCIPLES

The Complete Personal Preparedness Resource Guide

Barbara Salsbury
and Sandi Simmons

Horizon Publishers
Springville, Utah

ISBN 13: 978-0-88290-806-9

Published by Horizon, an imprint of Cedar Fort, Inc., 925 N. Main, Springville, UT, 84663
Distributed by Cedar Fort, Inc., www.cedarfort.com

LIBRARY OF CONGRESS CATALOGING-IN-PUBLICATION DATA

Salsbury, Barbara, 1937-
  Preparedness principles : the complete personal preparedness resource guide for any emergency situation / by Barbara Salsbury.
    p. cm.
  Includes index.
  ISBN 978-0-88290-806-9
  1. Preparedness. 2. Emergency management. 3. Disasters. 4. Safety education. I. Title.

  HV551.2.S24 2006
  613.6'9--dc22

                          2006013844

Cover design by Nicole Williams
Cover design ©2006, 2009 by Lyle Mortimer

Printed in Canada

10 9 8 7 6 5 4 3 2

Printed on acid-free paper

DEDICATION

Images created by the cataclysmic events of the past few years are indelibly stamped on our minds. We recognize that many, many people all over the world have experienced catastrophes beyond comprehension and, against all odds, have risen to unfathomable challenges. We look to them as the epitome of survival, the strength we all wish we had, and the hope we all need in challenging times. This book is dedicated to them and to those who will inevitably encounter similar challenges in the future.

TABLE OF CONTENTS

Section IV: Principles for Dealing with Disasters

Section V: Principles for Emergency Evacuations

ACKNOWLEDGMENTS

A book such as this one cannot be described properly as just a book, as far as I'm concerned. It is a part of me. It seems it's been in the process of "being born" for almost a lifetime—an ongoing project that would not remain in a box on a shelf. It is the result of years' worth of experiences, rough times, research, and learning that filled up and spilled over onto pages. Along the way many individuals encouraged, prodded, put up with, and prayed for and with me so that this dream became reality. To mention just a few:

First and foremost, the thanks and appreciation that go to my husband, Larry, for putting up with having an author in the house for all of these years probably cannot be measured. He not only prodded, praised, pushed, and prayed for, he was always there as my number-one supporter, holding my hand through those experiences that became visual aids for chapters. If there was ever a real knight in shining armor, he is one.

Without the talents and contributions of Sandi Simmons, this book could not have been accomplished. Her editing skills and ability to bring the thoughts and words together are invaluable. Her knack at making the grammar obey is a skill that few possess. The thesaurus doesn't contain enough adjectives to describe the asset that she has been toward the completion of this project, called *the* book. Appreciation and recognition, added to credit where credit is due, add up to so much more than the word *thanks*. But I couldn't find a word that says it all!

Duane and Jean Crowther, as the stalwarts of Horizon Publishers, have been there since my first book, which seems like eons ago. Duane edited the book to meet critical deadlines. Helena Hannonen has always been the Sherlock Holmes I needed at the moment. The crew of Cedar Fort have become good friends that constantly encourage, as well as fine associates to work with.

Dave Sibley of Ready Reserve Foods, Inc., has discussed at length many preparedness scenarios with me. He graciously provided the dehydrated foods needed to continue creating the recipes and concepts using dehydrated foods discussed in the book.

My thanks to all these and many more. Without them, this book—this part of me—could never have happened.

INTRODUCTION

Recognizing the seriousness of this subject, and how difficult it is to get most people to appreciate delving into it at any depth at all, I feel it's important to put the proper perspective on preparedness right at the beginning. Many times during the discussions that take place at my seminars or workshops, those attending like to hear our personalized version of what it's really like to go through trauma and tough times. Preparedness is much better understood if one can catch the vision. Therefore, to begin, I will share what it was really like to have a near-death experience in the immediate aftermath of the October 1989 7.2 Loma Prieta earthquake in California.

We had survived the first several hours of the aftermath. The floors were still rolling and the walls shaking. There was no power, and the water was shut off because of broken water lines in the next block. Our floors were covered with approximately a foot and a half of rubble—the remains of the contents of every cupboard and cabinet. Glass shards were everywhere. We were just trying to cope as aftershocks pounded the area. We had been working at sorting through our portion of the disaster. It was now late evening and we decided to try to create a meal of sorts while there was still a little light.

We pulled a can of tuna out of the rubble of our pantry in the garage and rescued a loaf of bread out of the drawer to make sandwiches. We pushed the piles of "stuff" to one side of the kitchen table and sat down to eat. All of a sudden, the table started shaking again. My blood pressure skyrocketed and my fear was instantaneously full-blown. I cried, "Oh no, not again!" and grabbed for Larry's hand to hang on for dear life. Larry looked at me doubtfully. The table continued to shake. About that time Larry almost

lost both his life and his head! I looked over and discovered his nervous habit of bouncing his leg was occurring at a most dangerous time—dangerous for him! He lived to describe his near-death experience and how it cured him of a nervous habit.

Crises and disasters don't make appointments before they come calling.

Many of us have our lives pretty much under control as long as nothing major goes wrong. We go through the days with our fingers crossed and our eyes closed. We can keep the bills paid, food on the table, and the family reasonably happy as long as life is smooth. But just glancing at the newspaper is enough to scare us to death because it proves that life is not smooth at all. How would you cope if *that* earthquake were in your city? If *that* flood was devastating your community? If gas prices tripled in a matter of months? If a member of your family was involved in *that* accident? All these things, and more and worse, have happened to real people in just one recent year. No doubt most of them had also thought, "It can't happen to me." But crises did happen to them, and they also could happen to you.

In today's society, few of us are geared to rely solely on ourselves for the necessities of life. In a world where electricity and technology reign, we are accustomed to an instantaneous response to the dial, the switch, the remote, and the button. There is a grocery store in every neighborhood, a convenience store on every corner. Turn the tap and fresh water is yours for the taking. Turn up the thermostat and you can be cozy in the middle of winter.

However, crises and disasters don't make appointments before they come calling. Emergencies *do* happen, and the time may come when you have to rely on yourself. It's time you open your eyes and stop counting on your crossed fingers to keep you safe and happy. It is possible to keep going even when the floor drops out from under your feet, but it doesn't happen by accident. It happens because you are prepared.

Some people choose not to be prepared for emergencies or hard times because the prospect of dealing with a crisis is too frightening. Others don't plan for adversity because sufficient preparation seems to be too big an undertaking. Still others avoid preparation because they don't have a clue how to go about it. This book is your answer to all these roadblocks, and more. You have in your hands the solution and answers to getting through the worst that life can throw at you as well as the merely annoying things life can serve up.

BEING PREPARED REQUIRES TIME AND EFFORT

Being prepared is not just a matter of keeping a flashlight in your cupboard or tons of whole wheat under your bed. It is a matter of understanding the principles involved in being prepared, pulling the different aspects into a personalized program tailored to your own situation, and then putting that program into practice slowly and steadily. You'll need to realize right up front that being prepared requires time and effort as you learn new principles, begin new habits, and adapt the things you've already begun. It takes money and space—two things few of us have enough of. But don't be discouraged by that—we'll show you how to find both of those without setting up a printing press in your cellar.

This book offers workable solutions to meet your individual and family needs in an emergency. It provides you with the knowledge and skills necessary to set up a realistic, organized program of personal preparedness suitable to your circumstances, environment, and budget. It's a personalized "action plan" that will enable you to cope with most of Mother Nature's temper tantrums and the majority of the man-made disruptions of normal daily life with a minimum of discomfort and a maximum of confidence!

If, as it has been said, experience is a good teacher, I have been taught well. Let me share with you what I have come to call the "'Salsbury Saga." It's true. One year when my children were young, severe chest pains put me in the hospital two days after Christmas. The following February I returned to the hospital with a blood clot in my leg. In March, our young son tried to telescope (or pass) his own bowel. He was rushed to the hospital and given several hours to live. He survived.

Spring came, and that meant baseball. My husband loves baseball. One April evening, playing in the outfield, he stretched to catch a long fly ball when his cleats caught in the mud and he ripped the hamstring muscles in his right thigh. During his hospital stay, he caught double pneumonia. In June that year, I was again in the hospital, this time for my third surgery of the year.

July arrived, and my husband obtained a job in northern California. He packed and labeled everything, then left to begin the job. I was to stay until the house sold. Our house was broken into the night that Larry left and most of the packed boxes were stolen.

The following week, I discovered we had been victims of a land fraud scheme and really did not own our house after all. After discussing it in vain with several lawyers, I called Larry and said, "Come and get me!" Larry arrived, but the rental truck, which had been half-loaded by friends, was too small. At this point, I was not well enough to drive a second truck. Faced with the question of whether to take all of the furniture or just the provisions we had for our preparedness program, we decided to take the provisions. Two weeks later, when we returned for our furniture, it was gone—stolen. We went back to northern California nearly empty-handed.

All of this happened in just one year! But these and other similar experiences taught us much about preparedness. Through that whole unbelievable year we were able to take care of ourselves. Not once did we have to choose between proper medical care and feeding the family. Not once did I have to worry how my young children would be fed while my own hold on life was so precarious. We didn't go under. We survived! We began that awful year prepared to face crises, and we emerged a year later with a firsthand knowledge of what works and what doesn't, and with a strong determination to be even more ready for anything the future might hold. In the years that followed we have weathered our share of peace, trauma, and tribulation. Through it all, I have never worried that our family would go under. We have been prepared to cope with it all.

This book, the results of years of research, has been written to share with you some of my family's experiences: our trials and errors and successes, as well as experiences that others have shared. Some of these principles you may have heard before. Some will be new to you. Some are just good common sense. I'm going to show you how to take the ideas you've heard of already, combine them with the ones that are new, and make them work for you.

SECTION I
ESSENTIAL ELEMENTS

CHAPTER ONE

UNDER THE UMBRELLA OF PREPAREDNESS

If I were to tell you that you need to be prepared, your first question might be, "For what?" It is a very valid question. If you need to be prepared to survive an earthquake, you would go about preparing your home and gathering supplies in a completely different manner than if you are preparing to survive an extended period of unemployment. Likewise, if you're ready to face a hazardous chemical spill on a nearby highway that requires you to leave your home immediately, you'd have different supplies and equipment than if you were ready for a three-year drought. Being prepared to triumph over one kind of crisis does not necessarily make you ready to laugh in the face of all problems. When life rains on your parade, what you really need is an umbrella to protect you.

THE UMBRELLA: PROTECTION

The umbrella has long been a symbol recognized to represent protection, a shield from the elements. The goal of *Preparedness Principles* is to help you design a personal-preparedness umbrella that will provide protection, confidence, and comfort to suit your needs and circumstances.

Personal experience has taught that being prepared does not make the crisis disappear! Even if you're ready, it's still there, only in more manageable proportions. Commodities, combined with knowledge and skills, create confidence and lessen chaos.

> *Preparedness is being in control during out-of-control situations.*

Preparedness is much more than just "food storage." Food certainly factors into it, but it is more than just that. It is self-sufficiency applied in a very personal manner. It is being in control during out-of-control situations.

On September 22, 2004, President George W. Bush, in his address to the United Nations said, "In this young century, we need a new definition of security." For the nations of the world, his answer was Homeland Security. For the families of the nation, I suggest that what we need is Home Security. I encourage you to do what you can, where you can, when you can. As individuals, you and I can't resolve the frightening situations in the state, country, or world. But we can resolve to do something—to create our own safe haven through attitude and action in our preparedness programs.

HOME IS A SAFE HAVEN

Your attitude figures heavily into the formula. On the one hand, you can hide your head in the sand and keep your fingers crossed, hoping bad things won't happen. On the other hand, you can head for the hills with your gun and your gas mask. Neither attitude is particularly appropriate or reasonable. The better choice is to walk the middle of the road by making your home a safe haven, where you live confidently for today and prepare securely for tomorrow.

Practical preparation now could very well make the difference between coping and chaos. You are in charge of tailoring your preparedness program to your needs, to your circumstances, and within your budget. Unlike riding a roller coaster or being pregnant, being prepared is not an "all or nothing" thing. Being a little bit prepared is a whole lot better than not being prepared at all. Being well prepared is better than being a little bit prepared. You determine how much you are willing to do. Practicality reigns. I am not advocating you turn your home into a wall-to-wall storage unit, or that you become so obsessed with what "might" happen that you stop living in the here and now. Instead, I am urging you to learn the principles of preparedness and determine what is going to work for you. Then, get to it! You can do what needs to be done to feel secure. You take it one step at a time, with a personalized plan of action. Positive preparation minimizes panic and fear.

	Under the Umbrella of Preparedness *Helping you to help yourself always be prepared*			
Type of Disaster	Worst-Case Scenario	Provident Living	Dealing with Disasters	Emergency Evacuation
Description	Long-Term Calamity	Rainy Days and Hard Times	Natural- or Man-Made Disasters	Natural- or Man-Made Disasters Requiring Evacuation
Shelter	You are in your home with normal utilities. However, no food or supplies are available anywhere or at any price. Your survival depends on your supplies.	You are in your home with normal utilities. Food and supplies are available but you do not have sufficient money or means to aquire them. Frugality is required.	You are in your home or have access to it, but you are without utilities, services, or transportation.	You are forced out of your home. There are no utilities, services, or supplies available other than what you take with you.
Duration	Long Term; many months to a year or more.	Short term or long term, a few weeks to a year or more	Short term, anywhere from a day to a month or two	Short term, 72 hours (three days) at least.
Causes	Widespread catastrophe due to: • War • Drought • Devastating storms • Terrorism, etc.	Economic Crises: • Unemployment • Personal financial difficulties • Death • Medical problems • Hospital stay • Extended family needs, etc.	Localized Emergencies: • Natural disasters • Weather related disasters, e.g. hurricanes, storms • Power outages • Civil unrest • Riots • Terrorism, etc.	Localized Emergencies requiring evacuation: • Natural disasters • Weather-related disasters • Chemical spills • Wildfires • Terrorism, etc.
Special Emphasis	• Core Concept: Bare-Bones Basics Bare-Bones Basics Complements Bare-Bones Basics Companions • Long-Term Storage	• Pantry Principle: Practical Prudent Provident	• Emergency supplies • Emergency skills	• All essentials need to be in a manageable, portable container • Small, compact, lightweight
Overlap	<-- Many Foods -->			
	Long-Term skills (repairing, mending, making do)			
		<-- Some Foods -->		
	<-- **Essential Elements** --> (affect all categories) • Attitude • Coping Skills • Money Management • Finding Room for a Pantry			

THE FOUR CATEGORIES: SEPARATE, YET RELATED

This book has broken down the different types of emergencies any of us are likely to face and explains the principles required to successfully deal with each of them. Under the umbrella of preparedness are four separate yet related categories. The first three categories are preparedness principles for dealing with crises and problems while remaining in your home or at least on your property. In the fourth category, proper preparedness principles teach you how to survive an evacuation when you are forced out of your home. The four categories are (1) Principles for surviving Worst-Case Scenarios, (2) Principles of Provident Living, (3) Principles for Dealing with Disasters, and (4) Principles for Emergency Evacuations. Each of these different sections covers a unique scope of problems with distinctive preparation methods, as well as the principles that will allow you to successfully deal with each.

While preparedness situations can be as different as night and day, there are some basic, underlying principles that apply to all situations requiring preparedness. Essential Elements gets you started by showing you these basics—from money matters to where to put the supplies you'll be gathering, and how to care for them when you get them.

Category 1, Principles for Surviving Worst-Case Scenarios deals with just what the name suggests: how to cope with the worst life can deal out. What if there was a famine so terrible that there was nothing left in the store to buy? There was no food available at any price. The photos in the newspaper of starving children with enormous eyes were not pitiful victims from some starving Third-World country, but from your own city? The time may come when these could be scenes from your city, but they don't have to be you or your family.

Category 2, Principles of Provident Living, shows you how to get through hard times with a positive attitude. Whether the crisis is a long-term bout with unemployment, a strike that interrupts the distribution of supplies to your city, or a national economic crunch, the result is that you have to take care of your family under drastically altered circumstances. Abiding by the principles of provident living enables you to accomplish more than one thing at a time. These principles will ensure you have on hand the knowledge, skills, and commodities you need to get through difficult times. Plus, you'll find that the Pantry Principle (chapter 14) is a sound money-management system, and the most effective financial way to live. We have survived serious economic hardships on several occasions, and I know from personal experience that the knowledge and skills needed to get through hard times are just as essential as those required to get through a 7.2 earthquake.

In Category 3, learning the Principles for Dealing with Disasters will qualify you to live through Mother Nature's temper tantrums (hurricanes, storms, etc.), or through man-made problems (civil unrest, widespread technological disruptions, or the aftermath of terrorist strikes). These are the situations where you are still in your home, but you are without the necessities of life that we take so much for granted: utilities, power, communication, running water, and so on.

Category 4, Principles for Emergency Evacuations, prepares you to cope should a sudden crisis or disaster force you out of your home at short notice. Statistics show that in an evacuation situation you will need to be completely self-sustaining for a minimum of seventy-two hours before you can count on receiving assistance from local or government rescue agencies. How well you prepare in advance will make a huge difference in how confident and comfortable, or how utterly miserable you will be until help arrives, or the situation is brought under control and you are able to return to your home.

DIFFERENT CATEGORIES, DIFFERENT METHODS, DIFFERENT SUPPLIES

Each separate category of preparedness requires different methods and different supplies to deal with its problems adequately. However, you will not find long lists of mandatory items to purchase and stockpile in these pages. Instead what you'll find are principles—fundamental truths upon which to base your own individual choices. These are concepts that, if adhered to, will enable you to face the uncertain future with confidence.

As you browse the categories, you'll find you may have heard some of the ideas before. Some principles will be new to you. There may be some ideas that you've heard about for years but never considered in a preparedness context. *Preparedness Principles* combines all the fragmented facets into a total program.

This is not the preparedness program of your grandparents' day. The attitudes and fads of twenty or thirty years ago are not necessarily practical or applicable for today's lifestyles. Research, technology, population growth, urban development—all have changed how and where we live. A higher percentage of people live in apartments or small homes with limited storage space. Very few homes have large yards, let alone acreage for growing crops. An uncertain employment market means many families will have to move several times during their lifetimes. Times have changed, and we have to move with the times and adjust our ideas and plans. For that very reason, *Preparedness Principles* is the answer. It provides a protective umbrella of principles for dealing with the challenges of the times, no matter what they are.

CHAPTER TWO

PLANNING PRINCIPLES: KNOWLEDGE, PRACTICE, AND LISTS

When you look at an umbrella, you'll note that the handle holds the working mechanisms and the connecting spokes to the structural framework. It unifies the separate sections, while supporting the whole. In a preparedness umbrella, this section, Essential Elements, is the handle. These are the elements, principles, and skills that affect all of the other categories of personal preparedness.

"BEFORE" IS A KEY PRINCIPLE

One of the key principles of preparation is that obtaining necessary knowledge and skills before a crisis occurs is absolutely vital. Knowledge and skills can make all the difference between chaos or confidence, confusion or calmness, crying or creativity. Just as it's too late to begin to fill the cupboard when the need arises, it's too late to learn the skills that allow you to live confidently through a crisis once that crisis is at your door. Someone once foolishly suggested that living through a crisis "only requires common sense." That might be true if your "crisis" is not having a thing to wear to dinner tonight. But if your crisis is not having a thing to eat for dinner tonight because you just had a 7.2 earthquake and your house is in shambles, that common-sense idea goes right out the window. Common sense alone is just not enough. Any time you compound a tense, unfamiliar situation with confusion and inadequacy, you have a big problem. The field of preparedness is not the place for on-the-job training. Mistakes that are made in the learning process could prove to be critical errors—not necessarily life threatening, but certainly "quality of life" threatening. On the other hand, some emergency preparedness skills could prove to be very dangerous if safety procedures were not adhered to. Learning the process of using a liquid-fuel lantern, or connecting the fuel canister to a camp stove for the first time should be done prior to the storm, not in the middle of Hurricane Whomever, with the electricity down and your roof half gone.

PREPAREDNESS UPDATING

Knowledge and skills, once acquired and practiced until they reach a usable level, can be "retired" with scheduled updating and refreshing. The important factor is to have them to fall back on. For example, I do not grind grain for flour and bake my own bread to save money. But I could if I needed to. Nor do I preserve bushels of fruits and vegetables any more, but I know how. We don't plow and plant a half-acre garden like we used to; we maintain just a small garden patch. But should there be a need to grow our own "crops" in greater quantity, we would be able to. We rarely use our camping equipment for camping these days, but if the power should go out, we have it and know how to use it.

I recommend that you calendar checking equipment, accessories, kits, and so on when it's time to change the clocks, or the month of your birthday, or some other annual event that you can mentally associate with preparedness updating. This is also a good time for a knowledge and skills refresher. Brush up on any preparedness skills that may be out-of-date or a little rusty from lack of use. Reanalyze the risks that might be lurking in your future and assess the skills that might be needed to deal with them. Set a plan for acquiring any new skills necessary. This would be especially important if you have recently moved, or if your household circumstances have changed. (Have any children grown old enough to learn skills that would help the family get through a challenging situation?) Keeping on top of things keeps your confidence strong.

Many times in this book, I'll recommend you add this item or that activity to your list to update or check annually. Before you're done, you'll probably have a long list of things to check annually to stay prepared. It may take you a couple of hours or even a couple of days to make sure everything is in order and in good shape for the year to come. It's time well spent, and when you're done, you can pat yourself on the back for accomplishing an important task necessary for keeping your family safe and prepared.

Speaking of lists, it's important that you remember to keep a hard copy of any charts or lists or worksheets you create as part of your personal preparedness planning. It's all well and good to have the information on your computer or handheld planner, but it's not sufficient. Remember, you're planning for events that quite possibly include lengthy power outages or other disruptions, in which case all your carefully thought-out plans stored only on your computer will be inaccessible. A hard copy on a shelf or in a binder doesn't require any electricity. These worksheets and lists are your personalized action plan. You want to make sure you can access them when you want them.

Having a shelf of resource books and manuals that you can occasionally lightly review is a smart idea (this one occupying the most important place on the shelf, of course!), but emphasis must be placed on the principle of "being prepared." The information between the covers of a book is essentially useless if you do not have the confidence or understanding of how to apply it. Having several cookbooks on the shelf will not make you a skilled cook. Likewise, having a book on how to survive a disaster will not keep you safe and warm if you don't know the skills or have the supplies before the disaster occurs. It's too late for preparation once the need arrives!

Preparedness is not an all-or-nothing thing. Something is much better than nothing, even if the something is just a little bit of something.

BEGIN NOW!

The nice thing about preparedness is that it is *not* an all-or-nothing thing. Something is much better than nothing, even if the something is just a little bit of something, so don't wait until you finish reading this book to get started. Don't procrastinate until you have all the knowledge and all the money you need (Ha! As if that could ever happen!). Start today with what's on hand and build on what you already have. Being prepared is a big undertaking, but like a journey of a thousand miles, it begins with a single step. Your first step (besides reading this book, of course) should be to find out what you already have. As you read each chapter and learn what you need and should have, take an inventory of what supplies you do have that apply to preparedness and would prove useful. This is the foundation upon which you can systematically build. Taking an inventory is not an enormous time-consuming project that will take over your life (and therefore will never be started). It's a simple task to help you, not hinder you. It doesn't have to be done within a limited time, and it doesn't have to be done all at once. It is also not a contest; only your answers, priorities, and ideas count. If your preparedness cupboard starts with a working flashlight and a bag of chocolate chips in a cardboard box in the closet, good for you! You've made a start.

LIST? WHOSE LIST? YOUR LIST

There is a lot of confusion about what to prepare and how to prepare. Many people are so overwhelmed by the complexity of the preparedness subject they don't even know where to begin. There are many people or companies ready to capitalize on your confusion with a photocopied list that specifies exactly what items you need to purchase to be prepared. If someone else has compiled the list, even though it may be professionally or commercially done, don't rely on it too heavily. The reason that someone else's list will not work is that being prepared involves too many important individual factors for a set list to

You need a plan tailored to you: your need, your situation.

apply to everyone. You need a plan that is tailored to your needs and your situation. Granted, many of the things you need in order to be prepared can be lumped under general headings that will be on anyone's lists: food, blankets, a cooking source, water, and so on. What I take the most exception to are the lists that suggest that you need exactly and only what they say, and that only the brands suggested will fulfill your preparedness needs. You know the kind: Under the food heading you'll find, "Whang-O! Bars—One bar provides all the protein, fiber, vitamins, caffeine, food additives, and artificial flavors a person needs for a full twenty-four hours! A case of twenty-four is only $99.95," or for warmth, "Nature's Best 100 percent natural polyester blanket. Made from hand-fed, organically grown polyesters. In its own genuine plastic cover. Only $29.99." If you don't like it, won't eat it, won't value it, don't want it, can't stand it, or can't afford it, then don't buy it! It's just a waste of your resources. For those with little money and whose

dollars are usually screaming for mercy at the end of each month from being stretched so far, chapter 14 is for you! (See page 107.)

If money isn't an issue with you, and if you really aren't worried about how appropriate or accurate your emergency preparedness supplies are, as long as gathering them requires a minimum of effort and time on your part, then these lists will be fine for you. You'll end up with something in case of emergencies, and as I said before, something is definitely better than nothing. It's just not as good as having the right things. The operative word in "personal preparedness" is *personal!* Making it personal makes it right.

Having a list is not a bad thing. In essence, this book could be considered a list, since I am suggesting things you need to be prepared. The difference is that the list you need is not someone else's list—it is your list, your plan of action, shaped by your individual factors to meet your needs!

CHAPTER THREE

MONEY MATTERS!

An integral part of preparedness is a piggy bank—*a large* piggy bank. To be prepared, you not only need to budget wisely to purchase emergency supplies and equipment, you also need to have a readily available supply of the actual green stuff. This is one of the most difficult areas of preparedness for most people to acquire. It's difficult enough to just keep up each month, let alone get ahead.

TOO MUCH MONEY CAN BE TROUBLE

There are a few for whom money is not a problem. In a general way of speaking, having plenty of money is a good thing. We'd all love to be in that situation. But when it comes to preparedness, affluence could cause a problem just because of a faulty mind-set. Money by itself will not keep you warm, or feed you, or give you light in an emergency situation. Having money can give you a false sense of security. There might be an inclination to think, "I don't want to worry about it right now. I'll simply buy whatever I might need when the need arises." This kind of thinking could leave you painfully unprepared in circumstances where your money is of little value. Circumstances can quickly arise where money is not the commodity required. Power outages can shut down computers and banks, making money inaccessible. You might theoretically have it on paper but have nothing in your hands to show for it. Crises can create situations where replacement items and supplies are not obtainable at any price. As I emphasized earlier, when the crisis arrives, the time for preparation has passed. Money cannot buy equipment or food to allow you to live through a crisis when you can't get to the store to buy it, or if the store isn't stocked or open. Money cannot replace preparedness when a need arrives on the doorstep. If you have sufficient funds, use them now in a wise, planned, and practical manner, so if there should come a time when things are more important than paper dollars, you and your family are still cared for.

THE OTHER SIDE OF THE COIN

On the other hand, one of the major dilemmas for most people, in attempting to have a working preparedness program, is finding a way to fill the box on the pantry shelf marked "money." For most, the concept of preparedness has not previously incorporated the concept of funds, but it should. The general attitude towards money today is drastically different than it was even one generation ago. Not only is credit card debt at an all-time high, but also the commitment (tendency) to set aside savings for a rainy day is at an all-time low. This double whammy (debt and lack of savings) is a lethal combination that can sink a person in circumstances that would otherwise only barely rock life's boat. Keeping in mind that crises and hard times don't make appointments before calling, having at least some money should be emphasized as an essential portion of any preparedness program. When, for whatever reason, the income that you are used to relying on is reduced, postponed, delayed, or terminated, you learn very

> *Debt and lack of savings is a lethal combination.*

quickly that the bills still must be paid. Financial crises require that you have sufficient funds on hand to tide you over, pay the bills, and fill the tank. You may have food on the shelf, but if you do not have at least some liquid finances, things become very difficult, very fast. We have lived through more financial crunches than I care to remember, and if there's one thing we've learned, it's that you can't put wheat in the gas tank!

Solid financial preparedness indicates that there are basically four areas of savings: You need some cash at home in a piggy bank for short-term emergencies, and you need accessible money in the bank as an emergency fund. Every family should have a rainy-day fund to fall back on in case of financial reversals, and of course, long-term planning is vital to everyone's future, whether or not that future includes emergency situations.

There are dozens of books and resources on the market to help you with long-term planning, so I will not delve into that subject, important as it is. However, to help establish a well-rounded preparedness program that will sustain you and your family through difficult times, let's take a closer look at the piggy bank, the emergency fund, and the rainy-day fund categories.

The Piggy Bank

Having a small amount of cold, hard cash on hand can be a lifesaver, even if it's only twenty to fifty dollars. In a localized emergency, you may need a bit of cash to make phone calls, buy bottled water, or any number of small things while banks are closed, or you can't get to an ATM. Put the money (don't forget to make some of it change) in an envelope or box, tucked away in a drawer where no one will be tempted to use it for other "emergencies," like to soothe a desperate need for a diet soda and king-size candy bar. You might need to seal it in a can, or use ten layers of strapping tape, or put it in a box marked "Hemorrhoid Ointment" to keep it safe from marauding family members so it's still there when you need it.

The Emergency Fund

Emergencies happen all the time; they're just not on the catastrophic scale. A tire blows out on the way to work and must be replaced. Flu season has struck again, bringing unplanned doctor visits.

Your teenage son needs new shoes because the ones you bought two months ago are already too small. The ancient washing machine finally threw in the towel. And so it goes. It's a well-known fact that there is always more month than money. For many people the grocery budget functions as the emergency fund. It is often the only flexible income available. But if your monthly budget is stretched to the last penny just keeping food on the table and a roof over your head, emergencies like this can be disastrous. Having your pantry established as a segment of your money-management system and as a "budget stretcher" can help, but few budgets are flexible enough to repeatedly cover these kinds of setbacks. It's crucial that you work into your budget a way to set aside a little money to cover these emergencies so they don't push you over the financial edge. Aim for at least a couple hundred dollars in an accessible bank account to start, and build that up to a point where it can cover the unpleasant little surprises life can dish out.

Early in our married life we struggled financially, as many newlyweds do. We strove to be independent, but living paycheck to paycheck without any savings in the bank at all put us on tenuous ground. Even small emergencies would wipe us out and put us in the undesirable position of having to be dependent on family to bail us out. Finally, we decided that we had to have an emergency fund in the bank, even if we had to sacrifice to get it. And we did. I don't remember now what we had to give up or do without at the time, but I remember it was painful, considering the tight budget we were on. However, after about eight months we had almost two hundred dollars in the bank. It truly was a satisfying feeling. And then, without warning, a blowout on the road meant we had to get new tires and repair work. It took every bit of the two hundred dollars in the bank and part of the month's grocery budget to get the car working again. I was depressed for days that all our money was gone in

For many people, the grocery budget functions as their emergency fund.

a single day after having sacrificed for months to build it up. But then one day I realized that our emergency fund had done exactly what it was supposed to. We'd had an emergency, and we'd come through it without faltering or going into debt. It was a success! We started building the supply back up the very next month so we could be ready for the next inevitable emergency.

The Rainy-Day Fund

Our grandparents used to set money aside every month for "a rainy day." Rainy days are those times when you face serious financial reversals: you've lost your job, or an accident prevents you from working for several weeks or months. Or, the financial crunch could come from skyrocketing utility and gasoline prices; a salary that had been sufficient suddenly is woefully inadequate. You need money in the bank to see you through until you can get back on your feet. The rainy-day fund should equate to several months worth of salary. Six months used to be the recommended amount, but even three months can be a staggering figure for many to try to accumulate, on top of all of the normal expenses of living. Again, having a working preparedness program can help considerably in these situations. But unfortunately, food on the shelves will not pay the mortgage or put gas in the tank. You have to have money. Your rainy-day fund can be part of your long-term financial planning, as long as it isn't tied up so tightly that you can't access it if you need it.

Back during the recession of the late 1980s my husband lost his job and we were without work for almost a year and a half. It was a tough, tough time, emotionally as well as financially. Because our cupboards were well stocked to begin with, we had plenty to eat (though I'll admit variety was somewhat lacking at the end there, and fresh food of any sort was a rare treat). The problem was that it takes cash to pay bills and keep enough gas in the car to be able to look for jobs. We stretched a few months' worth of money out to last a year and a half, augmented by temporary part-time jobs here and there, but it was hard! I can attest firsthand to the vital importance of having cash set aside for a rainy day.

I read once that a wise person always pays himself first. Anytime you earn a paycheck, take out a set amount to pay yourself before you pay any other bills or spend even a dime. Decide an amount and take that much out right up front. Ten percent is a good number—easy to figure but quick to add up in the long run. (Hey, it's less than the government takes from you!) Divide up that ten percent between long-term planning and a liquid, accessible bank account. It may hurt a bit to get started, but once it is a habit, you'll really be grateful that you do it. Setting aside money on a regular basis will help you get through rough times. Plus, when times aren't so rough, you'll find you can plan ahead for upcoming expenses as you need them, like replacing old cars or appliances without going into debt. It's a nice feeling.

The relief that comes when a "crunch" rears its head is incredible, and instead of causing all kinds of chaotic fallout, you are able to roll with the punches and keep sailing on.

Having an accessible amount of money should be as much a part of your Preparedness Pantry as peanut butter and batteries. Combined with food in the pantry, it could prevent an unexpected crunch from becoming a disaster in its own right.

THE PRINCIPLE OF BEING DEBT-FREE

One of the finest gifts you can give yourself is to live within your means and to stay out of debt. Debt is so very easy to acquire. Not a month goes by that you won't find half a dozen or more preapproved credit card applications in the mailbox. Even people with terrible credit ratings are encouraged to open new lines of credit (usually with extremely high interest rates). Students as young as fourteen years of age are targeted with credit card applications and can be thousands of dollars in debt before they ever

> *Keep working on that rainy-day fund. Then, when the rain comes, you don't have to buy an umbrella; you are the umbrella.*
> —Clark Howard,
> *The Clark Howard Show,* July 29, 2005

graduate from high school. Today's materialistic society encourages the notion that you are entitled to all the worldly goods you want, and that you deserve them now whether you can afford them or not. Being frugal, showing self-restraint, or doing without until you are in a position to buy something free and clear seem to be old-fashioned ideas to be laughed at or disdained. Well, society's notions on debt and spending are wrong. Debt is a crushing burden, and it can destroy your peace of mind, your self-respect, and your relationships. More marriages end in divorce due to financial difficulties than for any other reason.

If you're out of debt, do yourself a favor and stay that way. Throw those credit card applications right into the shredder the minute you get them. If you're drowning in debt, resolve today to end the nightmare. Prepare a plan to pay off your debts, beginning by cutting your credit cards into little bits. Live within your means, even if it requires you to go without some of the material goods you'd love to have. Many states offer free consumer credit counseling services that can help you get control of your spending situation and get out of debt. Check the front of your phone book in the Community pages for information about these services. Start today. The peace of mind that comes from living within your means is well worth foregoing material possessions.

MONEY MANAGEMENT SYSTEM TO BECOME DEBT-FREE

Trying to eliminate debt while still using your credit cards is like using a paper cup to bail out a rowboat with a hole in the bottom. Until you patch the hole, the best you'll be able to do is keep your head above water, and that will take all the energy you have. The first step to getting out of debt is to stop going into debt. Here are a few suggestions that you can build on for a healthy financial situation.

> *Learning how to discipline one's self and exercise constraint where money is concerned can be more important than courses in accounting.*
> —Marvin J. Ashton,
> *One For the Money*

USE A BUDGET

Draw up a workable budget and stick to it. *Budgeting* is not a dirty word. Rather, it is a means to an end. Having a realistic budget is the way to make the best use of your income and savings. It is how you can achieve financial goals and avoid financial pitfalls. Budgeting requires that you exercise self-discipline and patience. It also requires you to distinguish between wants and needs. Many of your needs are actually just wants that you think you need. I love this true statement I heard many years ago: "The greatest cause of disappointment in this life is trading what you want most for what you want at the moment."

To create an effective budget, you have to know how much your income is and where your money goes each month. Begin by listing all your expenditures from the previous several months. This may be difficult if you are used to spending cash without keeping a record of where it is spent. It is a little easier to see if you use a checkbook. Determine where your money went and whether the purchases were necessary or unnecessary.

Next, list all your set expenses like mortgage payments, utilities, food, car-related expenses, and so on. Don't forget to include major expenses that you only pay once or twice a year like insurance payments, automobile registration, or Christmas. Those may need to be budgeted, with money set aside each month in order to pay the large lump sum all at one time. Analyzing your past several months of spending should give you a pretty good idea of how much you spend on each of these categories so you'll know how much to allot for them.

Add up all the expenses you have each month, and hopefully, it will be less than your income after taxes. If it is, then you can use the difference between your income and your expenses to pay off debts, begin some long-term planning, set aside a liquid rainy-day fund (no pun intended), put some money in the bank as an emergency fund, and hide away a little as a piggy-bank fund.

If your expenses overwhelm your income, your choice is to either cut back expenses or increase your income, or both. It's difficult to cut back on spending, but if you look long and hard enough at where your money goes, you'll probably see places that can be trimmed. Often just being aware of your spending habits will result in cutting costs. Sometimes people purchase unnecessary fluff-stuff simply because it looks appealing at the moment, not because they need it or even really value it. But when you're watching every dime you can pass these things up quite painlessly. As Benjamin Franklin said, "Beware of little expenses; a small leak will sink a great ship."

Cutting back can sometimes be enough to slip your spending back into the black. Try some of the simple, obvious cuts and see what they do for you. Buy fewer convenience foods. Go out to eat less. Eat at cheaper places. Rent a video instead of going to the movies. Go to the dollar theater (if you're lucky enough to have one near you) rather than to full-price movies. Don't buy new clothes this month. Don't buy anything unless it's on sale. Go to the library instead of buying books or CDs. When you put each budget category under careful scrutiny, you'll probably find many ways you can trim the fat.

Some people will studiously cut out minor expenses like their fresh bagel in the morning, yet never think to review their major monthly expenses. Are you paying more for insurance than you need to? Before you send in your next car insurance check, call around and get a few quotes from the competition. That could save you hundreds each year. What about your telephone bill?

There is usually such fierce competition between

Even a small amount saved on a regular basis eventually adds up. In the early years of her marriage, my daughter wanted a piano for her family in the worst way, but it just wasn't in the budget. She took a job babysitting three hours a day, one day a week, and she saved every penny she made. Two years later she had enough to buy a nice second-hand piano, which she and all four of her children learned to play in the ensuing years. With patience and persistence, even a seemingly insignificant amount will add up eventually.

SAMPLE BUDGET

Income:
- Work: $
- Other Income $
- After Taxes: $

- TOTAL $

Expenses:
- Mortgage $
- Insurance $
  - Health $
  - Life $
  - Homeowner's $
- Utilities
  - Gas $
  - Electricity $
  - Water/Sewer $
  - Garbage $
  - Telephone $
- Charitable contributions $
- Loans/Debts
- 2nd Mortgage $
- Credit Card Debt
  - # $
  - # $
  - # $
- Savings $
- Vehicles
  - Car Payment $
  - Gas $
  - Maintenance $
- Lessons $
- Other Activities $
- Child care $
- Household Expenses
  - Food $
  - Lunches $
  - Bus $
  - Clothing $
  - Entertainment $
  - Emergency Fund $
- Annual Expenses
  - Christmas $
  - Vacations $
  - School Expenses $
  - Birthdays $
  - Other Expenses $

TOTAL EXPENSES $

phone companies that it's highly likely you could save on this bill. Even if you don't change carriers, you can call and ask if you're getting the best deals they currently have to offer. They usually can trim your bill somewhere, but they won't do it unless you ask first.

Anytime you make a major purchase, furniture or appliances for example, ask the salesperson if they can give you a sale price. More often than not, salespeople are authorized to offer price breaks if a customer asks for one. Consider replacing old appliances with new energy-efficient ones. The savings could pay for the purchase price in a year or two. So while it is good to cut small expenses, don't forget to cut the large ones also. One large decrease in a monthly bill might just justify splurging on a fresh bagel once or twice a week.

If you have cut expenditures back to the bone already and there's nothing left to trim, you may need to look into finding ways to increase your income. It may be necessary to look for a better-paying job or take on a second job. You may need to check into options for more education to qualify you for a better-paying career. Before you throw that idea out as pie-in-the-sky, remember to look at the big picture. It may be worth taking on some student loans and a heavy schedule if in the end you can earn a better living. Find out the facts before you toss the idea.

As a personal example, in 1974, when a major construction project came to an end, my husband (an electrical-safety inspector) discovered that, because he didn't have a college degree, his job with the company was at an end also. Faced with finding another job in an increasingly competitive business or changing careers, we knew we didn't ever want to be that vulnerable again. With two almost-teenage children and no prospect of financial security in sight, we decided to bite the bullet and return to the university so Larry could finish his degree. It was one of the hardest decisions we ever made. It meant I had to return to work, and Larry had to work part-time while carrying twenty-plus hours each semester.

We were so financially strapped that the national poverty level would have been living in the lap of luxury to us. We gave up safety nets and employee benefits like insurance and sick leave. Our children worked a paper route to earn their only disposable income. Holidays were meager and vacations non-existent during those years. It was a major sacrifice for all of us. We knew going into it that it wouldn't be fun, and we agreed at the outset as a family that we would support one another. And, it wasn't fun! But three and a half years later, thanks to a combination of tuition loans, determination, and miracles, we finished.

Although Larry's name was the one on the diploma, every member of our family felt like we had earned part of the degree. And in retrospect, that precious piece of paper wasn't the only thing we got from our experience.

We all learned a lot: we learned how to budget—and how to budget more. We learned that we don't have to keep up with the Joneses. We learned to make over and make do. We learned that money isn't the most important thing in the world. We learned that fun doesn't have to be expensive. And most importantly, we learned we can get through anything if we stick together. All these lessons have served us well in the decades that have followed. It's a source of pride and strength to look back and be able to say, "We faced that hard trial and we got through it."

ELIMINATE DEBT

In order to eliminate a current heavy load of debt, a debt-elimination calendar is a great help. As I said before though, it won't work if you are continually adding new debt while trying to pay off old debt. Cut up your credit cards, live within your means, and pay as you go. Financial responsibility now is the first and most important step to getting out of debt.

In a debt-elimination calendar you list all of your outstanding debts, the interest rates they carry, and how long until they are paid off at your current rate of payment. Begin by marking off several columns on a piece of paper. In the left-hand column, write the months, beginning with next month. Across the tops of the other columns, list your debts in the order you want to pay them. You may first want to pay off the debt with the highest interest rate, or it may be the debt with the earliest pay-off date. In that first debt column, list the payment down the column for that creditor each month until that debt is paid off completely. The trick is to make sure that as soon as the first debt is paid off, that dollar payment is immediately rolled over onto the next debt. Don't let that money be siphoned away for any other purpose. Continue that process of paying off a debt and rolling the payment over onto the next loan as long as it takes, until all your debts are paid in full. In the following illustration, you can see that this method will work if you just stick with it.

(See an example of a debt-elimination calendar on the following page.)

If your debt situation is grim and you own your home, you may want to consider more drastic measures, like taking out a debt-consolidation loan. This kind of loan is a second mortgage on your property that allows you to consolidate all of your debts into one payment, though not necessarily at bargain interest rates. If you're currently paying out a thousand dollars a month on debt payments with high interest rates (and there is no extra money to pay the loans down with a debt-elimination calendar situation), a debt-consolidation loan may be able to cut your monthly payments to, say, $600. This is only a good

idea if you scrupulously apply the newly available $400 each month right back to debt repayment. If the loan amount was sufficient to cover all your debts, immediately apply the extra money to paying off the consolidation loan. If it only paid some of the debts, add the consolidation loan to your debt-elimination calendar and treat it as another debt to be paid off as soon as possible. Once your debts are paid, resolve never to get in that situation again! Check with a credible bank or credit union to see if debt consolidation would work for you. Keep in mind that a debt-consolidation loan is a lien on your property. If you sell your home you must pay off both your first and second mortgages.

The way you spend your money today will determine what you have and what you can do six months from now, five years from now, and for the rest of your life. It also determines how well you are prepared to deal with financial crunches and crisis situations.

Sample Debt Elimination Calendar

	#1 Credit Card #1 18% Interest	#2 Credit Card #2 14% Interest	#3 Store Credit Card 21% Interest	#4 Furniture Loan 9% Interest	#5 Car Payment 8% Interest
January	100	85	50	120	275
February	100	85	50	120	275
March	100	85	50	120	275
April	100 PAID!	85	50	120	275
May		185*	50	120	275
June		185	50	120	275
July		185 PAID!	50	120	275
August			235	120	275
September			235	120	275
October			235 PAID!	120	275
November				355	275
December				355 PAID!	275
January					630
February					630
March					630
April					630 PAID!

*After debt #1 is paid off, the $100 is added to debt #2 for a new payment of $185.
Continue the process, adding the previous payment as it is paid off to the next debt.

CHAPTER FOUR

THE PANTRY SYSTEM: FINDING A PLACE FOR EVERYTHING

Next to money, or the lack thereof, inadequate space is the greatest challenge many people face when they decide to get prepared. Without actual, physical storage space, you can't possibly consider a program that recommends you gather supplies in large quantities. At first glance, you may be convinced that there is not one more square inch of empty cupboard space, let alone an entire pantry in your home. And you know the walls are not made of spandex. Since the success of your preparedness program is largely based on your ability to find a place to put it all, perhaps a pair of magic glasses would help you see more creatively. Remember the 3-D glasses in the theater that made a whole new dimension realistically pop out at you? Along those same lines, visualize in your imagination the pair of 3-P glasses that I'm giving you; your "Preparedness Pantry Possibilities" glasses. With the help of a new viewpoint, you'll be able to see available pantry space that was hidden from you until now. There is a pantry area just waiting to be discovered in your home! A few ideas, a little ingenuity and creativity, and some effort on your part will enable you to create a pantry system to suit your needs.

Creating your pantry system will probably be a challenge that you can't complete overnight. If you are starting at square one, this project might easily take several months or more. Set a goal and work toward it, if only a step—or a shelf—at a time. Continue to improve your system until it functions at maximum efficiency for you. Keep your evaluations and expectations realistic—it can be gratifying and rewarding. Just remember, a pantry in a less-than-ideal spot is better than no pantry at all!

And a special word of encouragement for those of you who might be renting or who must move frequently: a pantry is still essential in your home. It is worth it, both monetarily and from a preparedness perspective, to put forth the effort to create a pantry, no matter where you go, or how often. In fact, just as a personal insight, having a wonderful pantry really made a positive difference in the sale of several of our homes.

SHELF SEARCH

No matter how small your home or apartment is, or whether you own or rent your home, a pantry is not impossible. Very few lucky people will have an ideal situation to work with. For everyone else, their "pantry" will actually consist of a "pantry system," meaning a combination of mini-pantries in several rooms, closets, and transformed nooks and crannies. Generally, there is space enough, even in very small households. The problem lies in that much of the available space is unrecognized or used inefficiently. Here is where you begin to use those 3-P glasses. Your new goal? To discover how many different places in your home or apartment can be turned into pantries or mini-pantries. These mini-pantries do not have to be located in one place, nor do they even have to be in areas with optimal storage conditions (dark, dry, and cool), though of course, the more ideal the conditions, the longer your supplies will last.

> *A pantry in a less-than-ideal spot is better than no pantry at all!*

As you develop a pantry system, though, it makes sense to keep like commodities together. This helps you remember what and how much of each item you have. And maintaining an inventory of what is where makes sense also, particularly if your mini-pantries are spread throughout your house. Taping a list on the inside of a door of a particularly full cupboard identifying what's on each shelf is a good idea, since it may be difficult to remember what's stored there if some items are stacked behind or on top of other items.

> *Don't limit yourself to spaces normally identified as cupboard space or pantry space.*

The first rule for finding pantry space is work with what you have, and look for ways to make it better. The second rule for gaining a pantry: don't limit yourself to spaces normally identified as cupboard space or pantry space. Nooks and crannies and unusual places can play a significant role.

USE THE WORKSHEET

Examine each area of your home for hidden potential. Put on your thinking cap and start your creative juices flowing as you look around for different places that can be turned into pantries. Look up, look under, look inside. Rearrange, reevaluate, reprioritize. Expand your evaluation beyond spaces normally associated with groceries. Where can you find unused or underused space that could be put to work as pantry space? As you explore the pantry potentials in your home, jot down comments, dimensions, ideas, and sketches on the following worksheet. After you have reviewed the options suggested in this chapter, refer to appendix A for specific how-to details for creating many of these pantry ideas.

TO BUY OR TO BUILD, THAT IS THE QUESTION

When you find a likely-looking spot in your home, the next step is to transform it from just an empty space into a working, functioning pantry. That usually means with shelves, containers, or cupboards of some kind or another, or all of the above. If you are handy with tools, the only thing standing between you and a pantry is a little time and a little money. The following ideas and some of the plans in appendix A will get you started. If, however, you were standing in the wrong line in heaven when they handed out the handyman genes, don't despair. Your local home improvement store is loaded with terrific storage and shelving ideas that will work even for people who can't tell a hammer from a hangnail.

I suggest that everyone, no matter what their skill level is, take a tour through the storage-solutions section of a local store just to see all the creative options that are available. You may find ideas there to fit your situation that would never have occurred to you. You could then purchase their supplies, or build your own version of a particularly good idea, based on your skill and budget level. Either way, just knowing what's available could make a big difference in how you can take advantage of potential pantry space that you've discovered.

> *A student of mine, a young man who lived with four other bachelors, went home from a class on the Pantry Principle (see chapter 14) determined to find a place to keep his emergency preparedness supplies. After a thorough review of his apartment and ribbing from his roommates, he was totally discouraged. Spare closets and cupboards were not to be found. Refusing to give up, he went out and bought five cinder blocks, placed his bed on four of them and used the fifth as a step. He grinned as he shared his success at our next class.*

BE READY FOR INSPIRATION

Sometimes just getting your mind thinking in a certain direction can inspire creativity. For example, while at a home improvement store I happened on a display of pressboard cupboard kits. Even though I was at the store for plumbing supplies, when I saw that

Pantry Search Worksheet

Areas to Consider	How to Improve for Use as a Pantry
Cupboards • Space above cabinets • Space below cabinets • Receding corners • Deep cabinets • Above stove • Above refrigerator	Clean out/rearrange Turntables Double-decker turntables Additional shelves Purchased or custom drawers Boxes Step Shelves
Closets • Hall or guest room • Bedroom • Linen • Broom • Utility	Rearrange Add shelves/step shelves in space above clothes Use end or half closet for floor to ceiling shelves Use crates/bookshelves for shelves Shelf racks on the backs of doors Redesign the entire closet solely as a pantry
Odd Spaces • In laundry room • Above washer and dryer • Between refrigerator and wall • Under beds • End or corner of a room • Under stairs/stairwells • Attic • Basement	Rearrange Use space above Add shelves Add vertical drawers Make built-in pantry Use crates/bookshelves for shelves Create pantry space with a false wall (possibly made from the backs of bookshelves)
Under Sinks • Kitchen • Bathrooms	Rearrange Add shelves Install or build cabinets/shelves
Out of the House • Garage • Carport • Sheds • Covered porch • Other	Rearrange Add insulated walls to create an entire room Add shelves, floor to ceiling Add freestanding shelf units Build a loft Suspend shelves from ceiling

Copy this page and take it along with you to your home-improvement store to check out their storage solutions and/or closet renovation sections. Let your imagination go and you'll find you have lots of creative options to choose from. Use it as a worksheet; keep notes and jot down prices for future planning.

cupboard, I instantly visualized how effective it would be as a pantry. With more than one I could create an even bigger pantry! I'm sure the store clerk couldn't imagine why in the world a bunch of boxes stacked on the floor could bring such a smile to my face. You'll find that your brain will start reinterpreting what you see also. Once you start thinking about how to maximize your space for pantries, you'll discover all sorts of options that would have never before occurred to you. Think of me when you're grinning in a store!

ADD A SHELF

There are as many different shelf options available as there are things that need to be stored on shelves, and there are very few areas in a home that can't be made more useful by adding a shelf or two. You can build floor-to-ceiling shelves for lots of storage space, or you can add just a single shelf or two on a spare wall in a utility room or closet to immediately increase the usability of that space. Shelves can be simply functional, or they can be decorative as well. You'll find metal utility brackets and boards, or ornate wooden brackets and hardwood shelving, or you can install adjustable shelving tracks so you can change the height of the shelves to match the items you put on them. Shelves can go just about anywhere to take advantage of the smallest spaces.

Pantry shelves don't have to be beautiful; they just have to hold stuff. Many home improvement stores or lumberyards have cull lumber or scrap piles where very affordable shelving pieces can be found. They may not be perfect—they may contain a knot or not match. But it doesn't matter if the shelf is not destined for public view. One requirement that Larry, the master pantry-builder, has is that all lumber for shelving must be straight. Warped wood just won't work.

A SHELF SUGGESTION FOR RENTERS

Don't hesitate to contact your landlord for permission to install quality shelving (even at your cost) that you will leave when you move on. Almost all of our landlords responded positively to this request, especially when we took the time to explain exactly what we had in mind to do. (Sketches help, even if you're not an architect.) If you focus on upgrading closets, laundry areas, and so on, rather than altering main living areas, your success rate will probably be better. A few times our landlords enthusiastically came out and helped us with our projects!

SLANTED SHELVES

Some people endorse the use of slanted shelving for canned goods, particularly if you have a whole room devoted to a pantry. You slip your newly purchased canned goods in the back of the shelf unit and the slant automatically rolls the oldest product to the front to be used first. Thus, the cans are rotated out on a regular basis. Slanted shelves are a clever idea, but although we've tried them in several homes, I personally find them more bothersome than beneficial. Commercial versions are usually expensive; they don't easily accommodate different-sized cans on the same shelf system, and they take up much more room than regular shelves. In fact you can store much more on straight shelves than you can on slanted shelves.

A suggestion from Sunset Magazine makes sense if you live in an earthquake-prone area. If you are using metal utility shelves, install the shelves upside down in their frames. That way each shelf will have a lip on it to help keep cans and jars from falling off.

During a break at a workshop I was teaching, the discussion turned to the impossibility for most of those attending to have a real pantry. They all lived in very small apartments. The feeling of discouragement was evident. One young woman joined the conversation, saying that she had figured out why she had such a hard time being organized. It was an inherited trait. She went on to explain that in researching her genealogy, she discovered she had descended from the House of Pilot. And she could prove it with her preparedness supplies: she would pile it here and pile it there.

As for the rotation advantage, I find it's just as easy to pull my existing cans to the front by hand and put the newer items behind them when I bring them home from the store.

Some people believe that rotation refers not just to using the old stock first, but to actually turning the cans over on a regular basis in order to increase the shelf life of canned goods. With the exception of evaporated milk, this is just an old wives' tale. (Evaporated milk tends to coagulate and caramelize if not rotated occasionally. But canned milk is not a long-term storage item anyway. Rotating the cans can be accomplished by simply turning them over every now and again.) However, slanted shelves are an option if you want them.

FREESTANDING SHELF UNITS

There are freestanding, ready-made shelving units available in all sizes, just waiting to be filled with your preparedness supplies. These are especially appropriate for those of you who rent and don't have the option of putting nails in the walls or building shelves. They range in quality from metal to paintable pressed fiberboard (which doesn't necessarily have to be painted) to stained and varnished hardwood, and in size from small to full-room sized. Some shelf units are like bookcases, with sides and shelves, and with or without backs.

SHELF SPACING

Poorly designed shelving can waste a lot of usable space. If you are building your own shelves, decide in advance what you are going to put on them, and build accordingly. Lower shelves can be spaced further apart to accommodate taller five- or six-gallon buckets of bulk foods. You may want to plan shelves for No. 10 cans or gallon jars. Organize your cans, cases, and boxes so that each shelf holds approximately the same-sized items. If you stack individual cans or boxes more than two high, you'll spend too much time restacking fallen goods.

Do your existing shelves waste space? If you are dealing with existing shelves or with purchased shelf units with predetermined spacing, you'll have to make do or adapt. If the shelving is too far apart, or too deep (more than sixteen inches or so) you can add intermediate shelves or half-depth shelves to more efficiently use the space. If the shelves are adjustable, arrange them so there is a space of two inches between the top of the cans and the bottom of the next shelf.

MAKING SENSE OUT OF CHAOS: REARRANGING OR REASSIGNING YOUR CUPBOARDS

Are your cupboards a disaster area? Do you open the doors slowly—an inch at a time—to avoid the avalanche of dishes and junk that is stuffed inside like a bomb waiting to go off? If so, you probably have storage space there just waiting to be captured. Messes are very space consuming. But before emptying out all of the cupboards at once, plot out how to rearrange those disaster areas on paper first. Have a plan in place so that you don't take everything out, get discouraged, and shove it all back in without making any progress.

Reassign

As you try to imagine how the space can be adjusted for more efficient use, begin by looking at what is occupying the space now. Can you begin by reassigning? Do you have an abundance of specialized equipment filling shelf space, such as extra large cookware, serving platters, or unique pans or bowls that you use only for holidays or special occasions? These often-bulky items are essential when needed, but if you don't need them frequently, they shouldn't be taking up valuable shelf space all the time. I'm not suggesting that you throw out needed items, just reassign them to

No-cost, sturdy cardboard boxes can be cut to size for "custom-built" drawers. I recommend produce boxes that come with a top that slides down over the whole box. Place the box upside down inside the top for a double-strength "drawer." With a sharp knife you can even cut a handle-hole in the end. For smaller spaces, shoeboxes will work. Wrap several layers of strapping tape (the kind with fibers in it that is impossible to tear) around the upper edge and they will last for years.

a different shelf, closet, or area not as serviceable as prime pantry space ought to be. Reassign them to an accessible but less central location, perhaps the far back corner under the stairs, in a box in the back of a closet, or a high shelf in the garage. My large, seasonal utensils nest on a high, little-used corner shelf in the pantry, coming out as needed. That leaves quite a bit of prime shelf space to be used for pantry items.

Rearrange

The top shelf in many kitchen cupboards is usually too high to conveniently use every day, especially if your cupboards go all the way to the ceiling. Turn that top shelf into pantry space instead of a junk collector. Pull out all the extra mixing bowls or Cool Whip containers or decorative ice cube trays that are gathering dust up there and designate it as a pantry. All of the collective space of those top shelves will add up. If it's difficult to see what you put up there, tape a list on the inside of the cupboard door.

If you can't create more space on the shelves, you can add extra shelves, or you can purchase commercial space extenders. A turntable or pullout drawer or box in a hard-to-reach corner cabinet would make the space there more usable.

Is there wasted space between the top of your cupboard and the ceiling? Stack your pantry items there. Corral small items in boxes or bins that fit in the space. If you don't want to look at groceries above your cupboards, a short curtain (about the size of a valance) hanging from the ceiling would cover the storage space but still keep it accessible.

Is there room for a shelf between the upper cupboards and the counter? Move your flour and sugar out of the cupboards and into pretty canisters on the counter and use the empty cupboard space as pantry space. Spices can also look nice on a display shelf on the counter, in a rack on the back of a door, or compacted onto a double-decker turntable, freeing up cupboard space for pantry items.

The only exception in maximizing cupboard space is to avoid putting food items over the stove or in any other excessively hot area, if there's any possible way to get around it. Use that space for equipment, paper products, or other items that won't spoil.

MAKE ROOM ABOVE THE WASHER AND DRYER

Since many washer/dryer hookups are set back in an alcove, there is usually room to add several shelves, if not a set of cabinets, above them. If the alcove or closet is deep enough, the shelves could be on three walls, forming a U. Although heat and moisture make this a less-than-ideal spot for food, it still can provide needed space for nonfood items and emergency gear. If it's the only space you have, you can use it for food. Just be aware you'll have to rotate the food out more frequently than if it were kept in more desirable conditions. But that is the mind-set for a working pantry anyway—using it so that you're not losing it. (See appendix A-1.)

Some people actually have an entire small room for their washer and dryer. If you do, take advantage of it by installing shelves everywhere you can. My own laundry room is lined with store-bought ready-made shelving units. Since this room is much too warm and moist to be ideal for food items, the shelves are full of laundry soap, hand soap, dishwashing liquid, toilet tissue, paper towels, paper products, lightbulbs, batteries, dog food, and all manner of cleaning supplies. I also keep my upright freezer in this room. Every inch is converted to useful pantry space.

Recycled kitchen cabinets can find new life as a pantry above a washer and dryer (or outside in the garage). No matter how outdated or unattractive they may be, they will create useful pantry space out of wall space. Check the phone book for cabinet shops. Once in a while there will be seconds available at reasonable prices. Keep an eye out for used cabinets in yard sales if you want a real bargain.

CONVERT A CLOSET

Not every home can spare an entire closet, but even part of a closet, or parts of several closets, make fine mini-pantries if you use the space wisely.

The side or end of a closet also is a good place for a set of shelves. Even if the shelves could only be four to six inches deep, you'd find there might be a lot of usable space hidden behind your winter coats and galoshes. (See appendix A-2.) If building shelves is out of your league, measure the closet and look for a bookshelf with the proper dimensions. Another simple solution is to use the plastic crates or cubes found in office supply or bedroom décor departments. When fitted into the end of the closet, the walls will provide support, and the crates can be stacked from floor to ceiling.

Even a fairly small broom closet can be converted into a mini-pantry. Divide the closet in half with a tall vertical board. Build shelves on one side, and leave the other side open for your broom and mop and other awkwardly shaped necessities.

The shelf at the top of a typical closet is designed very inefficiently. You can gain quite a bit of additional shelving area without remodeling the entire closet, just by adding or adapting shelves at the top. The main shelf is usually quite deep. Take it out, and in its place, add one or two shelves that are narrower (twelve inches or so). This will allow you to reach up and in. Making even this small change in the majority of your closets would substantially add to your pantry space.

TRADITIONAL CLOSET USE REVISITED

You may have a whole closet that you can devote to pantry space without being aware of it. Begin by assessing how your closets are currently being used and then reevaluate, rearrange, and reassign them from a pantry perspective. During the years we lived in apartments in California, I simply changed the conventional use of my linen closet. This was a traditional wide-but-not-deep closet in the hallway. Sheets and blankets were stashed in boxes in the corners of the bedroom closets, and towels and washcloths were relegated to shelves in the bathroom. The entire linen closet was transformed into part of the apartment's pantry system. The floor of the coat closet is another unlikely pantry space, but that's where we kept our buckets of flour and rice and so on.

MAKE OVER A WHOLE CLOSET

If you can find a whole, large, square-shaped closet to transform into a pantry, put shelves from floor to ceiling on all three walls, leaving a step-in spot in the middle. Don't forget there is also space on the back of the door where racks can be hung to hold small containers. (See appendix A-3.)

If you are renting, or building-skill challenged, you can still create a very serviceable pantry out of a closet. A bookcase or shelving unit placed across the back, with two additional, narrower units on each side against the closet sidewalls will create a U-shaped step-in closet. For more stability, fasten the units to the walls. If you want to use taller shelf units to make better use of the space, remove the standard single closet shelf, if there is one. Simply save the shelf and the support strips for replacing when you move.

FREESTANDING CUPBOARDS OR CLOSETS

In years gone by, before built-in closets were invented, old-fashioned armoires were used to hold clothing. In a takeoff on an old-fashioned idea, you can use freestanding cupboards/closets/armoires as mini-pantries. In contrast to shelving units where everything is on display, these freestanding units will keep all your storage items neatly behind doors. Ranging from pressed fiberboard to beautiful hardwood, your freestanding pantries can be as plain or fancy as you wish, and come in a wide price range. Pressboard closets are fairly inexpensive, and even I can assemble them—so you know they're not too difficult to put together. But what a difference they can make! If the standard spacing between the shelves is too far apart for your purposes, you can put in additional shelves by using one-by-two-inch strips or brackets. Without question, most apartments lack storage space. During our years of living in apartments in California, we compensated for that by using freestanding cupboards whenever building shelves was not an option. We were willing to exchange floor space for pantry space. Our small apartment rooms became smaller, but our pantry space increased.

Don't forget there is quite a bit of room available up on top of freestanding cupboards also. Bright colored crates, boxes, or tubs can sit on top and make effective use of that bit of space. Label the ends for easy identification of contents.

Freestanding units keep all your storage items neatly behind doors.

A WALL OR TWO

If you're lucky enough to have a fairly large room in your house, take part of that room and turn it into pantry space. Use twelve to sixteen inches of floor space and build up! Wall space is one of the most overlooked opportunities for a pantry. Fill one wall, floor to ceiling, with shelves and hang a curtain in front of them. Or, for a more finished look, depending on the room, simple hinges and doors will make an enclosed pantry. In a standard ten- to twelve-foot bedroom, a whole wall of shelves would be an extra square foot or more of pantry space. Anywhere you have wall space is fair game: bedrooms, den, garage, and so on. (See appendix A-4.)

If you have a large enough room, build a false wall to form a sort of walk-in closet or room divider. This could be as fancy or as simple as you need and want it to be. If you're not handy with tools, buy tall bookshelves with backs. Line them up side by side with the backs to the room and the shelves facing into the little walk-in pantry area, leaving a couple of feet as an entrance. If you can spare just a little more floor space, move the bookshelves another twelve to fifteen inches further out into the living area and double your pantry space by putting additional bookcases (backs are optional on this set) against the real wall (facing the row of bookshelves with backs) in the newly created walk-in pantry. (See appendix A-5.)

When we were first married, we lived in a small rented home. We weren't allowed to make any permanent changes or mar the walls, but we still wanted to have a pantry. In the tiny 10-by-10-foot bedroom we used as a nursery, we created a walk-in pantry by stacking wooden apple boxes on top of each other, floor to ceiling, and almost the full width of the room, about five feet out from the far wall, with their backs to the center of the room, forming a dividing wall. We placed a second row of apple boxes against the wall. On the backs of the boxes nearest the bedroom area we tacked up peg-board, which strengthened and supported the boxes. We then painted it to match the nursery furniture and hung pictures and toys on it for decoration. A curtain, hung from the wall to the boxes, closed off the "doorway" to this small pantry. We placed the children's dresser in the closet, since none of their clothes hung very low anyway and the space at the bottom of the closet otherwise would have been wasted. This left a "bedroom" only 5 by 10 feet, just barely big enough for both cribs and room to squeeze past them to put the babies to bed. It was cramped and crowded but it worked, and the babies couldn't have cared less.

TAKE ADVANTAGE OF THE SPACE UNDER THE BED

There are better things to keep under the bed than dust bunnies. I suggest that you convert this normally ignored or underutilized space into a unique functioning mini-pantry. An under-the-bed pantry is a classic case of small spaces discovered and recovered. It can be done with very little effort (once you get rid of the dust bunnies). Depending on the size of the bed—twin to king—you will have available twenty-one to forty-three square feet of new pantry. This is worth getting enthused about, since most of us have only thought of this space as storage. If you are renting, or space is at a premium, with a little planning and organization perhaps this is the idea that can be adapted to become the pantry solution you've been looking for. Many under-bed storage containers are available to allow you to immediately put that space to good use. Some are plastic; some are cardboard. Either will work fine in an under-bed mini-pantry. Though they are designed to fit under the bed to hold bedding, sweaters, and so on, they can just as readily hold groceries and pantry items. Because they come in different depths, you'll want to measure your under-bed space before you buy and plan on allowing one half to one inch clearance to be able to slide them in and out. Some of them even have wheels on them. For the containers to be useful, you'll need to organize, categorize, and label the ends of these "drawers."

If your bed were higher, you could fit more pantry items under it. Very high beds are quite fashionable. If you have one, you may wish to sacrifice fashion for function, because you can store a lot under a high bed frame. (Add a deep dust ruffle to hide the pantry items if you wish.)

> *Anywhere you have wall space is fair game for a mini-pantry.*

If you only have a regular-height bed, there are some tricks you can do to turn it into a high bed to accommodate a "pantry down under." For example, commercial bed risers are available in different heights. You can usually find them in home improvement stores or home products catalogs. As a safety precaution, remember to remove the casters to prevent your bed from rolling off the risers. If you are handy, you can build a platform to serve as a bed frame.

A simple wheeled pallet made from one-fourth inch plywood, casters, a narrow one-by-two-inch edging to keep things from falling off, and a pull rope will make under-bed pantry items easily accessible. This kind of "drawer" will allow you to use all the space under the bed, not just the space around the edges. You just won't rearrange the furniture very often.

You can use poly buckets to accomplish the same thing as building a platform. If you use food-grade white poly buckets as containers for bulk flour, sugar, grains, beans, pastas, or small packaged items, a combination of five-gallon and six-gallon buckets will allow access to the buckets and create a working solution. Place six-gallon poly buckets under the four corners of the bed (and another in the center if the bed is larger than a twin) and top them with a piece of plywood cut to the size of your bed. (Home improvement stores will usually cut wood to the size you want for a nominal fee.) The mattress sits on top of the plywood with or without the box springs, depending on how high you are willing for your bed to be. Then, you can use the space under the bed to store five-gallon poly buckets full of things you consistently use like flour, sugar, and chocolate chips. (Keep canisters in the kitchen for everyday use and refill them from these buckets.) Since the five-gallon buckets are about two inches shorter than the six-gallon ones, you'll be able to access the smaller buckets (as well as any other tubs or containers that will fit) without a problem. Since most people are used to thinking about the

Under-bed storage containers allow you to put that space to good use. See diagram on following page.

space under their beds as storage space for blankets or out-of-season clothing at best, or as a junk collector at worst, using the space for a mini-pantry could be the new twist to an old idea that is just the solution you've been looking for!

FOOD AS A BED FRAME

If you have No. 10 cans of long-term storage foods like wheat, beans, or dehydrated foods that you aren't intending to eat for a long time, stack those in a single layer and use them as a bed frame. A twin-size bed sits neatly on about seventy cans. It's about the same height as a regular bed frame and you'll never see the cans if you put a dust ruffle on the bed. (You can do the same thing with a multitude of poly buckets also.) I know a woman who did this and she said it worked great for two reasons. First, it was a great place to store all those cases of dehydrated food that didn't have anywhere else to go. Second, the under-bed space was no longer a hiding place for dirty clothes, dirty dishes, and banana peels. It saved a lot of arguments with her teenager.

LONG-TERM STORAGE OR FUNCTIONING MINI-PANTRY?

When space is at a premium, finding places for long-term storage and finding space for functioning mini-pantries is difficult. Many of the same places can be used effectively for either one. You'll have to decide which you need most, and how to use your discovered and recovered space most efficiently.

A BUNK BED PANTRY

A bunk bed converted into a mini-pantry? That's exactly what a friend did. Her family (mom, dad, and daughter), lived in a cramped two-bedroom apartment with no storage space. So Linda turned her daughter's bedroom into a bedroom/pantry. Her bed was a twin-sized bunk bed. The lower bunk belonged to Ann. The upper bunk was the pantry. They reinforced the plywood pallet with additional screwed-in slats for strength, and stored the mattress for the upper bunk in the garage rafters. Cases of canned goods were stored on the floor under the bed, and all other pantry items were organized in boxes and containers on the top bunk. Linda commented, "It's the best I can do, and it's sure better than nothing." After a pause she added, "You'd be surprised how much

Creating an Under-the Bed-Pantry

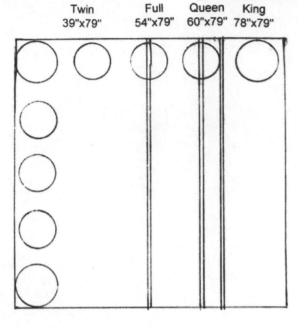

Twin 39"x79"	Full 54"x79"	Queen 60"x79"	King 78"x79"

Number of containers
that will fit under bed.

Twin	18
Full	24
Queen	30
King	36

5 gal. =25-33# ea

Fill a small container
from pantry under
the bed.

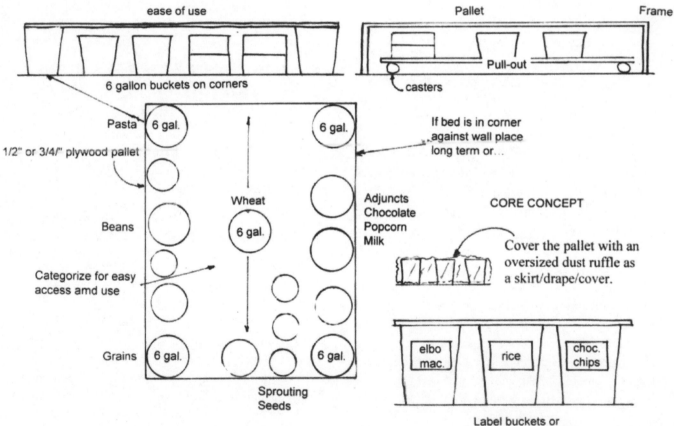

ease of use

6 gallon buckets on corners

Pallet   Frame

Pull-out

casters

Pasta   6 gal.   6 gal.

1/2" or 3/4/" plywood pallet

Beans

Wheat

6 gal.

Categorize for easy
access amd use

Grains   6 gal.   6 gal.

Sprouting
Seeds

If bed is in corner
against wall place
long term or…

Adjuncts
Chocolate
Popcorn
Milk

CORE CONCEPT

Cover the pallet with an
oversized dust ruffle as
a skirt/drape/cover.

elbo mac.	rice	choc. chips

Label buckets or
continers on side for
ease of identification

Purchase bulk on sale by pound
Purchase 25# - 50# bags
   Share and Save
Transfer Containers

space there is up there. It's just a closet laid sideways." There you have it: a bunk bed pantry—a closet laid sideways.

UNDER THE SINK

There often is dead space under kitchen and bathroom sinks where shelves can be built or set in—even if only to the side of the pipes. Even makeshift shelves, balanced on bricks, create room for storing soap, shampoo, deodorant and other nonfood items. If your bathroom has a sink without a cabinet, consider installing one to serve as a mini-pantry. If you have small children, don't forget to use safety latches if you keep anything down low that could be toxic or in the cleaning supply family. (See appendix A-6.)

LIVING ROOM/FAMILY ROOM/DEN

While no one wants shelves with soup and tuna lining their living room (though it would be a conversation starter), that doesn't mean the public rooms in your house can't be functional as well as inviting. Pull your couch two feet out from the wall. Stack case goods or equipment in sturdy containers behind it to the height of the couch, put a flat board across the tops of the boxes to even it out, and cover it all with a pretty tablecloth. It makes a slightly unusual sofa back table for plants or a table lamp. Of course, don't use this space to store items you'll be using all the time, since that would be really inconvenient. The same idea works for end tables. A pretty cloth can cover a multitude of surprises.

You would think, based on its name, that a beanbag chair would be a good place to store beans. It's a nice thought but a bad idea. First of all, do you really want food that you intend to eat someday to be sat on, rolled around on the floor, and exposed to all manner of dirt and dust? Of course not. Food needs to be kept clean and free from contaminants in appropriate storage containers. Secondly, if you put a sufficient number of beans in a beanbag chair to fill it out properly, the chair would weigh three hundred to four hundred pounds, maybe even more. It would be much too heavy to move around or conform to your body when you sat in it. The filling for beanbag chairs is shredded foam or tiny lightweight plastic pellets, not beans.

UNDER THE STAIRS

Homes with stairwells often have framed-in space underneath the stairs. The same concepts apply to this space as to regular closet space. Put shelves on as many walls as possible, or if the slanted ceiling is too awkward, consider putting shelf units on casters that can be rolled out for convenience. Under my daughter's stairs, they stashed No. 10 cans of long-term storage as tightly as they could in the furthest tip, where it angles sharply and is too narrow to get to easily. Then, where the ceiling got about three feet high, they put a small bookshelf in front of the cases of No. 10 cans. This formed a kind-of "back wall" for the closet. The far side of the under-stair closet is lined with twelve-inch shelves, and the near side is lined with six-inch shelves. That leaves a convenient two-foot space in the middle to allow them to reach anything on any shelf. It's a lot of storage space in what would usually be considered just a junk-collecting space. (See appendix A-7.)

If your stairs are divided, like in a split-entry home, your under-stair space probably extends back under a landing, and maybe even back farther again than that. You can still take advantage of all that space instead of it just being a messy catch-all. Use the farthest back, inaccessible dark corners for long-term storage foods or equipment. Under the landing, or far enough back that access is still difficult, store spices, canned goods, or paper products in wheeled containers that can be pulled out without too much trouble. Easily installed battery-operated touch lights can illuminate dark spaces without the need for electrical rewiring, as long as you remember to replace the batteries occasionally.

Adding 1-by-4-inch or 1-by-6-inch shelves between the studs can turn even wasted stud space into storage space that's the ideal width for canned goods, spices, or a multitude of small containers.

Beanbag chairs are not preparedness pantry containers!

In the front, build all the shelves you can, or at least stack clearly labeled plastic containers.

Now wouldn't that be a better use of the space than a black hole where socks and coats disappear for months on end until the dreaded clean-out day?

GARAGE, ATTIC, OR SHED

Many people will tell you that a garage, attic, or shed is a poor place for a pantry because they are too hot, too cold, too accessible to bugs, too dirty, and so on. In many respects, they are right. These places usually are too hot, too cold, too accessible to bugs, and too dirty. However, if this is the space that you have—adapt!

Garage

Creative assessment can get you a workable, wonderful pantry. Our family has spent most of their lives in California, where dark, dry, and cool basements (the ideal place for a pantry) are nonexistent. We also have moved a lot, which has given us ample opportunities to design and create many garage pantries. There is plenty of room in a garage that you may never have associated with a pantry. Is a garage ideal? No. Does it pose challenges? Of course! Is it an option? Absolutely! It merely requires planning around the fact that food or other items might not keep as long, due to the less-than-ideal conditions. Remember the rule: work with what you have, and look for ways to make it better!

A garage provides pantry options that range from just shelves to cabinets to walls of cabinets to a completely insulated walk-in pantry. In most of our California homes we've transformed the garage into an extension of the house, containing an entire pantry system of its own, including loft, insulated walls, cabinets, and customized shelves. Having our pantry built into the garage usually means our cars are not kept in the garage. It's inconvenient, but it's a choice we've made and a price we've been willing to pay in order to be prepared and live within our means.

If you are not willing to give up your entire garage, you can move all the tools and yard and garden equipment to one side (or to a shed) and dedicate the other side pantry space, lined with shelves or cabinets and cupboards. Try to put pantry shelves on the coolest side of the garage, usually the north wall or an inside wall attached to the house.

Garage Loft

Most garages have loads of wasted space if you look up. The area above the vehicles is usually empty and just waiting to be turned into pantry space, or at least storage space. If you have rafters, you can add a plywood "floor" to the rafters and stationary stairs or a ceiling-mount, pull-down ladder to create a loft that you can walk in. If your garage already has a ceiling in it, you can build from scratch, buy ready-made, or have professionally installed suspended shelf units that hang down from the ceiling. These wouldn't be particularly convenient for storing food items you use regularly. However, they would be great for storing emergency equipment, blankets, or holiday decorations. Then you could use the closet or cupboard space formerly occupied by the blankets and holiday decorations as pantry space!

Attics

Attics are generally much too hot for storing food, but perfectly acceptable for nonfood supplies and equipment. If you have an accessible attic that isn't filled with blown-in insulation, use it for blankets, paper goods, and things that won't spoil.

My daughters-in-law turned their attics into whole rooms full of storage space. They insulated everything, strengthened the floor, and installed fold-down stairs where the access panel in the hall ceiling originally was. They use their attics for all their seasonal storage, holiday decorations, camping equipment and so on. That left the closets and storage space in their houses for pantry items.

If you intend to store anything at all in your attic, fans or vents are a must to prevent combustion. I know one family who wanted to make their attic space usable for food items so they connected an air conditioning vent to their attic to keep it acceptably cool in the summer months. Sometimes it just takes creative thinking to turn what you've got into what you want.

Sheds

Sheds are often a prime example of the worst possible conditions for keeping food. They normally are exposed to all the extremes of temperature, humidity, and dirt all year long. But if that is the option you have to work with, then do what you can to make it function. Insulation and caulking will improve conditions greatly, as will carefully choosing a cool location when you set it up if you have a choice (and by "cool," I mean "not hot," rather than "really awesome"). Like attics, garages, and other less-than-ideal places, sheds do well for many nonfood needs, such as 72-hour kits, emergency equipment, sleeping bags, and tents. Consider them a functioning part of your preparedness pantry system.

If you already use your loft, garage, shed, or attic to store holiday decorations, off-season clothing, or stuff you don't really need but can't bring yourself to get rid of yet, try reorganizing it all. Stack it higher, deeper, more compactly, and more neatly to free up space. (Pretend you're practicing a real-life version of the computer game Tetris.) Then convert the recovered space into a mini-pantry.

PRETTY CLOSE TO IDEAL

An ideal pantry would be a cool basement room dedicated entirely to being just a pantry. Dark, dry, and cool, with shelves on all the walls, this is what everyone would love to have. If you have an unfinished basement, consider yourself lucky. Choose a corner that is without windows. Insulate all the walls as you build them, and remember to plan plenty of space for shelves galore. If the basement is already finished, use a room with as few windows as possible. Cut a piece of plywood to fit inside the window frame against the glass, then insulate the window space between the newly cut plywood and the room. Close and seal off all heater vents, add a multitude of shelves, and you're in business!

A room on the main floor makes almost as good a pantry as a basement room. Keep it as dark, dry, and cool as possible by covering any windows, blocking off the heater vent, and keeping the door closed. If you can permanently dedicate a room to being a pantry, consider insulating the walls also. Four-by-eight-foot sheets of Styrofoam insulation can be installed right on top of existing wallboard, with shelves butted up against it. If the room is still too warm, open the air conditioning or cooler vents during the summer, and keep the heater vents closed in the winter. A full-fledged whole-room pantry is hard to beat.

A REFILLABLE WORKING PANTRY

You'll agree that some of these ideas are pretty inconvenient when it comes right down to actual cooking. It just is not worth it to have to walk to the farthest reaches of the house each time you need a cup of sugar or a can of tomatoes. It is vital, however, to be able to use whatever space you can find to store the supplies and food you need to be prepared and to stretch your budget. What you need to make these distant mini-pantries usable is a small working pantry. This can be as simple as a cupboard or couple of shelves in or near your kitchen where you keep a can or two of the things you use most often, and canisters of flour, sugar, and so on that you can refill from bulk containers stored in other parts of the house. This way you get the best of both worlds: mini-pantries that hold your bulk-buying bargains and stock-up-sales items, and a working pantry that allows you to have the things you need most right at your fingertips. It is also the key to rotating and using, rather than just storing, the items you purchase bulk.

WHERE NO PANTRY HAS GONE BEFORE

Sometimes as you search for space for a pantry, you'll come to the conclusion that whoever drew up the plans for your home or apartment used invisible ink when including plans for storage. When it seems that finding a workable mini-pantry system is just impossible, take the words from Rodgers and Hammerstein's *Cinderella* as your theme song: "Impossible things are happening every day!" Your creative juices must work overtime if you want to create a pantry badly enough—either that or be related to me and have pantry in your DNA. Finding space may be the final frontier, and you must boldly go where no pantry has gone before.

Let me share with you some of our experiences to prove that you make the best of what you have until you can do better. You have to just keep making improvements on the worst until it becomes acceptable. Notice that I didn't say "until it becomes good." Sometimes acceptable is the best you can do.

When we moved eight hundred miles and went back to college in Provo, Utah, with two almost-teenagers, we rented a tiny house designed by the aforementioned architect who used invisible ink and had a strong aversion to storage space. Even though finding pantry space is programmed into my DNA, this house pretty much had me stumped: no basement, no attic, no garage, and almost no closets. Although the conditions were highly undesirable, Larry built some narrow shelves on one wall of the water heater/furnace room. He also reclaimed some otherwise wasted (though still less-than-desirable) space by building shelves above the washer and dryer in the corner of the kitchen. The only other option we could come up with was a rickety metal shed in the backyard. Larry repaired the sagging doors and added shelves to the inside. It was far from ideal, but it was all we had available so we made it work. Of course there was the time during one winter there that a fierce storm blew in, and in the middle of the night, when bitter winds were howling we heard a terrible crashing and banging. The next morning when we went out to inspect the damage, we had to walk to the end of the block to see how our shed had fared. We hauled it home from the neighbors' yard, beat it back into shape, and tightly secured it to its base. Were these storage options ideal? Definitely not. Were we desperate? Yes. Did they work? Yes, for the most part. Were they better than nothing? Absolutely.

ORGANIZING YOUR PANTRY SYSTEMS

After going to the work of finding pantry space to store your purchases, it's important to actually be able to use them and not lose them. You can lose your food and supplies in two ways: (1) You can forget you have it until it is so old it is unusable, or (2) You can literally lose it. You know you have it but you have no idea where it is, and it's too much bother to try to find it. Both are a sorry waste of money and effort. With a pantry system (mini-pantries located in a variety of places), being at least somewhat organized saves time and money, in addition to guaranteeing better shelf life for everything. To me the term "system" not only refers to the variety and location of pantry shelves, it also refers to the way the items are organized, categorized on those shelves, and listed on a master list. The most wonderfully remodeled closet or freestanding cupboard unit won't function properly if, when you open the doors, you're faced with a chaotic jumble of crammed, tossed, smashed, piled, and jammed-in stuff. The shelves may look like they're full, but what a waste! I have three suggestions for keeping

your valuable mini-pantries usefully organized. (1) keep like items together, (2) use containers, and (3) label, label, label!

KEEP LIKE ITEMS TOGETHER

Keeping like items together seems like common sense, but you'd be surprised how many people will just stash whatever they have in the nearest spot available. From the outset (or from this moment on) make a point to designate certain places for certain foods or supplies and stick to your plan. Until you are very familiar with your system, it may help to put a masking tape label on the edges of the shelves to remind you what is supposed to go there. All canned fruit goes on this particular shelf. Canned vegetables go on the shelf below. Medicine and first aid supplies go in the hall closet. Grains and beans go in the mini-pantry in the baby's room, and so on. The reason for this, besides not losing the things you have purchased, is so you can see at a glance what you have and what you need. For example, say you were looking at the grocery ads and saw that Ed's Grocery Mart is having a sale on canned peaches. Before you run down and buy a case of peaches, you can just walk to your mini-pantry and take a look. It may turn out that you already have plenty of peaches. It would be wiser now to use that money for stocking up on something you are running low on, like tomato sauce or flour or laundry soap. Or maybe the brownie mix shelf is in a desperate condition. By being able to see instantly what is or is not on the shelves, you can stretch your budget in the right direction.

USE CONTAINERS

You'll find there are some small items that just take up too much space if they are arranged neatly on a shelf. Toothpaste and dental floss, for example, or Band-Aids and over-the-counter medicines. For these types of items, instead of laying the items out individually, buy a container (or find the right-sized cardboard box) and lump all the like items together in it. You'll be able to keep three times as much on your shelves and it will still be easily accessible. This is especially important if one shelf or closet is going to contain several different kinds of items that could easily get jumbled together, such as hygiene products and cleaning supplies.

Plastic boxes, tubs, or containers are perfect for

this type of organizing because they come in so many different sizes. You're sure to find the size you want. Cardboard boxes or shoe boxes are great also. You can make them practically indestructible by wrapping several layers of strapping tape around the upper edges.

For example, one of my mini-pantries was in a narrow but deep hall closet, with fixed shelves set too far apart to be efficient. Without boxes to organize the closet contents, the closet would have been mostly wasted space. However, with tubs to hold soap, medicines, hygiene supplies, shampoo, washcloths, and so on, I was able to take advantage of almost every inch of the closet. True, I did have to take out a box and set it on the floor to access the box behind it, but that was easy enough to do, considering how much pantry space it afforded.

LABEL, LABEL, LABEL!

You might think that you'll remember what you put in each box on your shelf, but when you have several generic boxes or tubs in a row with no indication what's inside them, it's more difficult than it seems. You can save yourself much frustration by clearly labeling each box. You can write directly on the plastic or cardboard with a felt-tip marker if you choose, though if you later change the contents of the box,

you'll have to scratch out the previous identification, or try to scrub it off, which may or may not be successful. This won't change the usefulness of the box, but it isn't really attractive. If that doesn't bother you, there's no problem. If it does, you may wish to write on labels instead. I've found that self-adhesive labels have a tendency to curl and peel off with weather changes and time. To combat this, I usually firmly affix my container labels (either the adhesive type, or just a square piece of white paper) with clear plastic packaging tape. If the container is going to be stored outside in a shed or garage where the weather will affect it, I make sure to completely cover the label with clear tape, not just around the edges.

In *The Wizard of Oz*, one famous line says, "There's no place like home." I'd like to paraphrase it: "There's no place like a pantry!" The delight of bringing home a case of peaches or half a dozen cans of pork and beans (bought at superb sale prices, of course!) and being able to have a place to put it away is satisfying! The satisfaction of adding to my supply of wicks and candles is comforting! Feeling assured that you and your family will be warm as winter and blackouts return is security! Knowing that the chocolate shelf is full is wonderful!

Just remember, a pantry in a less-than-ideal spot is better than no pantry at all!

CHAPTER FIVE

KEYS TO STORAGE: WHAT TO DO WITH IT WHEN YOU GET IT

Now that you have found the shelf space for a pantry system, you need to learn a few of the keys to making sure the time, money, and effort you've expended in filling those shelves aren't wasted. The food you've stored needs to be edible when you want to eat it, and your equipment needs to function when you want to use it. That means there is more to maintaining a pantry than just stacking stuff on shelves. What you have to realize is that with an effective preparedness program you will never be "done." You can successfully acquire a three- or six- or twelve-months' supply of all the things you will need for that space of time, but even at that point you are not done. Your supplies need to be constantly used, replaced, rotated, and cared for. That way they don't spoil and end up being wasted.

> *Your supplies need to be constantly used, replaced, rotated, and cared for.*

USING, REPLACING, AND ROTATING FOOD

Using and replenishing your storage program should become a commonplace, everyday activity, as normal as preparing meals now is. And while it requires an initial investment to stock a pantry, eventually it becomes the most economical and convenient way to live. Instead of going to the store when you need something and paying full price for it (plus purchasing other impulse buys while you are there), you can go to your storage room or pantry to get what you need. Then you replace it next time it is on sale.

"Rotating your food" can be interpreted two ways: turning each can or package over so the food inside it is stirred up, or moving the position of the can or package so older products are used before newer products. For the most part, I don't bother with the first interpretation. With the exception of evaporated milk, which will settle if not turned over sporadically, your cans and boxes don't need to be turned over on a regular basis. However, it is very important to rotate your supplies so that you use the oldest stock first. When you bring home a half a dozen cans of tuna (purchased on sale, of course!), you must pull the cans on the shelf to the front and put the new ones behind them. If you don't, the old stock just keeps getting older and older, until it will have to be discarded. I find one of the best ways to keep my food effectively rotated is to keep a felt-tip marker in the canned goods pantry and scribble a quick date on my cans, packages, and boxes as I put them away. At a glance, I can see that the can of soup with the '05 on it needs to be used before the can with '06, or I should grab the bag of pancake mix marked "May '05" before I take the "December '05" bag. The one exception I make is chocolate chips; they don't stay on my shelves long enough to bother marking a date on them.

NOT AN INHERITANCE FOR YOUR GRANDCHILDREN

Food storage was never meant to be an inheritance for your grandchildren. Even with the excellent methods available for treating food to extend its shelf life, food does not last forever. Proper care and rotation of the food items in your pantry is essential. To have to discard and then repurchase things due to spoilage is to forfeit your original savings and defeats the purpose of preparedness. If you purchased a hundred pounds of flour and several cases of SpaghettiOs in order to be ready for a rainy day, put them on the shelf where they would be conveniently out of the way, then rested on your laurels for twenty-two years, you'd be in for a rude awakening.

SHELF LIFE

No food's shelf life is indefinite, no matter how it is packaged. In fact, any timetables for shelf life in this book are only approximate, in order to provide guidelines for a sensible use-and-rotation system. The idea of "permanent storage" or "food that will keep until the end of time" needs to be eliminated from your mind and vocabulary. The point is not to try to keep food forever. The shelf life of a food does not mean how long you can keep the food on a shelf without having to actually eat it. A better meaning for shelf life in a preparedness context is that you have learned to store your food properly so that it will give you life after it has been on your shelf. A main purpose of the Pantry Principle (see chapter 14) is to use the things you have stocked on your shelves and replace them when the price is right.

No food can be stored without eventual deterioration, even under the best circumstances. Proper storage conditions and practices, though, will minimize deterioration, and ward off contamination and insect damage as well as changes in flavor and appearance. Each food has an ideal shelf life beyond which nutrition, taste, and texture slowly but surely decline. For example, canned vegetables have a shelf life of approximately one to two years from the time you purchase them at the store. That means that the manufacturer guarantees that your can of green beans will have the same quality, texture, and nutrition a year after you buy it that it had the day it came off the conveyer belt

at the cannery. The shelf life estimates published by manufacturers, the government, and other sources are extremely conservative, since they can't account for the many different conditions under which consumers will store the food. Their figures are based on the time beyond which full nutrition cannot be guaranteed. That doesn't mean that if you eat your can of green beans a year and a day after you buy it that you will die of botulism poisoning, or that the beans will have deteriorated into an amorphous blob. It just means that there is no guarantee that you'll get 100 percent of the food value and quality the beans had the day they were canned. You still may, but it isn't guaranteed.

KEYS TO STORAGE

Keeping food dry, cool, and protected from light is the key to proper storage. The less light, heat, and moisture the food is exposed to, the longer its shelf life will be. Heat, light, and moisture are the real villains in your pantry and home storage areas. These three factors encourage bacteria and mold to grow, can cause spoilage, and will vastly reduce the shelf life of food, even canned goods. Too much heat can also cause flavor and appearance changes. The higher the temperatures in your pantry areas, the more rapid the deterioration. Ideal storage temperatures range between thirty-five degrees and seventy degrees for best retention of vitamins and least probability of spoilage. For comparison, remember a refrigerator keeps food at forty degrees. You recall how much longer fresh food keeps when it's refrigerated than

---

A main purpose of the Pantry Principle (see chapter 14) is to use the things you have stocked on your shelves, and replace them when the price is right.

Optimal Canned and Dry Food Storage Conditions:

Cool
Between 35° and 70°, cooler is better

Dry
At 50 to 70% humidity

You may store food in less-than-optimum conditions, but it must be used sooner.

when it's left on a counter or shelf. It's the same idea for foods in a pantry or cupboard. Cool temperatures retard spoilage. In addition to spoilage, heat and moisture invite insect infestation in dry foods and encourage rust in canned goods, especially along the seams or wherever there may be a slight flaw in the metal. Light can actually destroy the nutritive value of food exposed to it for an extended length of time.

HOW OLD IS TOO OLD?

Inevitably, even in the best-kept pantries, you'll run across a can or box or case of food that has been overlooked or not needed until it's probably past its prime. You hate to just toss that food in the dumpster, since you spent good money on it. For all you know, it's still perfectly good. But on the other hand, for all you know, it may be bottled botulism. How do you know? Who's to say whether it should go on your table or in your trash can? The safety of food should always be your first consideration in shelf life. The odor, flavor, and texture of all foods will change as food ages, with a commensurate decrease in food value. The more they deteriorate, the less we will want to eat these foods. However, if it was safe to begin with, and if it doesn't show any of the following signs of spoilage, then the food should be safe to eat, even if it isn't as appetizing as it was when you first brought it home.

CHECKLIST FOR FOOD SAFETY[1]

If any of these signs of spoilage are present, throw the food out without tasting it!

1. Bulging can or lid

On home-bottled food, the lid will be concave and seal cannot be lifted with fingers. Cans purchased in stores will bulge on the ends.

2. A milky appearance to the liquid

In older foods, the food may begin to deteriorate, forming a residue in the bottom of the jar or can. This is not an indication the food is bad, just old. The liquid may appear cloudy due to the sloughed-off food, but the appearance should not be milky.

3. Corrosion on the inside of the can, especially along the seam

4. Rust, especially along the seam or seal of a can

5. Slimy appearance or texture

6. Rancid odor, especially in foods which contain any amount of fat

7. Mold growth on the food or inside of the container

8. Frozen can or bottle

Freezing produces hairline fractures in the seal and allows spoilage to begin. If a can is accidentally frozen, keep it frozen until time to use. Once the can thaws, the food will begin to spoil, though evidence of spoilage may not be visible for some time. Just because spoilage cannot be seen doesn't mean it isn't there and isn't harmful.

9. Off-smell

Food generally changes in odor as it ages. If the smell has developed to the point where it is unpleasant, discard the food. Remember though, a changing odor is not the same as a spoiling odor.

10. Home-bottled food processed improperly?

If improper processing times, methods, and/or recipes were used for home-processed vegetables and meats, the jar may be sealed but the product deadly. Do not taste! Throw it out!

CHOOSING THE RIGHT CONTAINER

When you fill your pantry shelves, if you only buy a few extra cans and boxes here and there, you may be able to keep these products in their original packaging. However, bulk purchases of sugar, oats, flour and other foods, especially if brought home in twenty-five-, fifty-, or one hundred-pound sacks, should be transferred into sturdy, airtight containers that will shut out insects, rodents, and moisture. If

Only food-grade, airtight, moisture-proof, puncture-proof containers are acceptable for storing food.

you don't, you take the chance of losing the bulk of your bulk-buying bargains.

There are containers of every size, shape, and material to choose from. What you use will depend on how much of each item you have to store. Only food-grade, airtight, moisture-proof, puncture-proof containers are acceptable for storing food. Glass, plastic, or metal containers are all suitable as long as they have tight-fitting lids; rodents can penetrate most plastic, even if it is extremely hard and heavy; glass and clear plastic allow more light to reach the food, which sometimes makes them less desirable than other options, though they are acceptable if the pantry area is dark most of the time.

Don't store food in any container that is not specifically meant to hold food. Plastic containers are made of chemicals. If not specifically designed to hold food, those chemicals may leach out when they come in contact with food. Likewise, if a food-grade container has been used to hold nonfood products, chemicals from these products could be absorbed into the container and subsequently released into food stored later in that container.

You can buy new containers of all sizes, but perfectly acceptable used containers can often be obtained for free or at minimal cost. Bakeries, doughnut shops, or restaurants sometimes sell used four- and five-gallon plastic buckets which previously held frosting or pie filling or the like. Gallon mayonnaise, mustard, or sauce jars and metal lard cans are often discarded by fast-food outlets, restaurants, cafeterias, or other places where food is prepared in volume. Don't be afraid to ask if you can have these containers before they are thrown away. I suggest you pass on plastic containers that have held pickles, vinegar, or other strong-smelling contents. It is almost impossible to remove the residual smell. That smell will then be absorbed by anything else you put into the bucket. Just think: dill-pickle-flavored powdered milk or vinegar oatmeal! (I'll skip breakfast today, thank you!)

Large plastic buckets and metal containers may also be purchased new. Check with wholesale container or food outlets, or institutional and restaurant suppliers if these containers are not readily available in your local stores.

You will probably find it convenient to have containers of many sizes on hand. Large plastic buckets may store large amounts of food for future use, while smaller jars and containers with plastic lids (such as shortening or coffee cans) might be more convenient for everyday kitchen use. Gallon jars with

---

Container Options:

Quart jars with lids

Large jars, such as pickle or peanut butter

Gallon jars with lids—glass or plastic

No. 10 cans with tight-fitting lids

Coffee cans/shortening cans with lids

Old-fashioned canisters with tight-fitting lids

Large lard cans with lids

Medium to large plastic buckets with lids

Plastic food-storage containers such as Tupperware, Rubbermaid, etc.

This chart will help you calculate the approximate number of containers you'll need if you purchase in bulk.

Item	# of 5-Gallon Containers Needed per 50 lbs Purchased
Rolled oats	2
Wheat, whole grains	1½
Lentils	1½
Beans, pcas	1½
Soup mix, dry	1½
Macaroni	1½
Noodles	6
Flour	2
Sugar	2

tight-fitting lids are good for pantry storage, especially if they can be kept in a relatively dark pantry. A gallon jar will hold five to six pounds of grain or beans, or three to four pounds of noodles.

Another pantry principle is that some types of commercial store packaging are more apt to become insect- or rodent-infested than others. This is especially true in humid climates. For improved storage capabilities and longer shelf life, you might want to put items packaged in cardboard, foil, plastic, or paper bags—still in their original packaging—in metal, glass, or sturdy plastic containers with tight-fitting lids. These would be items such as gravy or flavoring mixes, pouch cookie mixes, corn bread mixes or muffin mixes, bags of chocolate chips, envelopes of drink mixes, flavored rice or pasta pouches, and so on.

I have heard people suggest that fifty-five-gallon garbage cans make good storage containers for bulk purchases (such as grains or beans or other dry products). This is not true. I don't recommend the use of plastic or metal garbage cans to store foods because they can't be made airtight. The lids don't fit tightly. Even if you lined the garbage can with a plastic bag, it's still a poor choice. A plastic bag is not airtight, and it certainly will not deter rodents or insects. They will chew right through it like it isn't even there. Besides that, these containers would be so heavy when filled that you couldn't move them. In addition, such a large container would take a long time to use. The chance of the last half of the product spoiling, being infested with bugs, or being eaten by rodents is high.

A recent trend is to purchase many storage foods like grains or beans in Mylar bags. These look like metal cloth (kind of like Mylar balloons are the aluminum-looking balloons). Mylar bags are airtight, and they stack well, but they are not even remotely rodent- or insect-proof. Mice will appreciate your thoughtfulness in providing a tasty, accessible meal for them. Once opened, bags are less convenient to use, less airtight, and more likely to spill than a container with a lid. I prefer a sturdy, resealable, rodent-proof container any day.

MARAUDING MICE

It's not unusual to have mice discover grains, pasta, or anything else in your pantry, especially if it's not cared for properly in rodent-proof containers,

and move in with all their family and friends for an extended party at your expense. To best combat invading mice, first and foremost, take care of your food properly when you bring it home. That will eliminate 99 percent of all future problems. Secondly, if you discover the telltale signs of mice, take action at once. Don't wait another two weeks or a month before you set out traps and mouse bait. The longer the mice are left to themselves, the more you'll have to get rid of. Mice reproduce rapidly. The more there are to get rid of, the more unpleasant the job is.

Usually you can tell that you have resident mice by the droppings they leave. Packages and containers will have telltale bite and chew marks. There may be scattered food and crumbs on the shelves or floor. To get rid of them, I suggest mousetraps and mouse poison, like D-Con. This poison has the benefit of killing the mouse and mummifying it for lack of a better term at the same time so they don't decompose inside your walls. People have been searching for ways to build a better mousetrap for centuries, with no avail. Bait your traps with cheese or peanut butter (harder to steal), watch your fingers, and set them in the area where you find signs of infestation. You have to be extremely cautious with both traps and poison if you have pets or children in your house. You may need to put the traps and poison on a top shelf and spread out a handful of grain to attract mice up there away from curious animals or children.

YOU MEAN THE BUGS ARE ALREADY THERE?

You get out a bucket of flour to make some cookies, remove the lid, and find—horror of horrors!—you have weevil! Before you throw out every bit of food you have, fumigate your house, and disinfect every surface with bleach, relax! Having bugs in your food is not the worst thing that could happen to you. Honest. An infestation of bugs does not make you a lousy homemaker (pun intended).

It's almost impossible to keep bugs out of your grains, flour, and cereal products. In most cases the eggs, if not the insects, are already there. The weevil or mealy moths come home with you in packages from the grocery store and in sacks of grain, flour, or foods from other outlets. If you see an occasional little brown moth flying from shelf to shelf in the grocery store it is likely that you will be bringing some home with your groceries in the food packages or in the folds of the brown paper sacks. If you live in an area where grains and beans are grown, they are already there, flying from fields to your home. Therefore, you must learn how to cure, kill, or cope with the bugs. Your goal should be to recognize them and prevent them from incubating, establishing colonies, and spreading.

DEALING WITH MEALY MOTHS

Mealy moths are as likely to attack boxes of cake mix, cold cereal, pancake mix—regular items that you use every day—as they are bulk containers of grains and beans. They're persistent and will destroy a lot of food if allowed to remain unchecked. In order to get rid of them, you have to find out where they have made their home. Pay attention to the cupboards where you see bunches of the moths clustered on the undersides of shelves or on the ceiling and walls of the cupboards, even outside of the cupboard as the colony grows. There will be webs or sticky strings on the inside and outside of boxes and down through the product, and the lumping and clustering of the product is a good sign of infestation. Look for pinholes in the packages where the insects have either come or gone. There will be a "grainy dust" on the sides and bottom of the package, as well as throughout the product.

The young are in the form of larvae, which will crawl from one box or package to another. One of the miserable things about the larvae is that they can get into jars of grain or cereal by crawling up the threads of glass at the top where the lid screws on and on into the product. They can chew through plastic as well as cardboard.

You will need to go through the items in your pantry, box by box. When you find packages full of the moth or larvae, don't chuck them into the wastebasket in the kitchen. The moths are attracted by light; they will quickly get out of the wastebasket and infiltrate any other food containers or cupboards that they can get into. You many end up spreading them instead of containing them. When an infestation is really bad, fill garbage bags with the boxes and packages of infested food. Take them outside and spray bug spray directly into the garbage bag before putting the bag into the main trash outside. Once you find the source of the culprits and clean out the cupboards, you may consider clearing the shelves and spraying the cupboards

and cracks (*not* the food!) with a good bug spray. Yes, it can be a big job, but if any surviving larvae grow and develop into moths, you will eventually have to repeat the same cycle all over again. It's better to do a thorough job the first time.

In order to control them, you will probably need to use a commercial product. After you have cleared out infested packages and sprayed your shelves, go to a store that has a good pest control section, where mouse traps, and such are. There is a pest strip for flying insects. Mealy moth is one of the first insects listed in their "target" listing. Dow makes a good product; there are probably other brands that are just as effective. It comes in a waxy cake form, approximately 2 by 4 feet, and is hung up with a hook. Simply hang several of them in your pantry and cupboards. They work quite well, though it may take more than one for a pantry or kitchen.

The bad news is that you can bring more mealy moths home from the stores on any given day, or they can come in from the neighbors. Another option is to give up trying to control them and just consider them as easy-care house pets that don't require any special pet food.

RECOGNIZING SIGNS OF WEEVIL INVASION

If you discover just a few bugs in your flour, you can be assured that all of their relatives and extended family are in that container as well. If left untreated, the entire container of food will be destroyed, and the bugs will move on to other containers until your whole pantry is infested. You need to learn to recognize the signs that they have taken up residency so that you can get rid of them—now!

If you have a weevil infestation, you will find weevil hulls or shells (the bodies discarded by the weevil as they grow) scattered about. There may be tiny pinholes in packages, dust or grit on the shelves, and live beetles—small, round black or brown beetles, some spotted, some not—or larvae. You may find highways of crisscrossing paths in your flour containers where weevil have crawled across the top. The creatures may also be hiding down inside the product itself.

In addition to finding the bug bodies or larvae, you can determine insect residency in larger containers of grains and beans by running your hands through the product. If it looks like or feels like sand or grit, there are weevil. If it feels as if there is a layer of grit or sand on the bottom there are probably a lot of them.

GETTING RID OF AND KEEPING AHEAD OF WEEVIL

One method of removing the bugs is quite simple. In cereals, such as oatmeal, simply bring a pan of water to a boil. Then add the oatmeal and wait. It only takes seconds and any bugs or weevil will float the top, where you simply scoop them off. Finish cooking your cereal and you have a fine weevil-free breakfast.

If the infestation is in flour, you can sift the weevil out of the flour and then heat-treat the flour to kill any remaining eggs. If the infestation is not severe, you can pick them out by hand. The insects will not spread as quickly if you keep dry ingredients in containers with tight-fitting lids. This is especially true in humid climates.

Heat-Treating

Preheat your oven to 140°F. or the lowest temperature your oven will consistently heat to. Spread the food evenly on a cookie sheet. Don't pile the food too thick; half an inch is a good depth. You can put two cookie sheets in at a time. Leave the oven door slightly open to prevent overheating. Place it in the oven for half an hour, then remove the cookie sheet and allow the food to cool. Gently bounce the cookie sheet up and down so that any hulls and weevil will come to the top. You may use a dry wash cloth and gently brush the hull off into a sink. Or use a fan or blow dryer, set on low, to blow off any remaining insect fragments. Make sure it is cool, and then store the product in an airtight container. Do not heat-treat dry milk or sugar (or chocolate chips). Heat-treated grain will not sprout.

Dry Ice

Many items can be purchased in bulk, at a good savings, and "canned" at home using dry ice. Dry ice is solidified carbon dioxide. It is not regular ice in any manner or use. It is nontoxic to you and to food, but dry ice will burn you! Use caution: you should wear gloves or use thick folded paper to handle it. Children should not be allowed to touch or play with dry ice.

Dry ice is placed in the bottom of a container and the container is then filled with grain or other dry food. At room temperature the dry ice will evaporate leaving carbon dioxide gas, which forces the air and moisture out of the container. Insects will suffocate in this inert atmosphere. This procedure does not kill the sprouting capability of grain. If a proper container is used, the inert atmosphere will remain as long as the container is kept sealed. Once opened, keep a lid on tightly in between uses.

It takes approximately two ounces (or two square inches) of dry ice per five-gallon can or bucket. Put the ice, crushed or in a small chunk, on the bottom of the container, then pour the food on top of the ice. To crush or break it up, put the large chunks or slabs of ice into several folds of newspaper or into several brown paper grocery bags, (one inside the other) and smack it with the side of a hammer. Then you must wait about thirty minutes before tightly securing the lid. During this time the carbon dioxide is pushing out all the oxygen. If you put the lid on too soon, the container will explode, probably ruining your can or bucket and definitely making a huge mess. After half an hour or so, put the lid on and keep an eye on it for five minutes or so. If the sides of the bucket bulge, pop the lid off and wait a while longer.

If you use a plastic container, put a few inches of dry food on the bottom of the container, place the ice on this, and then add food to fill the container. Dry ice creates such intense cold that the plastic might become brittle and crack if you put dry ice directly on it.

Do not use dry ice in glass containers! The pressure might cause the glass to literally explode.

Sugar is one food that rodents, weevil, and mealy moths are usually not interested in getting into.

Use Dry Ice on:

Grains, flours, beans, lentils, split peas, oats, oatmeal, pasta, dry milk, dry soup, mixes, cornmeal, and popcorn.

Many commercial companies use a nitrogen backfill process to can dehydrated foods and grains and beans. This process creates the same type of inert atmosphere as dry ice does.

Deep Freeze

If you only have a little bit of infested grain to deal with, your freezer will often take care of it. Put one to two pounds of grains or beans into heavy plastic food bags and place them in a deep freeze (one that freezes at 0°F.) for two to three days. Then spread the product on a cookie sheet to thaw and dry. However, that being said, keep reading.

THINGS THAT DON'T WORK

Freezing

If the temperature isn't cold enough, freezing your grains or other foods for a few days will not kill weevil or their eggs. I was doing research on this subject once to see if they would die if frozen, and a friend decided to help me with my research. She discovered a bag of pasta in her cupboard that had two inches of weevil thriving in the bottom of the package. She set the package outside her back door in the snow, and it remained there for over a week. As a joke, she wrapped a ribbon around it and brought it to me; a frozen block of ice with weevil in the middle "for my research"! I laughed, set it on my counter, and forgot about it. Later in the day, I discovered that my block of ice had come alive and was crawling with healthy, robust weevil. Being frozen had not deterred those creatures at all.

The temperature was just not cold enough to completely kill them. To paraphrase a line from *The Princess Bride*, "They were only mostly dead. There's a big difference between being mostly dead and all dead. Mostly dead is still a little bit alive." For freezing to kill bugs, it must be 0°F. or colder.

Diatomaceous Earth

Diatomaceous earth (finely ground sea plankton) has been used in some situations to control insects. However, according to the University of Utah Extension office, "We do not recommend diatomaceous (Fuller's) earth for controlling insect pests in stored foods. The problem is that it becomes a contaminant in the food product. It would not be suitable for use with flour or related food items. It may be used with whole grain products if a person has a good method of cleaning the grain before it is used."[2]

Commercial Fumigants

Do not use a commercial fumigant at home to get rid of weevil or mealy moths in your food. Products that kill insects can be dangerous to humans. No commercial fumigant, whether a do-it-yourself bug-bomb or a professional service, is meant to be applied to food. If the chemicals get on your food, you can no longer eat it. The residue left on the food can be deadly. Also, toxic fumes are deadly in enclosed surroundings.

Tape

Wrapping tape around the tops of your containers does absolutely nothing towards making them airtight. Not even duct tape, which is akin to sacrilege, since duct tape is the wonder tool of all home projects. Nor will tape keep insects out of buckets or jars. They will just chew through it. And all tape will eventually dry up, curl, and/or lose its stickiness.

At one time, Larry and I became energetic and decided to "can" six hundred pounds of wheat all at the same time, in our garage. Using five-gallon metal cans, we put in dry ice, poured in the wheat and waited. After awhile we became impatient and decided that we had waited long enough. We hurriedly tamped the lids on all the cans. I left and had gotten partway through the house on the way to the kitchen when I heard a horrible yell. Running back to the garage, I saw Larry standing with his arms thrown over his head as can lids and wheat whizzed past him like shrapnel. To this day some of those cans are contoured. We learned that it pays to be patient.

Wax

For many years, paraffin wax was the way to seal jams, jellies, butters, and sauces. Not any more. It does not seal sufficiently. If no additional lid is used, mice, ants, and other bugs can go right through the wax and have a feast on your food. I speak from experience here. Many years ago I sealed a batch of jelly with wax (several dozen jars). Several months later, I went to get a jar from the storage room for our toast. To my surprise, I discovered they were all empty! The wax was still in place at the top of the jars, but with the exception of little dabs here and there, all the jam was gone. Closer inspection revealed tiny holes around the edge of the wax. The ants had discovered my supply and industriously carried away my entire stash, bit by bit until nothing was left behind but the jars and the wax. Obviously they hadn't read any nutrition books to know that a diet of straight jelly was really bad for them.

Besides being susceptible to creatures, extreme heat will cause wax to melt and shrink, breaking any seal that might have been there. With the quality lids and rings that are available today, you should not even consider using wax as a sealant.

MYTHS AND OLD WIVES' TALES

If you have had any interest in storing food for the past several decades you've probably heard some of the far-fetched solutions for keeping bugs out of your foods: sticks of chewing gum, bags of salt, rolled-up newspaper, and of course, bay leaves.

I can conclusively state that bay leaves function well as a seasoning in soups but are completely useless as a deterrent for weevil. I tried valiantly to dispel this rumor for years and I was always greeted with disbelieving skepticism from my audiences. This wives' tale was so ingrained into people's heads that they refused to believe anything to the contrary. So I set out to prove beyond a doubt that I was right.

I called a local feed and grain store and asked if I might come down and catch some weevil. After

> *Bay leaves are completely useless as a deterrent for weevil.*

a few seconds of silence, the man on the phone responded, "You're kidding!" When I explained why I wanted them, he finally admitted they might have one or two. I entered the store with a bottle in hand and was quickly escorted to the back—behind stacks of large bags of grain. By moving sacks and climbing over, around, and under, I managed to catch six black Sawtooth grain weevil beetles for my experiment.

At home, I put two beetles into Canning Jar #1 (the control) with no bay leaf; I put two beetles and one large new bay leaf (crushed so that any "fumes" would be more potent) into Jar #2; two beetles and one old bay leaf (crushed) went into Jar #3. I added a small amount of barley and wheat flour to each jar and screwed lids tightly onto all the dated and labeled jars.

Nine months later there were approximately sixty beetles in each jar. The weevil showed no aversion to either old or new bay leaves. They ignored the leaves, crawling over, around, and under them.

Thinking that some people might not consider six weevils sufficient proof, I set out to find more. It is difficult to come right out and ask a friend if she has weevils and still keep her as a friend. But I found such a friend. I brought home fifty-two weevil. These were a different kind from those I'd previously used. These were carpet beetle weevils and they were in the larvae stage.

Larry designed a sophisticated "lab" of seven test tubes connected with glass tubing in such a way that the weevil had access to all seven tubes at all times. We laid this "lab" on a towel-covered cookie sheet, so that the tubes need not be disturbed while we observed the weevil. The numbered tubes contained the following:

1. Large pieces of new bay leaf, whole wheat flour, wheat.
2. Whole wheat flour, wheat, no bay leaf.
3. Large pieces of old bay leaf, whole wheat flour, wheat.
4. Fifty-two wiggling weevil.
5. Barley, whole wheat flour, no bay leaf.
6. Large pieces of new bay leaf, whole wheat flour, wheat.
7. Large pieces of old bay leaf, whole-wheat flour, wheat.

We placed all the weevil in the center tube. They varied in size from newly hatched and minute to good-sized and fuzzy. In order to obtain food, they had to go from the center tube into another tube of their choice. We kept a weekly log of their progress and reactions.

After six months there were tiny weevil and large fuzzy weevil and little black beetles traveling from tube to tube, crawling on or burrowing under all of the bay leaves. Every tube had happy and healthy weevil of all stages in it, bay leaves notwithstanding. So far as we could tell, none of them had died. Our conclusion? Bay leaves do not protect food from weevil!

To make sure this wasn't a fluke, my son, then in junior high school, replicated this study for a science fair project, and his results and conclusions were exactly the same. He also took a blue ribbon for the project!

According to the Utah State University Extension, "In regards to chewing gum, bay leaves, and ten-penny nails, if it appears that these methods are working, it is only because there was no infestation to begin with. There is no scientific evidence these and other old wives' tales prevent infestations or control infestations."

ATTITUDE REALLY MATTERS

If, in spite of your efforts, you end up with bugs, remember: attitude is important. It is hard to convince most people that there is nothing wrong with a weevil, but it's true. Weevils are not harmful if eaten. In some situations, you may not be able to afford to throw out infested food and buy more. It may not be available at any price.

Unlike the cockroach or mouse, weevils and mealy moths are clean bugs. As the popular saying (kind-of) goes: a weevil is what it eats. Raised in whole wheat it turns brown like the kernel; in whole wheat flour it is beige; in white flour it is white. You can sift weevil out and eat the food anyway; or you can ignore them altogether. A little weevil has never hurt anyone. And of course, if push comes to shove, you could always claim that they are high-quality protein.

CANNED GOODS

The dark, dry, and cool general storage rules apply to canned and bottled food products as well as to grains and bulk foods. In addition, there are a few pointers for buying canned food that should be mentioned. Don't purchase canned goods at salvage goods outlets or flea markets. They may be cheaper but you're gambling. Those products may be dented or damaged—even if you can't see the damage—allowing dirt and bacteria into the food. The food may be old or may have been stored for long periods of time in poor conditions, encouraging deterioration. Don't take chances.

Do buy canned goods in case-lot sales. Someone once suggested to me that case-lot sales were just the stores way of getting rid of old stock. This is not true. These products are new, high-quality goods. A case-lot sale is a sales tactic to generate business. The prices are usually good enough that the products fly off the shelves even faster than they would sell normally. They don't have time to become old stock. Even if the sale is held in a parking lot, and the food is exposed to the hot sun for several days, it is not a sufficient length of exposure to affect the quality of the food. You can buy with full confidence that the food is good quality.

KEEP IT ALL OFF OF THE FLOOR

Keep cases of canned goods and all storage containers off the floor. This can be accomplished rather easily and inexpensively by nailing narrow wooden slats (like furring strips) to boards laid on the floor, or by laying thin boards on top of a few bricks. Keeping containers off the floor prevents them from "sweating" and discourages the formation of rust and the growth of bacteria. This rule also includes case goods. Canned and bottled goods that are left in the carton should not be stacked directly on the floor, especially on concrete. The cardboard can act as a wick and, if there is any moisture, it will be sucked up into the carton. The carton could eventually fall apart, allowing the case goods to spill onto the floor and perhaps break. If you unknowingly pick it up, not realizing that it has become dilapidated, the cans or bottles can fall through the cardboard as it is picked up. The carton, slowly becoming saturated with moisture, can cause the metal of the cans to rust. This is true even if the box does not appear to be water-soaked. Mold, mildew, and bacteria can grow in these conditions.

FREEZERS

A freezer is a great addition to your pantry. It is an economical way to take advantage of sales. However, you must put foods in proper containers or they can be ruined. Don't think you're being economical by using regular plastic bags, bread wrappers, or cottage cheese cartons to freeze food in. These don't sufficiently keep air out. Freeze food in airtight, moisture-proof containers or freezer wrap. The labels on the packaging should specifically say "freezer use" or something similar. Improper freezer packaging will result in freezer burn, and the food will absorb flavors and odors. Then it won't be fit to eat and you'll probably throw it out. Most frozen food should be used within six months to a year, more or less, for the best quality. For information on what to do with your freezer in a power outage, see appendix L.

NONFOODS

If you're storing a supply of paper napkins, aluminum foil, plastic spoons, or the like, you can stash them pretty much wherever you can find room, regardless of storage conditions (except next to the furnace). Any nonfood item with a liquid or chemical base, however, needs to be kept in dark, dry, and cool conditions, and not directly on a cement floor. This includes cleaning products, medicines, household supplies, and more. What's more, you should avoid storing chemical-based items (soap, cleaners, and so on) in the same area as food. Some food will absorb the odor or "flavor" of the chemical-based item and no longer be desirably edible. For example, flour could take on the taste of soap, or rolled oats could assume a laundry detergent flavor, and so on. If all of your food and nonfood products have to be kept in the same cupboard, at least try to keep them on separate shelves.

The chemicals in nonfood products have a limited shelf life. After a period of time, the chemicals can either dissipate or intensify. For example, the cleaning agents in laundry detergents lose their potency after a few years and you are left with just a box of filler. The same goes for chlorine bleach; it begins to weaken in strength after only three to six months. For the best results, make sure all your household products are rotated and used on a regular basis.

Medications and vitamins also have a limited shelf life. They should be used by the expiration date printed on the package. After this date, the medication may change in potency, becoming either stronger or weaker. Either way, you're not getting the dosage you think you're getting when you take it, and it could prove dangerous to your health.

I highly recommend that every person who takes prescription medication on a regular basis speak to their pharmacist and obtain an additional month's supply of medicine to have on hand in an emergency. The pharmacist can advise you on the best way to care for your medical preparedness supply. It would prove invaluable in the event of a major disaster, when the pharmacy may not be accessible for an extended period of time. The same goes for any over-the-counter medication you use on a regular basis.

EQUIPMENT

There are storage rules for equipment like emergency stoves and lanterns. All emergency preparedness equipment and seldom-used food preparation equipment needs to be kept dry and clean. It should ideally be covered when not in use to keep out dirt and grit. Rust and dirt cause deterioration, clogging, and malfunctions. Gaskets need to be checked and replaced regularly so they don't dry out and shrivel; moving parts need to be oiled. You need to be able to rely on these items when you need them. That may not happen if you don't care for them the rest of the time.

For fuel storage you'll find guidelines in chapter 24. Just a reminder here: Don't store liquid fuel inside your home.

MAKE IT WORK FOR YOU

The Pantry Principle (see chapter 14) works because you buy things at good prices that you eat, use up, and replace again in a regular cycle. In order to stay prepared, with food on hand to feed your family each day and during emergencies, you have to take care of your food storage. Optimal storage conditions are dark, dry, and cool. The warmer the temperature, the brighter the room, the more humidity in the room, the shorter the shelf life of your food. However, if you can't come up with optimal conditions, do the best you can with what you have to work

> *Any nonfood item with a liquid or chemical base needs to be kept in dark, dry, and cool conditions, and not directly on a cement floor.*

with. When you get the Pantry Principle working for you, take care of your food, use it up, and replace it often. Let your grandchildren get their own.

Notes
1. Food Storage Cooking School, Utah State University Extension, Salt Lake County, January 1999.
2. "Food Storage in the Home," EC257, University of Utah extension office, 1988.

CHAPTER SIX

PYRAMID PLANNING FOR PREPAREDNESS: NUTRITION IN A NUTSHELL

One of today's most widely discussed and controversial subjects is nutrition. Whole sections in bookstores promote hundreds of books based on every conceivable nutritional tangent; all are guaranteed to make you slim, young, healthy, and energetic. Yet despite all the knowledge presented, confusion reigns about this subject. Book A is a complete contradiction of Book B, which discounts the concepts persuasively taught in Book C, and so on and so on. Who are you to believe?

Muddying the waters even more, you'll find some people who are willing to sell you a single food or even a pill they claim will give you all of the nutrition you need in your diet and pantry. These claims are false. There is no pill or single food that can replace a healthy, balanced diet. NASA experimented with food in pill form for the astronauts back in the '60s and ultimately rejected the idea. It is possible for scientists to put all the vitamins and minerals your body needs in a series of pills. But food is more than just vitamins and minerals. It is those, plus fiber and bulk and trace elements and psychological factors and much, much more. There are no perfect pills that can replace real food in your preparedness pantry. If it sounds too good to be true—it is! If it sounds too easy to be realistic—it is! Feed your family sensibly, intelligently, and economically, but by all means, feed them food.

Nutrition is important. Yet most people know very little about the nutritional value of the foods they eat (or should eat, or think they should eat). We are tossed to and fro in a nutritional ocean where health is more often than not a "buyword." Rather than be swept with the tide, we need to have a basic understanding of nutrition, sprinkled with a lot of common

sense. The human body requires a variety of nutrients for survival. These are, among others, proteins, fats, carbohydrates, vitamins, minerals, amino acids, trace elements, and so much more. You can't emphasize one at the expense of another without damaging your health. We need them all in their proper proportions. Good health and energy from the foods you eat are the goals you should have for yourself and family. In an emergency situation, these nutritional goals are even more important. Your aim is to maintain good health under all conditions. This goal should heavily influence the decisions that you make when you choose food for your preparedness pantry.

CAN YOU BUILD A PYRAMID IN YOUR PANTRY?

The essence of the nutritionally well-balanced diet has been broken down for us in what nutritionists call the Basic Food Groups within the Food Guide Pyramid. The basic food groups should be interpreted as just what the name (basic) implies—a foundation upon which to build good meals and sound nutrition. Each food group or section makes specific contributions to our bodies. Foods from all the food groups work together to supply energy and nutrients necessary for health and growth.

So, can you build a pyramid in your pantry? Can you obtain the proper nutritional food value

> *Basic Food Pyramid Categories: Grains, Fruits, Vegetables, Milk, and Meat and Beans*

from foods you store for day-to-day living, as well as from those you earmark for meeting the needs of the many different categories of emergencies that could arise? Daily pyramid meal planning is possible and desirable. It's fairly easy to plan healthful meals and menus when all the supermarkets are open and you have the ability to shop where and when you want. Being able to maintain a proper balance of nutrients during hard times or during an emergency is more difficult and requires conscientious planning and effort. It definitely won't happen by accident.

You may find that today's healthy pyramid meals will consist of whole grain breads or cereals, fresh fruits and vegetables, milk and cheese, and fresh chicken or beef, all appetizingly prepared, with a delicious dessert topping off the day several times a week. In a preparedness situation, the food may be completely different, yet it can still fit healthy food pyramid parameters. Your cereals may be hot, cooked whole grains instead of ready-to-eat from a box. Your fruits and vegetables may come from a can. Milk may be reconstituted from dry; cheese may drop off the menu completely. Fresh meat may be replaced with legume and grain protein sources. Decadent desserts may go by the wayside and Jell-O or an occasional made-from-scratch cake (unfrosted) will fill in on special occasions. The pyramid is still in place. It's just a little lopsided.

THE KEY TO SOUND NUTRITION

There is one word that is the key to obtaining the best-balanced nutrition possible from the food you keep in your pantry: Variety! Variety is the key not only to nutrition, but taste, texture, and appearance as well. Variety will make the difference between a "pile of" and pilaf; between "sop" and soup; between "not again!" and "more, please."

In every category of preparedness, variety is a key for maintaining health and wellness. For example, you may prepare for a Category One calamity by stocking up on food items that store well long-term, like wheat, dry milk, shortening, sugar, and salt. By storing these alone you have a very deficient diet, though it would keep you alive. But by planning ahead with variety in mind, you can have foods on hand that store well long-term, yet will work together to provide a healthier, less-stringent diet as

well. Grains—plural—are better than wheat only. Legumes combined with grains create the complete protein your body needs. Adding in some cans of dehydrated carrots or dried apples or the like could make a marked difference in both the healthfulness and desirability of a "long-term food storage diet."

Having variety in preparing to live providently is a natural. The more food choices you have on your pantry shelves, the more meals and menus you can create. The more variety you stock up on, the more likely it is you'll provide all the different nutrients needed for health and wellness.

In a disaster situation, your opportunities for cooking or meal planning for nutrition are severely limited. You have to plan in advance to have food on your shelf that is nearly ready-to-eat without further fussing. As you plan, variety should still be key. Several dozen cans of pork and beans may fit the parameters of the category, but it won't necessarily supply all your nutritional needs or satisfy your taste buds. A better choice would be a few cans of pork and beans, a few cans of stew, some MREs, some canned fruit, and so on. The more options you have, the more food value you'll have.

Variety is critical in evacuation situations. Preparation is also critical, since once the disaster occurs, your food options are immediately limited to only what you have already provided. A crisis situation will place great demands on your body; you may be running on adrenaline and nerves for an extended period. It's extremely important that you be able to refuel your body's resources in this kind of extreme stress. An assortment of food in your evacuation kit is the best chance of filling your body's needs. The nutrients missing in one food may be compensated for by the nutrients supplied by another.

I will emphasize and reemphasize the importance of having a variety of foods as you read on to learn the in-depth details of these different categories of preparedness. There is no one perfect food. No matter what the latest and greatest fad diet being touted in the media is, nothing assures your body of the nutrients it needs like eating a variety of foods. So, read on for more details on preparedness foods, but keep in mind that variety is the key, no matter what the situation.

PRINCIPLES FOR SURVIVING WORST-CASE SCENARIOS

IF WORSE COMES TO WORST

Your preparedness program begins with the realization that you don't want to be prepared for something. You want to be prepared for anything. It's not good enough to be prepared for the next big earthquake. That earthquake may never occur. You may be flooded out instead. If you're ready for an earthquake but you get a flood, you are up a creek without a paddle. You don't want to be prepared just for being out of work for six months. You may never lose your job (cross your fingers). Instead, a tornado could spread your neighborhood over half of the next county. You don't want to be prepared for any particular emergency. You want to be prepared for any emergency, period. Being truly prepared means being ready anytime to deal with anything. This isn't a pie-in-the-sky idea. It is a down-to-earth, doable option. By changing some habits and readjusting your priorities, you can be ready with the attitude and supplies to cope with almost any emergency.

It would be so nice if you could look into a crystal ball and see what was going to happen in the future. Then you would know which days to stay at home in bed, or when would be a good month to schedule a vacation to the Bahamas to avoid the earthquake. You'd know when to invest in the stock market and when to bail out of a shaky investment program. Sadly, no one has a reputable crystal ball available to help you plan your life. So it's up to you to live life to the fullest every day and to prepare to the fullest for whatever tomorrow may bring.

There are troubled times and uncertainty is everywhere. It's with a nagging sense of urgency we endeavor to be prepared. But prepared for what? What could possibly necessitate your needing a substantial quantity of supplies? Most people have half a dozen grocery stores within a five-mile drive of their home, and each of those stores has 10,000+ different items stocked on their ample shelves. You have access to fresh food twenty-four hours a day, seven days a week, and if you don't have cash, you can use your credit cards to pay for whatever sounds yummy at the moment. Then, you take your purchases home, where you flip on lights, crank up the heat, and get a nice, cool drink from the faucet without ever giving a single thought to any of these miracles of technology.

> *You don't want to be prepared for something, you want to be prepared for anything.*

> *In 1815 the Tamborn volcanic eruption killed more than 82,500 people. It was the most powerful eruption in recorded history. The volcanic cloud lowered global temperatures by as much as 3° Celsius. Even a year after the eruption, most of the northern hemisphere experienced sharply cooler temperatures during the summer months. The year of 1816 was known as "the year without summer." More people died from starvation than from the volcanic eruption.*

Why do you need an extended supply of anything (except maybe chocolate chips and ice cream)? The answer: We don't know. Many things could occur to make an abundant pantry necessary. Two or three years without rain would have a devastating result nationally, and even globally. Natural disasters (local or in distant places), war, nuclear accidents or attacks, truckers' strikes, drought, depression, terrorists, and technological problems: all are possibilities in this tumultuous world, and most could effectively shut down a country. Or, more personal disasters could be the loss of a job for an extended period or a devastating illness. If we knew the future, it would be easy.

But since we don't know what we're preparing for, the best idea is to prepare for the worst. By *prepare*, I mean that you have on hand sufficient food, supplies, and the right kind of equipment to be able to care for your family for a substantial length of time. I suggest that a year is a reasonable length of time—from the end of one growing season all the way to the next harvest. Up until this century, before electricity, refrigeration, and modern storage methods, families would have to prepare their harvest to sustain them

through the following year until the next season's crops were harvested. We are still dependent on crop harvest, even though it may not be you that is doing the farming. If bad weather destroys the fruit crops in California, Florida, and Chile, then we don't eat oranges until the next year's harvest season, whether we like it or not.

IMAGINE: NOTHING!

In deciding what to store, imagine that, for whatever reason, you cannot go to the store for an entire year. No zipping down to the corner for a gallon of milk or a little fresh fruit. No stopping in at the grocery store to buy a jar of spaghetti sauce or a dozen eggs. No McDonald's, no Arby's only what you have tucked away in your pantry or cupboard. Imagine that not only you, but no one, can go to the store for a year. The stores are empty. The only things left on the shelves are pots and pans, earwax remover, and greeting cards. People are starving, and there is no food available anywhere.

When you have this picture in your mind, then you are at the right point to truly think of what to have on hand for an entire year. No one likes to consider that a grim situation like this could be possible, but it is. Consider the Great Depression. It's doubtful that the people so blithely dancing the Charleston during the Roaring Twenties anticipated that just around the corner would be a time so terrible that

> The blight of the potato crop that left acre upon acre of Irish farmland covered with black rot was the beginning of the Irish Famine of 1846–1850. It left 3 million people dead. But crop failure is not the only cause of famine. During the Indian grain famine of the 1940s, millions starved to death—not because there wasn't any food, but because it was too expensive to buy. In the 1930s, up to 25 million Russians starved to death, mainly for political reasons. Today, millions upon millions of Africans are in danger of starvation due to war, political tension, and drought. **Famine** is not just a word in a dictionary or a paragraph in a dusty history book. People are suffering from it now, and it is always a potential problem, even in this land of privilege and wealth.

> We have yet to see the final results of the disastrous Asian tsunami of December 26, 2004. We roughly know the initial death toll—300,000-plus. What remains to be seen, though, is the suffering that may result from the complete destruction of their crops and croplands, and rebuilding efforts hampered by desolation. It could be years before many of those countries are able to sustain themselves again, and without substantial support from other countries, the death toll from starvation could easily exceed the loss of life in the disaster itself.

starvation and black despair would stalk the nation. Not here! Not us! Do you remember seeing the television broadcast of the 1984 Olympics in Sarajevo, Bosnia? It was a thriving, beautiful, modern metropolitan city. Yet only a year or so later that beautiful modern city was destroyed, the country around it devastated, and families malnourished and starving because of war. Only a year or two without rain in Africa in the 1990s precipitated the deaths by starvation of hundreds of thousands of people. Two or three years without rain in America could feasibly bring the same result. We hope and pray that nothing like this will happen, but we shouldn't bury our heads in the sand because the picture is too unpleasant or because nothing like this has happened for a very long time. Think how grateful you would be, if times got that bad, that you and your children could go to bed each night with food in your stomachs.

Since the major portion of a preparedness program is food, put the focus on that for just a moment. Choosing, gathering, purchasing, and storing a large quantity of food and commodities for yourself or for an entire family can be a truly daunting thought. That's why you start with the basics first and when you have them, then you move on from there, if you desire. I suggest that you concentrate on bare-bones basic foods that sustain life and will readily store for a reasonable to long period of time without constant attention. The next step is to fill in all the holes in the diet so that not only do you sustain life, but so that you stay healthy and relatively happy also. This is the goal.

(If you're me, that means there must be chocolate involved somewhere, too!)

CHAPTER EIGHT

BARE-BONES BASICS

Many people think of "food storage" as the supply of food you have stashed in the basement or under the bed that you never have to think about again once you get it. You buy it, stick it in the closet, and forget it, and assume that you're prepared. You don't have to use it; you just have to have it—just in case. If someone mentions in passing about how bad things could get someday "with the way this world is heading," you mentally pat yourself on the back and feel smug because you've got it under control.

The Barest of Bare-Bones Basics:

- *Wheat and other grains*
  - *Pasta*
  - *Cornmeal*
  - *Tapioca*
  - *Legumes*
  - *Beans*
  - *Dry peas*
  - *Lentils*
  - *Dry milk*
- *Sugar or Honey*
  - *Salt*
- *Cooking oil/fats*
- *Chemical leaveners*
  - *Yeast*
  - *Baking powder*
  - *Baking soda*
- *Spices/seasonings*
- *Bouillon/soup base*
  - *Attitude*

Maybe you do. Maybe you don't. More about that later. What you probably do have stashed away under the stairs is a supply of bare-bones basic foods. Bare-bones basics are the kinds of items traditionally considered long-term storage foods.

A supply of bare-bones basic foods is a good place to start your preparedness program. The emphasis is on grains and legumes, augmented by dry milk, sugar/honey, salt, and a few other supplementary items needed to make these foods edible and functional in simple, easy recipes. In the face of a devastating famine or other crisis when food is not available for purchase, these foods would keep your family alive. They are considered basic because they are extremely economical, take a minimal amount of storage space (especially when compared to prepared foods), have a long shelf life (when stored properly), and provide the variety and calories to sustain life.

That said, I'd like to add right up front that the potential of bare-bones basics, especially grains and beans, goes far beyond just a survival stash. They form a firm foundation for the foods portion of provident living because they are the most economical, budget-stretching kinds of foods to have on your shelf to help cope with financial hard times. These core foods make the most versatile and economical base to build a more extensive pantry supply on. Don't limit them to a stash under the stairs. Bring them out and use them so they can be the heroes every day.

Even if you have never seen a whole wheat kernel or drunk powdered milk in your life, these foods are not as unfamiliar as you think. Believe it or not, these foods are the foundation for most people's diets, even in our fast-food, eat-on-the-run society. When you stop in at a restaurant for a burger and a chocolate shake, bare-bones basic foods are part of your order: grain in the bun, oil and salt used in the preparation, and milk and sugar in the shake. Granted, there is a substantial difference in form between the whole-grain, staple food you would bank for a crisis and the ultra processed product you buy at the drive-up window. The point is that bare-bones basic foods are basic to society and have been, in one form or another, since the dawn of time. Balancing these bare-bones staples with economy and sound nutrition is vital to a program where you want to be prepared for the worst that can happen.

Eating life-sustaining foods doesn't have to be a disaster in itself. Nor does it require a college degree in nutrition to eat healthfully in a preparedness program, not even in a bare-bones basic preparedness program. As I mentioned before in chapter 6 the key is variety! Variety is the key to nutrition, taste, texture, and appearance, all of which are problems generally encountered in a diet consisting solely of basic foods.

The fewer items you expect to have in your pantry, the more critical the understanding and application of the principle of variety becomes! If starvation is going to grip the nation and all you will have on your pantry shelf is a selection of the bare-bones basics, having a variety (even a small variety) of bare-bones basics will enable you to wring the most food value from your foods, and can make all the difference in the world. There is no one perfect food. While all food has value, no one food supplies all the nutrients you need. No one food is so versatile that it can be used to create all the taste, texture, and sensory appeal that we need and expect in our diets. Most people don't worry about this because their regular diets are so varied and substantial that they get the food value and satisfaction they need without giving it a second thought. But in a severely limited diet, as would be the case if you were relying only on a few bare-bones basic foods to stay alive, a lack of

If your diet is extremely limited, mixing and matching is vital.

nutrients could eventually cause severe health problems. Mixing and matching the right things in the right way is how to maximize the nutritional value of the food you have.

Protein is an example. Protein is a fundamental nutritional building block made up of amino acids. Our bodies have to have it. Meat is the most common source of complete protein you can find. Legumes also are a source of protein, but by themselves they are only an incomplete source of protein. They don't supply all the essential amino acids that your body needs. However, if you mix and match beans with grain, the grain fills in the missing amino acids and the combination of the two provides a complete protein. For example, when a grain, such as corn, is eaten with a legume, such as beans, the combination will be much higher in high-quality protein than either one eaten alone. Combining improves the protein quality of your diet as a whole.

Many different societies have been mixing and matching foods for centuries, without ever having a scientific explanation of why they should be doing what they are doing. In Central and South America, beans and rice or beans and tortillas are a common combination. Rice and lentils are a staple in India; rice and bean curd (tofu) is a mainstay in China and Japan. And in the United States, thousands of people sit down to lunch with a sandwich made of bread (a grain) and peanut butter (a legume) every day.

You can mix and match grains and beans together in the same recipes or meals. Mix multiple grains together in the same recipes. You don't even need to eat the two foods at the same time; just eat them in the same day and you still get the improved nutritional value of the combination. If your diet is extremely limited, mixing and matching is vital.

BUT WHAT CAN I EAT?

Wheat, beans, dry milk, sugar, salt: I often show this abbreviated list in my classes and workshops and ask, "If this is all you have, what kind of recipes can you fix for meals? The usual response is either "boiled grain" or "bread." Boiled grain is a correct answer. Bread is not. It takes more ingredients than just grain and dry milk to make bread.

There is no doubt that a stringent, stripped-down diet of only these four or five items would be extremely difficult to cope with. I've had people relate to me the troubles they've had coping with, and the dietary problems caused by a strict diet composed primarily of wheat. One man in the Midwest told of having to rely solely on such a diet when he was laid off. The entire family struggled with diarrhea and nausea and had difficulty eating the same thing day after day for so many weeks. The children especially had a hard time dealing with the lack of variety. It's not difficult to understand their point. A diet of these foods would become monotonous in a very short period of time, and any marked alteration in your diet can cause digestive problems. It would be hard to find any enthusiasm whatsoever to come to the table if all there was to eat, day in and day out, was boiled grain and powdered milk.

There are a few solutions to this problem. The first to remember that is even the strictest of long-term storage programs should be more than just four or five items. Don't store just wheat; store wheat and barley and oats and rice and more. Don't store just beans; store pinto beans and navy beans and lentils and split peas and pink beans and more. Thus, you will be able to have a bit of variety, even in a severely restricted diet. A small variety of basic foods provides a marked nutritional improvement over a diet of only one grain, like wheat.

The next solution is to accustom your body to eating these foods before you are forced to eat them. Make it a point to consistently incorporate grains, beans and other whole foods in your current meal plans. It won't change the monotony of the diet if a Worst-Case Scenario descends on your doorstep, but being accustomed to them will prevent you from becoming ill from the marked change if they suddenly become the greater part of your daily diet.

This is important enough to say again. I don't recommend that you "store and forget" your bare-bones basic foods. These types of foods are good, tasty, healthful, and extremely economical. The wisest course of action is to not just have these foods

Don't just have bare-bones-basic foods on hand as security in an uncertain world; use them as part of your regular diet.

on hand as security in an uncertain world, but also to use them as part of your regular menus. Start today to incorporate these long-term-storage type foods into your diet. Whenever you bake something, even cookies, replace part of the white flour with whole-wheat flour. Add a handful of barley to a soup or stew. Cook oatmeal or whole-wheat-flour pancakes for breakfast. Make a point to use your bare-bones basic foods, even if only on a limited basis so you become accustomed to them. They're good, and they're good for you. (If you have discovered the goodness and economy of these foods and use them regularly already, you get a gold star for the day.)

The next solution, and one of my strongest recommendations, is that if you are considering, for whatever reason, that all you want to have in your pantry are the bare-bones basics, you must put in a few other items to make them adaptable and edible. However, that is the subject for the next chapter. If you have nothing but bare-bones basics, there are still a few things to do with them beyond just boiling the grains. Here is a rundown on the bare-bones basics themselves, and I'll follow it up with some suggestions on what to do with them. (An enormously helpful hint is that you really need to know how to prepare them long before you need to eat them.)

BARE-BONES BASICS

Bare-bones basics have two strong appeals when you look at them strictly from a preparedness perspective: (1) these foods will sustain life if they're all you have to eat, and (2) they have a long (even a very, very long) shelf life, so *if* you aren't willing or able to work them into your regular diet, you can still store them for a future time of need and they'll wait for you without constant care.

Grains

Wholesome, versatile, and economical, whole grains have sustained and nourished the world for thousands of years. They are affordable and adaptable, and are the place to start for most meals. Wheat is one of the most common grains, and is probably the most valuable and versatile due to its gluten content or bread-making qualities. Very few other grains will grind into flour that will make bread or raised dough on their own, though they can be mixed (up to 25 percent) with wheat flour to make breads with unique flavors and textures. (Spelt flour also has a high gluten content and will make raised bread by itself.) This makes wheat an extremely useful grain; plus, it is the one we are most familiar with, and probably the least expensive. It isn't the only useful grain, by any means, so even if a large portion of your stored grain is wheat, you should still stock a wide variety of other grains for their flavor, variety, nutritive value, and recipe versatility. Remember, variety is the key for health. Rice, barley, millet, cornmeal, oats, popcorn, quinoa, tapioca and more all have a valuable place in a Bare-Bonus-Basic long-term food storage program.

Grain to Water Ratio for Cooking Grains:

Grain	Cups Grain to Cups Water
Amaranth	1:2½
Bulger	1:3
Kamut	1:3
Millet	1:3
Oats, rolled	1:3
Pearl barley	1:3½
Quinoa	1:2
Spelt	1:3
Wheat, whole	1:3
Wheat, cracked	1:3

FOOD ALLERGIES?

If someone in your family is allergic to wheat (or has a gluten intolerance), there are other grains that are often acceptable and trouble-free. Check with your health-care provider for suggestions and information. Because food allergies are all different, the grains that will be acceptable in your situation will differ also. In filling your pantry shelves, pay attention to grains, nuts or other ingredients that may be similar, but not the same as the exact allergen that you have dealt with previously. They may also be a problem for you. For example, wheat, spelt, and buckwheat are similar in makeup; if you're allergic to wheat, you may also have a reaction to the other two. Most tree nuts are also allergenic; an allergy to one often means an allergy to others. Before you stock up on other grains,

or potentially allergenic foods, make sure you are okay with them. If not, don't buy them or store them. Don't assume that because times are hard and that problem food is all there is to eat, that somehow you'll be able to eat it. You won't.

MILD BARE-BONES BASICS

Some grains and beans are just too harsh for little children, or even for adults suffering from illness. If your preparedness foods consist of only bare-bones items, you will want to make sure that there is some way to provide mild or bland meals; foods that would not be harsh or too strong in flavor or effect. The mildest grains are oats, rice, barley, and millet. Tapioca, though technically not a grain, also fills the bill here. It can be easily made with

Should you buy your grains and beans at a supermarket or a healthfood store? Either one. Grains and legumes from either place will meet the requirements for a Bare-Bones-Basic pantry. Your decision will depend on what is most important to you. In a supermarket, you'll probably find grains and legumes in larger bulk quantities (twenty-five- and fifty-pound bags). You'll also probably find the best prices and sales, especially during case-lot sales or other bargain times. In a healthfood store, you'll find products that are generally grown without pesticides and chemicals. As a rule, you'll pay more for them also. You'll also usually find a much greater variety of grains and beans in healthfood stores than you'll find in supermarkets. The choices are plentiful and delightful. They could add exciting variety to otherwise plain fare. Whether you chose the grocery store selections or the organic, natural choices in healthfood stores, the food storage guidelines in chapter 5, Keys to Storage, apply to both.

dry milk to be soothing on the throat or stomach. You may have an occasion to need rice water or old-fashioned barley water to sooth an upset stomach. Think ahead and have sufficient amounts of the mild grains on hand. Additionally, consider having some canned or dehydrated fruit tucked away with the rest of your bare-bones basics for the same situation. Fruit is not technically a bare-bones basic food, but in the case of illness, the blahs, or whatever other malady may waylay you or your family during hard times, it would be very much appreciated.

BASIC COOKING INSTRUCTIONS

Presoaking hard grains, like whole wheat, is optional, but it can reduce cooking time. Soak hard grains for six to eight hours or overnight. Cook them in their soaking water. The softer grains, like rice or pearled barley, can just be cooked without soaking. To boil grain, as a general rule, bring the water to a boil, add grain, and return to a boil. Then, reduce the heat and simmer, covered, until done. The grain is done when the water is absorbed and the grain is softened. Most grains will still be slightly chewy when cooked. When the grain is done cooking, remove it from the heat and fluff it with a fork. Re-cover and allow it to sit for five to ten minutes. Cracking will shorten the cooking time.

RICE

Yes, rice is a grain but since there are more than 7,000 varieties of rice, a few of the better-known ones deserve mentioning. In your preparedness pantry, rice is economical as well as versatile. It can be used for desserts as well as main dishes. Long-grain rice cooks up dry and fluffy and is good in curries, pilafs, and casseroles. Short-grain rice is more tender and sticky and is good for breakfast cereals, puddings, Oriental dishes, and casseroles too. The flavors and textures differ from variety to variety, but all can basically be used interchangeably. Mixing different lengths can add textural interest to any dish. I include wild rice here, though it isn't technically a rice.

Cooking rice: Don't rinse rice. Rinsing rice before cooking causes the starches to release more quickly than they should, and the rice will not thicken. Measure the rice and cold water (or other liquid, for example, juice or broth) into a saucepan. (Add ¼ to ½ teaspoon salt per cup of rice, if desired.) Bring to a boil, reduce heat to low, cover and simmer twenty to thirty minutes for regular white rice, thirty to forty minutes for brown rice, until the water has been absorbed. Don't peek—lifting the lid interrupts the cooking and can leave the rice dry and undercooked. Remove from heat. If you want drier rice, fluff with a fork and let stand, covered, ten additional minutes.

Mild Bare-Bones Basics
(Children, Chills, Comfort)

Millet
Rice
Barley
Regular/quick oats
Tapioca
Fruit*

*Not technically a bare-bones-basic food, but in case of illness, it would be very much appreciated.

Grain to Water Ratio for Cooking Rice:

Grain	Cups Grain to Cups Water
Basmati—white	1:1¾
Basmati—brown	1:2½
Brown—medium	1:2
Brown—short	1:2½
Brown—sweet	1:2
Jasmine—brown	1:2½
Jasmine—white	1:1¾
Long grain	1:2
Short grain	1:2
Texmati—brown	1:2
Texmati—white	1:1¾
Whani or red	1:2
Wild and brown mix	1:3
Wild	1:3½

A PET POINTER

You can prepare your dogs for hard times as well as the other members of the family. If hard times come and you are no longer able to obtain dog food for your pet, rice can come to the rescue. We have two dogs, and as a general rule, we don't allow them to eat people food. I make an exception for rice, though. I will occasionally mix plain cooked rice in with their food, and once in a while, if they are sick, I will feed them a bowl of just plain rice. I checked with our veterinarian and he agreed rice will not hurt them, and it would be a good thing, in difficult times, if they were acclimated to rice. If the time should ever come when you can no longer buy dog food for your pet, begin mixing cooked rice in with their food a little at a time as you use up the last bag of dog food. Then their systems will be used to it when rice is all that is on the canine menu. The same principle applies to your other pets. Maybe your gerbil or parakeet or cat can't eat rice, but they certainly deserve to be considered in your long-term planning. They are part of your family, and therefore your responsibility. Make sure a space in your long-term storage pantry is set aside for food for them.

It's not unusual for my kitchen to resemble a mad scientist's workshop. I often have multiple projects going on that are related in some way to preparedness. One day, Larry had to go in to work really early, earlier than I was willing to get up. I woke up enough to tell him I'd just made some really good rice pudding with one of my new recipes and he should try some for breakfast. When he got home that afternoon, I asked how he'd liked his breakfast. I expected rave reviews because the rice pudding really was quite delicious. He said, "I had Wheaties. I found three cauldrons on the counter and I didn't know if you'd kill me because I messed up one of your experiments, or if I'd just die from the experience. None of them looked like rice pudding to me." (That was because the rice pudding was in the refrigerator.)

TAPIOCA

Tapioca is not actually a grain; it comes from a root. It is used and stored like a grain, so it's included here. Tapioca is a versatile food, not usually considered a basic. Think beyond pudding for a minute. It can be used as a main dish for lunch, as a dessert, combined with rice or other grains for a main meal, or used as a thickener for sauces, soups, and so on. Cool tapioca with a dollop of jam on it is beyond good; it's great! The beauty of tapioca is its mildness. If a family member were feeling under the weather, the mildness of tapioca would be helpful and comforting. For small children also, tapioca is easier to digest than some grains. For storage, transfer it out of the cardboard boxes you buy it in and put it into a sturdier, airtight container.

POPCORN

Popcorn should be included in the bare-bones basics if for no other reason than because of its taste and texture. In hard times, bad times, good times, insecure times, anytime, it tastes good! And to top that off, popcorn is a good-for-you nutritional grain that fills the variety requirement very well. It doesn't have to be relegated to the sidelines as a snack either; I often have a bowl of popcorn and an apple for lunch. (Some seasonings or butter-flavored sprinkles would be a useful addition to your bare-bones basic pantry shelves.) Popcorn is extremely economical; you could say that you really get your money's worth when one cup unpopped gives you twelve cups popped. For a morale booster, popcorn is probably right up there with chocolate. Almost.

If you have old popcorn that has lost its pop, it most likely is because it lacks moisture. You simply need to put the moisture back into it. Work with a small amount of corn at a time. If you add water to a large container of popcorn it will probably mold and you'll lose the entire container. Put two to three cups of unpopped popcorn into a quart jar and add a tablespoon of water. Put the lid on and shake the bottle to distribute the water throughout the corn. Then set it aside for a day or two so that the water can be absorbed. The key is "absorbed," not soaked.

Microwave popcorn is fun and fast, but not a long-term storage item. Because of the oil in each package, its shelf life is only a few months. For long-term storage, be sure to have regular popcorn properly stored in an airtight container.

Another fun popping note: the grain amaranth can be popped the same as popcorn. It will make teeny-tiny popped kernels.

FLOUR

Boiled grain is all well and good, but nine times out of ten, the reason I want grain is because it can be made into flour. With flour, I can have bread and pancakes and cupcakes and cookies and pizza crust and a million other things that I know and love (providing I also have the other ingredients required to make them, of course). You might wonder why I don't recommend you skip right past the grain and simply stock up on flour. Shelf life, that's why. Wheat and other grains will store for years and years; flour will only store for a year or so before it goes rancid. Since flour is such a desirable commodity, it's vitally important that you not only store grain, but also a way to turn that grain into flour. You need a grinder or mill. If you only intend to use it for the occasional odd emergency, and not on a regular basis, a good hand grinder is all you will need. You won't be looking at grinding fifty pounds of grain all at once. You will only grind a batch or two to make just as much flour as you'd need at the moment. A good hand grinder will produce good flour. It will also crack or grind beans and nuts as well. Besides, it will keep on working in a power outage, which an electric mill

won't do. You don't need to purchase a costly appliance with a lot of miraculous attachments unless you really want to. If you want to incorporate fresh grains into your healthy diet frequently, you should consider buying an electric grinder or mill. It's a good way to use your bare-bones basics. Besides, it's wonderful to take a batch of muffins or a loaf of bread out of the oven and know that your whole grain flour was as fresh as could be and packed with vitamins and nutrients.

If you have a good blender to work with, you can use it to grind grain into a fine-enough flour to make breads, pancakes, or any baked goods. It may not be flour as fine as a commercial mill can grind, but it will work. Only blend/grind small portions at a time.

LEGUMES

Legumes (beans, split peas, lentils, and more) play an important part in a bare-bones basic diet. Without animal sources to provide protein in your diet, beans step up and fill in the deficiency. They (combined with grains or other beans) are your source for protein, the body's building blocks. Even if you've never cooked a dry bean in your life, it is imperative that you number them with your bare-bones basic supplies.

When you select beans, look for smooth skins and bright colors. Cracked, split, or dull, wrinkled skins indicate that they are dried out. I know, they're supposed to be dried out—but not like that. There is a quality difference between dried and dried out. Before cooking, spread your beans on a clean kitchen towel or on a cookie sheet, or sift them through your hands and remove shriveled beans and rocks. Little rocks do get past the cleaning process. Then, rinse them in cold water. Beans must be soaked before cooking in order to be digestible. Before the beans can

If your oil supplies are running low and you aren't able to replace them, you can make them last longer by substituting pureed beans for some of the oil in baked goods. Up to half the required oil can be replaced with pureed beans and still have a successful end product.

really start cooking, they must rehydrate—that's the purpose of soaking them. If you fail to soak the beans first, some of your cooking time is wasted while the beans rehydrate. So, soak the beans first—especially the denser varieties, such as kidney, pinks, and small whites. There are two methods of soaking beans: the short soak/boil method, and the long soak method.

(a) **Short-soak/boil method.** Boil beans in water for only three minutes in a heavy pot. Cover and set them aside for an hour. Dry beans absorb as much water in one hour, when soaking is started by first boiling the beans for three minutes, as they do in fifteen hours of cold water. Drain and discard the water and rinse the beans. Proceed with cooking. This method reduces hard-to-digest complex sugars by 80 percent, which helps cut down on intestinal gas. (Note: you do not need to soak jelly beans, not even the black ones, since 100 percent of the sugars are not complex.)

(b) **Long-soak method.** Soak beans for eight hours or overnight. Drain and discard the water, and rinse the beans. Proceed with cooking. This method is better than no soaking at all, but it doesn't remove the complex sugars as well as the short-soak/boil method.

After soaking, cook beans in fresh water—not the water used for soaking—in a large covered pot. Use three to four cups of water for each cup of dry beans. Don't add salt or any acidic flavoring (tomatoes, lemon, and so on) until the beans are cooked all the way through. Each cup of dry beans yields two and one- half cups of cooked beans.

Note: Baking soda has been used for years to hasten the softening of dried beans. Baking soda is an alkali. Some nutritionists do not approve of using baking soda because it tends to destroy the thiamine or vitamin B content of the bean.

OLD BEANS? USE THEM ANYWAY

Don't throw out beans you may consider too old. As beans age, the skin becomes tough and the beans will not soak up the water. Instead of discarding them, crack them. If you have a grinder, simply put them in with the burrs open, ¼ to ½ cup at a time, so that the beans are cracked, not ground. You may want to run a handful of grain through the grinder afterwards to clean out the beans. No grinder? Use a sturdy blender. Put it on the coarsest grind possible. If you have a pulse button, use it. Just put in a few beans, ¼ cup or so at a time, to crack the tough skin. If you don't have a grinder or a blender, use two grocery bags, one inside the other. Put several cupfuls of beans inside the bags and double fold over the open end. Put the bag on a sidewalk or driveway and smack it with the side of an ordinary hammer. (The regular round end of the hammer will punch holes in the bag and your beans will spill out.) The cracked beans can then be soaked and used as you would newer beans.

Don't mix old beans with new beans in the same container. The newer beans will cook faster and become soft much quicker than the older beans, leaving beans with "bones" in your recipes.

Bean Cooking Times:

Bean	Hours
Adzuki	2
Black turtle	1½
Black-eyed peas	1–1½
Chickpeas/garbanzo	3
Great northern	2
Green lentils*	45 minutes
Baby lima	1½
Navy	2½
Red kidney	1½
Red lentils*	20–25 minutes
Soy	3
Split peas*	1–1½

*Do not presoak

Although there are many, many different kinds of beans—each with its own unique flavor—they are all basically interchangeable. If one particular bean doesn't work out to your satisfaction in a recipe, or you don't have the kind the recipe calls for, there's always another to take its place.

Most non-bean legumes don't require soaking before cooking. Lentils, split peas, and so on can just be cooked from their dried state. They don't require the lengthy cooking time of beans either. There is a surprisingly large variety of lentils available in size, color and taste and there are other things to do with lentils and split peas than to put them in soup. Try putting them in pilafs, for a start, or cooking them in bouillon and serving as a side dish.

PASTA

Pasta is a processed form of wheat flour. It has the advantage of being familiar and easy to fix. It comes in a wide variety of forms and flavors and is an integral ingredient for an infinite number of delicious recipes. Though it doesn't have the extensive keeping qualities of whole grains, it stores well enough, under proper conditions, to qualify as a long-term storage item.

The best "white" pasta is made from durum wheat, which is refined and ground into a yellow-white semolina flour. Semolina flour makes pasta that can be cooked al dente—soft enough to eat, yet firm so it will still hold its shape. Pasta that is made from regular white flour will quickly cook into mush.

There is a lot more to pasta than just plain spaghetti and macaroni. You can find enriched high-protein varieties, whole-wheat pastas, and those with vegetable powder added, such as spinach, artichoke, or tomato pasta. These, of course, add to the nutritional variety in the pasta family. Additionally, the variety and thickness of the different forms of pasta add a visual difference as well as a textural difference, which is important if the foods in your pantry are limited.

BEYOND GRAINS AND LEGUMES

If you distill an average person's diet down to its most basic factors, take out all the filler and cut

While walking through a store one day, I discovered jars of the most amazing pasta I'd ever seen. The pasta was a work of art—absolutely beautiful! It was so pretty I'm sure I could never bring myself to cook it. I'd never seen anything like it before: bows three inches long by two inches wide, striped in shades of cream, strawberry-sherbet pink, and pumpkin orange; twisted, striped ribbons sixteen inches long by one and a half inches wide in chartreuse green, lemon yellow, and orange; pasta "hats" with rolled brims, colored by beets, spinach, paprika, and curcuma. You could decorate your house with your food storage if it were all this type of pasta. The instructions on the package should read something to the effect, "Arrange in a beautiful glass container, display in a prominent place, and enjoy." Cook it? Never!

Vitamin Tablets:

These don't technically fall into the category of "food," and I'm the first to say that pills cannot replace food. However, if all that is available is an extremely deficient diet, something as simple as a daily vitamin tablet will ward off a multitude of ills. Scurvy, for example, is a painful disease caused by a lack of Vitamin C. A hundred years ago, it was common for sailors on long sea voyages to contract scurvy because they didn't have any access to fruit or fresh food. Today, a doctor could practice his entire life and never see a case of scurvy because foods containing Vitamin C are plentiful. A Bare-Bones-Basic diet, though, does not contain any food with Vitamin C in it. A common, over-the-counter multiple-vitamin tablet could save so much pain and suffering. Beware though: vitamins are not store-and-forget items. Bottles will have expiration dates printed on them. You need to be aware of these dates and replace them before they expire.

right to the fewest number of items necessary to stay alive, what you have left is a bare-bones basic diet. Up to now, the lion's share of this chapter has been concerned with grains and beans. Grains and beans are vital in a long-term storage program, but they are not enough on their own, not even to make up the most stringent diet. Even the barest of the bare-bones basics includes more than grains and beans. You must also have a supply of a few additional crucial items: dry milk, cooking oil/shortening, salt, sugar/honey, leavenings, spices and seasonings, and bouillon/soup base. These items are as indispensable as the grains and beans themselves. The grains and beans provide the bulk of a bare-bones basic diet; these other things make them edible. They make simple recipes possible. Since they all provide nutrients grains and beans alone don't have, they are essential items.

DRY MILK

Dry milk is exactly what its name implies: milk that has had almost all the moisture removed. Dry (also called powdered) milk has a far longer shelf life than liquid milk (years compared to weeks) and doesn't need to be refrigerated due to its low moisture content. It's less expensive and easier to store than fresh milk, but has an unfortunate disadvantage in that it never tastes quite as good as the real thing. Dry milk may or may not be fortified with vitamins A and D.

Regular nonfat dry milk is typically made by spraying skim milk into hot air in a low-pressure chamber where the water instantly evaporates, leaving behind fine particles of powdered milk solids. Instant milk is regular dry milk that has been further processed, causing it to clump together. The resulting product is easier to reconstitute with water than regular nonfat dry milk. There is no difference in food value or storability between regular and instant. The most common type of dried milk you'll find in grocery stores is instant nonfat dry milk. Dry whole-milk powder and dried buttermilk are also available, though they aren't as common.

Though powdered milk may not be able to pass a taste test against fresh whole milk, it tastes a lot better than it used to. If you haven't tried it in the past few years, it's worth another try. Many people who are used to drinking skim milk don't notice a great deal of difference. It is wonderful for cooking. When a recipe calls for milk you can substitute reconstituted dry milk. Reconstituting is often not even necessary. When baking, simply add dry milk solids to the other dry ingredients and add the water with the liquid ingredients. You can add more nutritional value to recipes by adding an extra tablespoon of dry-milk solids to the dry ingredients whenever you cook something.

For the maximum shelf life, purchase or repackage your dry milk in airtight metal No. 10 cans rather than keeping them in the cardboard boxes found at the grocery store, and then follow the standard food-storage rules closely. Dry milk needs to be kept dry, cool, and out of light. Unopened, in proper containers, in proper conditions, dry milk will easily keep for two to three years. That's a conservative estimate. Once a container is opened, the shelf life of dry milk is limited, so keep it tightly covered and use it as soon as possible. For this reason, it's better to buy milk packaged in smaller containers—the size that you would be able to consume in a few months. If it sits opened longer than that, the milk will likely go stale. It won't hurt you; it just doesn't taste as good. It can still be used in cooking.

Reconstitute instant nonfat dry milk by mixing or shaking the dried milk with the recommended amount of water. To reconstitute regular (non-instant) dry milk, use warm—not hot—water and begin with half the recommended amount of water. Add the dry milk and stir vigorously with a whip until dissolved. Then, add the remainder of the water and chill. Some people like to add a drop or two of vanilla or a teaspoon or two of sugar per half gallon of milk to improve the flavor. Reconstituted milk can be used immediately but it tastes best after being refrigerated for several hours. After reconstitution, the milk should be stored in the refrigerator.

MILK IS VERSATILE

In addition to its high-quality protein, one of the benefits of milk is its versatility; it can be used to make so many different things. Consider the following:

Sour Milk

Some recipes have buttermilk or sour milk as an ingredient. You can't just replace it with regular sweet milk because the success of the recipe depends on the chemical reaction of the sour/buttermilk. It's not a serious problem though because sour milk is easy to make, even with dry milk. For instance, if a recipe calls for one cup of sour milk or buttermilk, measure a tablespoon of an acid, like vinegar or lemon juice, into a measuring cup. Add reconstituted milk to equal one cup. Stir gently and let it sit for five minutes. This can replace sour milk or buttermilk in baking recipes.

Commercially dried buttermilk can be found in supermarkets in the baking items aisle.

Sweetened Condensed Milk

Need a sweet pick-me-up? Sweetened condensed milk can be used to make all kinds of desserts; it can even be used as a glaze on a cake made from bare-bones basics. Mix two cups of dry milk; a tablespoon of butter, margarine, or oil; and half a cup of boiling water. Blend thoroughly with an electric mixer. While beating, add a cup of sugar. Beat really hard until the sugar is dissolved. This yields about a pint of sweetened condensed milk. It will store, covered, in the refrigerator up to two weeks. You can even add cocoa powder with the dry milk for a chocolate glaze.

Cheese

Who would want cheese to be relegated to a distant fond memory? Not me. And it doesn't have to be, even in the worst of times, if you plan ahead. Two items should be on your priority list along with dry milk. They are vinegar and rennet tablets. You know what vinegar is, but rennet may be unfamiliar to you.

It is a natural enzyme that causes milk to clabber into a smooth, thick, custardlike curd. With these items, you can easily make cheese and cheese spreads. Although making cheese isn't as common as baking bread, simple cheeses are no more difficult to make than bread; easier, in fact.

Cottage (or soft) cheese can be made with just milk, rennet, vinegar, and salt, and equipment found in any kitchen. It's possible to make soft cheese without rennet, but your chances of success are greatly improved with it. And since it's so readily available and very inexpensive, it's not a problem to keep some with your bare-bones basic supplies. You can usually find rennet tablets on the same shelves as the puddings in the supermarket.

Cottage cheese is perfectly suited for anyone needing a mild or bland diet, in addition to being an important supporting ingredient in your menus. As a bonus, it solves the mystery of exactly what the curds and whey in Little Miss Muffet's bowl were. Simply, the cheese lumps from making simple cheeses are curds, and the liquid left as they form is the whey. You'd be wise to keep dry milk, vinegar, and rennet in your pantry. As for the "spider that sat down beside her," all my research indicates that you really don't want spiders in your pantry. They don't store well.

OTHER MILK OPTIONS: CANNED AND ASEPTIC

Other milk options for your pantry are canned milk and aseptic milk. Canned, evaporated milk is

Nonfat dry milk	+	Water	=	Reconstituted Milk
1½ tablespoons	+	¼ cup	=	¼ cup
3 tablespoons	+	½ cup	=	½ cup
⅓ cup	+	1 cup	=	1 cup
1⅓ cups	+	1 quart	=	1 quart
5⅓ cups	+	1 gallon	=	1 gallon

milk that has had 60 percent of its water removed by evaporation. It comes in whole, low-fat, and skim versions. When you mix it with an equal portion of water, it can be substituted for fresh milk in recipes. The high-heat process gives it a bit of a caramelized, "canned" flavor, and it is slightly darker in color than fresh milk. Canned milk can be stored at room temperature until opened, after which it must be tightly covered and refrigerated for no more than a week. Evaporated milk has a shelf life of twelve to eighteen months; therefore it's not necessarily considered a long-term storage item. You can't store and forget it for years and years. However, due to its versatility and high-quality protein, it holds an important place in a storage program. Just remember to use it and replace it regularly. Evaporated milk is one storage product that benefits from occasionally being physically rotated—turn the cans upside down or shake them.

As an added bonus, evaporated milk, when slightly frozen, can be whipped and used as an inexpensive substitute for whipped cream.

Aseptic milk is often called UHT milk (ultra high temperature) for the technique used to preserve and package it. It can be stored at room temperature because of the special pasteurizing process used. You've most likely seen it in the single-serving "juice box"-type package, but it also comes in pint, quart, or even half-gallon packages. Unrefrigerated aseptic milk has a conservative shelf life of six months to a year.

MILK INTOLERANCE? USE SOY

If you suffer from a milk intolerance, you may be one of the many people who have turned to soy milk or rice milk to fill the spot left in a diet by a lack of dairy milk. Both of these can be purchased in aseptic packages, which is a good thing from a preparedness standpoint. They have a shelf life of approximately six months to a year. Once the package is opened, the milk should be refrigerated and used within seven to ten days.

You can make soy milk yourself quickly and economically from soybeans. For two quarts of soy milk, use a pound (two and one-half cups) of dry soybeans. Soak the beans in two quarts of water overnight, or bring them to a rapid boil for three minutes, cover and remove from heat and let sit for an hour. Drain. Using three quarts of fresh water, grind the soaked beans in a blender. Put part of the beans with enough water to cover them in the blender. Blend for

---

Try making these cheese recipes. You don't even need to wait for hard times because cheese-making is a lot of fun and very satisfying.

Baker's Cheese
(Tastes like Ricotta or cream cheese may be used in any recipe calling for either cheese.)

3 cups non-instant (5⅓ cups instant) dry milk
¼ rennet tablet
½ cup buttermilk
2 quarts warm water

Dissolve rennet tablet in warm water. Thoroughly mix in dry milk and buttermilk. Cover and allow to stand at room temperature until set (about five to ten hours). Pour into a cheesecloth-covered strainer, close the cheesecloth, and squeeze out as much whey as possible. The whey may be saved for use in bread. Place the cheese in the refrigerator until well chilled (usually overnight). Knead the cheese until the texture is smooth. Cheese will freeze well for up to six months. Makes about one pound.

Day Cheese
(This is a popular cheese in Mexico. It is very quick and easy to make.)

1½ cups non-instant dry milk or ⅔ cups instant dry milk
2 to 3 tablespoons lemon juice or vinegar
4 cups water

Thoroughly mix milk and water together. Place in a heavy pan on low heat, or use a double boiler. Slowly add lemon juice or vinegar to the milk as it cooks. Stir continually to avoid scorching the milk. Bring just to a boil, but do not boil. The whey will be almost clear and the curds soft. Remove from heat and pour through a wire strainer. Rinse well with cold water. Season lightly with salt and serve.

two minutes until very fine. Repeat with the remainder of the beans and the rest of the water. Strain the beans through two layers of cheesecloth into a large pot. Squeeze as much liquid as you can from the puree. This is the soy milk. Boil the milk for half an hour, stirring occasionally to prevent scorching. You must boil the milk thoroughly to destroy a substance in the soybeans that interferes with digestive enzymes. While the milk is still warm, stir in two tablespoons of sugar and a teaspoon of salt. Cover the milk tightly and store in the refrigerator. You'll need to strain the milk again before use because a skin will form on the surface.[1]

Dehydrated soy milk is available in whole-foods stores and health food stores. It has a long shelf life if stored properly.

COOKING OIL/FATS/SHORTENING

Fat is downright essential for good health. Our bodies have to have fat to function properly. Most of the energy needed by the human body is provided by fat. In addition to energy storage, fat serves as a protective cushion and provides structural support to help prevent injury to vital organs such as the heart, liver, kidneys, and spleen. Not only that, but some vitamins and nutrients are fat-soluble and can only be carried throughout the body in the presence of fat. Fat makes us feel satiated after a meal and it adds a great deal of flavor to food.

Our bodies have to have it, and our recipes have to have it too. It serves an important purpose,

particularly in baked goods. Fat adds flavor and texture to baking products and is chemically necessary to achieve the proper consistency in cooking and baking. When you reduce or eliminate the fat from a recipe, chances are that the end product will be tough, flat, full of tunnels, and lacking in flavor.

For these reasons, it's important to have some sort of fat in your long-term storage program. Exactly which kind you store will be determined by numerous factors; you have to sort through the pros and cons of each choice and figure out what will work best for you.

Vegetable oil refers to oils extracted from numerous sources—soybeans, corn, peanuts, cottonseed, safflower seeds, rapeseed (for canola oil) and sunflower. Cooking oils that are simply labeled "vegetable oil" are made predominantly from soybean oil or a soybean-oil blend. Most vegetable oil has a bland flavor that doesn't interfere with the flavors of the recipe you're making. Vegetable oil is readily available and affordable in any grocery store. The problem is it doesn't have a very long shelf life—around twelve to eighteen months. Purchasing it in opaque containers rather than clear ones will extend its life a little longer, as will ideal storage conditions (that is, dark, dry, and cool).

If you have a choice, cold-pressed or expeller-pressed oils are preferred over those processed using heat, as typical high-heat processing may cause health concerns. Cold-pressed oils are usually more expensive and often more difficult to find than regular oil. Supermarkets may carry them in their natural foods aisle, or you can find them in health food stores. They have about the same shelf life as regular oils found in the supermarket.

Shortening is vegetable oil that has been hydrogenated (had hydrogen pumped through it), altering

---

One gentleman who survived the devastation and starvation in Europe during and after World War II recalled that cooking oil was the most valuable food item they could have. It was valued not only for its nutritional qualities but also because it could be traded for nearly anything else they needed. It was of such value that a quart of oil could be traded for several bushels of apples or several hundred pounds of potatoes.

Cooking Oil Options:

Almond, Avocado, Butter, Canola, Coconut, Corn, Grape, Lard, Nut, Olive, Peanut, Pumpkin, Safflower, Sesame, Shortening, Soybean, Sunflower, Vegetable blend

its chemical makeup. The advantage of this is that shortening will store for a long time—five years or more, which is great for a long-term storage program. The bad thing is that the hydrogenation process turns healthy fats into trans fats, which create all kinds of health concerns. You may wish to use unhydrogenated oils on a regular basis, yet keep some shortening on hand in your pantry as a backup in case times get really difficult and you run out of healthier oils, or they have gone rancid and you can't get any more.

You might want to look into coconut oil as a good choice for storage and daily use. It is a solid at room temperature (good for baked goods), and yet melts easily at 76⁰ F. It has a long shelf life—five years or more. Because it is a saturated fat, it fell out of favor for a few decades, but scientists lately have acknowledged that it is not the same as other saturated fats. It is made up of medium-chain fatty acids (as opposed to long-chain fatty acids) and reacts completely differently in the body. It actually is very healthy for you. The drawback to coconut oil is that currently it is difficult to find and somewhat expensive. You can look for it in health food stores or through Internet sources (Internet search word: coconut oil).

If you regularly use lard, you'll need to find another choice for your long-term storage. Lard has an extremely high rancidity factor and essentially has no shelf life outside the refrigerator.

SUGARS OR HONEY

Sugar is a type of food associated with one of our primary taste sensations: sweetness. We love our sugar! According to USDA data, "Surveys indicate that the average teenage boy eats at least 109 pounds [of sugar] per year, while the average American eats upwards of sixty-four pounds."[2] Sixty-four pounds of sugar a year per person is a lot of sugar! Now imagine going from sixty or one hundred pounds of sugar

A wonderfully easy pancake syrup can easily be made from one part white sugar, one part brown sugar, one part water, and a few drops of maple flavoring. Bring it all to a boil, reduce the heat and simmer for two to three minutes.

in a year to absolutely none. That would be a rough adjustment!

Sugar is not just something to sprinkle on your breakfast cereal in the mornings; it plays an important and necessary role in cooking besides merely providing sweetness and flavor. Sugar blends and balances flavors, much like a seasoning. For example, in most tomato-based recipes (spaghetti, chili, barbecue sauce, and so on), sugar softens the acidity of the tomatoes and blends the flavors. In baked goods, sugar reacts with yeast in a thoroughly natural process called fermentation that is vital to bread rising and baking. It's essential in the creaming process that incorporates air into batters; the sugar crystals help create air pockets that contribute to a pleasing texture in breads, cakes, and other baked goods. Sugar acts as a natural preservative in jams, jellies, and sauces. It's not just tasty; it's useful as well. It's easy to see why you'll want to have some in your preparedness pantry.

Granulated sugar should be kept dry, in airtight containers. You'll need to transfer it from the paper bags it comes in or it will absorb moisture from the air and become as hard as a brick. Brick-hard sugar can still be used; it's just not as convenient. You can break it apart into chunks with a hammer and then grate it, or you can warm it in an oven until it is soft enough to use. Sugar is one of the few items that I am aware of that insects don't usually bother. Sugar stores indefinitely.

In the past, brown sugar was semirefined white sugar where some of the natural molasses was left in. Now, brown sugar is made by adding molasses back into refined white sugar; the amount of molasses added during processing determines the color of the sugar. You can try it yourself! Mix two tablespoons of molasses with a cup of white sugar to make homemade brown sugar.

Because of its moisture content, brown sugar must be stored in an airtight container. If not, it can

My mother always put a slice or two of bread in her cookie jar. the bread would be dry and crumbly, but the cookies were always soft.

become even harder than granulated sugar due to lost moisture. (Funny, white sugar gets hard because it gains moisture; brown sugar gets hard because it loses it.) One method of softening sugar is to place a dampened paper towel or a slice or two of bread in a jar or plastic bag with the sugar. Keep it sealed for one or two days. It should be soft again. You can also warm hard brown sugar to soften it. Heat it in the microwave for thirty seconds at a time until soft, or you can heat brown sugar in a pan in a regular oven at 250°F. for five minutes or so. Putting a small bowl of water next to the sugar in the pan in the oven and covering both with aluminum foil also helps. The sugar becomes soft when warmed and you can use it immediately, or measure it into usable amounts. It will harden again when it cools. You can also break off chips and run them through a blender or food processor a little at a time. The sugar will be more coarse than the original, but just as sweet. If you're going to cook with it, the coarseness won't matter anyway.

Honey, that popular liquid sugar produced by bees, has a distinctive flavor, is sweeter than regular sugar, and produces moist and dense baked goods. It is usually more expensive than sugar. Properly processed, packaged, and stored, honey retains its quality for a long time, even decades. However, the shelf life is largely determined by the temperature it's kept at (higher temperatures shorten shelf life), which is why many charts will give it only a two-year shelf life. Honey tends to crystallize with age. You can reverse this by warming (not cooking) it to melt the crystals. Age will also darken honey and make the flavor stronger.

If exposed to air, mold can invade a large container of honey. Before you throw it all out, try carefully scooping the top several inches of the honey off. If you get down to pure honey, the rest of the bucket will still be fine. Transfer the good honey to clean, airtight containers, making sure it doesn't touch any mold on the edges of the old bucket, and keep it in a dark, dry, cool place.

Honey is now available as honey powder. It may be packaged as powdered honey blend, which also has fructose and cornstarch in it. It can be used as a substitute for sugar or liquid honey. One cup of liquid honey is equal to one cup of honey powder and ¼ cup water. It is usually available in health food stores.

Light and dark corn syrup are sugars as well. They follow all the storage rules and guidelines of honey. Dark corn syrup has a stronger flavor than light. Molasses is a by-product of sugar production in sugar refineries. It is not as sweet as sugar and transfers a dark color and strong flavor to baked foods. Molasses and corn syrup have a very conservative shelf life of about eighteen months.

LEAVENINGS

If you really want to be able to use all those healthy grains you have stored, you absolutely must have some form of leavening in your pantry. No leavening, no bread. Also, no pancakes, no quick breads, no biscuits, no cookies (perish the thought!). If you want to get a rise out of your flour, you have to have leavening.

The most common leavening agents are yeast, baking powder, and baking soda. When mixed with a liquid, they produce carbon dioxide gas, which causes batter or dough to rise when heated. Since they all have a reasonably long shelf life, I highly suggest you have all of these in your preparedness pantry. This will give you many, many different options for how to use your bare-bones basics.

YEAST

Yeast is a live, single-celled organism. One pound of yeast contains about 3,200 billion yeast

> *If you want to get a rise out of your flour, you have to have leavenings.*

cells! This organism lies dormant until it is activated by a combination of sugar, moisture, warmth, and air. Then yeast begins feeding on the sugars in flour, and the byproducts are carbon dioxide gas and other organic compounds. The carbon dioxide gas expands the baked good to produce the light, fluffy texture, and the other "waste" products create the subtle flavors and consistency that make a good loaf of bread. All yeast is very sensitive; too much heat will kill it, and cold will stunt its growth. (Almost sounds like a house pet, doesn't it?)

There are four types of yeast. Compressed fresh yeast is highly perishable, as opposed to dry active yeast. You'll find it in the refrigerated section of the grocery store. It needs to be kept refrigerated and used within a couple of weeks, because the life span of a fresh yeast cell is only forty days or so. It must be proofed before using. Proofing yeast involves letting the yeast sit in warm water for about five minutes before it is ready to mix with other ingredients. Although it produces great flavor in yeast breads, fresh yeast is obviously not suitable for long-term storage.

Dry yeast is the type to choose for long-term storage. Yet, even dry yeast must be stored in an airtight container, in a cool environment with no threat of moisture. And regardless of conditions, it will lose its life over time. It is generally labeled with a shelf life of one to two years, though it usually will last longer. If the dry yeast is stored in airtight packaging, in a cool, dry place, it's not necessary to refrigerate it. Once opened, yeast should be stored in the refrigerator. Yeast works better if allowed to warm up to room temperature before you use it. Dry yeast comes in three forms: (1) active dry yeast, (2) quick-rise yeast, and (3) instant dry yeast. Active dry yeast is sold in the familiar packets you see in the baking section of the supermarket. It's been around for a long time. It can also be purchased in larger jars, which are your best choice for long-term storage. Quick-rise yeast and instant dried yeast are relative

newcomers to the yeast market. Grocery stores carry them in the baking section in small quantities, but for storage, you want the size of package that looks like a foil brick.

Technology has made these new yeast granules smaller in size than conventional dry yeast and even more dehydrated. Consequently, the smaller particles make it possible to mix them directly into the flour without the proofing period, and it speeds rising times by as much as fifty percent, often eliminating the need for a second rising period. For most breads, any of these three yeasts work just fine. One-half an ounce of yeast will raise four cups of flour in about one and one-half to two hours under ideal conditions.

You can use these interchangeably:
- One ¼ oz packet of dry yeast (active dry, instance active dry, or bread machine)
- One 0.06 oz fresh, compressed cake yeast cube
- 2½ teaspoons of dry yeast (active dry, instant active dry, or bread machine)

In case you're wondering, brewer's yeast has no leavening properties, but it is sometimes added to food for its nutritional benefits, as it is rich in the B vitamins.

CHEMICAL LEAVENERS

Baking powder and baking soda are the leavenings you normally would use for things like quick breads, pancakes, biscuits, and so on. These kinds of

---

To test any type of dry yeast for viability, mix a teaspoon of yeast and ½ teaspoon of sugar into ¼ cup of lukewarm water (110–120° F. degrees—comfortably warm against your wrist). If it bubbles within about five to ten minutes, it is still alive and will work to leaven your bread. Even if there are just a few bubbles, the yeast is alive, although its rising power is probably decreased. You can continue to use it without any problem as long as you compensate for the drop in rising power by adding more yeast. If there are no bubbles at all, the yeast is dead and should be discarded.

A friend in college heard yeast was a healthy supplement to one's diet, so he bought a container of yeast and ate two big spoonfuls straight from the jar. He somehow missed the part that said brewer's yeast is healthy; he bought and ate straight cooking yeast. He laughed about it later (months later), but at the time he was so miserable he just wanted to die. The yeast did its job very well. He said he could actually watch his stomach rising and falling and bubbling.

baked goods are much quicker to make than traditional raised yeast breads. Baking powder and baking soda work by a chemical reaction instead of a biological one (like yeast) to produce the carbon dioxide necessary to raise dough or batter. Though the two products seem similar in color and texture, they are not interchangeable. The speed and timing of the leavener is what distinguishes one from the other. Baking soda begins to create carbon dioxide gas as soon as it is mixed with liquid. Double-acting baking powder (which most baking powders are these days) produces a first set of gas bubbles when initially moistened, and then a second set when heated. The first reaction forms many small gas cells in the batter; the second reaction expands the bubbles to create a light texture.

BAKING SODA

Baking soda is sodium bicarbonate, or bicarbonate of soda. Since it reacts immediately when combined with water, it should be mixed thoroughly with the dry ingredients before adding liquids to insure even leavening. When liquid is added, baking soda begins to produce its leavening bubbles immediately, so any item baked with it should be put into the oven as quickly as possible. In addition, since soda is an alkaline, any product made with baking soda needs an acid product as well (sour milk, molasses, lemon juice, vinegar, and so on) to cause the chemical reaction, or it will not rise at all. Once moistened, baking soda has been activated and is no longer good.

The bonus of baking soda is that is has more uses than just as a leavening in baked goods. It also can be used to brush your teeth, for bug bites, to sooth an upset stomach, and more.

To use it as an antacid: drink ½ teaspoon baking

soda mixed in an eight-ounce glass of water every two hours up to eight times per day (four times per day for those over sixty; don't give it to children under five years old).

To use as a tooth powder: use baking soda on a wet toothbrush to clean your teeth and freshen breath.

To sooth minor skin irritations (insect bites and stings, windburn, sunburn, minor rashes): mix a paste of two parts baking soda to one part water. Smooth on the affected area.

Baking soda has an indefinite shelf life and should be stored in an airtight container in a cool, dry place. As a note of caution, if you're on a sodium-restricted diet, you shouldn't use baking soda

BAKING POWDER

Baking powder is basically a blend of an alkali (usually baking soda) and an acid (often cream of tartar). It is known as a double-acting leavening

Baking powder loses its potency over time. To check to see if it still causes a leavening reaction you should "proof" your baking powder: looking at it is the first step. Stir it around in the can to see if there are any lumps. Lumps are an indication that the baking powder has picked up moisture and started a reaction in the can, thus rendering it useless. Next, mix a teaspoon of baking powder into a glass of warm water to see if it fizzes. If it doesn't, throw it out.

Baking powder and baking soda seem similar in color and texture, but they are not interchangeable. To test whether your baking soda is still active, pour a couple tablespoons of white vinegar into a small cup and stir in one teaspoon of baking soda. If it froths, even a little, it's still good.

Acidic Ingredients include:

Applesauce, buttermilk, sour milk, honey, molasses, brown sugar, lemon juice, vinegar, cream of tartar, chocolate, regular cocoa powder, orange and other citrus juices, pineapple.

because it begins to release carbon dioxide as soon as it is moistened, and again when heated in the oven. You are unlikely to find single-acting baking powder in a grocery store; double-acting is generally the only type available. If you run out, you can make your own (single-acting) baking powder by mixing one-half teaspoon cream of tartar with one-fourth teaspoon baking soda. (This replaces a teaspoon of baking powder in a recipe.) Since it is only single acting, it will create carbon dioxide only when initially moistened, so you need to cook the batter quickly or it will go flat. Because the chemical reaction starts as soon as it comes in contact with water, be sure to thoroughly mix baking powder with other dry ingredients before adding any liquid.

Baking powder has a limited shelf life—one to two years. Packages will have a use-by date printed on them. It also should be kept in a cool, dry place, and most will still be active well past the expiration date.

SALT

Salt is essential for life and for good health. Salt is a mineral, one of the few rocks humans eat. Salt flavor is one of the basic tastes, and we instinctively like it.

Every cell in our bodies contains salt. That's why tears and sweat taste salty. Salt plays a crucial role in keeping our bodies functioning properly. Too much or too little salt in the diet can cause severe, even fatal, neurological problems.

Table salt has been refined so it contains nearly pure (95 percent or greater) sodium chloride. It also usually contains substances that make it free flowing (anti-caking agents). Most table salt is iodized, meaning a small amount of potassium iodide has been added as a dietary supplement. Iodized table salt has essentially eliminated iodine deficiency disorders in countries where it is used. So when you salt your food, you are not only making it taste good, but you are also giving your body essential nutrients it absolutely must have.

Salt plays an important role in cooking as well. Salt brings out natural flavors and makes foods taste desirable; it retards the growth of spoilage microorganisms; and it helps foods develop proper texture, among a host of other things. Very few recipes don't call for at least a pinch of salt—even desserts.

Salt has an indefinite storage life. As long as it stays dry and clean, it will never go bad. The round containers it comes in from the store are all right to keep it in if you live in a relatively dry climate. High humidity calls for a different container. If it's not stored in an airtight container it can absorb moisture from the air, which will cause it to cake up. If so, you simply need to dry it in the oven and break it up again. Iodized salt may turn yellowish with time, but this isn't a problem.

SPICES AND SEASONINGS

Seasonings and spices play a minimal nutritional role in our diet. That doesn't mean they're not important though. They are very, very important. They appeal to our senses. They make us want another bite. They make a meal something to enjoy, not just something to eat.

You need to have at least a few spices and seasoning with your long-term storage items because they make such a huge difference in the taste of the recipes you can make from just bare-bones basic foods. They need to be ones that are familiar to you but additionally, they should be ones that will go the farthest in making the greatest number of simple recipes taste better. Salt and pepper, vanilla, cinnamon, and maybe some chili powder or basil are a few of those.

Spices should always be stored in airtight containers. As a general rule, they come from the store in sealed glass or plastic jars or airtight metal cans, but occasionally some will be sold in plastic bags or in cardboard. These need to be transferred to a better container right away. Keep spices cool because heat causes them to deteriorate.

BOUILLONS/SOUP BASE

Bouillon is a seasoning, but it is so valuable in a bare-bones basic preparedness program that it deserves a mention of its own. You see, it's not really just a seasoning. Bouillon cubes are compressed, flavor-concentrated cubes of dehydrated meat, poultry, or vegetable stock and spices. Instant bouillon granules are the loose, granular form of the concentrate. Salt is usually listed as the first ingredient; thus, both are very salty.

If that is a concern for you, remember the salt will be diluted in the recipe, and don't add any other salt. Soup base often comes in the form of a paste in a jar or as a granular concentrate that serves the same purpose.

Read labels before purchasing; soup base may list meat as a first ingredient rather than salt. Bouillon is often used as a clear broth for soups and stews. It needs to be dissolved in boiling water according to package directions.

The beauty of bouillon and soup base from a Bare-bones basic perspective is how completely they can change the flavor of plain grains or beans. They make a fine base for soup, or even if nothing else is added, the broth can serve as a comfort food. Simply boiling grains in bouillon or soup base instead of water provides a completely different and delicious finished product.

Bouillon or soup base has a shelf life of one to two years (unopened), though I have used bouillon stored in my pantry for much longer than this, and it was fine.

ATTITUDE IS A BARE-BONES BASIC

When and if the time should arise that you have to eat your bare-bones basics, and nothing but your bare-bones basics, I suggest that you may need a big box of good attitude and a sense of humor along with your beans and dry milk. You'll need to find the fun in making bare-bones basics function. It may mean you'll have to learn that it's fun when you're successful at making a recipe edible. It's fun to figure out a real meal from bare-bones basics. It can be fun when the family admits a recipe tastes good. It's fun when you know how to make treats from the simplest of ingredients. And it's fun to share those treats with someone else less fortunate. Some have said there is nothing fun about a stringent bare-bones basic diet. I say it's up to you. Is your glass half full or half empty? Consider that things could certainly be worse; you at least have food for your family, and you know what to do with it beyond boiled grain. Your attitude will be as vital as any other element in your preparedness pantry.

WHAT CAN I DO WITH JUST THE BARE-BONES BASICS?

I spent several months researching and experimenting with what could be done if all I had to work with was just the barest of bare-bones basics. While the results didn't include any traditional seven-course feasts, I did discover a surprising number of possibilities beyond just boiled grain. Creativity can't magically turn beans into fresh peach pie à la mode, but it can add some variety and different textures and tastes to an otherwise exceptionally monotonous diet. Here are a few options:

Baked Pilaf

1 cup basmati rice (or any rice)
½ cup wild rice
½ cup lentils
½ cup dehydrated onions (optional)

Chicken bouillon or soup base dissolved to make five cups rice

Mix uncooked rice, lentils, and onions together in a well-oiled 2½–3 quart casserole. Pour broth over rice mix and stir. Bake at 350⁰ for sixty to seventy-five minutes, or until the broth is absorbed and rice is tender.

Basic Baking Mix

9 cups all-purpose flour
4 teaspoons salt
⅓ cup baking powder
1 cup plus 2 tablespoons instant or non-instant milk powder
1¾ cups shortening

In a large bowl, combine flour, baking powder, milk powder, and salt, stirring to mix well. Cut in shortening with two knives or a pastry blender until the mixture resembles coarse crumbs. Store at room temperature in a tightly covered container for four to six months, or in the freezer up to one year. Stir lightly before measuring. Do not pack down in the measuring cup. Level with a straight-edge spatula. Makes thirteen cups.

Easy Dumplings

2 cups Basic Baking Mix, above
⅔ cup milk or reconstituted dry milk

In mixing bowl add milk to basic baking mix all at once; stir just until mixture is moistened. Drop from tablespoon in ten to twelve mounds on top of simmering soup, broth, or even hot fruit juice. Cook, uncovered, over low heat about ten minutes. Cover and cook ten minutes longer.

Country Biscuits

2 cups Basic Baking Mix, above
½ cup milk or reconstituted dry milk

Preheat oven to 425°F. Measure Basic Baking Mix into a medium bowl. Stir in milk until mixed well. Turn out on a lightly floured board. Knead about fifteen times. Roll out ½ inch thick. Cut with a floured biscuit cutter or top of a 2½-inch-wide drinking glass. Arrange on an ungreased baking sheet. Bake ten minutes. Makes about twelve biscuits.

Drop Biscuits: Increase liquid to ⅔ cup. Mix well, but don't overmix. Dough may be lumpy. Do not knead or roll dough. Drop by spoonfuls onto an ungreased baking sheet or into greased muffin cups. (Hint: biscuits and fruit make a good breakfast or lunch.)

Vary biscuits by adding nuts, raisins, or chopped fruit.

Fry Bread

4 cups flour
2 teaspoons salt
3 teaspoons baking powder
⅓ cup powdered milk (not reconstituted)
1 teaspoon vegetable oil or shortening
1½ cups warm water

Mix together first five ingredients; add water a half cup at a time; let set fifteen minutes.

Roll a ball of dough about two inches in diameter into a patty ¾ to 1 inch thick. Fry in deep oil or shortening until golden brown. Delicious served with honey.

Taco Shells or Wraps

Delicious with Baker's Cheese or Day Cheese
1 cup finely ground whole wheat flour
2 cups white flour
1½ teaspoon salt
½ cup shortening
water

Mix together dry ingredients. Cut in the shortening and mix. Add enough water to form a soft dough. Place on a floured board and knead a few times. Divide the dough into fourteen balls the size of an egg, cover with a cloth, and let stand for about twenty minutes. Roll the balls into flat pancakes or tortillas. Cook in an ungreased skillet at medium heat, turning once.

Crackers

1¾ cups whole wheat flour
1½ cups white flour
⅓ cup oil emulsified in blender with
¾ teaspoon salt and 1 cup water

Mix dry ingredients, add oil-water-salt mixture. Knead as little as possible. Make smooth dough, then roll it as thin as possible on an ungreased cookie sheet (not more than ⅛ inch). Mark with a knife to size of crackers desired, but don't cut through. Prick each cracker a few times with a fork. Sprinkle lightly with salt or onion salt as desired. Bake in moderate oven (350° F.) for thirty to thirty-five minutes, or until crisp and light brown.

Easy Split Pea, Lentil, and Grain Soup

½ cup alphabet macaroni
½ cup green and yellow peas
½ cup lentils and or red lentils
½ cup pearl barley
½ cup rice
3–4 bouillon cubes or 3–4 teaspoons bouillon granules or soup base
3–4 cups water
salt and pepper to taste

Combine all ingredients in large pot. Bring water to boil and then reduce to simmer. Cook until tender, about one and a half to two hours. Serves six.

Cinnamon Crisp Treats

1½ cups flour
¾ cup sugar
½ teaspoon salt
2 teaspoons baking powder
1 teaspoon cinnamon
⅓ cup milk or reconstituted dry milk
⅓ cup shortening
1 teaspoon sugar
1 teaspoon cinnamon

Cream shortening and sugar; add dry ingredients thoroughly mixed, then add milk. Roll thin, cut in strips, and sprinkle with mixture of sugar and cinnamon. Bake in moderate oven (350°F.) for seven to ten minutes or until light brown. Makes about four dozen.

Notes

1. "Soybeans in Family Meals," *USDA Home and Garden Bulletin,* no. 208, adapted.

2. "Sugar Intake Hits All-Time High," in www.cspinet.org/new/sugar_limit

CHAPTER NINE

BARE-BONES BASICS: COMPLEMENTS

In a preparedness survey I once conducted, one of the questions was, "How long do you think is a reasonable period of time to be prepared to rely totally on yourself? A woman in San Jose, CA, responded, "Only six months, because if you are still having to eat your food storage after six months, you're going to wish you were dead!" Speaking facetiously, I believe I'd have to agree with her. An unrelieved diet of straight bare-bones basic foods for an extended period would probably be pretty unbearable. And it would be even more so because you now know it was unnecessarily unbearable!

Transforming a bare-bones basic diet from terrible to tolerable is easy and doable. It just takes adding a few pertinent complementary foods to your supply. (That's complementary, not complimentary; you will not be telling the rice how nice it looks.) To complement is to complete, or add to, or perfect. A complementary food is one that adds to or completes another food. The companion foods and those that complement the bare-bones basics are foods that will increase the nutritional value, appeal, and taste of the basics while greatly expanding their simple recipe potential.

The nice thing about bare-bones basic complements is that most of them can be put on the long-term storage shelf with your other pantry items and they will also wait patiently until you need them. That is, if you don't discover that they work wonderfully well for everyday cooking. They don't take up oodles of space or send your budget into shock. Yet the addition of just a few simple items will make all the difference in the world in what are sure to be extremely difficult times.

EGGS

Eggs fit the priority role in the bare-bones basics family for several reasons. They are high-quality protein. They can be used as a food by themselves or as a functioning ingredient in recipes. The problem with eggs, beyond the obvious shelf life dilemma (can you imagine cracking a five-year-old egg?), is that they insist on rolling off the shelf. Thank goodness for dried eggs. Dried whole eggs, dried egg whites, dried egg yolk, and dried egg mix are all available commercially. You'll need to read the label to determine which you want and which you're getting because there are some differences between them.

Dried whole-egg powder is 100 percent egg that, when blended with water, will produce liquid eggs that can then be used just like fresh eggs. During the drying process, about ninety percent of the water is evaporated, so that one pound of dried egg is equal to almost three-dozen shell eggs. Dried whole egg has the same nutritional value as fresh eggs. Both dried egg whites and dried egg yolks are convenient ways to use either part without the hassle and mess of separating the yolks from the whites. Bakers frequently use dried egg whites to make meringue. Dried egg mix is generally a blend of whole dried eggs, nonfat dry milk, corn oil, color, salt, and in some brands, lecithin and/or whey. The egg mix costs considerably less than whole egg solids. Which product to choose will best be determined by what you're going to use it for. The egg mix can be used as an ingredient in baking or scrambled eggs. Dried whole eggs can do the same, plus can be used as a replacement for liquid whole eggs. All are good, just different.

Dried eggs are easy to cook with. In recipes, simply mix the dried egg with the dry ingredients and add the additional liquid for the egg when you add the other liquid ingredients. In a pinch, you can substitute plain unflavored gelatin for eggs in most recipes. You can find it by the other flavored gelatins in grocery stores, and it stores for years. For one egg, use one packet of plain gelatin mixed with two tablespoons of warm water. (Don't mix the gelatin with water until you are ready to use it or it will thicken and set up.) Substituting works fine for up to three eggs in one recipe.

DEHYDRATED FOODS EXPAND THE BARE-BONES POTENTIAL

Dehydrated and freeze-dried foods are the perfect complements to bare-bones basic foods. Today's food dehydration techniques take fresh, wholesome food and reduce the moisture level to a miniscule 2–3 percent (as compared to the 25 percent of commercially dried fruits, like the soft and pliable apricots or apple slices you'll find in packages at the grocery store). This gives the food important advantages as a long-term storage food, especially long shelf life, low weight and volume, and a host of other benefits. And the best part of all is the great variety of food available in this form. The many and varied options are perfect for fleshing out a bare-bones diet. Remember, variety is the key! Flavored boiled grain and plain bread give way to luscious stews and casseroles and desserts—food everyone would be happy to come to the table for.

Long Life

Food spoilage is caused by the growth of bacteria, and bacteria will not grow if there isn't sufficient moisture or oxygen to allow to develop. Because dehydrated food is so very dry, and because it is processed in containers that have had the oxygen removed, the food will last a long, long time and still retain its food value. A shelf life for sealed containers of fifteen plus years is not uncommon (except for items with a high

fat content; shelf life for these is shorter). Shelf life will vary somewhat with each individual item, but for the most part, dehydrated foods are ideally suited for long-term storage. Once a can is opened, keep a tight-fitting lid on it. The can will last until you use it up, within reason of course. The food may eventually absorb moisture from the air, causing powders to lump and fruit to stick together and so on, but that won't hurt it. It's still okay.

Low Weight and Volume

Dehydrated food is perfect for people who don't have a lot of room to sacrifice to storing food. Most of the weight and volume of any food comes from water. Once this water is removed by dehydration, the weight and space savings can be downright amazing. For example, as many as thirty fresh tomatoes can fit into a pint-sized jar after they have been dehydrated. Ten pounds of sliced carrots will fit into a quart-size jar after dehydration. One No. 10 can of dehydrated peas holds the equivalent of twenty-seven cans of canned peas from the grocery store. As a general rule, dehydrated foods take only 20 percent of the storage space of wet packed foods.

Other Benefits

Dehydrated food tastes good! Granted, it doesn't taste exactly like fresh, but this shouldn't strike you as unusual. Fresh, canned, frozen, cooked—all these various forms taste a little different, yet you've become accustomed to them all over your lifetime. You'll find, though, that after preparing and adding a little seasoning, dehydrated food is just as good as its cooked or canned counterpart.

Dehydrated Food Is Good for You

As a rule, only top-quality products are used to produce dehydrated foods. The foods are picked when fully ripe, cleaned and trimmed to leave only the best parts, and processed soon after picking. After processing, dehydrated food retains more of its nutrients than either commercially frozen or canned foods.[1]

> *Dehydrated and freeze-dried foods are the perfect complements to bare-bones-basic foods*

> *Only top-quality products are used to produce dehydrated foods.*

Dehydrated food is simple to use. It does take a bit of time to prepare dehydrated food, but not that much more time. Fresh foods have to be washed and peeled and chopped to use. That's probably more time-consuming than opening a can and adding a handful of dehydrated food to a soup. Both powdered eggs and powdered milk are great for baking, particularly because of their convenience. Dehydrated vegetables are great in Crock-Pot meals.

Dehydrated food is reasonably priced. It might seem expensive when you purchase a can of dehydrated food, but when you consider the quantity of food packed in that little can, the cost is actually very reasonable, no more than fresh or canned foods, and usually substantially less. If you purchase dehydrated food in bulk or on sale, the prices are even lower. These are just a few of the many benefits that make dehydrated foods a good choice for long-term storage as well as daily use.

FREEZE-DRIED FOOD

Freeze-drying is another form of food preservation that lends itself well to long-term storage. It has most of the advantages of dehydration and a few others besides. Freeze-drying is a different process than regular dehydration. When food is freeze-dried, it is flash-frozen and then placed into a vacuum chamber. The low air pressure causes the moisture to be drawn off in its frozen state. The result is food that looks more like the original product when rehydrated. The foods maintain their original shape and texture, unlike dehydrated foods, which shrink and shrivel during dehydration. Freeze drying also preserves virtually all of a food's fresh-food taste, color, aroma, and nutritional content, and yet it is very shelf stable. Almost any food, from apples to zucchini, can be freeze-dried. So can ice cream (yum!), scrambled eggs, meats, casseroles, and even entire meals. The shelf life of freeze-dried food is very, very long—twenty to thirty years for items commercially dried

Freeze drying is a form of food preservation that lends itself well to long-term storage. Almost any food, from apples to zucchini, can be freeze-dried.

in metal cans with the oxygen removed—quite a bit less for items packaged in pouches (five years). Storage conditions will definitely affect shelf life, so keep these things in a dark, dry, cool area. Once containers are opened, a tight-fitting lid must be kept on them. Once they are exposed to air, they deteriorate rather quickly, so you'll need to use them or lose them. The disadvantages of freeze-dried foods are that they take up quite a bit of space (remember they maintain the shape of the fresh product), and they are expensive. When you factor in the thirty-year shelf life, the cost may be worth it to you.

Freeze-dried foods can do the same things in recipes as dehydrated foods, but the two aren't directly interchangeable. In the following paragraphs, when I speak of dehydrated foods, remember that freeze-dried foods are just as useful and can be exchanged for dehydrated if you like; they just take different preparation methods.

GREAT FOR DAILY USE ALSO

After reading about the advantages of dehydrated foods, you may be wondering why in the world you aren't using them on a daily basis. They sound pretty good, don't they? Well, they are, and you could be using them regularly. I do. I'm not saying I've replaced all my fresh food with dehydrated—that would be silly since I love fresh fruits and vegetables. But my cooking habits are greatly influenced by dehydrated foods. Not a week goes by when I don't toss a handful of dehydrated vegetables into a pot of soup, or cook some dehydrated peaches into my breakfast oatmeal, or use powdered eggs or milk in baking. I detest chopping onions, so I rely on dehydrated onions any time I fry hamburger or make meatloaf or the like. Dehydrated foods are convenient and affordable, so I can't imagine why anyone would choose to not use them. There is such a large variety of dehydrated food available, you may not know where to start. Some of the things—like dehydrated custard mix or peach-flavored apple flakes or sour cream powder—though nice to have, wouldn't be on the top of the list for a survival stash. Consider first the items that will contribute to making your bare-bones basics into a series of successful suppers, breakfasts, lunches, and treats. As you read, let your mind reflect on your general eating habits and favorite flavors. Perhaps you'll come up with a few items that would work for you as bare-bones basic complements beyond the ones that I describe.

VEGETABLES AND FRUITS

If circumstances consigned you to living off a bare-bones basic diet, one of the things you would miss the most would be fresh fruits and vegetables. Dehydrated fruits and veggies aren't quite the same thing, but they would run a close second. Think of how your options expand. Would you rather have a bowl of hot, cinnamony apple crisp or a bowl of hot, cinnamony pinto bean crisp? How about a pot of soup simmering on the stove, the air redolent with the aroma of broth, green beans, potatoes, carrots, onions, and parsley, compared to soup simmering with beans and wheat? This one is obvious. Health-wise, recipe-wise, tastewise—vegetables and fruits should be one of the highest-priority options for your long-term pantry. Just about every fruit and vegetable under the sun is available in dehydrated or freeze-dried form. Apples, apricots, peaches, pears, beets, broccoli, carrots, mushrooms, peppers, and yams: they're all available, plus plenty you'd never think of. Here are just a few (by no means all!) of my favorites and some ideas how to use them to augment the bare-bones basics in your cupboards.

• Tomato powder, flakes, or crystals: Use as paste, sauce, juice, soup, or just for the tomato flavor in recipes.

• Onion flakes, slices, minced: Use as an all-around seasoning (minus the tears).

• Bell peppers, chopped or diced: Use in soups, pilafs, side dishes, or skillet dishes.

• Potato flakes, granules, shreds, cubes: Use for thickening; add to soups or breads; use alone as hash browns or mashed potatoes. Great as a mild core basic.

• Celery: Add to sprouts, salad greens, pilafs, and soups.

• Vinegar powder: Use for salad dressings and to make cheese. (Takes less space and stores longer than fluid vinegar.)

• Catsup powder: The convenience and flavor of catsup, only for long-term storage.

• Apples, slices, chunks, sauce: Use in hot cereal, or for nibbling.

• Pears, peaches, apricots: Use as a snack, in hot cereals, or in desserts.

Just a tip about dehydrated fruit: it should not be overcooked. The more you cook it, the mushier it becomes. In fact, sometimes the best thing to do is simply pour very hot water over the fruit and let it stand. It will double in volume and have the taste and appearance of cooked fruit. You shouldn't eat dehydrated fruit as is in large amounts right out of the can. One or two pieces to suck on like hard candy are fine. However, it isn't candy. Eating large volumes of unreconstituted dehydrated fruit could cause

When I first started using dehydrated foods and creating recipes, I learned a lot by trial and error. There weren't many recipes available then. One thing I learned was that a piece of dehydrated fruit was almost as good as popping a piece of candy in your mouth. I got into the habit of filling a sandwich bag with different kinds of dehydrated fruit and putting it in Larry's lunch sack. He would nibble on the fruit all day. Soon, many of the fellows he worked with wanted to share his snack. They were always asking, "What did you bring today?" Sometimes I would send two sandwich bags to make sure Larry had enough. Our family is a great one for teasing, so one day I filled one small sack with dehydrated fruit and the other with a well-known brand of cat food. Larry, being used to my teasing, recognized it immediately and decided to carry on the little joke. When one of his friends said, "What do you have today?" Larry replied, "A brand new food. Here you can have this bag, I have another." The unknowing friend snacked on cat food all day, trying to figure out what the "new food" tasted like.

stomach problems when it swells and reconstitutes in your stomach.

TEXTURED VEGETABLE PROTEIN

Textured vegetable protein, or TVP as it is usually called, is a food product made from soybeans. The style most often used for long-term storage is made from soy flour after the soybean oil has been extracted and is a good source of protein and fiber. TVP has a long shelf life if stored properly. It comes in small dry chunks or flakes. You can buy it either flavored to resemble meat or unflavored. Many vegetarians use it regularly. Personally, I don't use it frequently, but it's good to have in long-term storage for the value it would have for its protein and fiber, as well as its usefulness as a flavoring if meat were no longer a part of a regular diet. Some of the most popular TVP products are the granules used as hamburger, or the chunks resembling chicken or ham. There are TVP products found in health food stores and vegetarian outlets that resemble canned meat products such as Spam. Still made from soybeans, they are compact, condensed, and moist.

GIVE THEM A TRY

Some people hesitate to buy dehydrated foods because they think they'll taste funny or they'll be too hard to prepare. They're not really hard to use, just different. And they don't taste bad, just different. It merely takes some time to get used to them. Trust me. Don't let lack of experience keep you from storing or using them. Buy them and try them. Then try some more. Practice will make all the difference. Don't expect perfection the first time you prepare them. With practice and experience, you'll find these foods are very good, very convenient, and very valuable to have.

SPICES AND SEASONINGS

Seasonings and spices will make a huge difference in the desirability of a bare-bones basic diet. A pinch of this or a teaspoon of that will take boring grain or bean dishes and turn them into tasty meals. A wide variety of seasonings and spices can make the same old basics have a multitude of interesting tastes.

You, no doubt, already have a selection of favorite spices in your cupboard that you use regularly. (If not, keep reading for some good suggestions on what to start with.) These tried and true regulars are the things you should have a back stock of to make sure they're available when you need them. For example, I use garlic salt on just about anything I cook (excluding chocolate chip cookies). I wouldn't know how to cook without it, and I have a few jars on my pantry shelves to make sure I don't have to. Think of your cooking habits and look through your spice cupboard to determine what is important to you; then make sure you have those items with your long-term storage supplies.

Apple Crisp

3 cups dehydrated apple slices
4 cups water
1 cup sugar
1¾ teaspoon cinnamon
1½ teaspoon salt
Topping:
1 cup sugar
1 cup flour
½ teaspoon salt
½ cup soft butter/margarine

Bring apple slices to a boil in water. Remove from heat. Mix sugar, cinnamon, and salt, and stir in apple slices. Spread mixture in an 8 x 8 x 2-inch pan. Sift remaining sugar, flour, and salt. Cut in butter until mixture is as fine as cornmeal. Spread as topping over apple slices. Bake at 400°F for about thirty minutes. Serve warm or cold.

Variation: Half the flour may be substituted with dry milk. One-half cup of rolled oats may be added to topping. (Sometimes I double the amount of the topping.)

Seasonings and spices will make a huge difference in the desirability of a bare-bones-basic diet.

Spices and herbs won't last forever. They'll lose their color, taste, and aroma over time. So, how long will they last? A true gourmet cook would be appalled to have to use any spice that was more than a few months old, but that's pretty extreme. For best results you should use and replace spices within a year. That being said, the actual shelf life of spices (properly cared for in airtight containers in a dark, dry, and cool place) is much longer than that. If it smells strong and flavorful, it's still good. Old seasonings and spices will not make you sick; they just aren't as potent as fresh ones. You can technically use spices until there isn't any scent or flavor left in them but you don't need to go that far. Replace your spices every couple of years and you'll be in good shape. Whole herbs and spices last longer than their ground counterparts.

If you're debating which seasonings and spices you should stock up on, some of the most commonly used seasonings include:

• Herbs (such as rosemary, garlic powder, oregano, thyme, and basil)

• Spices (like cinnamon, cloves, nutmeg, chili powder, ginger, paprika, curry powder, and allspice)

• Flavorings (like vanilla or maple flavoring)

• Condiments (such as Worcestershire sauce, soy sauce, and mustard)

• Flavored vinegars

• Salt and pepper—the most common seasonings of all

SOUP MIXES

Soup mix from a dehydrated food company will generally be a mix of vegetables, grains or beans, small pasta, and possibly TVP. These have a shelf life of many years. Soup mixes found in the grocery stores are a different product. Usually they come in foil or cardboard packaging and contain broth mix as well as dehydrated or freeze-dried vegetables in the package. These need to be kept in a sturdy, airtight container, such as a glass gallon jar. Even then, their shelf life would be measured in months

A one-gallon jar will hold at least thirty-five foil sauce/seasoning mix packets. I counted them.

(nine to twelve) rather than years, due to the fat in the mix. One or two grains or split peas added to this type of soup mix and you would have a hearty meal.

SEASONING AND SAUCE MIXES

If there are only bare-bones basics in the cupboard, the foil seasoning and sauce mix packets at the grocery store may come to the flavor rescue. These mixes usually have a higher fat content, which shortens their shelf life. Shorter, yes, but still acceptable for long-term storage with a little awareness factored in. They will need to be stored carefully (airtight containers in a dark, dry, and cool place, just like everything else), and used and replaced within a year or two. Considering how valuable they could be, though, it's well worth the little bit of extra effort. There are sauce mixes for rice and for pastas: ordinary gravy mixes can transform plain noodles into "storage stroganoff." There are ethnic sauce and seasoning mixes: the oriental beef and broccoli mix would just as effectively flavor rice, sprouts, and dehydrated vegetables. Cheese sauces will work miracles with plain grain or plain pasta (what child doesn't love macaroni and cheese?). Check out those rows and rows of seasonings and sauces in the supermarket. Bring home your favorite flavors: some to use today and some to stash with your long-term storage.

NUTS AND SEEDS

As far as nutrition goes, nuts and seeds have more protein than other vegetable foods (except soybeans). In that respect, they are a great complement to bare-bones basics. However, there is one characteristic that prevents them from being considered as ideal long-term storage items: shelf life. Their oil content is high, which is good for nutrition, flavor accents, and for making butters, but not long-term storage. Even

Nuts and Seeds:

Alfalfa, Flaxseed, Pumpkin, Sesame, Sunflower, Almonds, Cashews, Hazelnuts, Peanuts, Pecans, Pine Nuts, Pistachios, and Walnuts

so, if you recognize the shorter shelf life and properly take care of nuts and seeds, they will complement and combine with the bare-bones basics extremely well.

You can buy nuts and seeds in plastic bags or in bulk, but don't if you're planning to use them with your long-term storage items. Even if you transfer them to an airtight container, you can't remove the oxygen from the container, and the oxygen is what makes the nuts go rancid so quickly. Nuts commercially sealed in No. 10 cans or in the glass jars you'll find on your grocery store shelves have had the oxygen removed, and they'll have a shelf life of about twelve months as long as they're not opened. After opening, use them within a few weeks or keep them in the freezer for a month or two.

When transformed, peanuts become the must-have staple for many people—the peanut-butter half of peanut butter and jelly. Peanut butter has a longer shelf life than plain peanuts (about twenty-four months according to most charts, but realistically twice that long if it's hydrogenated).

A FINAL NOTE ABOUT BARE-BONES BASICS AND BARE-BONES-BASIC COMPLEMENTS

When times get really tough, regular routines go out the door as trouble comes in; your comfort zone, job, and schedules may suddenly be topsy-turvy. You may be spending more time at home, or maybe less time at home. Either way, with regular, familiar foods and meals a thing of the past, you'll have to spend more time on domestic duties (like getting food on the table) than you're used to. Until you become accustomed to using bare-bones basics and their complements, it will seem like real work. And when you are accustomed to it, you will know that it is real work. Keep in mind, though, it isn't Mission: Impossible. Remember your box of attitude. Attitude and awareness are two of the keys to put in place now, while you are still dealing with preparedness, not endurance.

Building the basics first is important, but having them be edible is important too. These complements are a way for you to make the bare bones taste like your home cooking, even in hard times. That is one of the things that is so important to understand: It's not just having stuff on the shelves that counts; it's being able to make it taste good that is the real key to success.

Notes
1. "Analysis Charts Table: Nutrients in the Edible Portion of One Pound of Food," U.S. Department of Agriculture Research Services Division, *Composition of Foods Handbook*, no. 8.

CHAPTER TEN

BARE-BONES BASICS: WHAT DO I NEED AND HOW MUCH IS ENOUGH?

Do you recall the following nursery rhyme?

Old Mother Hubbard went to the cupboard
To fetch her poor dog a bone
But when she got there the cupboard was bare
And so the poor dog had none.

Apparently Old Mother Hubbard didn't plan very well when she was figuring out her preparedness supplies. (Hopefully she has this book on the bookshelf and a good stash of rice down in her cellar, and the dog can fill up on cooked rice (see page 60) until Mrs. Hubbard can find a new source of bones.)

Her failure to plan sufficiently may have something in common with the prevailing cooking practices of our current generation. Not many people in this century grind their grain into flour for bread or cook everything they eat from scratch. Consequently, not many people would have the slightest idea how much food they would need to store in order to feed themselves completely and solely from their long-term storage.

Utah State University Extension gives some clarification on the matter of how much is needed. "One pound of dry matter provides about 1600 calories of energy. Because energy is the most critical item in a food storage program (it will prevent the baby from being hungry), it should be considered first. Thus dried beans, flour, wheat, rice, sugar, dried fruits or vegetables, pastas, or dried skim milk all provide about 1600 calories per pound. While 1600 calories will not adequately meet the energy needs of a hard-working large man, it will quiet hunger pangs for individual members of a family. One pound of dry matter per person per day serves as the basis for a food storage program."[1] One pound of dry matter per day is 365 pounds for a year. This is a very minimal amount; 1600 calories is a seriously calorie-restricted diet for most people in the best of times. It would keep you alive though.

To clarify more expansively, the following chart[2] breaks down the average suggested amounts of basic home storage foods for one person for one year (as well as for three and six months, if those seem to be more manageable time frames for you). These amounts are for an average adult male; an average adult female would require a little less. Variety is the key, so a possible breakdown of items within each group is suggested; you should vary the items within groups according to your needs and tastes, while sticking fairly closely to the general category amounts.

As was mentioned, these might seem to be huge amounts: 400 pounds of grain for just one person! You may say to yourself, "I don't even use four pounds of grain or beans per year, let alone 400 pounds. These numbers are way too high." In reality, they are not exorbitant. If these were the only foods in your pantry and you had no other way to get more to replace them, these would be the amounts to keep you alive, day-to-day. You might need more than this. These are just-barely-get-by amounts.

Remember to not shortchange anyone. If you have children or young adults, it would be far better to have too much in a time of need than to be caught short with not enough. Don't assume that because your child is only three feet tall and hardly eats enough to keep a bird alive, you don't need to store quite so much food for him. Time passes. Children (and appetites, and caloric needs) grow. By the time you have to use your storage, that sweet little child may be a foot taller than you and be eating you out

Suggested Amounts of Basic Storage Foods (one person/one year)

Item	Per Year	Per 3 Months	Per 6 Months
Grains	**400 lbs**	**100 lbs**	**200 lbs**
• Wheat	175 lbs		
• Flour	20 lbs		
• Cornmeal	30 lbs		
• Rolled Oats	50 lbs		
• Enriched White Rice	80 lbs		
• Pearled Barley	5 lbs		
• Pasta	40 lbs		
Legumes	**60 lbs**	**15 lbs**	**30 lbs**
• Dry Beans	45 lbs		
• Dry Lima Beans	2 lbs		
• Dry Soy Beans	2 lbs		
• Dry Split Peas	2 lbs		
• Dry Lentils	2 lbs		
• Dry Soup Mix	7 lbs		
Fats and Oils	**10 quarts**	**2.5 quarts**	**5 quarts**
• Cooking Oil	5 quarts		
• Shortening	2 quarts		
• Mayonnaise	1 quart		
• Salad Dressing (Mayonnaise Type)	1 quart		
• Peanut Butter	1 quart		
Milk Group	**16 lbs (or equivalent in canned milk)**	**4 lbs**	**8 lbs**
• Nonfat Dry Milk	14 lbs		
• Evaporated Milk	12 12-oz cans		
Sugars	**60 lbs**	**15 lbs**	**30 lbs**
• Granulated Sugar	40 lbs		
• Brown Sugar	3 lbs		
• Molasses	1 lbs		
• Honey	3 lbs		
• Corn Syrup	3 lbs		
• Jams or Preserves	5 lbs		
• Powdered Fruit Drink	6 lbs		
• Flavored Gelatin	1 lbs		
Miscellaneous			
• Salt	8 lbs	2 lbs.	4 lbs.
• Dry yeast	½ lbs	2 oz.	4 oz.
• Baking Soda	1 lbs	¼ lbs.	½ lbs.
• Baking Powder	1 lbs	¼ lbs.	½ lbs.
• Water	14 gallons*	14 gallons	14 gallons

*Obviously, this would provide drinking and cooking water for only a few days—less than a week. Much more water needs to be stored, if possible.

Fruits and vegetables in any form would enhance the nutritional value of this diet.

of house and home. As you review these charts and begin to figure out the amounts that will meet the needs of your family, round all of the amounts up, not down. Count everyone as if they were adults. They will be before you know it.

Perhaps you are a more visual type of person and you need to see how you could possibly need this much food (food that you've never used before!) in order to believe that it is really necessary. Rather than looking at shelves full of cans and boxes and buckets, it might help if instead you could visualize shelves with loaves of bread or batches of cookies or an assortment of practical recipes. Let's use wheat as our example. Wheat is the preeminent food storage food. If you follow the above chart, you would purchase and properly store 400 pounds of wheat for just yourself. (For the purposes of this illustration, just assume all the grain is wheat—in reality of course, it will be a variety of grains.) It's possible that you will buy this wheat prepackaged (or package it yourself) in sixty-seven No. 10 cans, (about the size of a large coffee can). A No. 10 can holds approximately six pounds of wheat, which is the same as fourteen cups of wheat. Fourteen cups of wheat can be ground into approximately twenty-one cups of flour. Twenty-one cups of flour can potentially be made into:

- Seven large loaves of raised bread, or
- Ten to twelve loaves of quick bread, or
- Ten batches of pancakes, or
- Ten batches of biscuits, or
- Ten batches of chocolate chip cookies

If you had 400 pounds of wheat (and providing you were wise enough to also store the other items necessary to bake your bread, pancakes, or cookies), you would have the equivalent of 466 loaves of bread—about one-and-a-third loaves of bread each day for a year. Or, for variety, you could make 600 loaves of quick bread or batches of something else; enough to have a little more than a batch and a half of something every day for a year. Each batch of pancakes is approximately fifteen four-inch pancakes, which would work out to five pancakes each for breakfast, lunch, and dinner, for a year, with a loaf of quick bread thrown in every other day for a change of pace. It's certainly enough to keep you alive, if you don't die of the monotony. (Hint: store variety, variety, variety!)

The following chart and guidelines will help you assess the foods in your pantry so you can get a picture of what can be made with them, how long they might last depending on your individual usage, and how varying that usage might stretch a product further.

Sometimes when dealing with unfamiliar food or food in an unfamiliar form, it helps to have a conversion table to make things a little easier. You may find the charts and figures on the following pages useful.

Hopefully, you can now visualize why such seemingly huge amounts of long-term storage foods are recommended. If those cans and buckets are all you have and you can't get any more, you'll be grateful for every one there is. It's good to know that it isn't just grain and beans and other dry stuff in the cans; it's actually food you recognize and can rely on to see you through when the going gets tough. And you know what they say: when the going gets tough, the tough make chocolate chip cookies.

Notes
1. *Home Storage, Use It or Lose It,* Utah State University Extension.
2. Adapted from www.providentliving.org.

Approximate Weight, Yields, and Usage of Dry Product in No. 10 Cans

Item	Pounds Product Equals Cups Product	Possible Recipe Potential (other ingredients also required)
Beans (dried)	5.25 pounds = 10.5 cups	4 recipes of bean soup, 5 recipes baked beans
Dry Milk (regular)	4.13 pounds = 13.5 cups	90 cups of fluid milk, 90 cups hot cocoa, 22 custard pies
Flour	4.25 pounds = 17 cups	Almost 3 loaves of yeast bread, 6 dozen rolls, 4 batches cookies, 3 cakes
Macaroni/Pasta	3.38 pounds = 13.5 cups	7 recipes macaroni and cheese, 7 recipes spaghetti, 7 tuna noodle casseroles
Oats (regular)	3 pounds = 13.5 cups	4 loaves oatmeal bread, 13 recipes oatmeal muffins, 4½ batches cookies
Potatoes (instant/buds)	3.19 pounds = 13.5 cups	54 servings, 13 shepherd's pies, 40 recipes potato rolls
Potatoes (granules)	6 pounds = 13.25 cups	54 servings, 13 shepherd's pies, 40 recipes potato rolls
Rice	5.75 pounds = 11.75 cups	35 servings plain rice, 11 recipes fried or Spanish rice, 26 recipes rice pudding
Sugar	6.13 pounds = 12.25 cups	12 batch sugar cookies, 12 cups pancake syrup, 7 cakes
Wheat	5.75 pounds = 14 cups	72 servings whole wheat cereal, 3 baked whole wheat casseroles, 24 cups sprouts
Carrots (dehydrated)	2.5 pounds = 15 cups	15 side dishes, carrots in 60 soup recipes, 30 carrot cakes
Peas (dehydrated)	2.75 pounds = 11.5 cups	12 side dishes, peas in 45 soup recipes, peas in 45 casseroles
Corn (dehydrated)	2.5 pounds = 15.5 cups	15 side dishes, corn in 60 soup recipes, corn in 60 casseroles
Eggs (dehydrated)	3 pounds = 96 tablespoons = 96 eggs	Eggs for 48 cakes, 48 to 96 loaves of quick bread, 48 batches of cookies
Onions (dehydrated)	1.12 pounds = 14 cups	Onions in 56 soup recipes, flavoring in 112 casseroles
Apple Slices (dehydrated)	1 pound = 13 cups	Fruit in 104 bowls of cooked oatmeal, 6½ pies

Approximate Yield Amounts

¾ pound honey* = 1 cup	1 pound sugar = 2 cups
1 pound cornmeal = 3 cups	1 pound rolled oats = 6 cups
1 pound barley = 2 cups	1 pound dried beans = 2 cups
1 pound lentils = 2 cups	1 pound chocolate chips = 2 cups
1 cup regular white rice = 1¼ cups flour	1 cup oats = 1 cup oat flour
1 pound wheat = 2¼ cups 6 pounds wheat (No. 10 can) = 13½ cups wheat	1 cup wheat = 1½ cups wheat flour 13½ cups wheat (No. 10 can) = 20¼ cups flour

*Note: Do not give honey to children under the age of two due to the dangers of infant botulism.

Cooked Yield

1 cup macaroni elbow/shell = 2½ cups cooked
2 cups noodles = 2 cups noodles cooked
Spaghetti, 4 oz. about 1 inch in diameter = 2 cups cooked
Grains: 1 cup dry = 2 cups cooked
Barley: 1 cup dry = 3 cups cooked
Lentils: 1 cup dry = 2 cups cooked
Canned vegetables, No. 303 can = 1 cup vegetables/1 cup water
Canned fruit, No. 303 can = 1½ cups fruit/½ cup water

Average Quantity Needed for a Batch

Yeast: dry = 1 to 2 Tablespoon per batch
Vanilla = 1 to 2 teaspoon per recipe
Chocolate Chips: Fudge brownies = 1 to 2 cups per batch Cookies = 2 cups per batch Snitching = ¼ to ½ teaspoon per recipe
Vinegar = ½ to 1 teaspoon per recipe

CHAPTER ELEVEN

SPROUTING: GREENS FROM GRAINS

In hard times, good times, emergency times, and in-between times, you can have a vegetable garden right in your kitchen. Summer or winter, rain or shine, you can easily sow, cultivate, and harvest an entire crop within two to six days and never have to pull a single weed. This crop doesn't require a rototiller, a shovel, gloves, or even sunscreen. All you need is a jar, some seeds, and water, and before you know it, you're a "sprout-jar farmer." Sprouts are nutritious and delicious, cost only pennies per serving, and take only a minute or two each day. Simple as they may be, from a preparedness perspective, these tiny little garden harvests can add a new dimension to how you eat, particularly during difficult times and stringent diets.

There are two basic types of sprouts: the tiny ones that you eat when they form a set of green leaves (alfalfa, mustard, radish, cress, and so on) and the larger ones that you eat before the leaves open or turn green (mung beans, pinto or other beans, lentils, rye, wheat, and so on). The method for sprouting both kinds is the same:

- Only use seeds or beans that are packaged and sold specifically for sprouting. Seeds that are packaged for planting purposes may contain toxic chemicals. You can find seeds or beans for sprouting in supermarkets or health food stores.
- Sort seeds and discard any that are broken, shriveled, or unhealthy looking.
- A small quantity of seeds will go a long way. For a quart jar, two tablespoons of tiny seeds, ¼ cup of bean seeds or ½ cup of wheat kernels is sufficient. Seeds must have room for expansion. (See chart on page 92.)

- Soak whole seeds in about three times their volume of water until they are saturated. The tiny seeds only need a few hours; medium ones should soak for eight hours or so; the large ones may need to soak ten to twelve hours. Drain off any water that hasn't been absorbed and keep the seeds in a warm place.
- Keep the seeds moist by gently rinsing or spraying with lukewarm water three times a day. If the force of the water is too harsh, it breaks off the tiny growing sprout. Frequent rinsing will keep the sprouts from molding.
- The main factors for germination are water, air, heat, and darkness, so keep your "garden" well covered and out of direct light. After the seeds pop, the small leafy sprouts can be uncovered and put in indirect sunlight, but keep the larger beans and seeds out of direct light until ready to eat. Light causes the sprouts to "green up," which is not desirable in the larger bean and seed sprouts.
- Never let the seeds or sprouts sit in water after the initial soaking.
- Sprouts generally taste best and have the most nutrients if you use them soon after they reach mature size. (Mung beans can be eaten when they are smaller.) You may rinse off the loose seed hulls, or you can eat them, whichever you please. Sprouts are ready to eat when:
- Wheat sprouts are the length of the seed.

- Bean sprouts are one and one-half to three inches long.
- Alfalfa sprouts are one to two inches long.
- Lentil sprouts are about one-fourth inch long.
- Soybean or pea sprouts are one-fourth inch long.
- Mung bean sprouts are sweetest after about twenty-four hours, but may be eaten up to two inches long.

- If seeds are allowed to sprout too long, a bitter or strong taste develops. If they develop root tips, snip off the tops and stems for use just before serving.
- Use sprouts as soon as they are ready, if possible. You can store them in a covered container in the refrigerator for up to five–seven days.

> *Never eat potato sprouts. The plant is a member of the poisonous nightshade family.*

CONTAINERS FOR GROWING SPROUTS

Commercial sprouters are available at most health food stores if you want to purchase them. They work great, but they're not necessary. One of the beauties of sprouting is that it can be done without purchasing any special equipment if you wish. A regular quart-size glass jar is perfect. You can cut a piece of screen or mesh to fit inside the ring lid, or you can cover the open end with a piece of nylon stocking or cheese-cloth held in place with a rubber band. Air flow is necessary, so make sure the opening is not blocked off completely.

A plastic colander is a good container for growing the larger sprouts. (Presoak the seeds in another container first.) Cover the colander with a damp towel to hold warmth and reduce evaporation, as well as to block the light. A plate or pan underneath it will catch the draining water.

Sprouting is enjoyable and easy enough to do on a regular basis; it is essential during any prolonged emergency or famine situation where fresh vegetables aren't available. You can produce a fresh crop every three to six days, with only a minute or two of effort each day. They may be your only source of "fresh produce," and they'll certainly bring variety, taste, and appearance to an otherwise bland diet. Plus, they cost

	Growing Time	Harvest Size	Yield (Seed) (Sprouts)	Taste
Sprouting				
Alfalfa	3 to 5 days	1½ to 2"	1 Tablespoon makes 4 cups	Crisp, mild, grassy
Mustard	5 to 6 days	1½ to 2"	1 Tablespoon makes 2 cups	Pleasant bite, similar to mustard greens
Lentil	2 to 4 days	¾ to 1½"	1 cup makes 6 cups	Mild spicy, fresh vegetable flavor and crunch, slightly starchy when raw
Mung Bean	1 to 5 days (immature) 5 to 7 days (commercial size)	¼" and up	Depends on harvest size; 1 cup makes 5 to 12 cups	Pleasant legume flavor, crunchy Bland, crunchy
Wheat	2 days	¼"	1 cup makes 4 cups	Sweet, nutty, chewy

very little for so much value in return: sprouts cost only about a nickel per pound.

SPROUTS AS A SOURCE OF NUTRIENTS

There seems to be a controversy over the nutritional value of sprouts. On the one extreme, you'll find sprouting fanatics that claim sprouts contain all the nutrients needed by man and will cure and prevent most known diseases. On the other extreme, skeptics will argue that sprouted grain contains no more nutrients than the unsprouted kernels. Neither one is right. In the first few hours and days of sprouting, a kernel of grain exhibits intense enzymatic activity and attains what is probably the highest protein and vitamin content of its life cycle. Take wheat, for example. It has been incontrovertibly proven by scientists that the vitamin C content of a kernel of wheat increases 600 percent when sprouted. The controversy exists because wheat has very little vitamin C to begin with, so a 600 percent increase still isn't a huge amount. However, it can add up. In a study[1] done by the Food Science and Nutrition department at Brigham Young University, they determined the vitamin C content of various sprouts. One cup of four-day-old wheat sprouts had 38 milligrams of vitamin C. The USDA recommended daily allowance for an adult is 60 milligrams of vitamin C each day. Therefore, you would need to eat a little more than one and one-half cups of sprouted wheat every day to meet your body's vitamin C needs if this was your only source of vitamin C. On a similar theme, Dr. Paul Burkholder, of Yale University, found that in oats, wheat, barley, and several other grains, the greatest nutritional increase in vitamin value was in B2; up to 1350 percent after sprouting[2]!

This is important news from a preparedness perspective. If you must live on a very restricted diet, you'll want to be able to squeeze every last bit of nutritional value out of the food you have. You'll find, though, that the greatest benefits of sprouts are not necessarily the vitamins you'll get from them. The attributes you'll find most desirable are the texture, the taste and variety you'll get from sprouted grains. In a stringent bare-bones basic diet, sprouts can serve as your "green leafy vegetables" and be a blessed respite from unrelieved starchy foods. They add new freshness to soups and casseroles, crunch to pilafs, greens to plain grains, and a new taste experience in every pancake, loaf of bread, and sandwich.

Notes
1. "Sprout Project," Dr. John Hill, Food Science and Nutrition Department, Brigham Young University, 1976.
2. motherearthnews.com/library/_November_December/Sprouts_A_Miracle_Food_For_A_Nickel

CHAPTER TWELVE

INDOOR FARMING: THE ANSWER FOR YEAR-ROUND PRODUCE

Have you ever been to a commercial greenhouse where the bedding plants stretched out for acres in a giant, muggy, glass-walled building? That's not what this chapter is about. It's not even about how to install a greenhouse in your kitchen, although that's certainly an interesting and thought-provoking idea. No, this is not even about making your ordinary, traditional backyard garden more productive. Nope—the useful, significant, and delightful principle I'm talking about here is being able to grow a variety of produce year round without the benefit of any yard, even in the middle of frozen winter! Otherwise known as indoor farming!

Can't you immediately see how this principle could be like a ray of sunshine on a dismal day in a worst case scenario? When the only food available is stored in your pantry, fresh food may be just a fond memory or a birthday-candle wish. The more restricted your diet is, the less variety you have to supplement the bare-bones basics. The longer a famine-type situation continues, the more welcome and appreciated a little fresh food will be. However mild or severe a worst-case situation you may find yourself in, you'll need an indoor farm.

Pure economic survival is another reason to become an indoor farmer. Really tough financial times and not being able to afford to go to the store underscore the advantages of growing your own little indoor farm.

Here's one last reason for indoor farming: it's fun! I don't need to grow greens and vegetables inside my home; there are plenty available in the stores at this writing. There's just something soul-satisfying in seeing things grow. If you come to stay for a day or two in our spare room, you'd go away happier for having shared the space with organic aromatherapy: spearmint, thyme, apple mint, lettuce, onions, spinach, beets, and a garlic clove that has gone crazy in a little flower pot. In addition to good nutrition, this little garden has a whole bunch of optimism, cheer, and enthusiasm planted in it, and who can't use those, no matter what the circumstances?

CROPS INDOORS?

As an indoor farmer, you'll be planting and harvesting crops of vegetables, though probably not crops with the traditional meaning. If you're thinking of crops that have to be gathered in with a tractor and an army of farmhands, scale back your imagination—way, way back. You can have a harvest of vegetables sufficient to make a difference in your diet and your health but it's unlikely that you'll have enough to eat everything you want and also supply the neighbors. When your choice is some or none, some can seem like a lot. Just as an example, half-a-dozen containers of greens or lettuce at peak production would supply a family of four a small green salad each probably twice a week, or some greens on sandwiches every day, or cooked spinach for dinner once a week. How large your harvest is will be determined by you. How large an indoor farm are you willing to work with? How many are in your household? How much space are you willing to find, give up or create for garden greens? You may even choose to exchange houseplants for fresh produce in order to meet your goals.

WHAT CAN I GROW?

In the last chapter, you learned the ins and outs of sprouting. Sprouts are tasty and desirable and easy, but why settle for just sprouts when you can have more? One of the most exciting things that I have discovered is that you can have fresh veggies year round. The key is understanding what you can and can't grow indoors.

Any vegetable that does not need to be pollinated in order to produce will work: lettuce (all kinds), greens (all kinds), broccoli, radishes, baby carrots, herbs, onions; the list goes on and on. Another clue is that most vegetables that are considered cool-weather crops will work.

Lettuce and Salad Greens

Leaf crops are the easiest of all vegetables to grow indoors. These include all the different leaf lettuces (Bibb, romaine, red leaf, and so on) and other salad greens including chard and spinach. They flourish in winter or indoor window light, as well as under fluorescent lights. You can sow a container with lettuce seeds and eat the thinnings within three weeks. Succession planting will provide the most produce; when the first planting is about three weeks old, start a second crop. Continue to sow every three weeks.

Larger salad greens like romaine and chard can be started in peat pots and then transplanted into their final container.

Broccoli and Brussels Sprouts

Broccoli and brussels sprouts adapt well to indoor farming. One healthy plant can provide produce for months, if not years. Once they start producing, you have to keep them pruned and picked. Broccoli leaves are edible as well as the stems and crowns. With brussels sprouts, you harvest the sprouts off the stem from the bottom up. They will continue growing and re-growing at the places where they were picked. I once bought a stalk of brussels sprouts at a farmer's market in California. I rooted it, planted it, and picked sprouts from it for over two and a half years.

Root Crops

Root crops, such as beets, carrots, onions and radishes are practically foolproof to raise. The trick with these types of vegetables is to think small; harvest them when they are still very young. Succession planting is your best bet to keep the vegetables coming; plant a dozen or so seeds every three weeks. Then you'll continually have something ready to harvest. Radishes are the vegetables that mature the quickest. You can interplant them with a slower-growing root crop like onions to take advantage of the space. The radishes will be done and harvested before the onions are mature. Beets and carrots should be kept baby-sized. You can plant beets for eating when tiny, or you can plant beets and let them grow to be able to continuously harvest the beet greens. For greens, don't ever cut off all the leaves at once or the beet will die. Just harvest the outer leaves every couple of days or so. Ditto with onions. You can pluck them up early and eat them as tender green onions, or you can leave them to grow and cut the tops for flavorings in cooking.

Herbs

One more family of crops that will grow well in your indoor farm is herbs. A large variety of herbs

---

Indoor Farm Crop Choices

Vegetables:

Bibb lettuce
Romaine lettuce
Loose-leaf lettuce
Onions
Radishes
Spinach
Chard
Mustard greens
Arugula
Tomatoes (possibly)
Carrots
Broccoli
Brussels sprouts
Peppers

Herbs:

Chives
Parsley
Nasturtiums
Thyme
Oregano
Mint

---

take kindly to indoor container gardening. The more you trim them for use in your cooking, the better they will grow. Warm herbal tea and fresh seasonings can go a long way to making tough times better. I even have chocolate mint growing!

Simple Herbal Tea:
1 to 2 teaspoons fresh herbs per cup of boiling water. Let steep five minutes. Sweeten to taste.

Other Vegetables

Just about everyone I tell this principle to wants to know, "Can I grow tomatoes?" And the answer is: maybe. Tomatoes require a great deal of sunlight, more than you'll be able to provide indoors. Adding a grow lamp or fluorescent lights may solve the problem. People with glowing green thumbs may have great success with tomatoes indoors; others less richly endowed may never see enough success to warrant the effort. If you want to give it a try, choose Patio Pik tomatoes or tomato plants designed for container growing. Tomatoes are the exception to the rule that I mentioned (only using plants that don't need to be pollinated). Tomato blossoms need to be pollinated by gently shaking the plant when it's in bloom.

Those same green thumbs that can grow indoor-container tomatoes can probably also grow just about any other vegetables. In theory, any vegetable should be able to be grown indoors. In actuality, why would you want to? Some plants are just too big to grow successfully indoors. Pumpkins, for example. One vine would take up most of an average-sized room and give half-a-dozen pumpkins at best. On the other hand, there are many seed varieties that are specifically produced to be grown in containers or small spaces. Tom Thumb seeds and plants are one such variety. You can check garden seed catalogs and gardening outlets for other midget or miniature vegetables. For some (like carrots), the vegetables themselves are small. For others, the plant is what is compact. Bush squash, for example: the vegetable is standard size, but the plant stays very small. Remember, these plants will need more care and more light than the ones ideally suited to indoor gardening. You may or may not be successful. I can't wholeheartedly recommend them,

but I don't want to discourage you from trying if you want to.

THE NEED FOR SEED

One of the things you will need to have on hand will be a batch of fresh seed. Your success could well hinge on the age of the seed. The older the seed, the less the sprouting capability of that seed. Heat will cause seeds to deteriorate also. One good thing is that seeds will remain viable for a year or two if you keep them in a very cool place, like your refrigerator. Put your seed packets in a resealable storage bag, squeeze out all the extra air, and keep them in the fridge. When you need to take some out, only take out the packet you need and only keep it out for exactly as long as you have to. If not fresh and if not kept very cool, don't expect all the seeds to germinate the following year. Some may, but if you're dealing with a worst-case situation and you desperately need your seeds to grow, do you really want to take that chance? The good thing about seeds in the stores is that the seed packets are dated and you can see that they are packaged fresh for the current year. Even the economically priced seed packages have fresh seed in them and their seeds will grow if you care for them properly.

If you are ready and enthused to start your indoor farm today, it may only be a matter of going to the store, buying the supplies you need, and doing it. Pots and potting soil are always available, even in grocery stores. Seeds may be a bit of a problem if it's the dead of winter. Even then, a quick browse through the gardening catalog sites on the Internet would allow you to order a wide variety of vegetable seeds and you'd have them in hand within a few weeks.

If you want to start an indoor farm because your finances are tighter than a straitjacket, you may have to save for a bit or creatively juggle your finances to find seed money to start your little enterprise (pun intended). It's one of those situations where a few dollars up front can bring exponential rewards down the line.

It may be a different story if you want to sow an indoor farm because there is no other food available. This could be a crucial point, because seeds, as well as food, may not be available at any price. This is a situation you have to anticipate and prepare for. The easiest way, of course, is to garden (indoor and outdoor) on a regular basis, long before you ever have to. That way you have supplies and experience always at the ready. But whether you do or not, seeds should be an important part of your long-term storage. You will need to trade them out every single year, but it really is a minimal investment. Buy a nice assortment at the beginning of the season when the seeds are freshest, store them carefully in your refrigerator, and use or replace them every spring. It's easy, it's inexpensive, and the rewards would be invaluable. Remember, this is not your ordinary garden. If you have a crop failure in a worst-case scenario situation, you may not have a store or corner fruit stand to rescue you.

FAST FOOD

Don't want to wait weeks and weeks for your little seeds to get big enough to harvest? Here is such a fun idea, I have to let my enthusiasm run over onto the page. To jump-start your indoor farm, one of the things that you can do is to visit the produce section of the local supermarket. (This idea obviously won't work if no one has any food, but it is too fun for words if grocery stores still have food in them.) They don't know it, but grocery stores sometimes get your indoor farm crops started for you. Look closely at the vegetables in the supermarket produce sections and you'll see what I mean. To begin, look for vegetables that have the potential to cooperate and grow. (These will be the same ones you'd start from seed and expect to succeed with.) You'll find that some greens, like spinach and leaf lettuce, will still have tiny roots attached because the whole plant was harvested and sold as one picking. Bibb and romaine lettuce do better than gourmet lettuces. Green onions, also, will have small but healthy roots attached. Look for whole cloves of garlic, full and not dried out, with tiny roots. Beets should have leaves and the long root still attached, and there should be tiny root hairs on the main root. Kohlrabi should still have leaves attached. Bring these treasures home and get ready for some fun!

You'll need a container of root-start, a transplanting concentrate found in most stores. Mix up a gallon or so according to the instructions on the label and have it ready. Now you need to prepare your crops to grow! Put beets, kohlrabi, green onions, and garlic right into small bowls or jars with root-start

solution. The solution should only cover the lower part of the vegetable; it shouldn't be completely immersed. Kohlrabi and garlic are fine in small bowls. The beets and onions are a little easier to prop up in jars. Lettuce roots will probably have sealed themselves off. Simply shave off the sealed part with a sharp paring knife, snip off outer, older leaves, and drop it into a jar with the solution just deeper than the roots. Sort through the spinach to find the plantlets that have the best roots with the most tiny root hairs. Trim off the large outer leaves and drop the plant into its own jar of root-start.

In my first experience with this, even though I had high hopes and talked to the plants every day, there weren't any overnight miracles. It didn't take long to start seeing results, though. The beets were the first to respond with new, long roots. Within two and a half weeks, the root systems of all the plants showed vigorous growth, all the plants were transplanted into new pots of soil, everything was growing, and I'd harvested onions twice. The romaine lost all of its original leaves, but shot up new baby leaves soon after. I planted the cluster of garlic just deep enough to cover the root base with soil and before long, it expanded and each separate clove sent up greens which I used in cooking. The little kohlrabi went crazy and was soon covered in leaves. I trimmed them and used them as greens in salads. They tasted like cabbage.

Remember, your harvest will not necessarily be vegetables per se; it will be the greens and the variety they can provide. It's another area where fun can be part of a serious situation, helping to turn negatives into positives.

FINDING YOUR INDOOR FARM PLOT

Your indoor farm does not have to be all in one spot. If you have a window or a place for a container—go for it. I have a container of rosemary growing in my bathroom. The "plant stand" is a metal clothes hamper that once belonged to my grandmother. It is just the right height and just the right circumference to hold a ten-inch farm. It grows in front of a small window. Your indoor farm does not have to be measured in feet or yards or acres. It can be successfully measured in inches. Grown in pots or boxes in sunny places or artificial light, your indoor farm will only be bounded by your enthusiasm and patience.

If you were to ask me where my indoor farm is growing, I'd have to reply, "Which room would you like to look in?" My main "acreage" is half of a white folding door resting on top of three plastic crates in front of the window in our spare bedroom. It has no less than fourteen containers in various sizes in an area eight feet long and fifteen inches wide. My kitchen "greenhouse" window is always full of edible plants, as is the set of shelves in the sunny corner near the sliding glass door.

Any out-of-the-way place with sunshine will work for indoor farming. Window sills are a good choice. You can buy decorative containers only four inches wide or so, designed especially for window sills. Hanging baskets, shelves, tabletops, bookcases, anywhere you would put a houseplant, you can put a farm. If you don't have enough natural sunlight, install a grow light or fluorescent light to help nature along. As I said before, you're only limited by your imagination and determination.

By the time you fill a clay pot with soil, add the plant, and water it thoroughly, it can end up weighing quite a bit. Keep that in mind when you're deciding where to put your farm. Shelves need to be sturdy enough to be up to the challenge.

In cold climates you may have to insulate the containers, windowsills, window gardens, or greenhouse windows. When we moved from California to Utah, I was delighted to find our new home had a small greenhouse window in the kitchen. I proceeded to plant containers with plants and seeds, placed them on the shelves, and waited—and waited. The wheat grass grew, but nothing else. Then one day the light dawned. I felt the potting soil and, sure enough, it was beyond cold—not quite frozen, but very cold. The greenhouse window that projected out into the sunlight also projected out into the frozen winter air. I replanted the containers, placed folded towels on the metal shelves as insulation, and left the can-light on above the sink during cold nights. My potted chives, thyme, and Bibb lettuce then consented to grow.

*Any out-of-the-way place
with sunshine will work
for indoor farming.*

Some windows, especially single pane or poorly fitted windows let in too much cold in winter to allow plants to comfortably grow. Try some of these solutions to see if they help:

- Place pieces of cardboard across the base of the windows.
- Affix material (cloth, cardboard, Styrofoam) to the window itself.
- Close the blinds or drapes at night or on very cold days.
- Wrap the container with a folded newspaper "blanket" held in place with a rubber band.
- Wrap the container with bubble wrap.

In terribly hot climates you may have to figure out how to insulate for just the opposite reason. The sun blazing through the glass of a window can be more intense than direct sun, somewhat like sunshine intensified by a magnifying glass. When sitting in full sun, with the plants in containers rather than in the ground, the entire container can heat up and cook the plant. A gauzy curtain or waxed paper taped in the windows can protect your plants from those intensified rays.

CONTAINERS

If you want esthetically color-coordinated containers, pots, and planter boxes that match the pillows and drapes and wall color scheme, it's a sure thing that you will be able to find them in the posh corners of the garden shops and interior design outlets. All types, sizes, and kinds of decorative and utilitarian containers are available in the garden departments of discount department stores. If it's not the gardening season and you want to get started anyway, check out thrift stores and dollar stores for containers of a more eclectic stamp.

The key to an acceptable container is good drainage. Good drainage holes in the containers are essential. Clay pots are good because they allow the soil to breathe and water slowly evaporates through them so that the plants don't stand with wet feet. You'll need drip plates under all your containers to avoid ruined woodwork, carpet, or floors. You can buy matching drip plates, or use old pie tins or the like. Even in the middle of winter you can buy inexpensive clear plastic pans to protect furniture at any florist shop or in any grocery store, in the section where they sell houseplants.

In order to grow, the plants need growing room. That means that the minimum-sized container should be six inches across the top and the depth should be at least six to eight inches. Bigger is fine; just remember the weight when water is added, and plan accordingly.

SOIL

It is important for the indoor farm to have rich soil. Most supermarkets, discount department stores, hardware stores, and so on carry potting soil. You can use it as is, or for an additional boost for your plants, go to a pet shop and buy a box of fine sharp sand mixed with ground oyster shells generally used in birdcages. Mix some of it into your potting soil—the sand lightens the soil, and the oyster shells provide lime. These two ingredients are beneficial for your soil and plants.

Just because your indoor farm is a lot smaller than a typical backyard garden plot, don't imagine it is completely care-free. You can't simply plant and expect the farm to grow and produce by itself. It still takes care, work, and patience. It must be watered. It needs to be fed. It must be continuously harvested. It is a living, growing thing, and as such, it needs your frequent care.

FEEDING YOUR VEGETABLES

Your plants will need to be fed. Just because the plants are growing in your house, it doesn't make them houseplants. They are vegetables and they need vegetable food. Full-strength vegetable fertilizer like you would use in an outdoor garden is too strong for a container plant. Dilute it to about half the strength recommended on the fertilizer container. Use this weaker solution every week.

LET THERE BE LIGHT

One of the most difficult indoor requirements is to maintain sufficient light. You'll probably have to supplement the natural sunshine with artificial light, especially during the darker winter months, but

Leaf and root vegetables need six hours of light a day; fruiting vegetables need eight.

that's done easily enough. Grow lights are available at garden supply houses or department stores, complete with specific directions for use. A standard fluorescent-tube-reflector fixture that accommodates two bulbs—available at any home improvement store—will also do the trick nicely. Since you'll need to raise the bulbs as the plants grow taller, buy the kind of light fixtures that can hang from the ceiling on chains, or on an adjustable stand. The lights should be hung about four inches above seedlings and raised as the plants grow. You can have some success simply using a sixty-five- to seventy-five-watt light bulb in a table lamp or floor lamp. Leaf and root vegetables need six hours of light a day; fruiting vegetables need eight.

If your crops receive window light or light that comes from only one side, you'll notice before long that your plants are leaning hard towards the light. You'll need turn or rotate the pots every few days so that the plants will grow straight and strong.

WATER

Too much water is a real problem with container plants. In fact, more houseplants die from overwatering than underwatering. But at the same time, not enough water also means death for a plant. With that conundrum, you have to find the middle ground between not enough water and too much. There isn't a hard-and-fast rule because it depends on what type of containers you have, how big they are, where they are located, the temperature, the humidity, the type of plant, and on and on. Unlike houseplants, a vegetable should never droop from lack of water; that's a sign the plant is in stress and it greatly slows down its production. Generally, if the top inch of soil is dry, it's probably time to water again. That may be as often as every day or every other day. You'll have to figure it out with trial and error.

How you water can be as important as when you water. For example, I had an indoor crop failure once because I didn't water the seeds properly. I sprinkled them. This gave the seed sufficient water to sprout. But when the baby plants tried to grow, the water did not go deeply enough into the container to soak the roots and encourage sturdy growth, so they cocked up their tiny roots and died. The next time around, I gently poured sufficient water to soak, but not fast enough or strong enough to wash the tiny seedlings away by disturbing the roots, which were as tiny as the plant. That crop of Bibb lettuce grew successfully.

Icy-cold water in the middle of winter can cause shock in plants. Use lukewarm water instead. Either adjust the faucet so the water is tepid instead of cold, or fill a pitcher and leave it out on the counter to warm to room temperature.

In some climates, a little humidity helps. To create humidity for your indoor farm you can simply fill a tray or dish an inch deep with pebbles or gravel. Fill it with water and place your farming containers on top of the pebbles.

OTHER PROBLEMS

You may get some bugs in your farm. To control them you can spray them occasionally with a mixture of cool water and alcohol; add one or two tablespoons of rubbing alcohol to a pint of water. Use it once a week. It should usually take care of the problem.

You know that the bane of all gardeners' lives is weeds. The pesky things are a constant bother. Container gardening is no different. I had a weed once. I pulled it and then had to rest for a while with a tall glass of lemonade. It was hard work.

Indoor farming is something that can turn a worst-case situation into a much better situation. It's not difficult, it's not an impossible dream, but it is something you need to plan for in advance. You may just want to find a small corner in the garage or a box on the balcony to compactly stow some potting soil and a few containers. Buy your fresh seeds annually and keep them in the back of the refrigerator. It doesn't take much to be prepared. Indoor farming is so much fun that you don't need to wait for hard times to try it. It won't be long before you'll find yourself talking to the veggies and bursting with excitement when a new leaf finally pops up. I must warn you, you may get hooked and discover that you are talking about your mini-farm almost as much as the kids and grandkids.

SECTION THREE

PRINCIPLES OF PROVIDENT LIVING

CHAPTER THIRTEEN

LIVING PROVIDENTLY

Living providently is more than making ends meet by tightening the belt another notch, turning down the thermostat, and doing without your favorite treats and activities because you can't afford them. It's not about deprivation in order to keep your head above water financially. It is about wisely caring for your resources. It's about living happily while living prudently. It's showing foresight and providing carefully for your future.

Nearly everyone faces hard times at some point in his or her life. It may be a job layoff or an injury that lays you up for months. Chronic illness may make it impossible to hold down a job. Perhaps skyrocketing costs and insufficient income are a continual worry for you. Whatever the problem, it's likely that at some time in your life you will come to a point where you simply can't make ends meet. When that rainy day is here, your preparations can make the difference between making it through and financial disaster. Living providently, stretching your budget, and obtaining the security of a reliable, well-maintained preparedness program all go hand in hand.

Living providently requires the wise use of your finances even when times are not particularly tough. Especially when times are not tough! As I discussed in Money Matters! (chapter 3), the time to be prudent with your money and provide for your future is when you have money. If your job is going well and you are able to meet your financial obligations today, then now is the time to be looking to the future. Use wisdom and build up your long-term planning, rainy-day, and emergency funds while you can. Who knows what tomorrow will bring? If it's continued financial solvency, good for you. If it's a pell-mell plummet toward financial disaster, wise preparations today may be able to save the day tomorrow. Besides money, a reliable preparedness program is fundamental to a secure future. If you have prepared yourself with the supplies needed to care for yourself in difficult times, setbacks or disasters lose much of their power over you. You are not at the mercy of your circumstances. This is a very comforting feeling.

If your income is sufficient for today, but insufficient to provide for tomorrow (or so you think!), relief is on the way! I am going to show you how to save money, increase your buying power, and have more to show for the dollars you spend. The Pantry Principle is the solution to the insufficiency. The essence of the Pantry Principle is to buy at the right price and have sufficient provisions on hand to meet any need that might arise. It is preparedness with a capital P. Provident living is not deprivation. It is penny-wise good judgment, and it will provide peace in a society where instability is the norm.

I recall reading a fairy tale when I was young about three old hags who shared one eye between them. As one passed the eye to the next hag, the other would call out, "Sister, do you see good times returning?" Without being prepared, we would be like these hags, feeling our way blindly along through difficult circumstances while anxiously looking for good times to return. If you live providently and prepare practically, you'll find that even bad times can be fairly good times.

CHAPTER FOURTEEN

THE PANTRY PRINCIPLE

If your bank account is bulging, and your idea of staying in your budget is to not spend more than your weight in gold daily, you can skip this chapter and move straight on to the next chapter. This chapter is for everyone else for whom money is a little harder to come by, and whose dollars are usually screaming for mercy at the end of each month from being stretched so far.

The foundation of your preparedness program lies in the Pantry Principle.[1] In essence, the Pantry Principle means storing commodities today for use in tomorrow's situations—whatever they may be. Stocking up when the price is right on all the food and nonfood items you use on a regular basis is the key. Not only is this the most economical way to shop and live, it provides security as well. When

> My husband went to work on a Friday and at 3 P.M. they called him in to tell him they were eliminating his job classification from the organization. We went on our food supply in our cupboards and it helped tide us over until he was working nearly ten months later. Then he started his own business and things were slow in the beginning. You need to have a backup. A job making $125,000 and partnership in the company guarantees nothing!
>
> —Glenna E.,
> San Carlos, California

emergencies arise, whether major or minor, you are never found wanting if you live by the Pantry Principle.

The Pantry Principle is not just food storage. It is much more than that. It is an effective money-management program that also enables you to be prepared for almost any emergency situation that could arise. It provides a personal buffer against outside forces (economic, political, natural, and so on), When you stock up on the items you use regularly, your pantry becomes your store. You go to the pantry for what you need, instead of to the market. And since you stock your pantry when commodities are at sale prices, you may never have to pay full price again. The goal is to get to the point where you do not have to go to the store. You may want to, but you don't have to. When you choose if and when you go to the store, then you are in control of both your budget and your preparedness situation.

Now, this is not to say that you'll never need to go to a store again, nor that you should boycott supermarkets. I frequent them often and regularly. Rather, the goal is mastery over your shopping situation: you only go to the store when you want to, not because you have to. Some people can reach the point where, if they have a financial crisis or some other problem, they can painlessly stay out of stores for a week or a month or two months. Some people will reach a level of pantry preparedness where six months could go by without needing a major shopping trip, other than maybe for fresh milk or produce. It would be entirely possible for my family to not set foot in a store for a very long time and still eat well. We would really miss fresh produce and dairy products, but we could make do with powdered milk and canned produce.

However, even I couldn't go forever without replenishing my shelves. I would eventually have to start again from scratch and build up my supplies.

The point is, first of all, that when you have a full pantry to rely on, emergencies lose much of their power over you. You need to catch the vision of why this principle works. Many people have told me that the only discretionary money they have is their grocery budget. If something goes wrong, the grocery budget has to cover it. Consider how it would be if you lived with the Pantry Principle every day of your life. Your shelves would be stocked with food your family likes to eat. The cupboards would be full. When an emergency came up, say, the transmission went out on your car—you wouldn't have to choose which bill you wouldn't pay this month or dig deeper into debt with a credit card nearing its limit in order to cover the car repair. Instead, you could take most of the grocery budget to fix the car, and live mainly off the supplies in your pantry for a month or two.

There was a day when every family maintained a fruit cellar as a matter of survival. The bounty of the summer was preserved so that no one would be found wanting during the winter. Fruits were bottled; spices were dried; cheeses and meats were smoked and hung to age. All that was gathered was carefully prepared for storage. Thus there was plenty on hand all year round. Today, some people might think a well-stocked pantry is an oddity, a luxury for the wealthy or a symbol of the past in someone's quest for security. Yet in the current economy, a pantry could be as essential to your survival as it was back in the days when food wasn't readily available every month of the year, unless you planned ahead to make sure it was. Today your pantry may be stocked with purchased canned and frozen goods instead of homegrown, hand-bottled produce, but the end result is the same. With the Pantry Principle you are never caught short! When emergencies arise, whether major or minor, you can free grocery money to pay unexpected bills and still eat well out of the cupboard. The commodities you stock in your pantry are not only a savings, they're an investment.

As an added bonus, with a full pantry you only have to go to the store when you want to, not because you have to. Therefore, you don't have to pay full price for anything. You can buy when things are on sale, garnering substantial savings and increased buying power. That's the ticket to stocking up effectively—buying what you need at the best possible prices.

TAILORING YOUR PLAN TO YOU

Many different factors affect your grocery budget: the size of your family, how many store options there are in your area, how many meals you eat at home compared to how often you eat out, and more. The trick is to work with these factors rather than letting them make chaos out of your plans. You need to reach out and grab the reins on your spending and buying so you are really in charge. You can't make store prices go down, and you probably can't print more money in your basement. But you can double your buying power with a little effort, and that amounts to almost the same thing.

You may think your grocery budget can't possibly be stretched even one more inch to incorporate stocking up into it, not even for just a can or two a week. I'm here to tell you that it can! Really! Here you will find a step-by-step program designed to help you get control of your grocery budget, no matter how small, and wrest more buying power from it (and therefore provide a way to get started stocking your preparedness pantry).

GETTING STARTED

Your goal of a fully stocked preparedness pantry (and control over your grocery budget) can begin on your next payday. As payday approaches, get ready with these steps:

Inventory Your Cupboards

Take a close look at what you have on hand. This shouldn't be a hard or lengthy process. Jot down the

When my husband lost his job as a corporate attorney and decided to open his own practice, he lost about 40 percent of his income. We did serious belt-tightening on our budget, helped our kids understand the situation, and ate significantly more food from our emergency storage.

—Suzi M., Santa Rosa, California

names of items and how many of each you have on the shelves on a sheet of paper under general headings such as "canned goods," "meats," "frozen foods," and "dairy products."

Plan Menus from Foods on Hand

Pretend that there is no way for you to get to the store until payday. What meals could you make from what you have on hand? (Don't forget breakfasts and lunches also.) Most people are surprised to discover that, even in a rather empty-looking kitchen, they can usually gather up supplies for several meals. Try to create enough simple meals to last until the following payday, even if you have to eat the same thing several times.

Assess Your Basic Needs

You'll find there are some meals you could make if you only had this or that item. Begin a "needs" list and add these things to it. Also list other must-have items: the things you cannot do without until next payday. Are you out of milk? Does the baby need formula? Is all the bread gone? Make sure you include as needs only those items necessary to nutritiously feed your family from this payday until the next. Have you squeezed the last bit of toothpaste from the tube? Be sure to include essential nonfood items also. Don't include wants (those things you would like to have but can live without). Be tough on yourself in determining what is a need and what is a want. When your list of needs is complete, estimate the cost of each item and add the prices together for an estimated total.

FIRST PAYDAY PROGRAM

Look at Your Paycheck

You've done the preparation work, now your "first" payday is here. Begin by determining what your grocery budget is, if you don't have a set amount already. Subtract from the net amount all of your bills and other obligations that have to come out of this paycheck, like rent or house payment, utilities, insurance, bus fare, car payments, etc. Also, deduct the out-of-the-ordinary but necessary expenses for this pay period (for example, upcoming birthdays, school pictures, and haircuts.) When all these fixed expenses are subtracted, what remains is your grocery budget. (Stop crying and keep reading.)

Subtract from your grocery budget the estimated total of your grocery needs. The remaining figure is called your "workable amount." It is the amount of money you can spend on groceries other than absolute needs. (Don't be discouraged if this amount is small. Even a few dollars of workable money will get you started.)

If your finances are so tight that creating a workable amount each payday seems impossible, consider this option: Set aside an amount, however small, from each paycheck as if it were another bill. Use this preselected amount as your workable amount. No matter how small your beginnings, this system can work for you.

Read the Ads

Study the grocery ads in your local newspapers. If you don't take the newspaper, many stores will mail

---

Barbara's Must-Haves: Chocolate-covered raisins, supplies for s'mores, and chocolate chips.

In addition to traditional supermarkets, there are many other outlets that sell groceries, many of which don't advertise. For the greatest buying power, you should consider all of them, big, small, and unusual. There are discount drug stores, membership clubs, mass merchandisers, day-old bread outlets, dollar stores, small specialty shops, and many others that may have great deals for your dollars. Many times they offer traditional supermarket items—paper goods, health and beauty products, detergents, soaps, canned goods, and so on—at significantly lower prices than you would pay for the same items in a grocery store.

their weekly ads to you if you add your name to their mailing list. Pinpoint the good buys on items that you frequently use, particularly those that are different from the items you already have on hand (to increase your menu options—remember variety). If possible, choose foods that will combine with those foods you already have to increase the number of simple meals you can prepare. Check carefully for sale prices on the items on your needs list also. Add these bargain-priced items to your shopping list. Since your workable amount may be limited in the beginning, dividing your money between food categories makes good sense. For example, if your workable amount is $48, limit your bargain spending to $10 for meats, $10 for canned goods, $10 for nonfoods, $10 for produce, and $8 for wherever it will buy the most at the best prices. You will get the most mileage out of your workable amount on an ongoing basis if you choose a variety of bargains.

Shop Using Your Best Skills

Being familiar with regular prices in order to recognize a good bargain when you see one is absolutely vital. This is a very important skill to develop, and an important step in controlling your grocery budget. Always comparison-shop prices in the grocery ads, and compare prices on different brands of the same item any time you're at the store. Become familiar with regular prices on items you frequently use and comparison-shop regular prices at different stores whenever you're there. Use these comparison-shopping and price-recognition skills to purchase the items on your needs list. Buy just enough regularly-priced needs items to get by until you see a sale on these items, when you can stock up. Then, buy your selected specials as wisely as you can with your workable amount. However, whereas you bought just enough of your regularly priced needs items, now you'll buy as much as you can of these bargain-priced specials. The idea on buying the bargains is to buy more than you absolutely need in order to get a ready supply at home. This is how you save money. When an item is on sale at a good price, you stock up. Then, when that item returns to full price, you needn't buy it again (since you already have a supply) until the price drops once more to what you're willing to pay. Stocking up on sale items you use consistently is crucial in filling your preparedness pantry.

Just for the record, rest assured that "stocking up" doesn't mean you need a semi truck to bring home your groceries. For some people, "stocking up" means bringing home a case or two of canned goods every shopping trip; for others it means buying four cans of soup instead of one. Some people may "stock

Price recognition is a vital, yet easily obtainable skill. Before you can take advantage of good deals, you have to learn to recognize good prices.

Begin by creating a worksheet with columns in which to record items, dates, and prices. Next, list ten to twenty items that you consistently use. These things should come easily to your mind: bread, milk, oranges, cornflakes, chicken, toothpaste—these types of things. Over the next several weeks, jot down the price of each of these items whenever you see it in the ads or in the stores, even though you may not be buying it at that time. (Or, create the worksheet all at once by devoting several hours to this project. Visit several different stores and jot down the various prices on the different brands for the forty or fifty items you use most.) Though prices may fluctuate, you will soon recognize a normal price range for each item.

As you gain confidence in recognizing good prices on those twenty listed items, move on to a new list of ten or twenty more and do the same thing again. Keep doing this until you are familiar with the regular prices of all the items you frequently purchase. It won't take long. Keep track of these pages in a notebook. They will serve as a reference until you are familiar enough with the average cost of each item and can recognize a good price when you see one.

up" with bulk buys: a hundred pounds of oats or fifty pounds of dry milk. Others have "stocked up" by buying a twenty-five-pound bag of flour instead of a five-pound bag. It's not a competition of who can buy the most the fastest. It's figuring out what will work for you and following through.

Reassess Your Needs

Add your new purchases to your cupboards and update your inventory list. Again, pretend that there is no way for you to get to the grocery store until your next payday. You have to make do with what you have on hand. Begin a new needs list, since your needs will have changed since you last wrote your list. You may have used up some of the commodities that figured heavily in your first menu plan. Or you may be running low on different items that were in stock last time. However, your new menus will reflect all the bargains you were able to purchase with last paycheck's workable amount.

SECOND PAYDAY PLAN

Do It Again

Determine your workable amount by following the same formula you used the first payday. If you are scrupulous preparing your needs list and creative enough in menu planning to provide many of your meals from your cupboards for another week, you may notice an increase in your workable amount, even if only a small one. But don't be discouraged if it's an unremarkable difference. Sometimes it takes several pay periods before you see progress.

Again, Read the Ads

With your workable amount in mind, scrutinize the ads for items on sale that you consistently use. Following the same pattern as last pay period, check for bargains and list those that will extend your budget by providing you with well-balanced meals.

Shop

Using your sharpest skills, buy your necessities and stock up on the best buys available. After you admire your growing stockpile in the pantry, add the items to your inventory and start the process again.

As you repeat this process payday after payday, you'll find your workable amount keeps on increasing. Eventually, a large percentage of your grocery money will be allocated for specials and bargains.

KEEPING THE BALL ROLLING

This plan should be repeated until most of your grocery money is being allocated for specials, sales, and bulk buys. Of course, you may choose to go to the store a little more frequently to stay stocked up on fresh produce, dairy products, and other perishables, but even fresh-food shopping follows the rules: buy only when the price is right, and stock up as much as possible, using a specific list of items and dollar amounts. Your refrigerator and freezer are definitely part of your pantry system. Eventually, your pantry should contain a sufficient variety of foods (including perishables) in sufficient amounts that you could serve several weeks of well-balanced meals without going to the store. The same goes for nonfood items as well. You will only need to go to the store when you see prices you consider low enough to pay. Although it will take different people different periods of time to attain this goal, it can be done. I think this is the most exciting point: you can make these principles work for you, no matter your income or the capacity of your pantry.

As you work with your new meal planning and shopping skills each pay period, you will gain more and more confidence in your abilities. The fuller your pantry grows, the more in control you will feel.

The habits you develop as you progress are meant to be ongoing. Don't allow yourself to slip back into the old way of menu planning (or not planning) and shopping. Forevermore, menus should be planned from what's on hand and what's on sale. Forevermore, shopping should be done from the specials in the ads. If a shopping trip or a meal you plan doesn't work out, you now have the flexibility to shift plans and adjust meals at will. You are no longer going to the store each week to buy specific foods for specific meals. Your meals come out of your well-supplied cupboards. Instead, you are buying just what you need to keep the pantry stocked. If, during the course of a pay period, you don't see a bargain that meets your current needs, don't buy. In fact, if nothing you want comes along for several pay periods, don't buy. Save the money to really stock up when you see something you want.

On the other hand, if a family member needs a new pair of shoes or a car needs repairs or a doctor bill must be paid, you can use the grocery budget to cover it and still provide well-balanced meals and a snack or two. You don't have to go to the store. Remember: you are now in control.

Short of inheriting a fortune from a long-lost rich uncle, the Pantry Principle is one of the best money-management strategies you'll ever learn for extending your existing budget as far as it will go. The monetary benefits are great, but the Pantry Principle is just as important as a preparedness program. It is the first and most important step for almost all of the different areas of preparedness because it provides the way and means to obtain and afford your preparedness supplies.

Notes

1. This chapter is adapted from Barbara Salsbury, *Beating the High Cost of Eating: The Essential Guide to Supermarket Survival* (Springville, Utah: Horizon, 2005).

CHAPTER FIFTEEN

MY PANTRY: WHAT DO I NEED AND HOW MUCH IS ENOUGH?

Now that you're aware of how to afford a reserve of food and supplies in your home, the next burning questions are "what do I store?" and "how much is enough?" You agree that it's important to have a good stock of food in your home to be prepared for emergencies, but what exactly do you store, and how much of it do you need? The information and charts in chapter 6 indicated an average necessary amount of bare-bones basic foods, the kinds that will sustain life in a worst-case scenario. But to live economically and be prepared for anything (including an extended period without work or a serious financial reversal), merely sustaining life isn't enough. The idea is to be able to continue living in a comfortable and familiar manner, even if everything else is falling apart around you. That requires having a healthy supply of regular food and everyday nonfood items on your shelves.

The question of what to store has a million correct answers (and a few incorrect ones). Here are two things *not* to store:

1. Foods you don't like. If you loathe beets, don't

store beets, no matter how healthy they are and no matter what a terrific sale there is on them today at Al's Corner Market. It is not necessarily true that if you get hungry enough, you'll eat anything. A more likely scene is that you'll hide your beets in the back of the closet and ignore them until a disaster happens. Then you'll dig them out of the dark recesses of the closet and find the cans are rusted and bulging. At that point, your choices are death by starvation or death by botulism. All right, maybe this is an extreme example, but you get the point. Storing food that you don't like is a waste of time, space, and money.

2. Exactly what the family next door has stored. Your storage plan should be just that, yours. Not the Joneses' or anybody else's. Every person's needs and tastes differ, and you'll do yourself a disservice if you copy precisely what someone else has, or if you unquestioningly purchase a "program" put together by a food-storage company without considering first if it is right for you. For all you know, the neighbors may be putting aside food for sixteen people (all their children and grandchildren, plus themselves), all of whom are allergic to wheat and are vegetarians besides. That wouldn't work for your family of two, who are avid hunters and love whole-grain bread. Or maybe the neighbors really love beets. You need to store what's right and appropriate for you.

Now that you know what to not gather for a rainy day, how do you determine what would be appropriate for you? Remember, the idea is to have a sufficient supply of the foods you regularly eat so in times of trial you can continue on with as little disruption to your normal eating patterns as possible. This is not to say that you need a supply of every little thing you eat now. You don't need to stockpile potato chips

> When our five boys were young, they liked fresh or frozen spinach. I bought a case of canned spinach, trying to have more variety. The boys wouldn't eat it after tasting it. Then they saw a cartoon of Popeye and how he got his strength from canned spinach, and that case of spinach disappeared quickly— but I never bought any more.
>
> —Mary S., Alhambra, Calif.

and licorice and TV dinners, nor candy bars, soda pop, and string cheese. But stocking up on standard foods like canned or frozen vegetables, canned soups, tomato sauce, canned fruit, cake and muffin mixes, spices, ketchup, and frozen meat is one of the first steps in being prepared. To determine what to store, look to your grocery list, your cupboards, and your recipe box for inspiration. Begin compiling a list of things your family eats on a regular basis. Make the list as long as you like, and include everything you can think of. Your list will probably look something like this:

The list can go on and on. Put everything on

oranges	ketchup
hamburger	mustard
chicken noodle soup	pickle relish
butter	canned corn
milk	frozen peas
eggs	barbecue sauce
salt	canned tomatoes
pepper	muffin mix
egg noodles	walnuts
poppy seeds	syrup
baking soda	cinnamon
broccoli	cream of mushroom
cauliflower	soup
cucumbers	cream of chicken soup
tomatoes	canned peaches
garlic salt	chicken
chicken breasts	potatoes
Rice Krispies	cold cereal
Cheerios	mustard
bananas	ice cream
sugar	chocolate chips
hot cocoa mix	baking chocolate
bacon	coconut
cheese	

the list. Don't be afraid to make it long. You're not going to run out and buy a large supply of all these things today. This just gives you something to look at to help you see what you use regularly. With a little bit of thought you can list all the foods you regularly use. Now, look at the list with a "preparedness pantry eye." What things on your list could be stored for several months to a year, and which are impractical? Some things lend themselves nicely to food storage, like canned foods and frozen meat. Some do not, like

potato chips and ice cream, which spoil too quickly. Some things may or may not be good for food storage, depending on your individual circumstances. Cold cereal, for example. While you could reasonably expect that the quality of a box of cold cereal would be good for several months, the chances of a box of cereal staying on the shelf for any length of time if you have teenagers in your home is nil. A six-month supply of Wheaties and AlphaBits would require a 10,000-square-foot warehouse for a single sixteen-year-old boy. Some items, like fresh fruits and vegetables, will not last more than a week or so. These may require a bit of creative thinking. Perhaps you can buy fresh food as long as you have the opportunity to do so, but purchase the canned or frozen counterparts to keep in storage for times when fresh is not available.

After you eliminate from your list the items that obviously don't fit the parameters, the next step is to prioritize what is left. Which items on your list could you easily do without, and which would you find it difficult to do without? A number system may help you in setting priorities: 1 = items I can't live without; 2 = things I'd wish I had but could get along without if I had to; and 3 = things that are nice but not necessary. Keep meals in mind. What are you going to feed your family if you only have your storage to draw from? If you could only have a few items on your list, which could you use to make the most meals? With some thought and effort you will end up with a fairly accurate list of food items that you use regularly, that will be most useful in making meals, and that would last a reasonable time in your pantry.

YOU MEAN THERE'S MORE?

Food is not the only thing you can and should have in your personal preparedness pantry.

Consider the following:

toilet paper	pencils and pens
toothpaste	cold medicine
aspirin	dishwashing soap
feminine hygiene	laundry detergent
soap	rubbing alcohol
batteries	notebook paper
shampoo	staples
Band-Aids	rubber bands

antacid   hand lotion

vitamin tablets   dental floss

matches

The lack of some of these things could make life utterly miserable. Figure out what you need in the same way you made your food list above. Make a list and set your priorities. These lists answer the first burning home-storage question you had: "What do I store?"

HOW MUCH DO I STORE?

The second question that most people pose is, "How much do I store?" Before you can come to any conclusions on this subject, you have to make another decision. That decision is, "For how long do I want to be prepared?" Two weeks? A month? Three months? Six months? A year? This is a personal choice. You have to decide what is going to work for you. If your business went under today and you were out on the street without a paycheck in your near future, how long do you think it could take to find another job and get money coming back in regularly? If an earthquake devastated your community, how many weeks or months would elapse before things got back to normal? What emergencies would necessitate you living off your provisions for an extended period? We all hope, of course, that any problems we face will be short-term and relatively painless, but there are no guarantees. Therefore, choose a time frame for being completely on your own with which you feel comfortable.

A good short-term goal is to gather a two-week to two-month supply of the things you eat now and eventually work up to a several-month supply that you feel comfortable with.

Having a thirty- or sixty-day supply serves a twofold purpose: (1) it is a jumping-off point for getting a more comprehensive supply and, (2) it works as an emergency supply in case of serious short-term emergencies. For example, a devastating winter storm could knock out power, put all roads out of commission, and empty store shelves easily. While it might not be the type of emergency to last more than a few days to a few weeks, you could nonetheless get pretty hungry in that amount of time. Could your family survive if you couldn't leave your home for a week? Would you be out of milk, bread, peanut butter, cereal, crackers, baby formula, soup, everything? Chances are an emergency could hit the day before you were going to the store for your weekly shopping trip rather than the day after.

Assume you've decided, for instance, that you'd be satisfied with food and supplies in your home to last six months (or three, or twelve). Now, you can begin getting actual figures to work toward. To help determine long-term food needs, you'll probably need to first measure short-term consumption. How much of those items on your "what to store?" lists do you generally use in a set time frame? For instance, perhaps you drink a can of orange juice about every three days. There are four weeks in a month, so you'll use twelve cans of juice in a month. Multiply that by six (or three, or twelve) to know how much you would need for a six-month period (or three months or a year, depending on how long you've chosen to prepare for). Six months' worth would be seventy-two cans, or three twenty-four-can cases.

If you generally use a can of peaches (or other fruit) 4 days a week, you would use approximately 16 cans of fruit in a month. Multiply that number by 6 months to determine that your family consumes 186 cans of fruit in half a year (or seven-plus twenty-four-can cases).

When your lists are finished and prioritized, when you have in mind how much you'll need to put away, then you're ready to start acquiring the items you've prioritized on your lists. Watch for these items to go on sale. When they do, buy more than you usually do and put them back as "storage." When you see soup on sale, buy three or four cans instead of just one. If the price is terrific, buy a case instead of a can. Consistent overbuying, especially when things are on sale, will accomplish your goals, slowly but surely.

> *How long you wish to be prepared for is a personal choice.*

CHAPTER SIXTEEN

HOW CAN I STORE A McDONALD'S IN MY CUPBOARD?

Some families live on farms, with chicken coops and cows and root cellars and gardens the size of city blocks. These people will probably roll their eyes and then skip this whole section because they tend to be naturally prepared. At the other end of the scale, you'll find some families who live in apartments in cities. The closest they come to farm life is keeping a canary in a birdcage. They wouldn't know a root cellar from a root canal. The only thing they make for dinner is reservations, and a home-cooked meal means they reheated last night's Chinese take-out in the microwave. The rest of us fall somewhere in between.

So what do you do about preparedness if you tend to eat more of your meals in restaurants than at your kitchen table? Take heart. You are not doomed to being a statistic at the first sign of trouble because you don't know how to bake a loaf of bread or whip up a casserole. However, you will have to put a little more time and thought into being prepared than someone who is used to cooking regularly.

If you truly never cook, you'll have to adjust to the idea that you may just have to try it sometime. There's a good possibility that the power outage that will shut off your heat and lights will shut down the local KFC also, leaving you on your own. Or if you are out of work for several months, your good looks alone won't keep the french fries flowing. The restaurant will want cash. So plan now and practice, in case you have to cook later.

To start, you'll have to have some ideas about what to cook. Check out a bookstore or library for easy beginning cookbooks with simple recipes in them. Or ask your neighbor, mom, friend, coworker, or relative to give you their favorite easy recipes. Or check the appendix for some easy meals from storable foods. Then buy the ingredients to make

those recipes and try them out soon (consider it an adventure). When you have a few recipes that you know you'd be able to prepare and are willing to eat, you can put the ingredients for these meals in your cupboards. Select two breakfast menus, two lunch menus, and two dinner menus. Keep them simple. Then, stock up on all the ingredients it takes to make each of them seven times. Once assembled, this assures you of two-weeks' worth of meals.

For example, I may choose oatmeal and pancakes as my two breakfast meals, and soup and tuna salad with canned fruit as my lunch meals. For dinner, I select spaghetti with canned corn as one choice and shepherd's pie with applesauce for my second choice.

Now I determine what ingredients are required for each of these meals.

Breakfast One: Oatmeal—oats, milk (dry or evaporated), sugar, cinnamon, salt.

Breakfast Two: Pancakes—pancake mix (or flour, baking powder, and so on), jam or syrup (or ingredients to make syrup).

Lunch One: Soup and canned fruit—soup (canned or dry mix), canned fruit.

Lunch Two: Tuna Salad and crackers—tuna, pickles, mayonnaise, crackers.

Dinner One: Spaghetti—pasta, spaghetti sauce (or ingredients to make sauce, or just canned spaghetti), hamburger (if you have a freezer), canned corn as side dish.

Dinner Two: Shepherd's Pie—hamburger (if you have a freezer), potatoes (instant), tomato soup, canned green beans, applesauce as side dish.

You will probably also want to have some ingredients or mixes for some snacks or treats. Old-fashioned non-microwave popcorn stores well and is a good option.

When you have stashed away all these ingredients, choose two more sets of meals and repeat the process. Then you will have four weeks' worth of meals set aside. Keep it up until you feel satisfied that you'll be able to take care of yourself for a while. Be sure to check out chapter 25 to find out about emergency cooking options that will work for you when your own power is out, as well as your favorite restaurant's. I strongly recommend that you practice several times so that a minor inconvenience doesn't compound into major chaos if your electricity is out.

With this process, you can be at least somewhat prepared to care for yourself, even if you have no intention of changing your current lifestyle.

But, you say, "I'm probably not going to cook and eat that food unless times get really bad, so it will probably spoil. What's the use of that?" I suggest that you take that into consideration and make regular replacement part of your plan. Set aside your cans of fruit and soup and packages of whatever now, so you're prepared. Then, in a year or so, while it is still good, donate it all to a homeless shelter and buy new for your preparedness program. (Mark your calendar or you'll probably forget!) It's not a waste if you've gotten a year's peace of mind out of it, and it ends up feeding someone less fortunate than you. That's a great investment.

CHAPTER SEVENTEEN

GROWING YOUR OWN GROCERIES: MIGHTY MINI-GARDENS

There are innumerable articles, magazines, books, Web sites and probably even libraries devoted to the joy and practicality of gardening; the benefits to your health, your psyche, your fitness level, your emotional well-being; the value for your home, your neighborhood, the earth, and the ozone layer. I'm a big gardening fan myself, so I can shake my pom-poms and give a heartfelt "Rah-rah-rah!" anytime someone gives a plug for growing things. For the moment, though, I'd like you to look at the benefits of gardening from a preparedness perspective.

You needn't have a ten-acre farm, a tractor, and a government subsidy for gardening to be financially advantageous. A surprisingly small plot can supply all the fresh vegetables a family can use, with plenty left over to freeze for the winter, if you go about it the right way. I suggest that everyone at least dabble in gardening on a regular basis, for preparedness's sake. My reasoning is this: If you prepare and cultivate your little ten-foot-square garden each year, growing a few tomatoes, maybe some cucumbers and a little squash, then should you lose your job and your finances get very tight, you can devote some real attention to your little garden and its produce. With only a little work, your previously prepared but probably underutilized garden plot is ready to rise to the challenge and provide for your family in your financial crisis. If you had to start from scratch and put in a garden where lawn or weeds flourished before, you probably could not do it because gardening is not cheap to begin with. But if the garden is already there (from years of dabbling) and the supplies are in your shed, then you're ready to capitalize on the opportunity. Every pound of produce you raise will cut your grocery bill. With a little work, you can expect these savings to continue for months and months. I remember many difficult jobless years when the vegetables from our garden and the fruit from our trees were the only fresh produce we had.

If you have the aforementioned ten-acre farm and the tractor, you don't need any help from this chapter. You're probably a whiz at irrigation and fertilizer and crop rotations (not that you'll read much about any of those in this chapter either). For the rest of us, garden space may be at a premium, or even nonexistent, but that's no excuse to not have a garden! Stay with me here and you'll see what I mean.

SMALL PLOTS

If you have the space for a typical square-plot garden, great; but don't be discouraged if you don't. There is no rule in the gardening rulebook that says your garden has to be a neat, rectangular space with straight rows and furrows. It doesn't even have to be all in the same place. A square foot here and a patch over there can become a successful, productive garden. A lot of food can be grown in a skinny strip of soil by the garage or a pocket of land at the side of the house. It is perfectly acceptable to have a four-foot square of peas by the back door, tomatoes mingled with the zinnias in the flower bed, and squash and carrots out back behind the lilac bushes. Put your fence to work supporting a crop of peas, pole beans, cucumbers, or even certain varieties of squash. Plant lettuce as an edging in front of your floral borders. You're only bounded by your enthusiasm and patience and by the amount of sunlight that is available. These tiny garden plots—little gardens—will give you just as much enjoyment as big gardens can, providing flavorings, fragrance, beauty, and a surprising quantity of produce.

It is important to begin with a plan before you begin to plant. Where are the little gardens in your yard? How much sun do they get? It will make a difference. Some plants require more sun than other plants (corn, beans, tomatoes, radishes, squash), but even the plants that are satisfied with less sun (lettuce, chard, parsnips, celery) still require at least six hours of sunlight a day. Chard may grow perfectly well on the north side of the shed, but your tomatoes would never develop to their full potential in such a shady place.

Can you find more little gardens if you do some rearranging? If you move the recycling bins to the shady side of the house, it might free up a good-sized square of sunny space to grow things in. Could the firewood be stacked behind the shed instead of along the fence where the sun always shines? You might find more space for little gardens if you threw out some long-standing traditions. Sure, petunias have always looked nice in the flower bed by the gate, but maybe this year squash and beans could take their place.

Look closely at all the little garden plots before you begin your plan. A well-organized plan will help you determine how many seed packets or plants you'll need, saving money and trips to the store in the long run. Your little gardens should be easily accessible. If your squash plant ends up being swallowed by shrubbery and you have to fight your way in to check on it, chances are you won't check it very often. Consequently you'll end up with zucchini the size of watermelons, and not even very many of those. The key to successful gardening is starting right.

As with a big garden, little gardens have basic needs that must be met in order for them to flourish. These are fertile soil, an ample water supply, plenty of sunshine, and a little regular tending to keep weeds down and produce picked.

SOIL PREPARATION

I can't emphasize enough the difference good soil will make to any garden. My daughter, who has always claimed to have black thumbs, discovered the startling difference good dirt makes when she put in a flower bed one year. Previously, she would prepare a hole for a new plant, put the plant in, and watch for the next few weeks as it clung limply to life before finally cocking up its roots and dying. She said she might as well have planted twenty-dollar bills for all the difference it made. But when she put in the new flower bed, she bought several yards of high-quality topsoil mixed with fertilizer to raise the bed a little higher than the surrounding grass. Every plant she put in practically leaped out of the ground as it began to grow. It was astonishing, particularly for one with thumbs the color of hers. Good soil can make all the difference in the world.

Vegetables prefer light, fluffy soil—not hard-packed ground. Your soil should drain well and have six to eight inches of loose, crumbly texture for plant roots to freely penetrate. You may have to add a good soil conditioner like peat moss or compost before your plants will thrive. Even when you start with good soil,

We have always made it a point to have a garden wherever we lived. While Larry attended Brigham Young University, we lived in a small rental house. We started a garden in the little plot out back, but before it had a chance to produce, we had the opportunity to buy a little house around the corner. We jumped at the decision, but that meant having to leave our garden behind. Our daughter (who was eleven years old) insisted that the garden should "move with us." We tried explaining that the plants would likely die, but she was adamant and promised she would take extra care of them. So we moved as much of the garden as we could—plant by plant.

For several months we could look out the back window and there she would be, sitting in the garden rows, talking to the plants. Almost all the plants lived—how would they dare to not! But then, this is the daughter that brought home a dead-looking stick and begged us to plant it so she could have her own tree. She did—one of the tallest in the neighborhood. The moral of this story? Never give up on your gardening opportunities.

you'll need to add fertilizer throughout the growing season for a successful garden. Plants need certain nutrients to flourish—mainly nitrogen, phosphate, and potassium, with a few other things thrown in. If these aren't available in the soil, the plants unfortunately can't get up and walk over to a more nutritious spot of ground to meet their needs. You are their only hope. Find a good fertilizer in a gardening center and feed, feed, feed.

TIMING

Vegetables fall into two groups; one does well in cooler weather and should be started before the last killing frost. The other group is very susceptible to frost and must wait till after the last frost date before planting. Your state university extension service (the number will be in the phone book) will be able to tell you the dates of the last frost for your area—these can vary even within states.

Beets, broccoli, brussels sprouts, cabbage, carrots, cauliflower, chard, chives, lettuce, onions, peas, potatoes, radishes, rutabagas, spinach, and turnips can be planted one month before the last frost.

The warm-weather vegetables are beans, corn, cucumbers, eggplant, melons, okra, peppers, pumpkins, squash, and tomatoes. These shouldn't be planted until after the last frost date in your area, although many of them can certainly be started indoors several weeks earlier to get a head start on the season, and then be transplanted outdoors after the danger of frost is past.

PLANT FOR BUMPER YIELDS

To get big crops from little spaces, it's vital to plant at the right time and keep every spot in production all of the growing season.

Interplanting Two Crops

The idea is to use the same little garden space simultaneously for two or more crops. Plant fast-growing plants in the same space as slow-growing ones. Radishes, lettuces, onions, and spinach grow quickly, so they can be intermixed with slow growers like cabbage, tomatoes, and broccoli. Corn, beans, and squash are a fine example of companion plants. Plant all three in the same spot of ground at the same time. The corn will quickly grow tall, get the first sun, and the most moisture. Pole beans will climb up the cornstalks to get the sun. The squash will grow along the ground and begin setting fruit at the same time the corn and beans are harvested and cleared away. Try planting carrots (slow) with peas (fast and early), onions (slow and below ground) with beans (fast and aboveground), or lettuce (somewhat slow) with radishes (very fast).

Succession Planting

Many cool-weather plants go in the ground early in the spring and are done producing about the same time warm-weather plants are ready to go in the ground. To get the most from your little garden plots, don't let space stand empty. As soon as the peas finish, pull them up, toss them into the compost pile, and plant squash (get a head start by planting seeds indoors in peat pots several weeks earlier). Start lettuce early; as soon as it begins to bolt, send it to the compost pile and put in a planting of bush cucumbers. If you have a long growing season, you might even get in a third planting in the fall. Replant as quickly as one crop is harvested. On the back of all seed packets, it indicates the number of days it will take for those seeds to mature for harvesting. That information, along with knowing whether plants do better in hot weather or cool weather, will help you determine which vegetables can be used in succession planting.

Stretching the Harvest

It takes planning to produce a continuous supply of vegetables in an amount your family can use, especially when you only have little gardens to work with. The best way to waste space is to plant more of one crop than you can possibly eat. Instead, sow small spaces at one-week intervals (they don't have to be in rows—they can be small spaces anywhere you can find). You can keep radishes, lettuce, pole beans, and more coming over a long period of time if you plant a little at a time on a regular basis.

> *Companion crops and succession planting will allow you to grow a lot of vegetables in a small amount of space.*

Companion crops and succession planting will allow you to grow a lot of vegetables in a small amount of space.

WATERING

Vegetables need ample water on a regular basis to grow best. A good rule of thumb is an inch per week for small plants, two inches for large ones. However, that's a general rule at best. Your soil, the humidity, and extreme heat will all have an effect on your garden's water needs. During dry spells, it's especially important to make sure your garden is watered. Even a week with insufficient water is enough to dramatically slow growth or reduce yields. Letting your plants wilt before watering will cost you almost three weeks of recuperation time for the plant; it takes that long for the plant to get back to the point it was before it was deprived of water.

Watering by irrigation (or letting a hose run until the ground is completely soaked) once a week is better for your plants than sprinkling, if you have a choice. One of the best gardens we ever had was in a house that had irrigation shares. Once a week we'd open the ditch and the water would flow into our garden until it was a foot deep in water. Some of the smaller plants were completely covered. I loved the sound of the water gurgling and flowing through my yard, nourishing my plants and making them grow.

CARING FOR PLANTS

Is there anyone who thinks weeding is fun? If you raised your hand, you are in luck; I have plenty of fun to share with you! Weeding is one of those unpleasant jobs that just has to be done if you want a lovely and productive garden. If not, the pesky things will take over the space and nutrients and sunshine and water that were meant for your flowers and vegetables. An hour weeding when weeds are little will save two or three hours digging them out when they are mature. You might try black plastic before planting, or mulch after planting to help keep weeds under control.

If you want bumper crops, it's imperative that you keep vegetables picked before they reach full maturity. Full maturity (overripe tomatoes, giant squash, lettuce going to seed, and so on.) sends a message to the plant that its purpose in life (reproducing itself by setting seeds) has been accomplished, and it will slow or stop production. Keep your vegetables harvested

if you want to keep them coming for a long time. Besides, vegetables taste so much better when they are young and tender. It's heaven!

CONTAINER GARDENING

No yard for even a little garden? No problem. You can be a backyard gardener and harvest your own crops even if you don't have a backyard. Land is optional. All you really need is a doorstep, a balcony, a patio, or even just a sunny windowsill (remember your indoor farm?). Container gardening is the answer to your gardening woes. We live on a very large lot, and we have plenty of room for a big garden. Nevertheless, my deck is covered with plants in pots and containers of all sizes. I love being able to step outside my door and be surrounded with growing things. It is just a joy to me.

Containers

Just about anything can be grown in containers, and just about anything can be used as a container. Pots, wicker baskets, tubs, pails, laundry baskets, wooden crates, planter boxes, hanging baskets, and even plastic bags of all sizes are acceptable container gardens. I once saw a pair of old leather work boots arranged artistically on someone's porch with pansies growing profusely out of them. Ready-made plastic, metal, and wood containers are so widely available that it isn't necessary to make containers yourself, though you can if you want to. At the end of our upstairs deck, we have a wonderful stack garden that my husband designed out of stair risers and old fencing. This year it is filled with a variety of leaf lettuce, herbs, radishes, and onions. In past years we've had abundant harvests of squash, peas, and pole beans also. (See appendix D for instructions.) Pretty much, if it will hold soil, it can be used as a planting container.

Your container should be large enough to hold the plant when it is fully grown, though in many cases that is smaller than you would think. Patio tomatoes grow just fine in a ten-inch pot. A half-bushel basket is great for squash or potatoes. Generally speaking, the larger the container, the better the results you can expect when growing vegetables, because deeper soil means less chance of the soil drying out. If the container doesn't have drainage holes, you'll need to create some, or at least add a one- to two-inch layer of gravel at the bottom of the container.

Soil

Container gardens have different needs than yard gardens. Soil is one of them. The soil in your containers must provide better drainage than your regular garden dirt. No matter what the size or shape of your container, make sure you start with a good commercial planting mix, available in most garden centers. These have the right proportions of sterile soil, organic matter, and fertilizer already mixed, providing all the nutrients needed for initial plant growth. These mixes are free of disease organisms, weed seeds, and insects. They're ready for immediate planting. See Indoor Farming (chapter 12) for an added hint about planting mixes. It works for outdoor containers just as well as for indoor containers.

Another advantage of planting mixes is their weight. Planting mix weighs less than half as much as garden soil when both are soaked. This is important when you want to move containers from one spot to another, or if your "garden" is a large number of containers on a roof or balcony.

Water

Whereas your yard garden may need to be watered once or twice a week, your container garden will need watering much more often than that. Since all sides of the container are exposed to the air, the water evaporates off substantially faster than in the ground. You'll need to water well when the top inch of soil in the container is dry. Big containers may need watering every two to three days. Small containers may need watering daily. Hanging baskets could even require twice-daily waterings in hot weather. On the other hand, overwatering will kill a plant as easily as underwatering. Wait till the top inch of soil is dry (½ inch in small containers).

Fertilizer

A vital part of growing vegetables in containers is fertilizing regularly. It's not enough to add fertilizer at the beginning of the plant's growth and then forget

> *Some vegetables are bred specifically for small-space gardening.*

about it. Generous feeding results in generous crops. I suggest a weak nutrient solution weekly, added to the soil in liquid form, mixed in with the regular watering. I usually have an old gallon milk jug on my deck that I keep filled and ready to use. It's just a matter of a few minutes' work to feed all my plants weekly.

Plants

Technically, any plant that will grow in your yard will grow in a container, provided the container is big enough and you have enough space. There are vegetables, however, that are bred specifically for small-space gardening. Patio tomatoes, bush squash and beans, miniature cucumbers, even pumpkins and watermelons have been developed to grow in compact form, just perfect for container gardens. Ask at your local nursery for the miniature and bush varieties, both as seeds and as plant starts. If you're ambitious, you can even grow dwarf fruit trees, grapes, and berries in containers.

With care and proper fertilizing and watering, your container crops could feed your family well. (The real secret is talking to them nicely.) Four five-gallon-sized tomato plants should produce eighty to a hundred tomatoes over the course of a growing season; four cucumber plants trained on a trellis will produce about 120 cucumbers. A 2-by-3-foot box with Swiss chard growing in it will allow fifteen to twenty-five pickings. These are all optimistic numbers, assuming decent growing conditions and regular care, but you get the picture. Even a container garden has the potential to be a contributing factor at your dinner table. See appendix C for some possible layouts for a functional container garden on a patio or balcony.

HERBS

Grown indoors or out, herbs are a must for any gardener. Many are as beautiful as they are useful, and they are wonderful additions to any flower garden. Many adapt readily to being grown indoors; some need no more sunlight than you'll get on your kitchen windowsill. Outdoors, herbs make delightful container plants. I love having a pot of chives on my windowsill. On a shelf beside my sliding door I have a compact container herb garden that I constantly use as I cook. There's nothing to compare to the taste of fresh basil in your spaghetti sauce or thyme in a simmering pot of stew. I love to plant lemon balm near my front walk so when I brush past it, that heavenly aroma is released.

COMPOSTING

When you hear the term "black gold," most people think of oil. Not me. I think of compost. Compost is organic material (leaves, grass clippings, straw, kitchen materials, and so on) that has been worked by bacteria and broken down into rich humus. It's full of nutrients for your plants when worked into your soil or used as mulch. Compost makes your soil rich. Why rake and sack up leaves and lawn clippings to send to the dump, and then turn around and buy peat moss and fertilizer to enrich your soil? Making compost yourself is easy, easy, easy, and it can save a lot of money.

You can make compost in a pit, in a commercially purchased container, even in a garbage can or you can make compost right on the ground, as I've always done. My compost pile is in the back corner of my lot, between the fence and a shed. Here are some very basic instructions:

Start with a pile of garden material: leaves, grass clippings, or whatever. Kitchen waste (peelings, stems, leaves, egg shells, and so on) can be used, but not grease, fat, meat scraps, or bones because they will make the pile smell terrible and attract flies. You can also use shredded newspapers and sawdust. Sprinkle a cup of bone meal or standard 12–12–12 fertilizer on top. Add an inch or so of dirt.

Continue building up the pile in layers until it's about as high as it is wide. Some composting experts advise that you turn the pile with a pitchfork every couple of weeks, and that you sprinkle it regularly with water. I don't bother doing either; I just ignore it and it's always worked for me. The rich, loamy compost will be ready to spread in your garden or flower beds in four or five months' time. Generally, you'll use compost the most in the spring, but the preparation of it is a year-round process, especially in the summer with grass clippings, and in the autumn when the leaves are falling and you're clearing out the dying plants as winter approaches.

There are so many benefits to gardening that it surprises me when I find people who don't do it. The financial aspects of it from a preparedness perspective are some of its best advantages. Remember, every pound of produce you produce will cut your grocery bill. Plus, gardening is therapeutic, delightful, and healthy—and is it spring yet? Hand me the trowel!

PRINCIPLES FOR DEALING WITH DISASTERS

CHAPTER EIGHTEEN

EMERGENCY PREPAREDNESS: GETTING STARTED

To this point, the emergencies we've discussed have resulted in a need for having food stored, a pantry built up, a long-term supply in place to help us get through. These are not the only requirements that crises will demand. Some emergencies rock the very foundation of our world, and everything is topsy-turvy for a time. This type of emergency requires not just food on hand to survive, but a rethinking of all the common necessities we take for granted each day. For some emergencies, even the bare necessities of life are threatened. In our fast-paced lives, most of us are not geared to rely solely on ourselves for these. But disasters do happen, and hiding your head in the sand like an ostrich will not keep them from happening. The time may come when you have to rely on yourself. That is why you need to get prepared now, before the need arises. When a disaster occurs, it's too late to prepare!

SAME CRISIS, DIFFERENT OUTCOME

Not everyone in any particular disaster will be affected to the same degree. For some the recovery may mean coping with injuries and personal loss, while for others it may simply be waiting for the power to return. For some, recovery will mean figuring out how to stay warm and fed, or dealing with structural damage or loss of income. All of the above-mentioned events might be occurring at the same time in your own corner of the same crisis. Coping with the aftermath may last anywhere from several hours to several weeks, depending upon the scope of the disaster and the enormity of the destruction.

In the wake of the 2004 Florida hurricanes, it took days for the relief organizations to get in and get set up because the destruction was so widespread and there was so much need. Some areas took five to six weeks to get the companies and organizations in place that would help with the rebuilding process.

I have had the opportunity to attend meetings with city officials responsible for municipal emergency preparedness. One of the major concerns discussed was the lack of sufficient preparation on the part of residents. "A critical point that you must understand," said one director of emergency services, "is that in an emergency there are not enough policemen or firemen to get to all people and all problems quickly—or even soon. It's just not possible. It's unlikely that city and county personnel will be able to meet the needs of individuals or individual families. Even in a localized crisis, individuals essentially are on their own while the needs of the majority are met. Therefore, emergency preparedness is everyone's responsibility!" (Ken Kraudy, Director of Emergency Services, Sandy City, Utah, 2004).

The United States has only one firefighter for every 480 people and one police officer for every 385 people. That means in an emergency, most people "are going to be on their own for possibly 48 to 72 hours," says David Paulison of the Federal Emergency Management Agency (FEMA).

—Mimi Hall,
"Survival Planning Starts at Home,"
USA Today, February 11, 2003

All relief organizations—the Red Cross, Salvation Army, National Guard, and so on—work to meet the most critical lifesaving and life-securing needs for the most people as quickly as possible. They are trained to move in, set up, and help, but not necessarily to meet individual needs. They are there for those who have lost everything, and to protect and help maintain order in the middle of chaos.

However, it's our job as individuals and families to be part of the solution, not the problem. We can't prevent the disruptions or the disasters that take away the normal elements of our lives (such as power, heat, light, and the ability to run to the store for supplies) and leave chaos in their wake. But we can determine how we will deal with the aftermath of these emergencies, when everything that's normal and reliable is in disarray, but we still have the security of our home for shelter. Let me share with you just one of my experiences that proves this point.

THE LOMA PRIETA 7.2 EARTHQUAKE—FIRSTHAND

On October 17, 1989, I was working in my home office in Santa Clara, California, preparing, of all things, a presentation on emergency preparedness. I was just completing the finishing touches when everything felt weird. I could hear a dull roar and thought, "Oh no!" I jumped and ran for the doorway as the 7.2 Loma Prieta earthquake exploded around me. I can remember that I couldn't hear anything except the awful, terrible roaring. Everything was shaking so hard that it was all I could do to hang on.

It slowed down eventually, but it seemed like it would never stop. The floor was like Jell-O, and it continued to quiver. Immediately there was no power, no phone, no communication, and darkness was setting in.

Although I knew as well as anybody what to do during an earthquake, my mind was a blank. It was so terrifying that I had to force myself to calm down and think about what I should do. First, I had to find shoes so that I could get through the rubble and broken glass. I next found my purse, and then the battery-powered radio. I crawled over, around, and through the mess, trying to get to the front door to see if it would open, just in case I needed to be able to get out. Then I got our 72-hour kits and put them by the front door. The house quivered continuously, and

I could tell this was going to be bad, but at that point, I didn't realize how bad.

About twenty minutes later, as my husband somehow made it home and came through the front door, the second quake hit. The nightmare escalated. By now my anxiety and trembling had probably climbed to a 7.2 also. We struggled through the rubble to get to our lanterns, first aid kits, and the items we knew we'd need to get us through the night.

Our next step was to check on our neighbors, especially the two elderly sisters who lived alone across the street. We discovered another neighbor going house-to-house with a wrench, tool pouch, and large flashlight to see what he could do to help his neighbors. Most of the neighbors, especially those with children, stayed outside all night, many seeking strength and support just by being together.

About midnight, it was unbearable to be inside any longer with the continuous aftershocks, so we walked the neighborhood streets with a lantern. It was eerie. It was quiet in the middle of the city except for the sound of the sirens. Total darkness replaced the brightness of city lights and streetlights. About 2:00 or 3:00 A.M. we finally attempted to sleep. Every time another aftershock would hit, we would head for the doorway, not knowing how bad it was going to get. I don't think anyone in the entire Bay Area slept that night.

For the next few days, as we dug our way out of the wreckage, our battery-powered radio was our lifeline. The rest of the country knew how severe the earthquake damage was before we did because the local communications channels were down. Fortunately for us, our home sustained only minor structural damage, though the inside looked like, well, like it had gone through an earthquake!

We were fortunate. We had our home and we had on hand the necessities we needed to sustain us for the next days and weeks. Others weren't so fortunate. Many lost everything, including their homes; they had to stay in evacuation shelters or set up tents in the park. The people who stayed in parks had to rely on water wagons, standing in long lines with cups, bottles, buckets, or anything they could find to carry water. Stores and gas stations were shut down for several days, and in some areas, for weeks and months. The power came back on sporadically, so you couldn't rely on the stores or gas stations being open. Bottled water, convenience foods, and plywood became extremely scarce as stores opened occasionally and only for short periods of time. Flashlights and batteries completely disappeared off of shelves.

Being prepared did not lessen the seriousness of the calamity all around us, but at least it made it bearable. Because we were prepared, we were able to take care of ourselves and assess what we could do to help others. We were able to cope and live through the crisis.

HOW PREPARED DO YOU WANT TO BE?

The recommended time frame for disaster preparedness is usually three days to three to five weeks. The extent to which you wish to be prepared for an emergency is an individual decision, and the manner you go about accomplishing it is individual also. Your unique plan is based on personal distinctions, all of which can change from person to person and place to place, and all of which influence how you prepare to care for your family. Many preparedness suggestions may seem like a lot of bother to carry out, some may even feel unnecessary. Being prepared for anything is a bit of a bother—like repairing your tent before you go camping, or fixing the screen door to keep the mosquitoes on the outside. But getting prepared for a disaster is a bother that can help you stay alive.

CONTRIBUTING FACTORS FOR PREPAREDNESS DECISIONS

The following issues (among others) will have an effect on how you prepare to care for your family. What disasters are likely in your area because of these factors? What can you do to prepare for these possibilities? You'll want to evaluate the ways they will personally impact your disaster-preparedness efforts, and how you will deal with them.

• How will your location impact you? Do you live in a rural area? In the suburbs? On the outskirts of a metropolitan city, or in the inner city? On a hill? In a floodplain? Near an earthquake fault? In the tornado belt?

• Is your home in an apartment complex or in a high-rise? Is your home a condo, retirement complex, a mobile home, cottage, duplex, a single-family home, a tree house, or a mansion?

• Is your budget limited? How can you creatively juggle in order to find the funds to get the supplies you will need?

• How many are in your household or family? What are their ages and health?

• Do you have health or physical limitations?

• How close do you live to individuals or families that you can rely on?

• What is within five miles of your home, in any direction, that could create localized disruptions of services for any length of time (such as industries, utilities, or power plants)?

Many of us are still thinking "72 hours." After experiencing firsthand the aftermath and recovery process during the chain of hurricanes in Florida in 2004, I'm convinced we need to encourage people to be able to be on their own for a minimum of three to four weeks.

—Ken Kraudy, Director of EOC, Sandy, Utah

We lived in Santa Cruz, California when the big earthquake hit in 1989. I had a van and I got all the neighbor kids to drop their bicycles they had been riding and get in the van. The earth was shaking and they were so scared. Anyway, they got in and were safe. I had water and blankets and some snacks. Eventually the parents came (when it was somewhat safe) and they were so happy I had protected their children. It's a good thing I thought of my van. It protected all of us from loose wires, and it was sturdy if anything fell on us, and I could move it if I needed to get to a safer place.

—Howey K., San Jose, Calif.

• What kind of temper fits does Mother Nature usually throw in your area? Tornadoes, hurricanes, snow, floods?

• Your climate will probably affect at least two different aspects of your planning (a) weather that you must cope with and the supplies necessary to do so, and (b) variations in the shelf life of supplies due to climate.

All these things, and many more, will affect how you prepare to care for your family. Don't rely on someone's printed or computerized list to cover your needs. If you really feel the need for a paper list in your hands, read this book, adapt it to make a list for yourself, and then make a dozen copies that you can hang all over your house to remind you of your preparedness goals and what you need to achieve them.

WHERE TO BEGIN

If you were without regular utilities and services for two weeks or more, what would you need to be prepared? A few of the obvious things would be shelter, sufficient food, a way to prepare it, some water, alternative sources for heat, light, sanitation, and so on. So, where do you start? It's a big job to be prepared, but every big job starts with a first step. The first preparedness step you need to take is to build on what you already have!

Begin by taking an inventory of what you already have that would prove useful in an emergency. The purpose for an inventory is to help you recognize the supplies that you presently have on hand. This is the foundation that you can systematically build on.

If you have already begun stocking a pantry as discussed in Section 3 (Principles of Provident Living), you'll have a head start on the food supplies necessary for disaster preparedness. Remember, though, you will need not just food, but also nonfoods and equipment to take care of yourself on your own. The

following chapters will give you sound suggestions on items that will see you through a crisis. Study them thoroughly to determine which suggestions will fit your needs. After deciding which things you'll need to see you through, begin by stocking up in sufficient amounts in all areas (foods and nonfoods) to get you through at least two or three days with all of the necessities. Then, follow the process again to increase your supplies to carry you through a week, then two weeks, then three weeks, always maintaining a balance, until you are satisfied with what you have prepared. The preparedness pantry rule of thumb should be "Always maintain a well-rounded balance." Don't ever spend your entire budget on just one or two items. Consistently buy, in balance, the greatest variety possible.

For example: should you have $100 set aside for preparedness, don't buy $100 worth of just tuna and canned beans, but rather, purchase smaller amounts of several things such as fruits, soups, pancake mix, lamp oil, matches, and soap. Then, should a need arise, you would be somewhat prepared in all areas, even if only for a short time. This is one subject where you don't want to start at the top of your list and work your way through it with military precision, checking off each category as you acquire it. What if a tornado blows through town, wiping out the gas and electric lines? If you've spent the last several months concentrating solely on purchasing the foods your family will need in an emergency, you may have food to eat, but no means of preparing it, no means of staying warm while you eat it, and no means of finding it in the dark even if you do have it somewhere. Conversely, if you gather all your supplies before you put aside any food, you might find yourself one cold, miserable night wrapped in your sleeping bag in the gentle glow of lantern light, staring glumly at an empty cupboard. The idea is to maintain a balance. Too much emphasis on one category of supplies or another may leave you kicking yourself in a time of need.

PRACTICAL PLANNING MUST INCLUDE PRACTICE

As you develop all of the facets of a sound emergency plan, build practice into it. The "drills" at home could prove to be priceless if and when the real thing occurs. The main reason for planning and practicing is that that you will be more likely

Remember, disasters create stress. You'll want to turn that around and make it work for you. And stressed spelled backward is desserts! So chocolate comes to the rescue again!

to keep your head about you in an emergency, and remember what needs to be done *and* what your priorities are. I know from firsthand experience how hard it is to keep your head when you're out of your mind with fear. Make it a point to sit down with your family and talk over your emergency plans so everyone knows what to do and what's available to help you.

Consider discussing these points (and any others that you think will benefit your family). You'll find more specific information in appendix M.

Earthquake

How do we take care of ourselves during the shaking? What steps do we take immediately afterward to account for each other and to secure our house? What could be the possible outcomes of an earthquake? (for example, our home is destroyed—then what? Our home is intact, but without power or heat—then what? Our home is intact structurally, but looks like a war zone inside. What next?) What supplies do we have to help us through until normalcy is restored? Does everyone know how to use them?

Tornado

What are the warning signs a tornado is coming? What do we do, and where do we go? What if we're not home? What steps do we take immediately afterward to account for each other and to secure our house? What could be the possible outcomes of a tornado? (For example, our home is destroyed—then what?

Our home is intact, but without power or heat—then what? Our home is intact structurally but looks like a war zone inside. What next?)

Fire, Flood, and Storm

What does our family need to know to get through, and recover from the different disasters that could occur in our area? Are we familiar with the supplies we have? Do we know how to operate any emergency equipment we have?

Do we have a plan in case our family is in separate places when an emergency occurs? What if Mom and Dad are at work and all three kids are in three different schools? These can be frightening concepts, but they *must* be discussed before an emergency occurs.

YOUR SHARE-AND-CARE INSURANCE PLAN

No man is an island, and that is doubly true during disasters. Start today to form a support group in your building, complex, or neighborhood. Make sure that your Care-in-a-Crisis plan is in place. This is an essential part of being prepared. Make arrangements, assignments, and commitments now, so that you know whom you will be able to rely on, or whom you need to help. It's your "share-and-care insurance plan." Planning, preparation, common sense, and knowledge and skills will enable you to cope with, and confidently live through the crises that may come your way. With awareness in place and a plan to get ready, you're off to a good start!

CHAPTER NINETEEN

SHELTER:
A STORM SHELTER,
A SAFE ROOM, OR A SAFE PLACE

A shelter is any place or structure that gives protection. While a tent, a cave, a lean-to, or a bomb shelter all qualify as shelters, the only shelter that really matters for our purposes in this book is your home. (If your home has just been destroyed or rendered uninhabitable by a disaster, then tents and community centers are also important shelter subjects. You can read more about these in the Emergency Evacuation section.) As stated in the previous chapter, disaster preparedness is all about situations where a crisis may leave you without normal utilities and features of life, but you still have your home as your protection and stability.

The hurricanes affected all of Florida this year [2004]; in fact, I really don't think Florida has ever seen this kind of unforgiving torment until now. Lindy and I rented eight movies and thought we would sit downstairs with the rest of the crew and ride out the storm. About 9:30 or so, the electricity went out, so we peeked outside to determine whether we would sleep in our beds upstairs or stay together in the basement. Florida doesn't have underground basements but our house is on a hill so the back is next to the hill. It wasn't bad out and the other three hurricanes didn't do much to us, so we went to bed. There was a strange humming sound from a distance but we rationalized that it was wind. Still, several times that night I awoke and walked the hallways just to make sure everything was all right. When we awoke in the morning, we were covered in pine needles, branches, and had several fallen trees around us. We still didn't have electricity and the radio warned us not to leave our homes, for several tornadoes had hit, tearing through a large brick building [Sykes]; lifting a trailer house and placing it on top of another home, killing four; and destroying two trailer parks on opposite sides of our town. The Sykes computer building is less than a mile away from our house, and the humming we heard was not the wind, but the tornadoes. Next time we will sleep downstairs. We did not have electricity for two days but found, since we were prepared, we were well taken care of. We had water to flush toilets, and plenty of food to eat. I was feeling pretty blessed and you might say a little smug, thinking that all I cared for was safe, when one of my students came to my house. He said his trailer was totally demolished and he had no idea what his family would do. That's when it hit home—the people hurt really were a part of me—people I care for and love.

—R. H., September 2004, Fla.

Your home can be a safeguard to prevent harm, as well as a defense after a crisis. In some cases, shelter is the difference between safety and injury, and even between life and death. The preparedness purpose of a shelter is to put as much protection as possible between you and the adverse conditions raging outside. Usually, simply staying safely indoors may be all the shelter you need. The part of the country you live in and the kinds of storm patterns you have to deal with indicate the lengths to which you need to go to provide adequate shelter. And, unfortunately, because of the threatening conditions in the world, all of us need to provide some protection against terrorism, no matter where we live.

SHELTERING IN PLACE

"Sheltering in place" is a proper first response to a biological or chemical attack, which would be, in all probability, instigated by terrorists or war. In such a circumstance, you will be directed by the Emergency Alert System (through the media) to take shelter immediately and provide as much protection for yourself and your family as possible. The main security measure you must take is to avoid breathing in the contaminated air. The best way to do this is to retreat to a room as far from outside air as possible and seal yourself into it by covering window and door openings, air ducts, and heater vents with plastic sheeting, and sealing the edges securely with tape. Your shelter-in-place room should be on an upper floor or as high as possible because biological or chemical agents are heavier than air and will settle to the lowest point. It doesn't have to be a particularly small room, nor a room standing empty for that purpose only. For example, my designated shelter-in-place room is a large bedroom with an adjoining bathroom. There is only one window in the bedroom and a small window in the bathroom. Since it is at the end of a hallway, if the time comes, I will only need to seal off those two windows and the doorway into the

> *Your shelter-in-place room should be on an upper floor or as high as possible because biological or chemical agents are heavier than air and will settle to the lowest point.*

bedroom to secure my area. I will still have access to bathroom facilities. The bedroom has a television in it, in case there is still power, which is as likely as not. Most biological or chemical attacks could cause great destruction of human lives, but not necessarily great physical destruction of buildings and services. With a few supplies, including food, water (even if the water is still running, don't drink it until you have been assured it is safe by proper authorities), and battery-operated radios and flashlights (in case the power is out also), we are set. You may want to keep a supply kit in the room on a regular basis, or it may be just as effective for you to tape a list of instructions and needed supplies on the back of the door of the designated room. With a list as your guide, it would only take a few moments to gather your family and supplies and secure your area. Sheltering in place usually only lasts for several critical hours, not weeks. You don't need to worry that you are effectively sealing yourself into an airless box and that you'll suffocate before it's safe to come out. (See appendix O for further details and instructions on how to prepare to shelter-in-place.)

SAFE ROOM

Your home is one of the safest places to be during a tornado or severe storm, but most homes aren't built to withstand sustained winds exceeding ninety miles per hour. If you live in an area where extreme windstorms, hurricanes, tornadoes, or severe lightening storms frequently occur, you may want to consider building a safe room. A safe room is an interior room without windows. It is built so that the walls and ceiling can protect you from flying objects and falling debris, yet remain standing even if your home is severely damaged. Safe rooms can be installed in basements or in an above-ground area such as a large closet. They usually have reinforced ceilings and thick concrete walls. Should you wish to further investigate creating a safe room, one of the best places to go for reliable information and detailed construction plans is the FEMA Web site www.fema.gov/mit/saferoom/. Be aware as you search for information on safe rooms that the focus of some Web sites is crime prevention and having a place to be secure during an in-home burglary, and so on, rather than natural disasters. Those may have their place also, but don't be distracted and forget to follow the specifications to keep you safe in destructive storms.

Just as with a shelter-in-place room, you should stock a safe room with supplies to last for a day or two. Your supply kit should include an adequate supply of food and water for everyone that will be in the shelter, a battery-powered radio, first aid kit, flashlight, cell phone if possible (grab it on the way in), some small games or other morale boosters, and any specific personal needs you may have (for example, baby needs, medications, and so on). The crucial point is to make sure the supplies are immediately replaced when the storm passes, especially if it is the storm season. You never know how soon you'll get hit again. I have a friend who, living in the panhandle of Florida, endured the astonishing 2004 hurricane season. She said in their particular area they called Hurricane Ivan "the storm that would not die." They would think it was over, but then it would swing around and clobber them all over again. And again. And again!

THE NEXT-BEST THING TO A REAL SAFE ROOM

If you are not willing or able to build a concrete safe room, you can create the next-best thing by strengthening a closet or other small, windowless room. It has nothing at all like the protection concrete can provide, but it is unquestionably more secure than

if you did nothing. Choose a small interior room on the lowest level (unless you live in a floodplain or on the coast). The point is to put as many walls between you and the outside as possible. If the closet is not finished with wallboard, you can increase the strength of the walls and keep them from buckling or twisting by screwing lengths of 1 by 4 lumber diagonally from the top of one corner to the opposite bottom corner. If you are handy with wood, you can notch the studs so that the 1 by 4s fit flush with the edge of the studs. In addition, you can line the walls and ceiling with plywood. The thicker the sheet of plywood, the more protection there is. Use screws rather than nails to hold the plywood sheets in place. You place the plywood right over the diagonal 1 by 4 supports. If your closet is already finished, you still have the option

---

It is estimated that a specification-built safe room will cost between three and twelve thousand dollars. One CBS meteorologist in Texas, doing a report on tornadoes in March of 2004, indicated that tornadoes are the nation's most violent windstorms. Texas has many more tornadoes each year than any other state, approximately 130 annually. She summed up by saying, "Safe rooms are a little pricey, but the closer a tornado gets to you the cheaper they become."

—Kristine Kahanek
CBS11's Chief Meteorologist, CBS11
Dallas/Fort Worth, Tex.
March 5, 2004

L. H. N. related the following childhood experience: "When my family bought a home in Provo, Utah, my father built a windowless underground cement bomb shelter in the back-yard. The memory of looking in, let alone going down in, still brings me shivers of dread, because in Utah, dark, enclosed places invite an overabundance of black widow spiders. Twice a year—before the practice drills—Dad would make huge, twisted newspaper torches. With the torches lit and brightly burning, he would muster all the 'Dad's kind of courage' he could find, go down into the dark recesses of the shelter, and burn out the black widows. Then, buoyed by lots of reassurance that it was now safe, our family would reluctantly descend for the shelter drill."

—L. H. N., West Jordan, Utah

If it were me I'm sure I'd always be looking over my shoulder for the creatures that I knew had survived and were lurking and looking, waiting to pounce. Ugh! Spiders are not my friends!

of diagonal braces and lining for further protection. Simply make the addition on top of the wallboard, or take the wallboard off, put in the extra strengthening lining, and replace the wallboard. And yes, it will decrease the inside space by an inch or so. But what space remains will be much safer. A solid core door (usually referred to as an "outside" door) will also provide more protection than a regular hollow closet door. You may even wish to add a dead-bolt lock to more firmly secure the door from the inside. (Make sure it's high enough to not be a temptation for small children, who could accidentally bolt themselves in and not know how to unfasten the bolt.) Add a vent to insure adequate ventilation.

Since your safe room has no windows, you'll definitely need a good, reliable source of temporary light. Flashlights and plenty of batteries are the first ideas to come to mind. Another suggestion for light is battery-powered touch lights. They are easy to install, and the glow of light from several of them used simultaneously would feel more natural (and therefore more comforting, probably) than individual flashlight beams wheeling around in the dark. As with flashlights, though, extra batteries are a must. Fluorescent, battery-powered lanterns will also fill the bill.

Keep your small supply kit stocked and ready in the back of the closet to help the frightening hours pass while cloistered in your safe room. I remember hearing once about a family that made it into their safe room closet with only moments to spare, and then spent several hours sitting anxiously in the dark as a hurricane raged and spread destruction all around them. At least they were safe. But I'll bet they wished they'd thought ahead enough to provide for themselves some light, maybe a few bottles of water, and a game or two to get their minds off their fears.

SHARED SPACE

Very few people have enough extra space to justify a closet sitting empty all year long in anticipation of a future event that may or may not ever occur. To use your safe room space wisely and yet still have it available as a safe room the minute you need it, consider using rolling racks to hang your clothes in the closet. Then, when the need arises, you can quickly get most of the clothes out at one time. If the closet is used for storing boxes or containers, buy or build a set of rollout shelves. In the back recesses of the closet, keep the supply kit you will need to have on hand in an emergency, as well as a stack of the blankets for warmth or to protect your head if things get really bad.

STORM CELLAR

A storm cellar is an actual cellar, a room or place below ground level, not necessarily connected to the house or basement. It's a place designated to go when the storms get so bad that it is not safe above-ground. I grew up in Ohio, in the path of tornadoes. We learned from an early age to recognize the signs of tornado weather. The sky would turn an ominous black with kind of an orange tint. The air would feel strange and eerie. My grandparents had a storm cellar in the yard, with two huge (to a child) wooden doors that opened outwards. They were not set flush with the ground, but at an angle. (Think of the opening scenes of *The Wizard of Oz*, when the family goes down into the storm cellar and pulls the doors closed, and a few minutes later Dorothy runs up and stamps on the doors to be heard, then runs back into the house. That's really what stormcellar doors look like.) When the sirens would sound, the children would all be sent home from school. We would run like crazy to make it home as the winds grew stronger and stronger. Then, with Grandpa and Grandma, we would go down into the musty-smelling, dirt-floored cellar. Grandpa would close the doors and we would wait. I think I felt more security from having Grandma there than from the fact that we were in the storm cellar. Her calming words and comforting touches reassured us that we would be okay. She may have thought differently, but we didn't know otherwise.

MOBILE HOME CAUTION

For some inexplicable reason, mobilehome parks seem to be tornado magnets. They are not safe places to be when Mother Nature unleashes all her fury. Choose a place now to seek shelter if you live in a mobile home. In some instances (hurricanes, for example) you'll have time to drive to the home of a friend or relative before the storm actually hits, but not all weather threats are so accommodating. Look around and find a sturdy building nearby where you can go to ride out a storm that hits without warning. When it does, don't wait. Go immediately and directly to a safer place. See Section Five for details and helps to make an evacuation situation more comfortable and secure.

SAFE PLACE

You may live in a part of the country where building a concrete safe room would be absurd overkill. Even restructuring a closet isn't necessary. For example, Larry and I have spent half our lives in Utah and never been more than mildly threatened by storms of any sort there. Tornadoes and hurricanes are just not indigenous to this area. Drought, yes. Treacherous ice-covered highways, yes. Winter storms that knock out the power, yes. But hurricanes and tornadoes, no. And although we live only ten miles from a major earthquake fault, safe rooms are ineffective for earthquakes because you don't have sufficient warning to get to them in time. That does not mean, though,

We actually did have a tornado in Salt Lake City in 1999. A freak Level 4 (very serious) tornado sprang up out of nowhere one August afternoon and destroyed a few blocks of the downtown area. It was the first tornado of that magnitude in Utah in all its recorded history. Even if you don't live in a likely area for disastrous storms, Mother Nature is notoriously fickle. It pays to be prepared.

that we disregard storm safety. Windows could always shatter, we could be hit by flying debris, trees could blow over and crush the house, and so on. It just means that instead of a safe room in our home, we have determined and designated a safe place. We chose the safest spot in our home to gather if storms blow severely enough to pose a threat. Our safe place is downstairs, in the end of the family room that doesn't have any windows, and near a bearing wall (the strongest wall in the house). Our family knows that when the wind blows hard enough to be worrisome, we head downstairs until it blows over.

SAFE HAVEN

No matter how severe the tumult going on outside your home, your can turn your designated place of shelter into a safe haven. Begin by discussing with your family the whats, whys, and hows of disaster preparation: what could possibly go wrong, why you are getting prepared now, how you are going about it, and how that will provide needed security during dark and stormy times. Then, when the crisis comes, speak in comforting words. Reassure your family that all will be fine, that you have prepared for this situation and it is under control as much as is possible. Your comforting tone and encouraging attitude will set frightened minds at rest, just like my grandma did for me in the storm cellar so many years ago. Your shelter is your refuge from the storm. You have it within you to create a safe haven in the midst of chaos.

CHAPTER TWENTY

JUST ADD WATER:
WHEN THE WELL RUNS DRY

Next to oxygen, water is the most essential element in the survival of human beings. A person can go without food for several weeks or more, but without water you can survive for only a few days. Day in and day out, water is vital! Water in an emergency situation is even more critical.

We are spoiled in our affluent society. We take clear, clean water for granted. We rely on turning a handle and having a cold drink or a hot bath whenever we want. We don't realize how easy it could be to lose that blessing. A natural disaster could easily drain wells or rupture pipes, disrupting service to our area, or leave the water contaminated and not fit to drink. And even if water is still available after a natural disaster, a hazardous materials crisis, or radioactive contamination, you should consider all water from wells, cisterns, or other delivery systems in the disaster area unsafe until it has been tested and cleared by civic authorities. Contaminated water is only marginally better than no water at all. Did you know, though, that having water in your pipes is dependent on electricity as well? Without electricity, there is no way to pump that water to your home. Since most of us don't live by a creek or have a well, we must find another way to have a sure supply on hand in case something should happen to our water source.

HOW MUCH IS ENOUGH?

At least some water needs to be in your preparedness pantry. But how much? FEMA and other emergency services recommend that we have at least a two-week supply of water on hand at all times. Bare-bones survival rations would be half a gallon per person per day just for drinking and minimal food preparation purposes. Half a gallon is only eight eight-ounce

glasses of water—the same amount nutritionists and dietitians recommend you should drink every day for good health. You might say that you don't come close to drinking half a gallon of water each day, but I bet you'd be surprised if you tallied up all the liquids you drink daily. If you added up all the water, juice, milk, soft drinks, broth, and so on, you'd probably be close to the half-gallon mark, if not over. And that's on a normal day, when food and water is plentiful. In an emergency, you'll find you probably want more liquid

---

Homework Assignment:

How Much Are
You Really Drinking?

Keep track of your daily liquid intake for at least three days. Write down how much you drink every time you take a drink of:

- *Water (bottled or tap)*
- *Milk*
- *Juice (fruit or vegetable)*
- *Soda pop*
- *Sports drinks*
- *Coffee/tea*
- *Any other liquid*

Is one-half gallon per person per day really enough for you?

Now, keep track for the other members of your family/household for three days.

than in regular circumstances.

In addition to drinking water, you will need half a gallon, per person, per day, for other uses, such as bathing, brushing teeth, and washing dishes. Again, this is just a bare minimum amount. On a regular day when you take your cereal bowl to the sink and turn on the tap to rinse it out, half a gallon of water splashes down the drain easily without you paying any attention. During a crisis, it will take watchful care to make half a gallon stretch to cover a whole day. Remember, these figures are the absolute minimum amount you should plan on having for an emergency.

Fourteen gallons is a good general starting amount, but you may need more than that. For example, when our son was in high school, he was energetic and active. He ran cross-country and track, and even when he wasn't running, he was constantly on the move. He drank so much water he should have sloshed when he moved. Half a gallon of water per day would not have been nearly enough for him.

> *Going through a difficult time requiring extreme measures can sometimes create habits that last years. Our family lived in the Union City/Fremont area of Northern California during the 1976–77 drought. We had slow-flow showerheads. We displaced water in our toilet tanks. We didn't use the dishwasher, but did use the water from hand-washing dishes to keep a few fruit trees alive. Our lawns were brown and brittle. We were extremely careful with our water in every imaginable way. I formed the habit of reserving my drinking water. If, after I took a drink of water from the sink, there was any water left in the cup, I'd set the glass at the back of the sink to drink later. To this day I still do that. I cannot bear to throw water down the drain.*

Consider some of the individual preparedness needs for water that could require you to store more than the bare minimum:

• Do you have a baby in your house? How much water do you need for preparing formula or baby food? Babies are notorious for spitting up and making messes, and they're usually in constant need of cleaning up. You'll need to have sufficient water to keep your baby tolerably clean, even if she can't have a full-fledged bath.

• Teenagers generally have more energy than any three adults put together. Energy output requires liquid input. Make sure you store plenty of water for active teens. In a crisis, you'll probably need to have a discussion up front about what your child's allowable rations are, to make certain there's enough for everyone.

• Is any member of your family an invalid or chronically ill? Do they have an increased need for water to take medications or for personal care?

• Do you have pets? If so, you will need to have additional water on hand for them.

• What kinds of foods are, or will be, in your preparedness pantry? If the majority of your food choices are dry or dehydrated rather than canned or ready-to-eat, you will need additional water to prepare them.

• Do you live in an area where extreme heat is a factor? If an emergency occurs in August and you live near Death Valley, California, you can bet you'll need more water than someone who lives in a more temperate climate, especially if your power is out, as well as your access to fresh drinking water. Emergencies can happen any time of year. Prepare for the worst possible case, and you won't be sorry.

• Are you accustomed to drinking a lot of water for good health on a regular basis? Many people carry a bottle of water with them wherever they go. To suddenly have that intake cut back dramatically, especially in a time of crisis, could be very difficult physically.

WHERE IS THERE ALREADY WATER IN YOUR HOME?

If a catastrophic earthquake occurred five minutes from now, before you had any chance to stash away your supply of gallons of water, all would not necessarily be lost. You have some water in your home that you may not be aware of.

Hot-Water Heater

There is clean, drinkable water in your water heater. Depending on its size, there are twenty to fifty gallons of water in a hot-water heater. The trick is knowing how to get the water out when just turning on the faucet doesn't do it. Opening the drain faucet at the bottom of the tank can access the water. (Have a bucket or bowl ready before you open the faucet so you don't lose any.) To get the water to flow, you'll first have to turn on a faucet somewhere else in the house. This releases pressure in the line and allows the water to drain out of the hot-water heater. Don't rely on this as your only source of water. If an earthquake causes your "emergency situation," your water heater could tip or break and the water could be lost, let alone causing gas and water lines to break. You should reinforce your hot-water heater (a good idea even if you're not relying on it as a drinking water source) by securing it to the wall with straps, or by using a kit designed specifically for this purpose. They are readily available at your local home improvement or hardware store.

Your water pipes also have water available in them. To access it, you must first turn on the highest faucet in the house to allow air into the pipes, and then turn on the lowest faucet in the house to drain out the water. When your water services are turned back on, and you turn on the faucets for the first time, all that air in the pipes will cause the water to pop and bang and "explode" as it comes out the faucet, almost like it had gone crazy. It hasn't. It's just the water pushing the air out of the pipes, and it only lasts a few seconds. It will be the same in every faucet in the house, which makes for a startling moment when you turn on a little-used faucet a week later and it spits and pops at you when you're not expecting it.

However, before you use the water from your water heater or the existing water in your pipes, you may have to take steps to insure that water remains uncontaminated. Broken pipes due to a landslide, flood, or earthquake can allow pollution to seep into your home water supply. To avoid this, you must first turn off the water intake valves to your house. That keeps the existing water pure and drinkable. I wish there was a hard-and-fast rule that tells you when you need to turn off your water lines and when it's not necessary, but there's not. It's a judgment call. However, unlike natural gas lines, which must be turned on by a professional once they are turned off, you can turn your water back on by yourself. Remember, it's better to be safe than sorry.

Toilet Tank

Another resource for clean water is the toilet tank (not the bowl, the tank in the back). There is anywhere from three to five gallons of water in each tank. You can dip the water out with a cup or ladle when the time comes. If your attitude makes you balk at drinking this water, it could at least be used for other purposes, like pet water or cleanliness. However, since it is a source for clean water, don't spoil it by putting chemicals in it to clean the bowl below. I also schedule a time once a year or so to scrub the inside of the tank, if for no other reason than it makes me feel better.

In the Pantry

If you have cans or jars of fruits, fruit juices, canned vegetables, or ready-to-serve soups on your shelves, you can obtain supplemental liquid from these. The liquid used for processing can be counted as part of your "emergency water supply." You'll find anywhere from one-fourth to one cup liquid in each can, depending on the size of the can and what it is. Drinking green bean water or peach liquid is clearly not as good as a glass of pure water, and obviously you can't wash your face in chicken broth but, if push came to shove, it's better than nothing to drink. Part of the mind-set of preparedness is to be able to adapt to make the best of the resources that you have on hand. If your drinking water needs are met (even

---

Caution

Before using the water from your water heater, it's imperative that you switch off the gas or electricity that heats the water. Leaving the heating part on while the water heater is empty could cause an explosion or burn out the elements, destroying your water heater. Don't turn on the water heater again until water services have been restored and the water heater is refilled.

barely) through another source, liquid from canned goods can still stretch a meager supply of water for food preparation. For example, you could use the light syrup from canned fruit to cook oatmeal, or as the liquid in pancake batter. You could use the liquid from canned vegetables to boil the noodles for boxed macaroni and cheese, or to prepare condensed soups.

Pool or Hot Tub

A pool or hot tub may or may not be a source of water for you. Depending on the crisis, you could have gallons and gallons of water to work with. However, an earthquake or severe storm could crack your pool or tub, and your water would drain away. Don't count on it as your only source of water. Pools and hot tubs are generally so full of chemicals that the water is unfit for drinking. They can't be boiled out, nor are there any more chemicals you can add to get rid of the chemicals that are there. It would be a good choice for gray water though, to wash or bathe with, and certainly to flush toilets.

Water Beds

The water in waterbeds is chemically treated to retard the growth of germs and algae. It isn't fit for drinking, but would also be acceptable as gray water for washing.

GETTING READY

There are some emergencies where you have a little notice before the catastrophe occurs. For example,

often there will be warnings and sightings to alert you to the possibility of tornadoes. People usually are aware days in advance of hurricanes heading in their direction. If you have a warning that trouble may be heading your way, you can increase your freshwater supply by filling bathtubs, pots, pans, containers, and buckets before the problem arrives. Then, shut off the main water valve just prior to the storm's arrival to protect the clean water already in your water system, and close the valves on the water lines leaving the house. If you're lucky, the tornado or storm will miss you completely, and all you have to do is drain the tub and containers, and turn the water back on. But if you're not so fortunate, you'll appreciate having those extra gallons of clean water. I can remember, as a young girl in Ohio, when the tornado warnings would come we always filled the bathtub upstairs and the big galvanized tubs by the washing machine in the basement. And in the aftermath of earthquakes in California, while there was still water, we would fill the tub and all of the empty buckets and pots that we could find in case an aftershock should break water lines weakened by the initial earthquake.

STORING YOUR OWN

Your best bet for being sure to have water when you need it is to store it in the first place. Many different types of containers are appropriate for water storage. Some are designed specifically for that purpose; others are acceptable for water storage, though it's not their primary function. New, used, big, small, glass,

Typical Amounts of Liquid in Canned Goods (No. 303 Can)

Canned Item	Weight	Amount of Liquid	Amount of Product
Fruit Cocktail	17 oz.	1 cup	1 cup
Green Beans	16 oz.	1 cup	2 cups
Peach Halves	17 oz.	1 cup	1 cup
Peach Slices	17 oz.	1 cup	1¼ cups
Peas	17 oz.	1¾ cup	¾ cup

plastic—you have a lot of choices. Each has advantages and disadvantages. You choose what will work best for you. However, before you rush out to build up a water supply, take a few minutes to review where you will realistically keep it.

COMMERCIAL WATER

A good place to start with water for emergency preparedness is to take a look at what's ready and waiting for you on the store shelf. There are a large variety of commercially processed, sterilized, and sealed water options to choose from. These would not have to ever be replaced or have their water changed unless they were opened, and they're relatively inexpensive. It's one item that you could plan to pick up each shopping day until you have a good supply.

Smaller bottles, such as the single-serve twelve- to twenty-four-ounce bottles, could easily be tucked into cupboards or closet corners, nooks and crannies. However, you'd need a lot of them, seventy-five twenty-four-ounce bottles to be precise, to equal fourteen gallons of water (the recommended amount for one person for two weeks). You may not have that many nooks and crannies in your house, especially if you're collecting water for more than one person. You can still use single-serve bottles, but you may want to plan on buying them by the case and stacking them in a corner rather than stashing them individually all around.

Single-serving water pouches are also available where camping, backpacking, or emergency supplies are found. These metalized pouches typically hold only four ounces of water each, so you would need cases and cases to reach the minimum recommended allotment. They are typically more expensive than water bottles for a commensurate amount of water. However, they are a good choice to put in 72-hour emergency kits, or in emergency car kits, where space is at a premium, but you still want some water.

Supermarkets also carry water in gallon jugs (similar to milk jugs). You'll want to stay away from these because, just like milk jugs, the plastic is just too thin for storage. It disintegrates rapidly and you could lose all the stored water.

You can buy water in heavy-duty two-gallon containers designed to slip onto a shelf in your refrigerator. These are a good choice.

You've seen the five-gallon jugs of water, often delivered to offices, which are put upside down on water coolers, and you get a drink out of a cone-shaped paper cup. Those jugs of water are perfectly appropriate for water-storage use. The plastic is sturdy and strong, and the jugs come sealed. You don't have to have a water-cooler unit to use them, either. When it's time to use the water, you just pour it out as you need it into a smaller, more manageable container, like a pitcher. One advantage is that bottled water companies will deliver the filled jugs right to your door. The disadvantages are that you have to pay a deposit for (or purchase) the bottles themselves (in addition to the water), the bottles are not stackable, and they weigh just as much as other five-gallon water containers (40 pounds when full).

TYPES OF CONTAINERS

If you don't want to purchase commercially packaged water, you can choose containers and store your own. Here are some of the alternatives.

Water Barrels

Large plastic water barrels can be a great option. They take up less space than a lot of smaller containers, and they can hold fifteen to fifty-five gallons. They do have some disadvantages, though. A full fifty-five-gallon water barrel will weigh 440 pounds! Once you fill it, it is not portable. You must have some way of getting the water out—without tipping it, wasting it or breaking your back. A siphon-hose

M. S. of Alhambra, California, wrote to tell me about her friend who had kept a full fifty-five-gallon water barrel in her garage for fifteen years. When the need arose, she discovered she didn't have a pump. So, desperate times requiring desperate measures, she poked a hole in the side of the barrel with a screwdriver and caught the water in a cup. The water was still good to drink after all those years, but her barrel wasn't any good after that day. I have to recommend a siphon pump over a screwdriver.

pump is the easiest and most logical way to access the water. You should be able to buy one in the same place you purchase your barrel for ten to fifteen dollars. Water barrels have two plugs, or fittings, on top, one for the siphon hose, and one to allow the airflow necessary for the hose to work. You will also need a bung wrench (a wrench with strange-looking "teeth") to open these special plugs. If you do, you can usually buy one in the same place you bought the barrel and the siphon hose. A decidedly second-best solution is to use a rubber tube to siphon the water out of barrel, like a thief would do to siphon the gas out of your car. First, open both plugs on the top of the water barrel. Next, get an eight- to ten-foot length of flexible rubber tubing (a section of narrow garden hose would do in a pinch) and stick one end well down into the water in your barrel. You'll want to clean it first if it's been outdoors in the mud all summer, watering your garden. Then, start sucking on the other end of the tube like a straw. When the water hits your mouth, quickly place that end of the tube into a bucket on the floor. The water should start pouring out of the tube. Make sure the bucket is lower than the water level in the barrel. The trick is that there must be water in the hose in order to start the siphon action flowing. If sucking on the hose like a straw just isn't going to work for you, another option is to have some additional water and a funnel on hand to begin with. Put one end of the empty hose into your water barrel. Put the funnel into the other end of the hose and use your additional water (a two-liter bottle, for example) to fill the hose. When the hose is full, put the end into your bucket and the water should start to flow out. These methods are not nearly as convenient or easy as a siphon pump, but they are options if a disaster should happen today, before you get a chance to buy your pump.

When siphoning water from a large barrel, remember to shut the siphon off before the water reaches the top of the smaller container you're using to catch the water. There is still residual water in the siphon hose that will fill the container the rest of the way to the top. When water is in short supply, you have to be careful to not waste a single precious drop.

If your barrel is made of white or transparent plastic, you'll want to keep it in a dark room or shed, or wrap it in a tarp to keep it away from light as much as possible. Exposure to light allows algae to grow.

Algae will grow in small containers also. However, they are much easier to clean and care for than a large barrel. Keeping algae from growing is easier than getting rid of it in a large barrel. See appendix E for suggestions on cleaning algae out of barrels.

Five-Gallon Water Jugs

You can purchase five-gallon water jugs. These measure approximately 15 by 15 by 20 inches and have a built in handle. A filled five-gallon container weighs forty pounds. Some water jugs have spigots built in. Others have a place for an optional spigot you can screw in. Some jugs are designed so that they can be stacked. The stackable ones cost a bit more but they can be a real space saver.

You can also buy heavy-duty five-gallon jugs designed specifically for water. Not that the other-shaped water jugs aren't designed specifically for water also. However, these water jugs are a different shape, and sold in a different department of the store (usually the automotive section or the sporting goods section). They look just like red gas cans, only they are white and are imprinted with the word *water*. These are about 16 by 18 by 24 inches. A word of caution is appropriate here: you should *never* store water in the red gas cans (or vice versa). They are designed to be readily recognizable as containing what they say they contain. To use them for other purposes could be disastrous. Perhaps you are aware that you are storing the wrong liquid in a certain can, but no one else may know that. It could result in an unsuspecting person pouring water into their gas tank or lawn mower, or even worse, trying to get a drink or put out a fire with gasoline that should have been water.

Previously Used Containers

Many previously used containers are acceptable to use. Thoroughly washed, clean food-grade plastic jugs with tight-fitting lids, or glass jars or bottles with screw caps can be used. Plastic has an advantage over glass by being shatterproof if it should fall or be bumped. I discourage the use of plastic milk bottles, because the plastic is thin and disintegrates rapidly, sometimes in as little as just a few months. It's not a bad idea to fill your milk jugs as a temporary water supply while you are in the process of getting better containers, but don't be surprised if you walk by your milk-jug water-storage area in a month or two and find an empty jug with a puddle underneath it. They just don't hold up. (If you intend to use them on a temporary basis, rinse milk jugs thoroughly with cold water first. Hot water will cause the protein in the milk residue to coagulate, making it much more difficult to remove.)

Two- to three-liter soda pop bottles are also perfectly acceptable. It just takes a lot of them to add up to fourteen gallons of water per person. One advantage of them being small is that you can stash them in a variety of small, lesser-used locations if you don't have room to keep them all in one place.

The gallon- or half-gallon-sized containers that hold fruit juice are a good choice, being made of sturdy, heavy-duty plastic. Rinse them thoroughly and mark them with a permanent marker so you don't have a very disappointed person looking for orange juice and finding only water.

Some used plastic containers do have a disadvantage. Sometimes even food-grade plastic will absorb a strong flavor, such as pickle juice or vinegar, from the original contents. Then, that flavor will leach back into the water you store in them. This is not a problem as far as health goes, but it might offend your taste buds or change a recipe's flavor. You can try to eliminate the offensive flavor by filling the container with a mixture of one tablespoon baking soda per one quart of water. Let the container soak for at least twenty-four hours (don't forget the lid too). Then rinse it again and check again for odor. If your container maintains a strong smell even after you've washed it out, at the very least the water could be used for cleanliness. For this same reason, it is important to not use containers for water storage that have previously held any sort of chemicals. For example, don't store drinking water in used five-gallon laundry-detergent buckets. The detergent chemicals will have been absorbed into the plastic, and then will be released back into your drinking water.

Plastic doesn't just absorb chemicals from ingredients stored inside it—it can absorb from the outside, too. Make sure that your water supplies, if in plastic containers, are not stored near gasoline, kerosene, pesticides, or similar substances. Plastic is permeable to these vapors.

Canning Jars and More

Glass containers can work. A distinct disadvantage is their breakability. Many people bottle their own fruits and vegetables each summer. When they use a bottle of peaches for breakfast, they will then fill the clean, empty jar with water before storing it until the next harvest season. If you store canning jars in your attic or garage or wherever, it's easy to keep them filled with water. Jars full of water don't take any more space than jars full of air, plus it puts you a step ahead in being prepared. You don't need to process these bottles in a water bath. Simply fill the jars and put on rings with lids. In this instance, clean, previously used canning lids are completely acceptable. One way to store them and reduce breakage is to keep the original sectioned box they came in. Put the filled jars back in the box. Full boxes can then easily stack, instead of having individual bottles spread out on shelves.

Metal Containers

I don't recommend storing water in metal containers for the simple reason that metal plus water equals rust. Besides, even after only a short while, metal containers will often give the water an unpleasant taste. (The only exception would be stainless steel containers, which would end up costing a small fortune.) Choose glass or food-grade plastic for storing water.

PROPER FILLING OF A CONTAINER

Once you've chosen your containers and brought them home, it's time to fill them. If you're using soda pop bottles or other small containers, you can fill them at the kitchen sink. If you're using larger containers, you can fill them in a bathtub or use a garden hose. If you have a fifteen-gallon barrel or larger, you'll need to fill it right where it's going to stay since it will be extremely difficult if not impossible to move it after it's full. A utility room with a floor drain is a good choice for keeping large water barrels. You can run the hose in a nearby window and fill the barrel right there. When you want to change the water, you can siphon it out right into the floor drain without having to carry heavy buckets out of your house. If you store your barrels in a garage, part of the water can be siphoned out, and the rest dumped on the lawn when it's time to change it.

If you are using a hose to fill your barrels, wash the hose with soap and rinse it at least two or three feet back from the nozzle. Then, continue with these steps for filling containers with water:

1. Fill your container, large or small, to overflowing. Let a small amount of water run over the top. This eliminates all the air in the jug. The exception to this rule is if your water has to be stored where it might freeze. Then, allow an inch or so of headspace for expansion. You'll need to change this water more often. If there's any chance of freezing at all, store in plastic, not glass.

2. Filling will cause air bubbles to form, so pat the sides of your containers to get the bubbles to rise to the top.

3. Top it off. Refill that inch or so left by the air bubbles again until a little water flows over the top.

4. You do not have to add any purifiers to the water. Water from your tap is safe and good. It does not need to be purified when you put it in the containers, and probably not when you end up using it, unless it has not been cared for properly, or unless something has polluted it. According to the Utah State University Extension, you purify water only if the purity of the water is in doubt.

5. Put the lid on.

6. Store in as dark and cool a place as possible, and preferably not directly on a cement floor. (Lay down some slats before you set your containers down.)

7. Check your water a couple times a year. If it's not slimy or cloudy, and if there are no frogs in it, leave it alone. Change it out for fresh every year or so to make sure it is still good.

8. After extreme weather conditions, check for leaks.

PURIFYING WATER

As I said above (step 4), if you have stored clean water in clean containers, checked it regularly, and occasionally replaced it to make sure it stays clear, you do not need to purify it! Just drink it! The same goes for water in your water heaters, and so on. If the water coming into your house when the containers were filled was clean, that water is still clean.

You need to purify stored water that is cloudy, or that comes from other sources that may be contaminated. The water in a city near my home became contaminated a few years ago. Nearly 100,000 people were without safe drinking water for almost two weeks while water-treatment officials scrambled, trying to find out the source of the problem and fix it. In the end, it turned out to be a dead raccoon in the bottom of one of the treatment plants. The citizens of West Valley City, Utah, had plenty of water; it just wasn't safe to drink. For two weeks, they had to purify their water, or buy bottled water, or drive out of their area to fill containers to take back to

While I was writing this book, our son was called to active duty in the army and assigned to a mobile hospital unit. That got me thinking, and I came to the conclusion that surely the army—which takes soldiers all over the world into places where unsafe water conditions exist—would have the definitive answer on which ingredients or methods are most effective for purifying water, and therefore that method would also work for the rest of us.

So I sent him an e-mail and asked him to find out what kind of water purifiers or methods the army uses. What is the critical ingredient they use to get rid of the nasty germs they deal with all over the world? How do they make the water safe for the soldiers?

A month later came the reply:

"Mom:

At long last here is the secret recipe: Bleach. That is all that is in those big water trailers. In the soldiers' personal kits, they have standard camping water tablets. Nothing special."

There you have it. Our U.S. Army has resolved the situation for us.

their homes. It was a real pain, but it was certainly an appreciation lesson to all of us about the importance and convenience of clean running water.

WATER TREATMENT METHODS

Water may appear crystal clear (or not!) and still be contaminated. Harmful microorganisms can exist that can cause diarrhea, cramps, nausea, exhaustion, and serious illnesses. Protozoa, such as cryptosporidia and giardia, are relatively large and easy to filter out. Bacteria, such as salmonella and cholera, are smaller than protozoa and harder to remove. Viruses, such as hepatitis A and B, are the tiniest of all. Only boiling, chemicals, and purifiers can handle viruses.[1] If there is any question about the safety or cleanliness of the water you intend to use for drinking, food preparation, brushing, or dishwashing, purify it.

Because it is difficult to store a large water supply, it is wise to know how to properly purify water, and to be prepared with water purifying agents.

Filtering Out the Obvious Lumps

If your water is obviously contaminated with debris, or even if it is simply cloudy instead of clear, prefiltering it is your first step in purification. This is true whether you intend to use a commercial filter to clean your water or any other treatment method. An easy way to prefilter is to line a colander or strainer with several layers of coffee filters, cheesecloth, or towels (paper or cloth). Then, just pour the water through. A cotton plug in a funnel also will work. Note that prefiltering is only the first step in purification—your water is not yet safe to drink.

Filters and Purifiers

You can purchase water filters and purifiers in all sporting goods stores. Filters trap protozoa and bacteria. Purifiers also handle viruses, which are too tiny for most filters. (Combining a filter and chemicals can achieve the same protection.) Filters trap microorganisms in an internal element or cartridge. These are made out of many kinds of materials, including ceramic, glass fiber, iodinated resin, and carbon. Although camping or backpacking water filters are very effective, their filtering capacity is limited. After a while, the filters become saturated and must be replaced (or in some models, cleaned). Their capacity depends in part on how dirty the water is

to begin with. Prefiltering, as mentioned above, can help extend the life of your filters. Commercial filters and purifiers can be quite pricey.

Boiling

Boiling is a very effective, recommended method of purification when water safety is in question. Five minutes at a rolling boil is sufficient to destroy the bacteria that might be present. However, it's very important that you pay attention to the words "at a rolling boil." It's not five minutes from when you put the pan on the stove. The water has to heat up first, and you can start counting the five minutes when there are big bubbles exploding all over on the top of the water. It can take anywhere from five minutes to half an hour to get to the point where you can begin timing the water, depending on how much water you're trying to purify, your source of heat, and what your altitude is. (It takes much longer to boil water at a high altitude than it does at sea level.) If you're not careful, you could end up losing a large portion of your water to evaporation in that amount of time. Using a tight-fitting lid will help, as it boils as well as while it cools, since most of the water will condense on the lid and drip back into the pan.

The 1.5 million residents of Phoenix were warned Tuesday to boil their drinking water or use bottled water. Muddy water stirred up by recent storms was flowing into one of the city's operating water treatment plants. Two other treatment plants were shut down and the fifth was closed because it was flooded by the storms, leaving only one of the city's five watertreatment plants producing at full capacity.

—Deseret Morning News
Wednesday, January 26, 2005

Chemical Treatment

Chemical treatments (bleach and iodine) are inexpensive ways to treat bacteria and viruses, but they won't work against cryptosporidia.

Purifying with Bleach

One of the more popular water purification methods is the easy household bleach method. Any household bleach solution that contains hypochlorite, a chlorine compound, as its only active ingredient will purify water easily and inexpensively. Regular bleach solutions with five and one-quarter percent sodium hypochlorite, or "ultra" bleach solutions with 6 percent sodium hypochlorite are most common. They are what you usually find in grocery stores. All it takes is a few drops of bleach in a gallon of water,

> *Don't have a dropper? Use a spoon and a square-ended strip of paper or thin cloth about 1/4" x 2." Put the strip in the spoon with an end hanging down about 1/2" below the scoop of the spoon. Place the bleach in the spoon and carefully tip it. Drops the size of those from a medicine dropper will drip off the end of the strip.*
> —Cobb County Emergency Preparedness, Cobb County, Ga.

and you're in business. However, it is common for people to apply the "if some is good, more is better" reasoning to bleach purification, and go way, way overboard. It's drops! Not cupfuls per gallon! One person I knew figured a good plan was to store her water in empty bleach bottles, and she would leave one-fourth to one-half inch of bleach in the bottle and fill the rest up with water. There wouldn't be any germs in her water, for sure, but she could end up sick, just the same.

To purify water with bleach, use the following chart to determine how much you need. If your water is clear but the safety is questionable, use the figures for clear water. If your water is cloudy or murky, strain it through a couple of layers of cloth to remove large impurities first, and then use the figures for cloudy water. Add the chlorine solution to the water and stir, then allow the mixture to stand for thirty minutes (sixty minutes for cloudy or very cold water). The water then should have the distinct smell or taste of chlorine. If this taste or smell is not present, add another dose of solution to the water and let it stand another fifteen minutes. The taste or smell of chlorine in water treated this way is a sign of safety.

Chlorine (bleach) is effective on most bacteria and viruses, but it doesn't kill cryptosporidia or giardia, which may be present in floodwater. These parasites can cause severe illnesses. Boiling is the best treatment in this situation.

Bleach has a limited shelf life. After three months, its disinfectant qualities begin to dissipate. Replace your bleach often. Also, only use "regular" household

Purifying Water with Household Bleach		
Amount of Water	**Drops per gallon of water if water is clear**	**Drops per gallon of water if water is cloudy**
1 quart	2 drops	4 drops
½ gallon (about 2 liters)	4 drops	8 drops
1 gallon	8 drops	16 drops (¼ teaspoon)
5 gallons	½ teaspoon	1 teaspoon

bleach for purifying water. For one thing, you don't want your water tasting like "Wildflower Meadows" or "Mountain Breezes." For another thing, the chemicals added to make your bleach smell like something other than bleach are not meant to be ingested. Stick with plain, regular bleach.

Remember, you don't need to add bleach to the water when you store it (providing you are storing potable drinking water in the first place). You add bleach to purify water when you are ready to drink it, but only if necessary.

Iodine

Iodine tablets or drops are the same as water purification tablets. There can be a distinct iodine odor and taste. The water will taste better if you can plan ahead and allow it to stand for about thirty minutes after mixing. Some iodine tablets are sold in two-bottle packages. One bottle is the iodine. The other bottle is tablets that remove the taste of iodine. Iodine requires a lot of contact time in cold or murky water. It's not recommended for pregnant women or people with certain medical conditions. Follow the usage directions on the package. One tablet usually is sufficient for one quart of water; double the dosage if the water is cloudy.

Ultraviolet Light

Rather than using chemicals or filtering, you can purchase a small device that irradiates water, neutralizing pathogens of all sizes, including viruses. Check with a local sporting goods store for these useful tools.

TASTE AND APPEARANCE

Stored water tastes "flat" (as does boiled water). This is because it has no air in it. It does not harm it in any way. Pouring it back and forth between two containers can add oxygen back to the water and make it taste better. Refrigeration also helps the taste, though this is a moot point if your water problems come with power outages. Taste-neutralizer tablets and commercial carbon filters will also get rid of chemical odors and tastes.

SHELF LIFE OF WATER

Water can be stored for long periods of time, even up to five years or more, if it doesn't react with the container or its components. From a taste standpoint, potable water stored in glass or polyethylene containers will remain safe, but may change somewhat in taste or odor. Although some of these qualities may be disagreeable, they aren't harmful. Check your stored water every year or so to determine whether the containers have leaked or if any undesirable characteristics have developed. If so, the water needs to be replaced.

You can take comfort in knowing that, with your water safety and availability issues resolved, it won't be another crisis if, in the middle of the storm, you hear a small voice saying, "I want another drink of water."

Notes:
1. Adapted from REI product information on water filters and purifiers.

CHAPTER TWENTY-ONE

MAKESHIFT MEALS FOR TUMULTUOUS TIMES

In an emergency situation, you may be limited to cooking on a camping stove by the light of a candle or lantern. If the situation is serious, your fuel usage will be restricted, your water cautiously rationed, and you may be dealing with these in the middle of chaos. It's important to choose food and food-preparation methods that will get you through these tough situations where you have to do without the essential services that we take for granted: power, running water, light, and a supermarket on the corner to run to for supplies. Your food choices should be a comforting relief, not an added catastrophe.

Consider this chapter a crash course in Disaster-Food Preparation 101. If you want to get an A in the class (and, more importantly, get through a disaster with the least amount of upset), you will carefully plan and stock up on the right food supplies. Your food choice is right if (1) it requires little or no cooking, (2) it requires little or no preparation, and (3) it requires no refrigeration.

Consider the situation of some of the victims of Hurricane Katrina in Louisiana in 2005 as a case in point—not the unfortunate ones who lost everything in New Orleans, but the ones in the surrounding areas who were faced with destruction and loss, yet still were able to stay in their homes. It was weeks or months before all of their utilities were back in place. Until then, they had to make do without utilities as they tried to put their lives back together. These are the ones whose stories didn't make it onto the news, but whose lives were nevertheless severely disrupted. Can you imagine how grateful many of them were to have prepared in advance to care for themselves; that they had cans of food on their shelves that they could open and eat, even while surrounded by disaster?

Food for emergency situations that requires little or no cooking or refrigeration need not be special food or food you have never tried. Consider your pantry shelves and use your imagination. The same stock of food will meet your family's emergency needs, and it can consist of preferred, familiar foods used in nutritious daily meals.

Food is available in many different forms. It can be fresh, canned, dehydrated, freeze-dried, instant, frozen, and so on. Some food types are very appropriate for disaster-type emergencies, and some are not at all appropriate. The kind of food (or food style, such as canned, dehydrated, or instant) that you choose to have on hand for an emergency situation should be determined by:

- The amount of water required for preparation.
- The kinds of equipment required for preparation.
- The kind/amount of fuel required for preparation.
- The storage space available in your home.
- The cost.
- Personal tastes.

When water is in short supply, spicy or salty foods should not be part of an emergency food supply.

WATER REQUIREMENTS

Your food choices will either have water already included in them (such as canned foods), or will need to have water added to them to make them edible (like dehydrated or instant foods). If you have to add water to prepare the food you store, you must include an equivalent amount of water to your drinking/food-preparation water supply.

EQUIPMENT REQUIREMENTS

It's highly likely that your regular means of cooking and heating food will be severely restricted. Without power, your kitchen stove may be just another surface to set things on; if the house is a shambles due to earthquake or storm, it may not even be that. Unless you plan ahead with an alternative, cold food will be your only choice. You can, of course, intentionally choose to not arrange for any alternate cooking options. If you do, you'll want to make very sure that you stock food that requires absolutely no cooking and is still edible when cold. When it comes down to it, though, there's a lot to be said in favor of warm food, especially when dealing with unsettling situations. Hot cocoa, for example, just isn't as soothing or calming when it's cold.

The pros and cons of the different emergency stove options are discussed in detail in chapter 25. Compare, for example, a three-burner butane camping stove and a tiny winged-tab stove that burns nickel-sized fuel tablets. You can cook a lot more on a camping stove than on the pellet-fuel stove, but the camping stove and fuel will require ten times more space to store than a three-tab pellet burner, and it will require a greater financial investment also. (Since different foods have different cooking requirements, you should decide how to approach the subject. Do you first acquire your emergency-cooking equipment and then match your emergency food choices to it, or do you select your food choices and let them determine which types of equipment you then need to acquire? Both ways work.)

Keep in mind that your food choices should not require any refrigeration, either before or after preparation. This means you'll have to cook smaller batches, more often, so as to not have any leftovers or spoilage. Nor will meals work that require cooking in the microwave or oven since the premise for needing these nearly ready-to-eat meals is that your electricity will be out for an extended period of time.

FUEL REQUIREMENTS

Once again, you can cook a lot more on larger cooking equipment, so you will have many more food options with it. But the larger the equipment, the more fuel is required. More fuel requires more storage space, more costs, and more upkeep. What is going to work for you?

STORAGE SPACE

Different food forms require different amounts of shelf space to hold them. If your available space is limited, your food choices will be limited also.

COST

Having food on hand for an emergency is possible on any income, from the Stretch-Your-Dollars-to-the-Screaming-Point Budget Plan to the I-Own-a-Gold-Mine-in-Alaska-and-Money-Is-No-Object Plan. Of course, if you are on a tight budget, your options are more limited (in everything, not just emergency preparedness, sadly enough). This just means you will need to be a little more creative, a little more patient, and a little more determined.

PERSONAL TASTES

Last, but not least, your likes and dislikes play a big part in the different kinds of food you will stock up on for emergency purposes. Remember, these should be foods you use regularly and are familiar with; nothing strange or unusual or untried should be on your shelf "for eating in emergencies." You may need to tweak your tastes a little bit, but your disaster-preparedness food should still be comfortable and common. For example, if you are used to eating fresh produce, canned vegetables may be a stretch for your taste buds, but they're still in the recognizable zone. Instant mashed potatoes may be an acceptable power-outage preparedness substitute for homemade mashed potatoes. If canned soup is frequently on the menu at home, then you're in luck because canned soup is a great emergency preparedness food. There are so many readily available foods that fill the bill as food for a disaster you shouldn't have a problem stocking a cupboard with choices that will work for your family.

You need not be resigned to weeks of uninterrupted canned chili or plain SpaghettiOs either. Even with limited stove and fuel options, you can create healthy and satisfying simple meals if you have a nicely stocked preparedness pantry. Planning seven-course sit-down dinners isn't the goal. Control, normalcy, and edible food is. Of course, in a terrible crisis, survival may be the paramount objective. In that case, a can of cold potatoes or tomatoes by candlelight will fill the bill. Hopefully, a preparedness pantry that remains standing will provide more than mere survival. Plan ahead to mix and match the canned and packaged goods you commonly stock in your cupboards to make easy meals during emergency situations. This ensures that, not only are you ready for an emergency, but also that your supplies get used and replaced regularly!

Take a look at some of the recipes in appendix B for ideas to get you started. As an example, canned potatoes, tomatoes, vegetables, and broth combined become a delicious soup. Doesn't that sound better than having a bowl of canned potatoes and a bowl of green beans? Both would keep you alive, but the soup would actually be enjoyable. Disaster foods don't have to be distasteful.

Keeping these points in mind, not every form of food meets the criteria for disaster preparedness. Some food forms are exactly right, some are completely inappropriate, and some are not recommended but could probably be tweaked to work if that's all you had. Here is a brief rundown on several different categories of food and whether they will work in emergency situations. Mix and match from the different categories to get variety in your diet.

CANNED GOODS

Canned goods—which also include products commercially processed in jars like pickles or peanut butter and jelly (the real staff of life!)—make up the majority of items in most people's pantries. A can of this and a can of that are reliable conveniences. Canned goods are an excellent way to have a stock of soups, pasta, meat, beans, juice, milk, fruits, and vegetables on hand for use in any emergency. They usually don't require any additional water, and many canned goods can be eaten straight from the can without being cooked if necessary. We're familiar with them and used to eating them. In a stressful situation, it would be one less new thing to have to deal with. They are readily available in stores, come in an enormous variety of options, and are affordable. In fact, if you haven't looked closely lately, canned foods have blossomed far beyond your basic green beans or tomato soup. You could use the soup aisle alone to stock a preparedness pantry and never eat the same thing for weeks on end. It seems when I was a child, there were three kinds of soup: chicken noodle, tomato, and vegetable. Now you can find entire meals in a can: steak and roasted potatoes, sirloin steak and vegetables, hearty chicken and rotini—and that's just the soup aisle! Nearby, you can also find an entire selection of ready-to-eat pasta meals.

You'll also find complete meals combining canned goods and packaged goods. These may or may not be a good choice for emergency preparedness planning. Before you stock your shelves with these, yummy as they look, make sure that they can be prepared in a limited power situation. If it needs to be baked, it won't work. If it can be prepared completely on a stovetop, it will probably adapt to being prepared on a camp stove or sterno stove.

Under proper storage conditions, most canned goods remain usable for at least eighteen to twenty-four months. This includes the new soft cans; soft-foil packaging now contains products you are used to finding as canned goods. You'll probably be seeing many more of these as time goes by. The same storage principles apply to these as to metal cans. Date/put older cans in front. Remember the rules for knowing when you've had a can too long (see chapter 5, Keys to Storage). One very important thing to keep in mind: A manual can opener is a must! You don't want to be stuck hacking away at your can of pork and beans with a hammer and screwdriver by candlelight because your electric can opener won't work.

In case you're tempted to save a step and heat your canned goods directly in the can, make sure you open the can first. If you don't, the pressure buildup inside the can will cause the seams to split, or worse, cause the can to explode. Either way, you'll have food everywhere and it will be another mess to deal with.

HOME BOTTLED/HOME CANNED

Home-bottled fruits are appropriate for use in emergencies since they are ready to eat without further cooking, and they don't require water to prepare.

In fact, they contain liquid that can be considered as part of your water supply. Home-bottled vegetables are acceptable also, with the caveat that they must be boiled before eating to destroy potential botulism toxins: ten minutes for watery food, such as green beans in water, and twenty minutes for foods with a thick or solid consistency, like creamed corn or pumpkin. If untreated, botulism poisoning is usually fatal.

The down side of food in glass jars is that you run the risk of the bottles breaking during the crisis (if the emergency should be an earthquake, for example).

PACKAGED GOODS

Another category with preparedness potential and great variety is packaged goods. Everything that's dry and in a package falls into this category, including puddings, macaroni and cheese, cereal, Tuna Helper, dry soup mixes, dry milk, and so on. Almost all items require some liquid to make them ready-to-eat, but that's easily countered by storing more than the minimum requirements of water. Some require cooking, and that can be fine also, providing you have planned ahead and acquired a source for cooking that doesn't require electricity (see chapter 25). If you don't have a cooking source and don't intend to get one, these are probably not the best choices for you. If you do, though, packaged goods are a great choice. They store well (under proper conditions), are generally affordable, are familiar, and are readily available in any grocery store.

MIXES

Although these do require some cooking, biscuit and pancake mixes are great to have on hand. During the aftermath of a disaster, there probably won't be sufficient fuel or proper equipment to be baking raised yeast breads or baked goods. But pancakes or crepes can take the place of bread in sandwiches, and such, and are filling and easy to fix. They can be quickly prepared with a minimal use of fuel, as long as you're prepared with a cooking source and the fuel to use it. If you prepare broth, soup, or stew, dumplings can be added as your "bread" without the additional use of fuel. You could also cook biscuit mix in hot oil to make scones or fritters.

INSTANT

Almost anything can be found in instant form: rice, puddings, cereals, soups, and meals (such as cups-of-noodles or cups-of-casseroles). Usually, these foods are completely or partially processed before they are packaged so you have very little cooking to do to make them ready to eat. They require a minimal amount of fuel and a minimal amount of water. Therefore, they meet the criteria for foods to use in emergency situations. Besides, instant chocolate pudding is the next best thing to chocolate chips to help you make it though several days without power.

SHELF-STABLE FOODS

Shelf-stable refers to "retort" processing, which stabilizes the foods so that they require no refrigeration. Usually the foods are packaged in plastic pouches (soft cans). Many are marketed as microwave meals and are found on supermarket shelves. You can even purchase milk in little boxes that can sit on your shelf until you want to drink it. These are great as an emergency source of food since most are completely ready to eat as is. Of course, they might be more palatable if they were heated, but cooking is usually optional.

MREs

MRE stands for "meals ready to eat." The current version of army C rations, MREs are the shelf-stable foods (which require no refrigeration) designed for the armed services. Most come as a single-serving entrée in a multilayered foil/plastic pouch that can be stored, under proper conditions, up to ten years. They can be purchased as individual entres, or packaged as a complete meal, with cookies, crackers and cheese, and the like, plus an MRE heater—a single-use chemically activated packet that heats your entrée. MRE heaters can also be purchased separately, if you don't want the complete meal, but would still like a way to warm your MRE entrées. They can also be heated in their pouch in a pot of hot water, or they can be eaten cold if necessary. Some varieties taste much better than others. Try one or two first to see if they meet your taste test. You could also ask some members of the armed forces which ones taste best. They'll probably have firm opinions! You can usually find all these in army/navy surplus stores, preparedness stores, or in the camping section of sporting goods stores. Be aware as you shop for them that the cases or units you see offered for sale are probably all the same item. Seventy-two pouches of unrelieved scrambled eggs could be a pretty depressing discovery when it comes time to eat them. The price may be great by the case, but it would probably be a better deal to pay a little more and buy them individually to ensure variety, or find a few friends to trade with.

COMMERCIALLY-DRIED FOODS

Readily available dried fruits are a good nutritional addition to your disaster pantry as long as you're willing to eat and replace them regularly until then. Commercially dried fruit retains a lot of its moisture. That makes it good to eat but also gives it a relatively short shelf life. The familiar raisins, apples, apricots, and other dried fruits fall into this category. Don't confuse dried food with dehydrated food. Dehydrated food is hard and brittle. Dried fruit is moist

A reporter went to Waveland, Mich., a few days after it was devastated by Hurricane Katrina. He had this to say about MREs: "An evening at the meetinghouse was an experience of survival, where even the most simple of human needs is a project. We dined on military-supplied MRE's, which defy opening but with a sharp instrument. This large-book-size packet contains a heating packet into which water is poured and it heats the main course, a solidly filling substance defined as such things as Chicken Tetrazzini or, my choice, an enchilada. It also has within its multiplicity of packets a cookie, crackers and cheese, refried beans, punch powder, candy and a wonderful towelette. A four-wick candle in a can illuminated the banquet around which, beneath the now-visible stars, conversations became intimate as people wondered of their uncertain future."

—John L. Hart, Deseret Morning News, Church News, September 10, 2005, 7–12

and pliable. You usually can find it on your grocer's shelves in plastic bags. You can make dried fruit last longer by storing it, in its package, in airtight jars. It will also last longer if teenagers don't know it's there.

Beef jerky is a reasonably good choice for preparedness also, although its saltiness may cause increased thirst. You can extend its shelf life, just like you do with dried fruit, by storing it in airtight containers. Make it a point to not mix *hot and spicy* flavors with regular flavors. If left very long in the same container, they all will be *hot and spicy*.

FREEZE-DRIED FOOD

Freeze-dried foods are sometimes referred to as home-storage foods but you are more likely to recognize them as backpacking foods. You may have eaten them as the raspberries in your breakfast cereal without knowing you were eating a freeze-dried food. Even complete meals are available in freeze-dried form.

Freeze-dried foods meet all of the parameters for the Category-Three-preparedness-food niche. They are easy to prepare. They can be quickly reconstituted with hot, warm, or, if necessary, cold water. The backpacking versions can even be prepared and served in the foil pouches that they come in. They have a long-term, stable shelf life, though the foil pouches are susceptible to insects and rodents. To make sure the product is there when you need it, you'd want to put the whole pouch, intact, into insect-proof containers. If you buy it in cans to begin with, make sure you use tight-fitting lids once the can is opened. They require some water for preparation, but it is minimal. (Nevertheless, add that amount to your water supply.) The best part is that they taste great. (Freeze-dried ice cream is fabulous!) Cost is the main disadvantage. If this were all you were putting away for an emergency of several weeks duration, it could be prohibitively expensive. If money is not an issue, freeze-dried food is a great way to go. If you're watching your budget, consider them for a meal or two.

NOT RECOMMENDED, BUT USABLE IF YOU HAVE TO

Some forms of food just don't fit the parameters set out for a disaster-preparedness pantry. Remember, food for getting through the aftermath of a disaster should require little or no cooking, little or no preparation, and no refrigeration. That said, some patently inapplicable forms of food could be forced to comply if they have to, and if you plan ahead to make them work. They are still not recommended, but if that's all you have, you needn't go hungry.

Commercially Dehydrated Food

Commercially dehydrated foods can have a place in short-term emergency preparedness situations but they are not particularly the best choice. Proper reconstitution requires lots of water, heat, and time—three things you won't have a lot of in an emergency situation. You would be better off stocking up on canned or packaged ready-to-eat food. However, if this is what you have, either because an emergency caught you unprepared, or because the aftermath of a disaster lasted longer than you had planned for and you've eaten your more suitable foods, there are ways to make dehydrated food work for you in the face of water and fuel shortages. Using thermoses is one of my favorite suggestions. A thermos will allow for more efficient fuel and water usage during crisis times than an open pan. Dehydrated foods that are placed in thermoses with hot water are reconstituted and ready to use in just a few hours. For example, peaches reconstituted in one thermos and oats in another can be combined for a very good meal. (Add a sprinkling of cinnamon and brown sugar, top it all with evaporated milk, and you have a delicious breakfast any day, not just during disaster times!) See appendix F for full details on how to use a thermos to prepare foods for the tough times after a crisis.

Whole Grains, Beans, Seeds

Whole grains, beans, and seeds should be an integral part of the Category One–Worst-Case, and Category Two–Provident Living segments of personal preparedness, as well as the mainstay of what is considered to be a very healthy diet. Since the preparation of whole grains and beans requires time and fuel for soaking and simmering, however, they hardly seem to fit the parameters of a Category Three, or short-term emergency situation. Or do they?

If you rarely or never eat whole grains and beans under normal circumstances, skip this whole little section now. Don't even consider using them in the aftermath of a disaster. If you're not used to eating

them, the results could be dreadful, physically. However, if grains and beans are an integral part of your regular diet, you don't have to totally give up on using them in times of emergency cooking. They should not be considered the mainstay of your emergency preparedness food, but they can certainly be a supporting part. There are a few solutions that will allow you to prepare these foods, even with cooking and fuel limitations. (Of course, you'll need to provide for additional fuel and water supplies if you're planning on using grains and beans. Make it a part of your plan.)

The supermarket can offer several options for keeping healthy food in your emergency preparedness diet. Canned beans can be substituted for home-soaked-and-simmered dry beans, and a good variety are available. Instant rice comes in both white and brown versions. You can make pancakes, dumplings, or fry bread out of whole-grain flour and mixes. If you have a hand grinder, you can crack grains for cooked cereal. The finer the grind, the more quickly it cooks.

THE THERMOS TO THE RESCUE AGAIN

This is another situation where an ordinary thermos jug can make a food work that would otherwise not be appropriate. Whole wheat or any other grain prepared in a thermos with hot water in the evening is warm and ready to eat in the morning. Here's how to do it. Measure whole grain kernels into a thermos bottle. Add very hot, but not boiling, water to the bottle. (Boiling water can cause plastic thermos bottles to melt and can shatter glass-lined bottles.) Cap the thermos tightly and wait. In about eight hours you'll have warm whole wheat cereal. And remember, hot grains are not just for breakfast. You can mix and match canned goods with thermos-prepared grain for greater flavor, variety, and nutrition—beef stew over hot rice, for example. Or, add lentils to canned soup or broth for a more-filling meal, and so on.

Pasta could also be prepared by allowing it to soak in very hot water in a thermos. Remember, it's really a grain—just transformed. Pasta in a thermos only takes thirty to forty-five minutes to be ready to use, and requires much less water and fuel than preparing it in an open pan.

SPROUTS AND SPROUTING

If, after the initial shock of your crisis situation has passed, you can see that it's going to be quite a while before your utilities are restored, you might consider sprouting as a replacement for the supermarket produce department on a tiny scale. Since it takes several days to go from seed to edible sprout, you'd better not rely on it to be the bulk of your diet. However, after a week of eating out of cans and dry packages, a little fresh green food could be a welcome treat. See chapter 11 for complete instructions on turning your grain into green.

ENERGY BARS, COMPRESSED-FOOD BARS

From a preparedness perspective, energy bars and granola bars are more often thought of in connection with the fourth category of emergency preparedness: 72-hour survival and emergency evacuations. However, they can be a part of short-term emergency preparedness planning. Some could function as breakfast bars or light lunches. Or they could stretch your emergency food supplies if you planned for one main meal a day and filled in with a variety of grain or energy bars. They have the advantage of being small and compact. If space is at a premium in your home, they could be a good choice. On the downside, our society is used to substantial meals on a regular schedule. I'm afraid that if all you had to eat was an energy bar for breakfast, you'd find it woefully inadequate before too much time had passed, and downright depressing if energy bars were all you had to rely on for days or weeks. Even though that energy bar offers 2000 percent of all your dietary needs, it's not as satisfying as eating real food. It would be better to plan grain bars or energy bars to be a part of, but not the whole plan for your crisis menu.

Although it is possible to tweak many different foods to fit the parameters of a disaster-preparedness situation, your best bet is to plan ahead with food that fits the bill from the start. If it requires little or no cooking, little or no preparation, and no refrigeration, then your choice is appropriate and you'll be in good shape if the time ever comes that you have to rely on it.

CHAPTER TWENTY-TWO

STAYING WARM WITHOUT A FURNACE

Murphy's law states, "If anything can go wrong, it will." There must be a corollary somewhere that adds, "If something bad is going to happen, it will happen in the most inconvenient place and at the most inconvenient time." Like winter. During a cold snap. When you have a house full of company.

Actually, it's logical that disasters are more prevalent in the winter. Winter weather, storms, hurricanes, tornadoes, floods, and so on, are the cause of many emergencies. So it makes sense, when getting prepared, to be ready to take on bad weather in addition to all the other problems you may face during a crisis. Then, if half your house is whirled off to Munchkin Land in the dead of winter, you'll be warm while you pick up the pieces.

It could be a real challenge to stay warm when the furnace hasn't worked for days and there is no other heat source. Some of the suggestions in this chapter are just common sense, but it's amazing how your mind can go blank in times of stress. Having the ideas all in one place may help. Other ideas are a new twist on old supplies that could make a major difference when it's winter indoors as well as outdoors. I can remember one winter when I was little—we lived in a house that was so cold that the windows had ice an inch thick at the bottom of the glass on the inside. It can get mighty cold in a house.

As an awareness reminder, be especially considerate of babies and the elderly who are living with you, or the elderly who may be living alone near you. If they are not able to move around, they can become very cold, very quickly.

These are a few ideas on how to take advantage of your body's natural heat to keep you warm.

BLANKETS AND QUILTS

Most people have at least a minimal supply of blankets, decorative comforters, and quilts on hand. You can wrap up in a comforter or quilt. A quilt is different than a blanket. It will have batting, or stuffing,

A few years ago in Utah there was a power outage in winter lasting several days. A mother and two small children lived in an area particularly hard-hit by the cold front. The mother related that it was as cold inside her home as it was outside, with temperatures in the twentys during the nights. She only had a few blankets for each bed, which were sufficient when the heater worked, but woefully inadequate without it. So she put her children in two pair of pajamas each, piled all the blankets in the house onto her queen-sized bed, and put the kids in it. That's where they stayed and played for three days until the power came back on.

The 2000 ice storm caught us without an alternate heat source. We had to go and live with our daughter for eight days
—W. M., Bonham, Tex.

and is created in layers, which increases its warmth capacity. Quilts usually have more warming qualities than blankets, though several layered blankets can have the same effect as a good, heavy quilt. However, I'm describing an old-fashioned quilt. You can go into almost any department store and buy an inexpensive quilt to decorate your bed. These are not the same thing. These are usually created just for decoration, with a skimpy layer of batting sandwiched between two layers of cloth. They will make your bedroom pretty but they won't keep you any warmer than a single blanket. Old-fashioned quilts are far superior in terms of weight, warmth, and quality. However, they may be difficult to find anymore. You can make one yourself, or you can probably find nice, heavy quilts in boutiques or specialty quilt shops. What you can readily find, though, is the modern-day equivalent to the old-fashioned quilt: down comforters. These may even be superior to quilts because they can be wonderfully warm without being heavy. A down comforter has a filling of duck or goose down and/or feathers, with stitching holding the cover and filling in place. They are usually white, and you purchase separate decorative covers to match your decor, as well as to keep the comforter clean.

Often you will see what appear to be ordinary bedspreads advertised as comforters. These may or may not be warmer than blankets or store-bought quilts. These are designed like store-bought quilts, in that they have two layers of fabric with batting sandwiched in between. However, in some cases, the inner batting is much thicker and more durable than in cheaper quilts. They are probably better than blankets, but not quite as good as a heavy quilt or down comforter.

If you are an electric blanket person, think ahead and have a backup plan in mind because you may not have enough regular nonelectric blankets to stay warm when the electricity is out. If you don't think you have enough room to store extra blankets, consider laying blankets out flat between your box springs and your mattress when they're not in use.

BLANKET ROBE

It's all well and good to say you can just "wrap up in a blanket" when your agenda includes reading a book or other sedentary activities. But what about when you still have to keep on the go at home and get things done? Trying to get around while hanging on to a bulky blanket is cumbersome and could prove to be dangerous—so use your creativity and adapt a blanket into a robe! The easy fold-and-pin directions in appendix G will quickly and efficiently transform any blanket into wearable warmth. You most likely already have a bathrobe hanging on a hook in your bathroom, but it wasn't designed to keep you warm when you're without power for days on end. This quick-and-easy blanket robe is just the ticket to ensure that every family member has a cozy extra layer of wearable warmth. A blanket robe allows freedom of movement, yet it stays warmly in place, unlike a blanket, which is just draped around your shoulders and is continually falling off. A nice thing about them is that blanket robes are temporary. You don't have to buy and store another bulky item in order to be prepared. Each cold and heaterless morning, you can take the blanket off your bed, quickly pin it into shape, and go warmly about your business. Then, in the evening, you remove the safety pins and it resumes its original occupation as a blanket on the bed to snuggle under. I have to add a disclaimer here: wearing a blanket robe won't put you on anybody's best-dressed list. Instead of looking like a fashion plate, you may look like a round dumpling on a plate—but hey, you'll be warm!

SLEEPING BAGS

If you are used to thinking of sleeping bags only as part of someone's camping gear, think again. Sleeping bags can serve a dual purpose, camping for the fun times, and emergency preparedness for the not-so-fun times. Sleeping bags are a great warmth source. They are readily available in most sporting goods stores and variety stores, and they usually come in a huge range of warmth ratings and price ranges.

If you should decide to purchase one, check for its cold-weather rating. The lower the weather rating (five degrees, ten degrees, twenty degrees below zero,

> *Sleeping bags can serve a dual purpose, camping for the fun times, and emergency preparedness for the not-so-fun times.*

and so on.) the colder the weather can be and you'll still stay warm. If your sleeping bags are rated more for summer camping, you can make them warmer by adding a blanket inside the sleeping bag! An extra blanket inside the sleeping bag will keep you warmer than the same blanket laid on top of the sleeping bag. Sleeping bags can be used on top of a bed in a regular bedroom, or they can be used on the floor wherever your heat source is, if you have one. An air mattress or pad will make sleeping on the floor in a sleeping bag a lot more bearable or, lacking an air mattress, you can lay your couch cushions on the floor and put your sleeping bag on top of them in whichever room has the heat source. During the day, sleeping bags can be opened up and used as a wrap, the same as a quilt.

Should you be caring for someone who is bedridden, a sleeping bag could serve as a cocoon for added warmth during the day.

If you haven't checked the condition of your sleeping bags in a while, now would be a good time to do so. If a Boy Scout took it on a weekend camping trip, or a giggly girl last used it at a slumber party, you may have surprises you weren't counting on. You can live with the dry leaves, twigs, dirt, and candy wrappers (annoying but fixable). However, surprises like rips, tears, and broken zippers could compound an emergency situation. Make sure your sleeping bags (and blankets or quilts, for that matter) are in good shape now, while they aren't needed desperately.

EMERGENCY BLANKETS

You've probably seen the small, compact, metalized emergency blankets advertised or sold in sporting goods or emergency preparedness stores. It seems unreasonable that something that small and thin could keep a person warm, but they do. NASA designed the technology for use in the space program, and it works by containing almost all of your body heat. Their drawback is that they don't "feel" like a blanket. You don't get the same physical and emotional comfort wrapping up in foil that you do wrapping up in a regular blanket or quilt. However, I recommend them because when you combine them with a regular blanket (with the blanket next to you and the emergency blanket on top of that), you get the best of both worlds. They aren't designed for long-term use; they tear fairly easily and aren't washable. You would only use them for an emergency situation and then replace them. But they are very inexpensive and so small you could toss half a dozen in the back of a drawer and still have room for socks and underwear.

The next step up in disposable—emergency blankets is sometimes called a survival-emergency blanket or emergency all-weather blanket. These are reusable, waterproof, and more expensive than the ones previously mentioned, but still affordable. They are insulated and layered with plastic film, aluminum, fabric, and plastic. These blankets reflect 80 to 90 percent body heat. You can find them in sporting goods stores or well-stocked camping departments.

Paramedics and hospitals also use emergency blankets, but these are a different thing altogether. Medical emergency blankets are just thin paper with about the same benefits and drawbacks as using very large, thick paper towels as a blanket. Don't mistake these for the recommended metalized emergency blankets.

CHEMICAL HAND AND FEET WARMERS

It seems that if you can keep your hands, feet, and head warm, the rest of your body will follow along. Hats work for your head, and now you can buy small chemical hand and feet warmers to warm your outer extremities. To activate, you just squeeze and shake. These items are small enough to fit into your glove or shoe, and once activated, will provide heat for eight to twelve hours. You can drop them into a pair of slippers, or into your pocket if you're not wearing gloves, or tuck them inside a waistband. They are a one-use only item, but since they are relatively inexpensive (usually less than $2 per pair), you could easily keep several days' worth or more on hand (no pun intended).

A second renewable version of chemical body warmers is available in sporting goods stores or in the section of drugstores where you find ice packs and heating pads. These look like square bags of clear liquid, yet when you flex a metal button inside the pack, it causes a chemical reaction that changes the look of the liquid and creates heat. These body warmers range in size from hand size to heating-pad size, and they also are reasonably priced. To renew the pack, you place it in boiling water for five to twenty minutes, depending on the size. That may or may not be a problem if the power is out. (Do you really want to float your hand warmer in your soup on your sterno stove?)

HOT-WATER BOTTLE

An old-fashioned hot-water bottle is a very practical item to provide added warmth. In a situation where heat sources are limited, a hot-water bottle could be just the item you need to tuck under a blanket or quilt. (No electric blankets, remember?) It's a little extra boost that would be a welcome relief to a cold person, especially for hands or feet. When properly filled with hot water and wrapped in a towel to prevent burning, a hot-water bottle retains its heat for more than an hour.

If you don't own one and have never seen one, and you're looking for them on a shelf, you're not going to find a bottle. "Hot-water bottle" is really a misnomer. "Hot-water rubber pouch" is probably more descriptive. They lay flat and do not stand upright. They have a narrow neck and a corkscrew plug. You will more likely find them in the health-and-beauty-aid department of the store, rather than with the sporting goods.

If you haven't filled a hot water bottle for a long time, or even ever, here's a brief rundown on how to do it. Prop the bottle bladder in the sink (or in a large bowl to catch leaks, drips or overflow if water is in short supply). Grasp it around the neck and insert a small funnel in the opening. You may wish to wear an oven mitt or cover your hand with a towel to avoid burns from splashing water. The water should be very hot but not boiling. Fill the bottle only half full. It will bulge at the bottom. Squeeze out most of the excess air and tightly screw in the stopper. Dry the bottle, if necessary, and wrap it in a towel. Keep in mind that hot-water bottles aren't supposed to be used under anyone; they're not made to sit on nor to lie on. They are not that strong, and they can pop—like an expensive water balloon. If you are heating water on an emergency stove for the hot-water bottle, heat more than you absolutely need, then fill one or more thermoses with the remaining hot water. When the water in the hot-water bottle cools significantly, you can refill it with warmer water from one of the thermoses. This saves time and fuel. (Reserve the cooled water to be heated again if water is at a premium.)

If you inherited your hot-water bottle from your great-grandmother years ago, or if you've had one hiding in the dark recesses of your closet since you moved in the last decade, you need to check it for cracking and leaks. Rubber deteriorates with age. To check for leaks, look it over carefully first. If you don't see any obvious cracks then fill it full of water (it doesn't have to be hot), tighten the plug, hold it over a sink, and squeeze it. If it drips or explodes, it needs to be replaced. If not, it probably still has some life left in it.

LAYERED CLOTHING

If you live in a climate that gets cold in the winter, you will already have coats and outdoor wear on hand. You're better off if you can stay warm in your home without wearing outdoor clothing all the time. Reserve them for when you need to go outside. You will want the additional warmth of a coat at that time. Should it be wet and storming, it is important for the indoor clothing to remain as dry as possible.

Several lighter layers of clothing will provide more warmth than one thick layer. Layering even everyday clothes will trap body warmth. Thermal underwear is a good thing to start with (or at least a T-shirt if you don't have thermals). Add sweatpants and a sweatshirt. Top those with a pair of pants and a flannel shirt. Add a sweater or jacket. Fleece is a good choice for layering because it keeps insulating, even if it gets damp. On your feet, start with a thin pair of socks, followed by a thick pair of socks—maybe even two; thermal socks if you have them. Finish up your feet with warm slippers when you're inside and dry boots when you're outside. Wear a hat all the time. Hats help trap body heat, which is important since almost 90 percent of the body's heat is lost though the head. Hats are especially important for toddlers, babies, or someone who is bedridden. Keep their heads covered, particularly at night while sleeping. Have several pairs of gloves, some for inside that can stay dry, and a pair for outdoors where they may get wet. You can keep adding layer after layer of clothing until your arms stick out straight and you can't sit

> *Several lighter layers of clothing will provide more warmth than one thick layer.*

down. You may look a bit funny, but who cares? Do what you have to do to stay warm. If you are moving around and remaining active, you'll be creating body heat and will probably need fewer layers than a sedentary person. Don't hesitate to wear warm socks, long underwear, and a warm cap to bed if it's really cold.

Avoid tight clothing when you're layering. You may be tempted to use a pair of tight jeans or a form-fitting T-shirt as your first layer, but that's really counterproductive. Tight-fitting clothing inhibits circulation so the body won't warm itself efficiently. Plus, layering works by creating pockets of heated air. Tight clothing doesn't leave room for pockets of warm air to be trapped for insulation. Several lightweight loose layers are best. Garments that fit snugly at the wrists, ankles, and neck (where warm air might escape) will provide better protection and insulation. Use common sense though. Obviously, if all you have is tight jeans and T-shirts, tight clothing with a blanket is better than no clothing with a blanket.

It's tough to keep growing children supplied with winter gear, even on a normal basis. One idea that may help to keep them prepared for a cold-weather emergency is to stash away some warm sweat suits that are several sizes too big. For more than one child, use the one-size-fits-all rule. It's better to have them warm in clothes that are much too big than cold in clothes that are much too small because they grew a lot more than you expected. It is more important for your children to be warm than stylish. Give some thought to your teenagers too. Because they want to be "cool," teenagers often refuse to wear winter clothing, no matter how cold it is. While this is irritating (for a parent), it might be a big problem in an emergency—not because they won't wear the warm clothing, but because when they really need it, they might

The more absorbent a garment is, the more it will allow perspiration to evaporate from the skin. This is essential for body warmth. Whenever possible, choose fabrics that will allow body moisture to pass through. Natural fabrics and acrylics are the best choices for this purpose.

not actually have very much warm clothing. Some large sweatshirts and thermals tucked away on a shelf far back in the closet would be a good idea, just in case. (This might be a good subject for a family discussion—when it's not "cool" to be too cold.)

Depending on your climate and the weather patterns of your area, water may be more of a challenge than snow. Do you face floods or heavy rains? Be prepared for them. In an emergency where you have no electricity to dry wet clothing, steady pouring rain could make your life utterly miserable, particularly if your regular means of transportation is out of commission and you have to do a lot of walking to get around. Plan ahead to be able to stay dry when circumstances require you to leave your home. Rain suits, ponchos, and rain boots are great. Remember to check on these while the sun is shining. Many times they crack, split, and peel as they age, which of course means that they will not function when you need them.

The layering rules for warmth apply in cold, wet conditions as well.

LIVE IN A SMALLER SPACE

If it's very cold and you're not sure of the predicted length of a power outage, cut down on the size of the area you are trying to heat. Live in one room rather than the entire house. Pull all your kids, in-laws, dogs, goldfish, sleeping bags, blankets, and pillows into one room. Do your eating, sleeping, worrying, playing, and reading in that room. Space heaters (the kind designed to be used indoors) are more effective in a small space. It conserves the fuel you have. Even a fireplace will function more efficiently if you are trying to heat just one room, as opposed to an entire house.

Close all the doors, or use a blanket or tarp to cover doorways if there isn't a door. This confines the heat to a smaller area.

To get the blanket to stay in place, pin your tarp/blanket around a wooden stick or PVC pipe and rest the pipe above the door frame on two or three angled nails, or use duct tape to hold the cover in place, though it may peel the paint when you remove it. Be careful. When the emergency is over, a journal entry and a few photographs are a much better reminder of what you've lived through than a ruined paint job.

163

INDOOR TENTS

It's easier to heat a small space than a large one, but what if all you have is a large space? Perhaps you have a fireplace, but it's in a room with a two-story vaulted ceiling. Or the room you are gathering in is too open to contain the heat with blankets over entryways. In this instance consider setting up a freestanding pop tent inside (not requiring stakes in the floor.) The tent would trap and conserve heat—even if it's only body heat. Have you ever been on a crowded dance floor and noticed how hot it gets with 500 bodies milling around? The principle is the same, only without the music, gymnasium, or 500 bodies. The idea is to contain all the heat you can in a small space. If all you could come up with was sleeping bags and some hot-water bottles, you're better off in a small, enclosed space than in a big room. If you've planned ahead with an indoor space heater, all the better. If you have a fireplace, set your tent up in front of it with the tent opening facing the fireplace. Then you could make do with smaller fires and your fuel would last longer.

You see, with a little creativity it is possible to keep warm without having to invite all your neighbors over to do the cha-cha in your living room.

CHAPTER TWENTY-THREE

DEALING WITH THE FLAME FACTOR

Most men and many women work full-time, and struggle to keep up with their families and myriad other obligations in the few remaining hours of the day. Emergency preparedness has a tough time squeezing its way into those precious hours. That means there is very little time, energy, or inclination to revert back to making everything from scratch. You'll find no emphasis in this book on make-it-yourself equipment, which could be tragically unsafe. Nor will people be hunting game, tanning hides, and making lye soap—let alone heading for the hills when times get rough. The majority of us will cope with crises from our homes in the inner city, urban areas, suburbs, or rural areas. We live in a modern world, and we can be prepared in and for a modern world. And that is now easier than ever to do.

PRACTICAL AND ADAPTABLE CHOICES

A short walk through a well-stocked sporting goods, emergency preparedness, or discount department store is all that's necessary to discover numerous options available to help you care for yourself in a crisis. It could take volumes to evaluate the pros and cons of each piece of equipment and every gadget on the market that could apply to preparedness, so I'm not going to do that here. Instead, in the following chapters I will discuss the choices that are the most practical and adaptable for the greatest majority of people.

Practicality and safety are of particular importance in preparedness areas that deal with the flame factor. Dealing with the aftermath of a crisis is a lot more than just "indoor camping." The everyday, mundane processes of cooking, staying warm, and

having light change considerably when interrupted by the uncertainties of a crisis, especially when exacerbated by fear. Nothing is normal. Nothing is quick. Nothing is automatic.

SAFETY FIRST

Many assume that all camping gear automatically adapts to emergency preparedness usage in times of crisis. That could prove to be a dangerous assumption if you don't take into account the safety limitations of that gear. There are many camping items that are designed to be used outdoors only and could prove to be dangerous or deadly if used improperly indoors. For example, fueled stoves and lanterns can give off low levels of toxic fumes during use. When operated outdoors, this isn't any problem. However, if used indoors in a closed room (as could be likely if it is cold or stormy outside), these fumes could cause illness or even death, if sufficiently concentrated. Fueled camping equipment should only be used with proper and sufficient ventilation at all times. It doesn't matter how cold you think it is outdoors, open a window a few inches so that there is a cross-flow of fresh air!

If you are purchasing new equipment for emergency preparedness (or for camping that you intend to have double for emergency preparedness if necessary), choose equipment that indicates on the directions that it is appropriate for indoor use. In general, propane or butane are the safest fuels for indoor usage. You'll find more about that later, in chapter 24, Fuel Storage Guidelines. If you already have camping equipment on hand, I suggest that you evaluate the kind and condition of it. Make sure that all gaskets and safety devices are in place and functioning properly. If you question its safety in the slightest, replace it. Don't take chances with your life. If you can't provide adequate ventilation in a room (for example, if your kitchen doesn't have a window), only use fueled equipment outdoors, on a patio, porch, or even in a driveway.

If you plan on using an open-flame source for heat, cooking, or light, figure out where you will put it when it is in use. Normally, you might think that the middle of the kitchen table or some other central place would be the best spot. However, if that table is the center of most family activities, then that might not be the most practical plan after all. Identify possible safe places that are solid, stable, and out of the path of a lot of movement or activity, then put your open-flame light source there. Remember to use caution, and always have working fire extinguishers close at hand, just in case.

THE ESSENTIAL FIRE EXTINGUISHER

Safety becomes even more important under disaster situations, when assistance from local government may not be available. Your local fire department may not be able to reach you during a disaster. Be careful. Be Careful. BE CAREFUL! Anytime you have to use any sort of flame for heating, cooking, or light, keep working fire extinguishers within easy reach. It's important that you be absolutely fanatical about

safety during emergency situations!

Fire extinguishers don't last forever without regular upkeep, so if you protected your home by buying a fire extinguisher back when Jimmy Carter was president and haven't given it a thought since then, you should stop feeling quite so safe. Extinguishers should be replaced or recharged regularly whether they've been used or not. Never, never test your fire extinguisher by spraying it. Using your fire extinguisher even once, even for only a few seconds, renders it unusable until it's recharged, so have fire extinguishers all around your house, and keep them accessible. Know how to use them, and make sure everyone in your family knows how to use them, but don't use them until you need them.

CARBON MONOXIDE DETECTOR

In addition to working fire extinguishers, every level of your home should have one or more carbon monoxide detectors, not just for disaster purposes, but also to avert preventable tragedies every day. They should also be considered as absolutely essential emergency preparedness equipment. During an emergency, when things are topsy-turvy and you may be using unfamiliar supplies, gear, and fuel, you must take every possible safety precaution to safeguard your family. Carbon monoxide detectors are vital! Battery-operated models are available, or you can

---

Different fire extinguishers are designed to put out different types of fires. Check the ratings before you buy.

Class A: *For fires fueled by ordinary materials like burning paper, wood, cardboard, or plastics.*
Class B: *For fires involving flammable or combustible liquids, like gasoline, kerosene, and solvents.*
Class C: *For fires involving electricity or electrical equipment, like*

appliances, switches, or power tools. Do not use water on electrical fires due to the risk of electrical shock.
Class D: *For fires fueled by combustible metals, rarely used for personal/home use.*
Class K: *For kitchen fires. This class was added in 1998.*

A standard ABC fire extinguisher is recommended for home usage. See Appendix J for more information on when and how to use your extinguisher.

have them permanently installed into your electrical system (with battery backup for times of power loss).

Fire extinguishers, fire alarms, and carbon monoxide detectors are three things that should be in everyone's homes all the time, not just in case of major emergencies. These three little things, which cost less than $30 each, can save lives and keep minor little emergencies from turning into major ones. If you do nothing else to be prepared, install a fire extinguisher, alarm, and carbon monoxide detector in your home today.

For any piece of emergency preparedness equipment, always follow the manufacturer's directions to the letter. If you're not completely confident in how a particular item works, take the time before the need arises to get proper instructions. Ask a competent representative at a reputable sporting goods store or emergency preparedness outlet for instructions, and then practice until it is easy for you to use. If you know absolutely nothing about camping or emergency equipment, take a reconnaissance trip through a large sporting goods store or two. Ask questions, and then ask more questions. Ask for recommendations. Find out the pros and cons of different pieces of equipment and the fuels they require. Make informed decisions based on facts.

One day without power can be fun, two days an adventure, and then we want to wave a magic wand and have everything return to normal. This is when you enter a danger zone. Open flames, short tempers, and frustration do not combine to create safe circumstances. Be aware, be careful, and be safe.

CHAPTER TWENTY-FOUR

FUEL STORAGE GUIDELINES

Most of the equipment used in emergency situations is dependent on some sort of fuel to make it function. Without fuel, the fanciest lantern in the world may as well be used as a doorstop or a boat anchor, since it won't be able to be used for light. Many different kinds of fuel are available, most of which are dangerous if not properly cared for. So, be careful! You don't want to add insult to injury by setting your house on fire in the middle of Hurricane Whosit.

The following are some general guidelines to show you what your options are, and how to care for your gear properly. The guidelines apply to emergency fuels whether used for cooking, heat, or light, though not all fuels can be used for all purposes.

FIREWOOD

Wood, in many areas of the country, is a plentiful and accessible fuel. The heating value of properly prepared wood compares quite favorably with other fuels, depending on the efficiency of your fireplace or heating unit. It's hard to beat as a source of heat in an emergency since it doesn't require electricity or natural gas. However, not a lot of apartment complexes, high-rises, or condos provide room to stack even a small mountain of firewood outside your patio door, so it won't be an option for everyone.

Wood is sold, most often, by the cord or fraction of a cord. A cord is 128 cubic feet when the wood is neatly stacked in a line or row. A standard cord would be eight feet long, four feet wide, and four feet high. How long a cord of wood will burn has so many variables that I can't begin to give even a ballpark figure. It depends on the type of wood, the dryness of the wood, the size logs the wood is cut into, the humidity of your area, how many hours a day you'll be using your fireplace, and so on. A general rule is that hardwood burns much longer and better than softwood, though what you buy is more determined by where you live than what you want. Hardwood is more readily available in the eastern United States and softwood in the west. One way to determine how much is enough would be to talk with neighbors who have burned wood to see what results they have had, and what kind of wood is available in your area. You can also talk to a firewood dealer. In many areas, particularly in the fall, signs advertising wood for sale appear on message boards, or on fences, or in newspaper classified ads. The yellow pages are also a source for firewood dealers (look under "Firewood"). If you have a chain saw, pickup, and time and energy, you can usually find opportunities to cut your own wood too.

The only firewood you may be familiar with is the neatly shrink-wrapped, uniformly sized bundles at the supermarket. It would be prohibitively expensive to buy a winter's worth of firewood this way, or even a month's worth for emergency preparedness purposes. If you only want fires three or four times a year for the fun of it, supermarket firewood is fine. Any more than that, and especially if you want firewood for preparedness's sake, buy it by the cord, partial cord, or pickup load.

> I saw a license plate that had me puzzled for a while. It said "4x4x8." The light dawned when I noticed the make of the car. It was a Honda Accord.

Some firewood needs to stand for several months to be dry enough to burn effectively, so don't wait until Halloween to obtain the wood you want to stay warm with at Thanksgiving. Once you have wood stacked and drying on the patio or out in the North Forty, keep it dry! Cover it with tarps or heavy plastic to protect it from the ravages of Mother Nature. Waterlogged wood is difficult to burn, and is prone to deterioration and rot. Rotten wood crumbles, smokes, and gives off very little heat. Be aware that creepy crawlies like black widow spiders are snug and secure in your woodpile. Always wear gloves when picking up an armload of wood!

PRESSED-WOOD LOGS

Pressed-wood logs fall into the "expensive firewood" category as well. They store and stack the same as firewood. Each log burns for about an hour. Although expensive, both the shrink-wrapped bundles and pressed-wood logs are an option if you live in a major metropolitan city and can't find a reasonably priced firewood source. To save the most money, buy them by the case in discount department stores instead of individually at the corner convenience store. And, of course, watch for sales and better prices at the end of the season when spring comes.

NEWSPAPER LOGS

Did you know you could make your own "logs" out of newspaper? See appendix H for step-by-step instructions for this project. It's an economical way to recycle. After all, you have already paid for the paper. Newspaper logs can be stacked and stored the same way you stack wood logs. It doesn't really take very long, and you can build your "log pile" all year long.

COAL

Since coal burns hotter than wood, coal is an option only if you have a firebrick-lined fireplace or a stove specifically designed for coal. Even then, coal has distinct disadvantages, as well as advantages. Coal fires are not as easy to start as wood fires, and burning coal requires patience. You must follow a specific and regular procedure of loading the coal, shaking or raking it, adjusting it so it's just right, and so on. If you don't follow the correct procedure, your fire will go out. Coal is dirty to handle and clean up. You must also have a plan to deal with the ashes

when your fire is out. (This goes for wood ashes also.) Ashes must be stone cold before you put them in a trash can, lest there be a tiny, hidden spark remaining that could set a major fire. Years ago, it was the policy of our local garbage company to not pick up trash containing ashes of any sort until they had seen them on the road side for a second week. That way they knew for certain that they were cold. They had had too many trash trucks burn up due to hot ashes to take chances.

Coal can be used in wood-burning stoves. However, if coal were your only heating source, one coal company said you would probably burn about one ton per month in a wood-burning stove or in the fireplace, depending on the weather and the type of coal. Hard coal burns longer and better than soft coal. Soft coal disintegrates into dust and crumbles much more quickly than hard coal, especially if it is not covered. Hard coal is available in the eastern states, soft coal in the west. Coal would take up less space than firewood for a commensurate amount of heat produced. Many coal yards or lumber supply outlets that carry it sell coal in bags or boxes, which would be appropriate for a limited emergency preparedness supply, as well as by the ton for continuous winter usage. If you decide to use coal as a fuel, keep it dry and covered, if possible in a bin or container. Discuss the pros and cons of coal in your area with a coal supplier before buying any.

CANNED HEAT

Canned Heat (also referred to by the well-known brand name Sterno) is a jelled petroleum product that comes in a small can, a little bit deeper than a tuna can. Canned Heat is a gel that is stable for storage indoors or out. It doesn't spill and it lights easily with just a match or lighter. All manner of backpacking stoves are made to be used with the jelled fuel because it's so light, compact, and easy to use (a real plus if you live in an apartment or condo where space is limited). In fact, you don't have to be camping up in the mountains to enjoy the benefits of this jelled fuel. Many professional caterers and amateur chefs use Sterno all the time for warming chafing dishes and fondue pots. You'll find it comes in handy during power outages and storms.

Sterno can evaporate fairly readily if exposed to air, so it's important that you keep the lid tightly closed when not in use. To extinguish the flame, simply replace the lid on the container. To use it again, just relight the fuel. As far as shelf life goes, we found a can of Sterno in our preparedness supplies that was at least ten years old. The fuel left inside was only about an inch in diameter and looked dried up. We assumed that it was a goner, but we decided to try it anyway. We were both surprised and pleased that as soon as we applied a match to it, it caught and immediately burned as big and bright as ever.

Canned Heat is a good choice for emergency cooking, but obviously not as a major heat source. You probably wouldn't gather round a little three-inch can on a cold night to sing campfire songs and toast marshmallows.

HEAT TABS

If you're looking for a cooking source that can be stored in next to no room, heat tabs are the way to go. You could store the stove and fuel for three week's worth of meals in a shoe box with room to spare. Three different types of heat tabs are available on the market for cooking, each made from different chemicals. They are hexamine tablets, trioxane tablets and Esbit fuel tablets, made of methenamine. They are roughly the same size (about the size of Alka-Seltzer tablets, though some are square and others round), and serve the same purpose but with minor differences. They burn at high temperatures with a high heat output, no smoke, and no visible flames. You need to be careful to not get too close or be careless, or you can get burned before you realize it. Use them in a well-ventilated area, especially trioxane, since its fumes can be lethal. Esbit burns completely and efficiently and leaves virtually no residue. Trioxane will evaporate if its foil packaging gets even a tiny prick in it, leaving you with an empty package when you need it, so handle it carefully. The other two do not evaporate. All heat tabs are shelf stable. You use them with a collapsible wing-tab stove (about the size of a pocket knife) or a pocket stove (about the size of a deck of cards). Two hexamine tablets will bring a cup of liquid to a boil in minutes, and will keep burning for twelve to fifteen minutes. The others give similar results. You can purchase the stoves and heat tabs in sporting goods stores or from your local army/navy outlet. If this is a resource you plan to use, I recommend that

you have several on hand to use at the same time. Be sure to place them on a solid, fireproof surface for use.

NOT NECESSARILY FUEL

Batteries and generators are not traditionally considered fuel, but in an emergency situation, they accomplish the same task as fuel: to make your emergency preparedness equipment work.

Batteries

Who could get along without batteries in this day and age? Take a look around your home to see how many things you have that depend on them. From toys to clocks to portable CD players, batteries are just a fact of life. As far as emergency preparedness goes, a whole raft of equipment is dependent on batteries, not the least being flashlights. A set of D-cell batteries will continuously power an average flashlight for about seven hours, more or less. Batteries will last about three years in storage if they remain unopened, and if your teenagers don't know where they are.

Keep your batteries for emergencies in their original package, in a cool, dry place at normal room temperature. Don't keep them in the freezer—that's an old wives' tale. Batteries contain acid. Freezing can cause the battery to expand and the seams to split. It would be a good idea to keep a stock of batteries specifically for emergencies in a special off-limits place (maybe in an underwear or sock drawer), and an accessible stock of batteries for Walkmans, tape players, and Game Boys somewhere else. Then you can be assured of flashlights and lanterns that will work when an emergency arises.

One way to make sure your flashlights have working batteries when you need them is to calendar consistent updating and changing of the batteries. Change the batteries in emergency flashlights on a regular basis—annually, whether they need it or not. A good time is when the time changes in spring or fall. Remember the battery-powered lanterns that are in the back of the closet waiting for the power outage as well as the flashlights you use regularly. Don't forget all of the flashlights tucked in the garage, closets, and sheds, too. Place the ones that are taken out of the flashlights at the calendared time into a box labeled "used but not dead." They can be used for portable CD players or handheld games or even in nonemergency-use flashlights. That way they are not wasted, but you can count on emergency flashlights working when you need them. Have plenty of extra batteries on hand because, not only do you exhaust batteries by using them, but they also go dead after extended periods of just sitting (especially if they're not sealed in their package).

Rechargeable batteries are fine and economical for everyday use, but when there is no power, there won't be any way to recharge them. So, from a preparedness standpoint, they don't have any advantage over regular batteries.

In addition to batteries, replacement bulbs are imperative to have on hand. There are basically three types of bulbs used in flashlights. The first type, vacuum bulbs, are the traditional bulbs used in flashlights. They cast a bright, far-reaching beam of light. They will typically burn forty-plus hours before they need to be replaced. Second, LEDs (light-emitting diodes, a simple type of semiconductor) drain batteries four or five times more slowly than regular vacuum bulbs, and they are very bright. They are very tough and can usually last up to 100,000 hours without replacement. The third type of bulbs are halogen, xenon, or krypton bulbs, which are gas-enhanced to prolong bulb life and to cast a brighter light.

For emergency purposes, you may consider buying a combination flashlight/portable radio. Some of these can be recharged with solar power or a crank handle, eliminating or lessening the need for quantities of batteries. Not every family member would need one, but one or two per household could be very useful. You'll find them in preparedness catalogs and stores as well as sporting goods stores and discount department stores.

> We had an ice storm and were without power for three days. We had no way to cook or heat our home. We now have a generator capable of running our furnace, a gas stove (that can be used to cook on) plus a propane gas cook stove.
> —M. S. G., Trenton, Tex.

Emergency Generators

When the power goes off for more than a couple of hours, a backup emergency generator can keep life humming along quite near to normal. There are basically two types of generators: permanent generators, which are installed as part of a building's electrical system, and portable generators. This book will describe only the smaller portable generators.

Portable generators can be an excellent idea for emergency use. Most run on gasoline or propane, and the more things they provide power to, the more gas they use. You probably wouldn't have the fuel stored to sail through a power outage with every light on in the house and the furnace turned up to 80 degrees, while you watch TV and eat four-course gourmet meals. But you could light one room, run the furnace an hour or so a day to keep the worst of the chill off, and use the microwave to heat your hot chocolate. You can even use a generator to take care of the food in your freezer or refrigerator (all it takes is turning it on once or twice a day for an hour at a time, and keeping the doors closed tightly). The fewer items you have running at one time, the smaller your generator can be and the longer your fuel supply will last. For general ballpark estimations, a 2200-watt generator (with a five horsepower engine) will run about an hour on a gallon of gas. A 1000-watt generator will run for about three hours on that same gallon of gas. Keep in mind that generators burn fuel and must be run outdoors. They should not be run in the garage.

It is important to get a generator that is adequately sized. Some electrical motors in home appliances and equipment can be ruined or damaged if they do not receive enough electrical current. The electrical cords used to connect the generator to the lights and appliances must be the proper size to prevent overheating or damage to your equipment as well. Because of this, as well as other safety concerns, it is critical that you do your homework with local reputable providers before purchasing or installing a generator.

FLAMMABLE LIQUIDS AND GASES

If you already have camping equipment that you plan to use during an emergency, then you definitely need to consider how to safely keep a small amount of liquid fuel on hand. For many families who live in rural or remote areas with unreliable access to electricity, propane heaters or generators are a winter necessity. People whose homes are heated primarily by propane store large tanks of fuel on their property to run them. This is legal and safe only because those large tanks are professionally serviced and safety inspected. In every other circumstance and with all other liquid fuels, you should only safely and legally store smaller amounts, enough just to get you through a short-term situation. Many areas even have laws that govern the quantity of fuel that can be stored on your premises. Check with your city or county fire marshal to find out what the laws are in your city. Safety parameters are the top priority for the storage of any amount of volatile fuel! Never consider stockpiling large quantities of any liquid fuel. Keep on hand only enough to get you through a difficult situation.

In spite of having identical origins, liquid fuels are not interchangeable. They each work in equipment designed specifically for that product. Knowing this, it would be a smart idea to buy pieces of equipment that use the same type of fuel, lanterns, stoves, and heaters that all use propane, or that all use butane, and so on. Then, you would only have to store one type of fuel, and your fuel would function in whichever piece of equipment you needed most at the time.

All liquid fuels are petroleum-based products. The difference between them is how their carbon atoms are linked together in chains. The fewer carbon atoms, the lighter the resulting product. After distillation in a refinery, components of crude oil are separated into gases (propane, butane), liquids (gasoline), heavier liquids (kerosene, diesel fuel), lubricating oils (motor oil, Vaseline —yes, the same stuff you put on your chapped lips or baby's bottom), and solids (paraffin wax and tar). All these different substances come from crude oil. The only difference is the lengths of their carbon chains!

Since they are flammable, all liquid fuels (white gas, gasoline, kerosene, propane, butane, and so on) should be stored outside your home and *never* kept in open containers. This is because fuel fumes are heavier than the surrounding air. The invisible, deadly, explosive fumes can sink to the floor and follow air currents directly to hot water heaters or other flame sources. Put them in a well-ventilated shed or unattached garage, preferably in as cool a place as possible. Use only proper containers that are clearly marked and approved with local and state codes. Just as an example, at one of our California homes, rather than keep them in the attached garage, we put our canisters of butane, several cans of white gas, and bottles of lamp oil in a large, sturdy forty-gallon Rubbermaid container with a tight-fitting lid. Larry drilled several holes on the sides, along the top edges, for ventilation. The tub protected the containers from the weather and the sun, almost as much as if they were in the garage. This large tub was kept on the north (and shadiest) side of a shed at the back corner of our lot.

Remember, all equipment that uses fuel and has an open flame will consume oxygen and produce hazardous fumes. You must provide adequate ventilation (one or more windows open a few inches), and you must have working carbon monoxide detectors and fire extinguishers handy. When it comes to any type of fuel storage and use, you can never be too careful, or go to too many extremes to make safety your first priority.

Propane and Butane

For preparedness purposes or camping, you can purchase propane in small cylinders about the size of a lunchbox thermos bottle, or in five-gallon tanks, the size typically used with gas barbecues. A small cylinder will last anywhere from one and a half to five hours on a two-burner stove, depending on whether the flame is on high or low. A tank can last about 120 hours. While under pressure in the cylinders, propane is a liquid, lighter than water. When released from the cylinder into your stove or lantern, it reverts to a gas. The cylinders are sealed, and all you do is screw the container on to the attachment of your piece of equipment. You never actually see the fuel. The cylinders are nonrefillable, and automatically reseal themselves when you remove them from the equipment.

Like all liquid fuels, store propane cylinders outside your home for safety's sake.

Butane is another fuel that comes pressurized in canisters. That means no liquids to spill that can cause fires. It is safe to use, and butane burns 100 percent clean, with no burning odors, residue, or smoke buildup. Each eight-ounce butane canister will burn from two to four hours in a stove, three hours in a heater, and five hours in a lantern. Because of its complete combustion during burning, butane is safe to use indoors, with proper ventilation and supervision, of course. Butane does not work well in cold weather, though. You may wish to have alternate plans or a backup plan if you live in an area where frigid weather prevails.

Kerosene

Some communities do not permit their residents to use kerosene appliances in certain environments. This is especially true of apartment tenants. However, in some communities this also applies to single-family dwellings. So, before you buy a kerosene lantern or space heater, check with the local building code authorities and/or fire department to find out if they are allowed.

Kerosene is used for heating and cooking and in lamps. Modern portable kerosene heaters are safe, reliable sources of economical heat, designed with safety in mind. Look for the kind that automatically shut off if they are tipped over or have a malfunction in any of the valves. Kerosene may have a reputation for smelling bad, though that is mostly a hangover from days gone by. Combustion in modern kerosene heaters is usually so complete that no smell remains, except a slight temporary odor during ignition and turnoff. It's important to use only water-clear 1-K-grade kerosene. Grades other than 1-K can release more pollutants in your home and pose a possible health risk. For this reason, you should only purchase your kerosene from a dealer who can certify that what you are buying is 1-K. Never use gasoline in kerosene heaters! They are not the same thing. Even small amounts of gasoline or other volatile fuels mixed with kerosene can substantially increase the risk of a fire or an explosion. Always store kerosene in a separate container intended specifically for kerosene, not in a gasoline can or a can that has previously contained gasoline. This helps you avoid using the wrong fuel by mistake. Kerosene

containers are generally blue, while gasoline containers are usually red. Although kerosene heaters are very efficient in the burning of fuel to produce heat, low levels of pollutants such as carbon monoxide are produced. (Ditto for other fuels also.) Keep a window open an inch or so to allow fresh air to effectively dilute the pollutants below a level of concern.

Lamp Oil

Lamp oil is highly refined, liquid paraffin oil. It's a clean-burning fuel and doesn't usually leave residual odors or soot. It is smokeless when the wicks are adjusted correctly. Lamp oil often is colored and scented. Colored fuel, which makes your oil lamp attractive as well as functional, allows you to quickly assess if a refill is needed soon. An ounce of lamp oil will last approximately five hours, give or take an hour. It stores well in the bottles or containers that it comes in. You can also keep your lamp filled and ready to light at any time. It doesn't hurt the oil or lamp. I have one filled with blue oil on my fireplace mantle year round.

White Gas

The common name for white gas is Coleman fuel, or, if it's a brand other than Coleman, simply camping fuel. It is unleaded gasoline that has been cleaned and modified to operate efficiently in camping equipment. It is one-third the cost of propane cylinders. Some people may think it is a little scarier to use since you have to pour it into the gas reservoirs of your equipment when they need refilling, and then pump up the pressure. It's not difficult once you know what you're doing. That is not to say that you don't need to be careful. Camping fuel is highly flammable and explosive. You need to follow the manufacturer's instructions carefully.

White gas stoves and propane/butane stoves look pretty much the same, and they work with the same efficiency and results. Lanterns are a little different, in that the bases of white gas lanterns are small tanks that you fill, as compared to propane lanterns, in which the base is the propane canister itself. White gas does not burn as efficiently as some other fuels, which means its carbon monoxide fumes could be more dangerous. Fire department recommendations are that you only use white gas equipment outdoors where there is plenty of ventilation.

Gasoline

Some pieces of equipment, though not all, use unleaded gasoline as their fuel source. Dual-fuel heaters do, and certainly generators do. Gasoline has a short shelf life, sometimes as little as a month or two. Nevertheless, if you have gasoline-powered equipment, you'll want to have a small supply of gasoline on hand, stored in a cool place away from your house. The best idea is to keep the small amount of gasoline in clearly marked, *red* metal or nylon fuel cans, and rotate your stock often. For example, if you have several cans, empty one into your car's gas tank each month, refill it with fresh gas, and put it to the back of the line. Then your gas is never more than three or four months old, and you'll be sure it will work effectively in your equipment when the need arises.

Matches/Lighters

Some canister- and liquid-fuel-powered equipment now comes with electronic ignition. No matches are involved at all. If your equipment is a few years old, or if you don't buy the top-of-the-line products with all the bells and whistles, it's essential to have some way, other than striking stones together, to light the fuel and create a flame. Matches are the most obvious choice. Wooden matches are much more reliable than book matches for emergency preparedness since they are so much sturdier, and they don't absorb moisture as readily as book matches will. The wooden fireplace matches that are approximately nine inches long are safer to use to light equipment than the regular shorter versions. You do not have to invest the added expense of purchasing the camping-style waterproof matches for emergency preparedness. Just keep the regular ones dry. If you live in a very humid climate or in a probable flood zone, store them in a container with a tight-fitting lid.

The long, skinny butane lighters are also acceptable, and in some instances, even better since you may be less likely to get burned with the flame six inches away from your hands instead of an inch and a half away. On the other hand, the barrels of butane lighters are too wide to insert in the little openings of some fuel lanterns. If this is the case with your equipment, make sure you have some matches on hand to use with those pieces. Some butane lighters are refillable, in the same manner as cigarette lighters are.

Speaking of cigarette lighters, I don't recommend using them to attempt to light equipment. With your thumb directly next to the tiny flame, you can't direct that flame down, or into a piece of equipment as needed without burning yourself. In an emergency or power outage it would be better to have a safer alternative.

If any of your emergency equipment needs to be lit to be used, make sure that you have plenty of matches or lighters on hand. The best equipment you can buy won't do you a bit of good if you can't find a way to light it.

CHAPTER TWENTY-FIVE

EMERGENCY COOKING-STOVE OPTIONS

After reviewing the different food options available, you probably have some inkling of what you'd like in your pantry for emergency times. Now, check out the options available for cooking the food. There are many to choose from, each with advantages and disadvantages. Evaluate each option based on its size, space, fuel requirements, safety factors, cost, and what you already have to determine what will work best for you.

SAFETY GROUND RULES

Whatever you choose, it will be very different from what you're used to using on a daily basis. All emergency cooking equipment has the potential to be harmful as well as helpful. From the very first moment, before you light the first match, you'll want to establish house safety standards and rules. Only use these cooking alternatives in a well-ventilated area, with an open window (one or two inches) nearby (even if it's freezing cold outside). Don't leave them on any longer than you have to, and never go to sleep with any fueled equipment left on. Always have carbon monoxide detectors in the areas where you're sleeping or congregating. If there are children in your family, there should be absolutely no running or horseplay when fires or open flames are in use. Take extra precautions with loose clothing or long hair. Have a family meeting to review and reinforce these ground rules. Be extra cautious, use common sense, and be alert. (After all, the world needs more lerts.)

When my new husband and I were on our honeymoon, we made the mistake of leaving a key to our apartment with my mother, so she could put our wedding gifts there for us after our reception. I didn't take into account that my mother loves practical jokes. She put our gifts in our new home, all right, but she also took the opportunity to arrange "surprise" homecoming decorations. She turned our furniture upside down, hung underwear on the walls like pictures (so embarrassing for a new bride!), and among other things, threw most of the electrical switches so there wasn't any power in our apartment. She didn't realize we would be returning in the middle of the night when it was pitch dark. We stumbled in and groped our way through the furniture maze. I knew immediately why the light switches didn't work (I know my mother very well), but I had no idea where the circuit breaker box was. I fumbled my way to the kitchen and found the gas stove. I turned all four burners on high, and by the light of the stove flames, we got settled safely in for the rest of the night. The next morning we found the circuit breaker box, turned the electricity back on, and went to get the key back from my mom!

—Sandi Simmons

NO GAS? NO ELECTRICITY?

Sometimes, when the electricity is out, you'll still have natural gas service. If you have natural gas appliances (heaters and stoves), you're in fairly good shape. Both will (usually) work without electricity. I remember a time in our early married years when we had a power outage of half a day's duration. We were one of the few families in our neighborhood that had a gas stove, so we had a party at our house. Three other families came over and cooked their dinners on our gas stove, and we all ate together by lantern light. It was almost a letdown when the electricity came back on toward the end of the meal.

More often than not, a power outage means the loss of electrical service. But once in a blue moon, it's the natural gas service that is lost. If your gas stove is not working but you still have electricity, a variety of electrical appliances can come to the rescue to fix meals. Use electric skillets, hotplates, toaster ovens, Crock-Pots, or even a coffee maker to heat food. This means if you are used to using natural gas for cooking, that an electric skillet on the shelf could be considered emergency preparedness equipment.

FIREPLACES

A fireplace can be used for cooking purposes as well as for heating your home, if you have a few pieces of equipment and a few of the right kind of pots and pans. A grill or rack is practically essential if you intend to cook in your fireplace. Without one, you're pretty much limited to cooking things that you can roast on a stick, like hot dogs or marshmallows. (And hot dogs aren't on the list of acceptable emergency food choices since they are perishable. What a shame!) While it is possible to balance a pan in the burning fire without a grill or rack, it's not practical, and it's certainly not safe. A grill, however, makes a world of difference since it gives you a stable surface for your pots and pans.

Camp grills greatly increase the functionality of your fireplace, transforming it into a built-in emergency-cooking place. You can buy them in sporting goods outlets. Some are made of heavy-gauge, chrome-plated steel and resemble an oven rack with legs. Others are made of heavy gauge metal that resembles a sturdy mesh. Most grill legs fold away for storage. The grills are sturdy enough to hold several full pots and pans at one time.

For fireplace use, pots and pans should be metal, with sturdy handles. Avoid pans with plastic or wooden handles. The pan should be stove top- and oven-safe. Cast iron is good, as are heavy, all-metal pots and pans. If you have some experience, a Dutch oven would come in handy. Dutch ovens are cast-iron pots with tight fitting lids. They have short legs and a rimmed cover on which hot coals can be placed (so the food is cooked from the top as well as from the bottom). A word of warning—they are heavy! When full, they are heavier! Some nicer cookware sets have a pot with lid that is called a Dutch oven. To qualify as a Dutch oven, the pot must be heavy with a thick bottom and sides. The lid is also heavy metal, not glass. It must be good for stove top and oven cooking.

Thick pot holders are a must for fireplace cooking, and those oven mitts that also protect your arms are even better. Provide a place to set hot pans as you remove them from the flames or coals so you don't burn your hearth or flooring. A wooden cutting board works very well. If you check out the camping sections of sporting goods stores, you'll find there are some fun and practical utensils available for campfire cooking that would work for fireplace cooking also, such as manual popcorn poppers and toasters. Many foods, if tightly wrapped in heavy aluminum foil, can be cooked right in the fire itself (like an original Boy Scout tinfoil dinner). Wait until the flames die down, then put the food packets in the glowing embers. Make sure that you have long-handled barbecue tongs to pull the food out of the fire and a cutting board or plate to put it on. (Note: Regular aluminum foil today is much thinner and weaker than it was several years ago. Be sure to buy heavy-gauge foil for foil cooking, or use two or three layers of the regular gauge.)

If you are considering adding on a fireplace or remodeling an existing fireplace, check out some of the options that can accommodate emergency cooking. Some fireplace inserts extend beyond the front of the fireplace and have a cooking surface that will accommodate pans for boiling water or heating soup. You could also have a hinged hook installed to hold a kettle or pot over the flames.

Absolute rule: Do not burn charcoal in the fireplace! The lethal carbon monoxide produced is not completely removed by the drawing of the chimney. You can die!

WOOD-BURNING STOVES

Wood-burning stoves can be practical and economical on an everyday basis, and a godsend in an emergency. When you have one installed, make sure you choose a model that allows for cooking on top, as well as heating, so it can be used to the maximum in a crisis. As with fireplaces, caution and safety must prevail.

> *Stove top s'mores are almost as yummy as campfire s'mores! Instead of cooking a marshmallow on a stick over the campfire and squashing the golden, gooey blob with a square of chocolate between two graham crackers, you make a sandwich of the ingredients and heat them in a pan until the chocolate and marshmallows melt. Cooking them on a wood-burning stove in a power outage is a delightful compromise!*

BUTANE/PROPANE PORTABLE STOVES

Some portable stoves are designed for use indoors; many are not. If you intend to use your butane/propane stove indoors, you must be sure to choose one that is approved for indoor use. Most butane stoves are acceptable for indoor use because butane burns completely and doesn't give off carbon monoxide emissions. My top choice for emergency cooking is a butane single-burner portable stove. It resembles a burner from a gas kitchen range. They are safe to use indoors and you can use your regular stove top cookware on them. If you had more than one, it would be easy to cook a normal meal during a power outage or crisis, and it would require no more time than it regularly takes to prepare a meal. These are ideal emergency stoves. The fuel is in self-contained canisters and burns cleanly and without odor. You can control the height of the flame in order to conserve your fuel. A fuel canister will last approximately two and a half hours on high, and up to seven hours on low. They

also have several safety features, such as automatic shutoff if the stoves are tipped or bumped. There are a multitude of accessories available. Set the stove(s) on a cutting board or heavy-duty cookie sheet right on your stove top or counter top and you'll hardly know the power is out.

Propane camping stoves come in models that have from one to three burners. You must check the manufacturers' instructions for these to determine if they are approved for indoor use or not. Propane gas doesn't burn quite as cleanly as butane, so if it is approved for indoor use, you must still be sure to leave a window open a few inches for ventilation.

STERNO STOVES/CANNED HEAT

Sterno stoves are small, lightweight stoves often used by backpackers, but equally effective for use in emergencies. They burn a jelled petroleum product that comes in a can with a flanged lid. (Sterno and canned heat are the most common brand names for this jelled petroleum product.) It's very flammable and it lights easily with just a match. This fuel burns smoke free, and is completely safe for indoor use. Sterno is shelf stable and stores for a long time, if kept tightly closed. If exposed to air, it evaporates rather readily.

Cans of canned heat are used with small collapsible stoves that fold down to a compact 2-by-4-inch size. The cans of Sterno simply slide into the stove. You'll probably want to use more than one at a time if you will be preparing food for more than a single individual. A seven-ounce can of Sterno will burn for approximately two hours. You can even buy accessories that make the stoves more functional, like grills that fit over one or two cans of Sterno.

HEAT-TAB STOVE

Heat-tab stoves and winged tab stoves are very small. When folded for storage, they take up only about 4 by 2 by ½ inches of space. They are also called pocket stoves. They use solid heat tabs as fuel. When the tabs are ignited, the burning flame is barely visible. Since these are so small, they require small pots or pans for cooking, such as backpacking gear or your tiniest pots and pans. It's doubtful that you'd be cooking any gourmet meals on these, but they are capable of boiling water and warming ready-to-eat foods. You could fry an egg in a very small frying pan. Have several stoves and packs of fuel tabs on hand if you're heating food for a family. And of course, take a reality check and practice cooking on them before the need arises. Each tablet will burn for fifteen minutes, more or less. They will continue to burn until the tabs are completely consumed unless you have a damper to extinguish the flame when you are through cooking. Any ceramic bowl turned upside down over the stove and heat tab will cut off the oxygen and snuff the flame. It can then be relit and used again. Because any fumes are odorless and nontoxic, heat tabs can safely be used indoors (though always with proper ventilation).

When these fuel tabs burn, you usually cannot see a flame. Be extremely cautious. They burn very hot. Do not allow anyone to wave his or her hand over the heat tab to see if it is lit.

Sterno stoves and heat tab stoves are a great preparedness choice if space is really at a premium and living quarters are cramped. They're not as versatile as butane single-burner stoves because you can't adjust the height of the flame. It is either on or off, nothing in between.

PATIO PROPANE BARBECUES

Many people already have propane barbecues on hand. These are a fine cooking source, and have the advantage of not taking up any more storage room than you've already allotted. Plus, most owners already know how to use them. Remember though, these are for outdoor cooking only! Do not bring your barbecue into your house, no matter how cold it is. You can wheel it right up to the back doorway so all you have to do is step out, stir the food, and step back in, but keep the barbecue outside. Don't take chances with carbon monoxide poisoning.

If your patio barbecue is your emergency preparedness cooking choice, think ahead now and figure out how you'll make it work during potentially stormy weather. If you live in an area where snow or rain are possible and likely, what precautions can you take now to cook outdoors then? Are you handy enough to rig up a temporary, slanted roof from a sheet of plywood and a couple of two-by-fours? If so, do you *have* a sheet of plywood and some two-by-fours? What about using an awning, such as those found on motor homes, or a heavy blue tarp with grommets along the edges? This tarp could be nailed

in place along the roof line and anchored on the other end to the deck floor or tied to a tree or fence or whatever you can find. Could a large patio-table umbrella be adapted somehow? What creative solution is going to work for you to keep the worst of the inclement weather off your head and your food while you safely use your barbecue outdoors? Now is the time to consider your options. One of these ideas, or something similar, might just make the difference as to whether or not you have warm meals or cold, canned Spam during the next weeklong winter whiteout or the six-day stormy blackout. We had a personal experience with how to make this work not long ago. It wasn't an emergency, but we had invited some friends over for a barbecue, and at the last moment, the heavens unzipped and the rain poured down. Normally, I'd have just broiled the chicken in the oven, but the oven was occupied with other food. So Larry pulled the barbecue under the eaves of the house, and then he pulled our patio table with the big umbrella over next to the barbecue to stand under. He tipped the umbrella to direct the rain away and proceeded to cook our meal without a bit of discomfort or mess. It worked perfectly!

LIQUID FUEL CAMPING STOVES

Camping stoves that burn liquid camping fuel (white gas, Coleman fuel) are designed to be used outdoors, and that's where they should stay. All fueled products consume air (oxygen) and release carbon monoxide. Since carbon monoxide is invisible, odorless, and deadly, it is much too dangerous to take chances by using liquid fuel stoves indoors. If you already have a white gas camp stove, think now how you are going to make it work outdoors if the weather is bad. Perhaps you could set it on a patio

> I am amazed at how many people run to their 72-hour kits during an emergency! I will run to the barbecue and the freezer without power. As food thaws, I'd rather eat it than let it rot. Too often, we forget to use common sense.
> —Pyper G., Salt Lake City, Utah

table just outside the sliding door: step out, stir the food, step back in. All of the options in the previous "Patio Propane Barbecues" section are applicable here also. If it's raining, you might need to put the stove under the table to protect it, or inside a large wooden crate (large enough to not catch fire from the stove flames!), or rig up a tarp to keep the rain off you and the food. Think it through now so you'll have the materials on hand to protect yourself from the weather when you need them.

Of course, if you live in a warm climate, or it's summer, the emergency cooking options expand greatly. Barbecues and camp stoves are naturally appropriate for use in the yard or on a deck, porch, or patio. You could even dig a pit and build a campfire in it. Of course, the prerequisite for a backyard campfire is that you have to have a backyard. Parks and Recreation departments usually frown on campfire pits sprouting up in public park lawns.

If you should have any qualms or insecurities about operating the stove options you choose, go to your local sporting goods store before the need arises, and have one of their trained people walk you through the steps for using your stove safely and confidently. Find the person who has the expertise and knows the specific equipment you're asking about (for example, camping stoves . . . not fishing rods or athletic shoes or how to work the cash register).

With these cooking options in mind, before you decide what type of cooking device you'll provide for your family, you have to take into account these factors:

• How many people will you be cooking for? Is the ability to prepare more than one food item at a time important? If so, consider a larger unit, or more than one unit in order to cook family-style meals.

• Do you want your option to be strictly for emergencies, or should you choose something more versatile that can also be used for camping or outdoor entertaining?

• How much space can you allocate for the cooking option and its fuel requirements?

• How much are you willing to spend?

The answers to these questions should pretty effectively narrow down your list of possible choices to just a few viable options.

CHAPTER TWENTY-SIX

WHEN THE LIGHT SWITCH FAILS

Most of us are not used to coping in pitch-black darkness. Even when the regular lights in the house are not on, there usually are streetlights, city lights, or neighborhood lights that penetrate into our homes. Take these away also and night can be very dark indeed. One night without lights can be fun, even an adventure. However, when we are used to having light at the flick of a switch, being without it for very long changes the experience entirely. Our activities change, our attitudes change, and our anxieties increase, especially if there are children involved. Certainly our frustration levels rise.

For those times when the light switch fails, we have to look to the alternatives that are available. Different light sources suit different circumstances: short-term, long-term, summer, winter, and so on. I would suggest that you choose several different options to meet different needs at different times. Read on for enlightenment on some, though certainly not all, of the choices you can find readily available in stores.

> *You can enjoy the darkness if you are prepared. During a severe ice storm we were prepared. We were able to cook, keep warm, and have light. We enjoyed our evenings together without TV, video games, or computer. However, we had to dig up a corded phone. We were without electricity for five days.*
>
> *—A. G., Trenton, Tex.*

FLASHLIGHTS

Flashlights are essential pieces of preparedness equipment. Even if there is never an emergency in your area, there will always be standard power failures, kids will want to read at night when they're supposed to be asleep, and boxes will need to be found in the attic. Flashlights are available in a variety of sizes and strengths. In fact, in just one store, I counted over forty different kinds and styles, from flimsy plastic throw-aways that only cost a dollar, to one giant rechargeable model I found that has the equivalent of a 10-million-candlepower spotlight! Some flashlights are designed to double as small lanterns. To use one as a flashlight with a directed narrow light beam, it stays snapped together. For the lantern effect, you set the flashlight down on its face and pull up the telescoping handle cover to allow the light to shine out the sides like a lantern. From mini to mighty, you can choose a flashlight with the lighting capacity, power, weight, and sturdiness that suit you best. It makes sense to have a working flashlight in almost every room (you can probably get away without one in the coat closet). If you always keep them in the same locations, everyone would always know where to find one when the need arises. While the light switch is still working, have a practice session for finding flashlights in the dark. Explain where they are in each room, including bedrooms, bathrooms, kitchen, and so on. Take the time to "walk through" finding the flashlights in each area—in the dark. (Pay particular attention to those who may have physical needs that will require placement of flashlights to be within easy, but perhaps not usual, reach.)

It isn't uncommon to reach for a flashlight in a time of need, only to find that the flashlight is missing or has dead batteries because it was used for other purposes, or ignored too long. Establish rules about when and where emergency flashlights can be used. This is easier to do if you have other flashlights available for use in nonemergency times, like when you need to find something under the bed, or when a child wants to read a scary book under the covers. I've found that a plug-in flashlight works great for these needs. These plug into an electrical outlet for charging and are always right there when you need them (as long as people remember to plug them back in after they're used). They hold a charge about as long as a set of batteries. Another option is the relatively new shake-and-charge flashlight. They don't require batteries. You just shake them for a minute and they give light for half an hour to an hour. Then you shake them again and you're good for another hour. They can be shaken repeatedly and last for years.

A standard-sized flashlight that uses two D-cell batteries will drain a fresh set of batteries in approximately seven hours of continual use, so consider them as a temporary light source rather than for long-term use as a lamp. Reserve them for the middle of the night, or as a light source while lighting a lantern, or for moving from room to room. For more about batteries, review chapter 24, Fuel Storage Guidelines.

As useful as flashlights are, since there is always the chance you may fall victim to a power outage that lasts more than just a single day, you'll want more than just a flashlight on hand to deal with darkness.

BATTERY-OPERATED LANTERNS

Battery-operated lanterns are one of the best choices for safety and light combined. They are much more reassuring if you have small children. They are safe (no flames, no potentially deadly fumes),

Flashlights or battery-powered lanterns are the only sources of light that are safe for use immediately after any disaster.

relatively bright, and easy. We keep one on a closet shelf all the time to use during run-of-the-mill power failures. Even if it's pitch black in the house, we can grope our way to the closet and immediately flood the area with cheerful light. They can use up to eight batteries at a time (or the large, square six-volt lantern batteries). Lanterns with fluorescent bulbs will burn much longer on the same set of batteries than will lanterns with incandescent bulbs. Even so, at eight batteries at a time, you'll want to make sure to have plenty of spare batteries so you'll have light the entire time you need it. If you have not yet purchased any kind of emergency light source yet, I recommend battery-powered lanterns over the open-flame style. Safety is the most important factor in difficult times.

CYALUME OR LIGHT STICKS

A small item that has become associated with emergency preparedness is a light stick or Cyalume stick. It can provide instant light just by shaking and bending the stick. You may recognize them as the glowing wands (or even the big glowing necklaces) that you can buy when you go to watch Fourth-of-July fireworks or any other nighttime outdoor event. They glow, but it's not a bright, penetrating light. You could use one while you locate and light other equipment, or it could provide security for children. If you taped one to the under side of furniture or tables in various rooms, you'd always have something to grab if the power went out to light your way while you went in search of a more satisfactory light source. They require very little storage space, are lightweight, and shelf stable. One disadvantage of Cyalume sticks is that they are one-use items. You can't turn it off to conserve the light for another time. After it's lit, it will continue to glow for eight to twelve hours, but once it's gone, it's gone.

CANDLES

Candles are an inexpensive option for emergency light, but they certainly can be a dangerous option, even more so than a lantern because you will be dealing with open flame. An open flame is not stable. Movement causes draft, which causes flames to leap and dance. Since most people are definitely not used to being around open flames, you must remember to take every precaution! Before the need ever arises, figure out where you will put your candle or lantern when it is in use. Somewhere safe, stable, and out of the way is your safest bet.

Limit who is allowed to be around or move a candle. Moving a lit candle is not advised, but should the need arise, be aware that the flame extends back toward you as you walk. Long hair and moving candles are a very dangerous combination. Don't blow hard and fast on a lit candle at close range to put it out. The splattering hot wax could burn you. Instead, snuff candles out with an upside-down spoon or other tool. (The only exception to this is birthday candles on a cake. In this case, blow as hard as you can so you can get your birthday wish!)

For safety's sake, you can buy solid candleholders or bases to hold your candles. These look like spiked plates. You secure your candle on the spikes to prevent it from falling over. The longer the spike, the more stable the candle will be. You can also purchase glass chimneys (such as are used with oil lamps) to cover the candle and make it safer to be around.

There is a difference between emergency candles and decorative or dinner candles. Decorative candles may smell good and cast a romantic light, but they don't cast a very bright or long-burning light. Emergency candles are generally made with different wicks and wax in order to burn brighter and longer. A general rule of thumb is the broader the circumference of the base, the longer the burning time for candles. (This goes for decorative as well as emergency candles.) The melting wax is the fuel for the wick.

One of the things we discovered going through the Loma Prieta Earthquake is the importance of the security that light provides. A friend related how a tiny tea light helped calm the terrible fear that her children experienced from the continual movement of the earth combined with total darkness. Every night for over a week, she placed a tea light in a jar lid in the room where they were sleeping to provide comfort and security.

Multiple-wick candles (from three to six inches in diameter) can have anywhere from three to five wicks. They burn longer and brighter than single-wick candles, plus they can be used for warming food if you place them under a grill or grid.

Consider using tea lights or votive candles as nightlights, or as comforting lights on a dark and gloomy day (in a safe place, naturally). This would allow you to keep your main source of fuel to meet normal light needs.

I learned by experience to store candles properly. If you are storing more than one in the same container or box, layer them flat with waxed paper in between them (not paper towels, as melted candles stick to them and make a big mess). Try to keep them as cool as possible. Attics are a bad place to keep candles because the heat will melt them all out of shape. Most of our warped, contorted, and funny-shaped candles still burned, but since they were on slanted and twisted angles, they didn't always drip where they were supposed to, besides being ridiculous to look at.

CANDLE LANTERNS

Small candle "lanterns" are available in many sporting goods sections that combine the safety features of candle, base, glass chimney, and carrying/hanging handle in one. Some brass or stainless-steel versions are designed to hold the standard white emergency candles (3 inches tall by 1 inch in diameter). Others hold tea lights, which will burn for two to four hours, as compared to nine hours for the emergency candles.

CANDELIER

A candelier is a large candle lantern (8 inches tall by 4 inches in diameter). It holds three standard emergency candles. The candles can be burned individually or simultaneously, depending on how much light you want. The candelier has a heat shield across the top that doubles as a small stove. You can boil water on it or heat soup, or use it as a warming burner. Candeliers produce enough heat to be a warmth source for one person, though not for an entire room.

STANDARD OIL LAMPS

Old-fashioned, standard oil lamps are a tried-and-true option. Some still burn kerosene, though the majority burn lamp oil, which is available in drugstores and/or the larger Kmart- or Wal-Mart-type outlets. If improperly lit, kerosene creates more, and darker, smoke than lamp oil, as well as having a definite odor.

If you are not familiar with operating an oil lamp, I suggest you go outside and practice lighting one and adjusting the flame a time or two before you need to rely on it during an emergency or power outage. You begin by filling the reservoir of the lamp with fuel. The wick needs to soak up the oil (or kerosene) before it will burn. Raise the wick to light it, and then lower it to eliminate smoking. Normally, the wick should not be visible above the burner when in use. You can raise the wick to create a brighter light, but if you raise it too high, it will smoke. The higher the flame, the faster the fuel consumption. To put out the flame, you simply turn the wick down until the lamp goes out. The lamp will be hot for a while after it's extinguished, so be careful. In between usage, when the lamp is cool, it's important to trim the wick. Trimming the wick means to simply cut off the charred portion. (Cutting, rather than just breaking off the charred parts, makes for a brighter flame.) The lamp will always burn better and brighter when the wick is trimmed. If the lamp is in constant use for any extended period of time you will use wicks quite rapidly. Keep several extra wicks on hand, as well as at least one extra chimney. Remember, most oil lamps are glass, which means they are fragile and break easily. Don't take a glass oil lamp that has been burning and place it on a cold surface. It could cause the glass to crack.

I have firsthand experience with smoking oil lamps. Even though I spent several childhood years on a farm in Ohio and had daily experience working with oil lamps, I forgot the little details over the years. A while back I decided to have a practice session to make sure our oil lamps worked. They did, but I had a few minutes of pandemonium trying to get the wick turned down fast enough and the windows thrown open before all the smoke alarms in the house went off!

If you are in the market for an oil lamp, look for the safer, more stable version that has the oil reservoir on the bottom rather than on a pedestal in the middle.

OIL LAMPS (A.K.A. LIQUID-FUEL CANDLES)

Back in biblical times, people burned oil lamps for light every evening. The clay lamps looked like small covered saucers with a handle on one side and a spout on the other. You would fill them with oil and light the oil in the spout. Today you can buy a distant relative to those old oil lamps. Now, instead of clay with a spout on the side, the lamps are made of plastic, with the wick on the top. They are generally about four inches in diameter and three inches high, and they'll burn from sixty to one hundred hours. You can't control the size of the flame, which means there is no increase or decrease in the brightness of the lamp. Since it is only a single little flame, they give only as much light as a dinner candle. Don't count on illuminating an entire room to the brightness of a one hundred-watt bulb with these. However, one would be a good choice as a night light since they burn for so long; provided, of course, you set it in a safe place. They are inexpensive and shelf stable for storage.

FUEL LANTERNS

For safety's sake, you are always safer with flashlights and battery-powered lanterns than with candles or fuel lanterns. But that doesn't mean you can't or shouldn't use equipment that has open flames. You just have to be extremely safety-minded. Lanterns usually associated with camping and outdoor recreation work well in power outages and disaster situations. Their advantages are that they are usually much brighter than battery-operated models, and fuel is cheaper than batteries. They are not as easy to use, so it's imperative that you learn how to light and

We had an ice storm and were without power for three days. Even though I collect miniature oil lamps and have over 200, I didn't have any oil! Now all my lamps have new wicking and oil!
—M. S. G., Trenton, Tex.

use one, and then practice often enough to remember the steps before you should ever need to use one in an emergency.

Propane/butane lanterns just screw right onto the propane/butane canister, using the canister as a base. The canisters are already pressurized. These types of lanterns produce light by fuel combustion in mantles. As a wick is to a candle, a mantle is to a lantern. That's where the fuel combustion takes place. Mantles are very fragile. They may last for weeks or even years if you are extra careful or you don't use them very often. Or they may break after only one or two usages. Changing a mantle isn't hard. It's just a matter of taking the broken one off and tying on a new one like you'd tie a shoe. It's impossible to do, though, if you don't have a replacement mantle available. Therefore, if you're planning on using a fuel lantern, you need replacement mantles tucked away with your fuel and other emergency supplies. Some spare lantern parts, such as gaskets or pump parts, wouldn't go amiss either.

You can also buy old-fashioned hurricane lanterns that burn either kerosene or lamp oil. They look like old-time, metal railroad lanterns. They are relatively inexpensive, generally have a broad, stable base, and burn with a fairly bright light.

My personal choice for fuel lanterns for emergency purposes is the butane variety, simply because they burn the most efficiently and are therefore safest for indoor usage.

SOLAR GARDEN LIGHTS

Take a second look at your garden or yard. Solar garden lights can be easily transformed into indoor security lights, either for stairs, hallways, or rooms. The bright-white LED lights are brighter than the amber lights. Though neither one is bright enough to light up an entire room like a hundred-watt bulb, the bright-white ones do a decent job of lighting a small-ish area. The amber lights could be used effectively for security and safety, illuminating a stairway, step, doorway, or a dangerous spot like a sharp corner on a low table. You can use empty quart jars or flower pots with dirt to hold them.

Their primary value is that they are a renewable light source. That means no batteries to buy, no dangerous fuel to store. During the day, simply put them

Fuel lanterns are more economical than battery-operated lanterns, but battery-operated lanterns are safer and easier to use. If you can determine that you may be without power for an extended period of time, you can balance your budget and light needs by using a fueled lantern in a safe spot as your main source of light, and using a battery-operated lantern like you would an especially bright flashlight, or as a secondary light source in another room.

outside or in a sunny window to soak up the sun's rays. In the evening, bring them in to provide a little security during dark hours. Even in cloudy winter gloom, most will recharge enough to create a comforting glow that will last for eight to ten hours.

MIRROR, MIRROR, THAT USED TO BE ON THE WALL

A simple idea that can double the lighting capacity of a temporary light source, but not double emergency fuel consumption during a power outage, is an ordinary mirror. It will reflect the light from your emergency light source, giving you twice the illumination. This can more efficiently light any area, and stretch a small amount of fuel or battery power.

During the aftermath of the Loma Prieta earthquake, we placed an oil lamp on the fireplace hearth and propped a 14-by-16-inch mirror (which, amazingly, had not broken) against the fireplace behind it. This one small thing greatly increased the light in the room. I vividly recall sitting on the floor, writing in my journal by the light of the mirror and lamp.

If no mirror is available, you could tape aluminum foil to the wall or backdrop behind a lamp or lantern. It's not as effective as a mirror but still better than a lantern or lamp by itself. If all you have is a flashlight, the principle will still work. Such a simple thing as a mirror or aluminum foil could have enormous benefits, when thought about and planned for ahead of time.

DON'T BE IN THE DARK ABOUT SAFETY

Simple power outages are not unusual. They don't fall into the category of "disaster," but they can easily range from "minor inconvenience" to "major annoyance." It's possible, though, for simple power outages (those not associated with emergencies, severe storms, or disasters) to have complications of their own. Hazards and dangers can lurk in the unfamiliar darkness.

For example, I learned the hard way. We were in the middle of the rolling blackouts of northern California. They had been occurring for several weeks, so I was used to them. I made the mistake of becoming nonchalant in my need for caution. It was dusk and getting darker by the minute. I was walking down the hall, trying to read some papers in my hand, and I was paying more attention to the papers than what was on the floor. "SPLAT!" I was what was on the floor. I had not remembered to pay attention to black dogs lying in darkened rooms on darkened floors. For days I had a bruised chin, elbows, wrists, and ribs to remind me of the dangers of not being alert in the darkness of a power outage.

Many of you are used to walking around in the dark at night in your homes. So what's the difference? First, the degree of darkness makes a difference. Without power, there is no filtered light from the streetlamps through the windows, no glow from the clock radio or the fish tank, no night-light down the hallway brightening things up enough to guide us through the maze of furniture. It may seem dark but it isn't completely. Second, the difference comes when you attempt to do those tasks and chores in complete dark that are normally done with sufficient light. You try to accomplish just as much, in just as short a period of time—but without the vital conveniences that you are used to, and without acknowledging that you are vulnerable. Therein lies the problem.

So, if you seem to have more than your share of power outages, use caution and don't be complacent. Have family meetings to review how to live through the inconvenience safely. Safety must be a first-priority consideration, particularly if you are using a light source with an open flame. For instance, it could prove to be a deadly mistake to trip over your dog if you were carrying an oil lamp. You can always blame the dog, but broken bones or worse is a high price to pay for inattention.

Since emergencies don't schedule a convenient time to arrive, it only makes sense to calendar a time to check all of your equipment to make sure that it is functioning and not in need of repair or parts, as part of your ongoing preparedness program. Obvious and easily remembered times are in the spring or fall when the time changes, or in the month of your birthday. Be ready for those inconvenient disasters.

EMERGENCY HEATING OPTIONS

There are many things you can do to stay warm without standard utilities but let's face it—unless you have some sort of heat source besides body heat, you're going to be cold. If you're reading this in the middle of an August heat wave, you may have a hard time summoning up the proper response to the thought of being cold. Here's what you do. Go down to a local restaurant and ask if you can stand in their walk-in freezer for five minutes in your shirt sleeves and shorts. Five minutes (or even two) should give you a proper appreciation for the misery that could await you if you're not prepared for a wintertime emergency.

You need to have equipment and fuel on hand and in working order to temporarily provide heat when circumstances have left you out (or in) in the cold. However, I cannot emphasize enough that safety is imperative. Caution! Caution! Caution! You *must* be extremely careful. You *must* practice beforehand. You *must* have a fire extinguisher and a battery-operated carbon monoxide detector on hand. You *must not* take chances! You don't have to be afraid of using emergency equipment, but you do have to be careful.

See appendix J for more specifics on fire extinguishers, and chapter 24, Fuel Storage Guidelines.

WOOD-BURNING FIREPLACES

The first obvious option for staying warm without a functioning furnace is a wood-burning fireplace. If you have one in your home, you're two steps ahead of the game already. This is assuming, of course, that you also have a supply of wood or coal or something to burn (without resorting to the Duncan Phyfe tables and Chippendale chairs).

Fireplaces are great in an emergency since they are not dependent in any way on utilities. They are good for heat, and as an added bonus, they can also function as a cooking source. They don't take any extra room to store (unless you're counting the large section of your backyard or patio where you stack your wood), and the fireplace itself won't cost you an extra penny since it's already in your house. What a deal! If you are used to curling up in front of a roaring fire with a good book, or snuggling with your honey in front of the fire on a crisp fall evening, then you are probably aware of the ins and outs of fireplaces already. If your fireplace has never seen a fire before and is used solely as a resting place for decorative green plants, now would be a good time to learn the basics of fireplace usage. Things like how to open the flu for fires, how to close the flu when the fire is out to keep warm air from being sucked up the chimney, how to build a fire and start it without burning yourself—these are all things you'll be glad to know if you ever have to use the fireplace to stay warm.

> *Fireplaces are often one of the first things to suffer structural damage in an earthquake. It may look safe from the outside, while the working flues on the inside are damaged. In this case, a fire in your fireplace could cause a house fire. After any earthquake or disaster, be sure to have your chimney professionally checked to be sure it is safe to use.*

In order to avoid using the furniture for fuel, make sure you have a supply of fuel on hand. Hardwoods burn longer than softwoods. To determine how much wood you need, light a fire (in the fireplace, of course) and keep it going for an hour. Notice how much wood is used in an hour and

> *If both your furnace and the electricity are not working, you'll find it's difficult to circulate the heat from the fireplace to other rooms in the house. Plan to live in the room with the fireplace and shut the doors to the other rooms in your home.*

multiply that by how many hours you'll want to stay warm. You can also recycle old newspapers to newspaper logs, which will burn about as long as a comparably sized piece of wood. (See appendix H for instructions.) If your fireplace is firebrick-lined, you can also burn coal. (See chapter 24, Fuel Storage Guidelines.) However, coal must be burned in a well-ventilated fireplace to be safe! If your fireplace doesn't draw well, don't use coal!

Freestanding wood-burning stoves have the same advantages that regular fireplaces do.

Fireplaces and wood-burning stoves cause creosote-buildup inside the flue pipes. As a precautionary measure, you should have your chimney professionally cleaned and swept after a season's worth of regular use. Another option is a chimney-sweeping log. These are similar in shape and size to pressed-wood logs. When

A friend of mine recently built a new home with a wood-burning fireplace, fully aware of its preparedness value. He told me that the way the fire smelled was almost as important to him as its fuel efficiency. He explained why the aromatherapy of a fire was important to his family. "Because we regularly love the wonderful smells and relaxing effects of a fire in the fireplace, it would be even more important to us during hard times. We associate the good smells of a crackling fire with happy times. The familiar smells would bring normalcy and calm to our family and help everyone feel like things are not so bad."

By planning ahead, you too can have morale boosters in your fireplace. To create aroma, use wood chips, chunks, twigs, or woody herbs or spices. You can add them dry to a fire, but you'll get better results if you soak them in water for half an hour or so first. The soaking will make them last longer. If you put the chips in a small can (like a tuna can) and put the can in the fire, it will also make the chips (and smells) last longer.

You can purchase wood chips at barbecue specialty shops or online. Or, you can make your own chips by gathering and chopping pruned branches and twigs from neighbors, or from parks or orchards, if the owners will permit. Pinecones are usually free in parks or neighbors' yards.

Here are a few ideas for aromatic fires:
Fruit woods:
Apple, apricot, cherry, etc.
Grapevines
Nut woods and nuts:
Chestnut, pecan, walnut, etc.
Evergreens: Branches and cones
Alder, eucalyptus, mesquite, sage, maple
Herbs and Spices:
All woody herbs, rosemary, thyme, sage, mint, cinnamon sticks, etc.
whole cloves, nutmegs
Dried citrus peelings

burned, they reduce creosote weight and thickness. These precautionary steps help reduce chimney fires.

We know firsthand the devastation that creosote buildup can cause. A cold, rainy day in a recent fall prompted building a fire in the wood-burning stove—the first fire of the year. Soon a fire was warm and roaring in the stove . . . and in the chimney and second floor of my brother's home. Fortunately, the fire department was quick to respond, and no one was injured. But what if this fire had been prompted by a disaster-related emergency instead of cool fall day? The fire department may have been too busy to respond quickly, and the results would have been much more grievous than "only" $50,000 in damages and a very upset family. If you have a fireplace or wood-burning stove, consider regular upkeep as a vital emergency preparedness precaution.

GAS FIREPLACES

Gas fireplaces may or may not work in emergency situations. It depends on the situation and the fireplace. If the emergency is an earthquake or some major catastrophe that ruptures the gas lines in your home, or anywhere along the line, your fireplace will be useless. If the electricity is down, your fireplace may not work either. Some gas fireplaces are designed to work without electricity. The blower may not blow, but the fireplace will still turn on and generate heat. Others require electricity to even turn on, in which case, your fireplace won't work, even if the gas lines remain intact. Check the manufacturer's manual or you local gas company to see what your options are if the electricity is out. If you are building a house or remodeling and are thinking of installing a gas fireplace, be sure to choose a model that can function without electricity if necessary. Check out several reputable companies to see all the different options available. In any case, since no gas fireplace is completely reliable in emergencies, having a backup plan is a good idea.

BUTANE SPACE HEATERS

If a fireplace is not in your emergency preparedness program, you are not automatically doomed to freeze. There still are a few options to choose from. There are portable butane space heaters on the market that have been approved for indoor use. These space heaters are designed to do exactly that—heat the space around you, though not necessarily a large room, and definitely not an entire house. They do work well and are easy to operate. Most have built-in safety features. On high, an eight-ounce fuel canister will last about three and a half hours, and approximately six hours on low. Most have an electric ignition, so you just have to turn it on; no matches or lighters are required. They are approximately the size of an average shoe box. As with the butane cookstove, the butane canister fits into a built-in well so the fuel canister doesn't extend beyond the heater itself.

CATALYTIC HEATERS

Catalytic heaters convert fuel (butane, propane, natural gas, or other hydrocarbon gas) to flameless infrared heat. They are safe to operate because no open flames are present. They attain nearly 100 percent combustion during usage with no measurable carbon monoxide to worry about. The only by-products of combustion, besides heat, are carbon dioxide and water vapor, which makes them safe and recommended for indoor use. They are ideal for places and times where power is not available on a continuous basis, such as unheated garages, recreational vehicles, and emergency preparedness situations.

KEROSENE HEATERS

Larger than catalytic heaters, kerosene heaters will heat a good-sized area extremely well. However, they are also larger to store when not in use, and use more fuel. One large model will run for twenty-four hours on the five gallons of fuel its reservoir holds. Some kerosene heaters function as a heating and cooking source. For example, a smaller model than the last one I mentioned still efficiently heats a large room and has a cooking surface. It holds about one gallon of kerosene, which powers up to sixteen hours of cooking and heating. The cooking plate on the top of the stove will hold several small pans or one large pot. One major problem with kerosene heaters is that the entire stove becomes extremely hot. The exposed sides are a real disadvantage. You run the risk

In trying to stay warm, remember you must not seal off all air circulation!

of someone accidentally getting burned if it is in the middle of the room, yet because of the heat they must not be placed close to walls or furniture. As with all types of heaters, for safety's sake, purchase only the kind that shut-off automatically if tipped over.

BARBECUES

Before you tell me that I'm out of my mind to suggest a barbecue can be used as a heat source, give me a minute to explain. I don't want you to haul your barbecue into the house and huddle around it until you keel over dead from carbon monoxide poisoning. (It's counterproductive to be warm but dead.) However, since many people own barbecues or hibachis, there are a few little tricks you can do with them outside to help ease the cold miseries, if disaster should strike before you have a chance to build your deluxe rock fireplace. Hot water is the first thing. Water heated on a barbecue can be used for hot-water bottles, for hot drinks, preparing foods, or for warming cold hands.

In the olden days, long before instant-heat hand warmers were ever dreamed up, people used potatoes as hand warmers. You can do the same. Wrap a potato in tinfoil and bake it in the coals. Remove the foil and drop the hot potato in your pocket. (Wait a few minutes first so you don't burn yourself.) Then you can put your hands in your pockets to warm them up. Or, you can put them in the inside pockets of jackets and zip the jacket. As an added benefit, you can also eat the potato! (No this is not a joke; you can do this.)

While you are using your barbecue—outside—for cooking or heating water, place clean bricks or rocks around the edges to warm also. (Don't place bricks or rocks directly in the flames since it is possible for them to explode, especially if they are wet.) When the bricks are hot, wrap them in a towel and put them in a sleeping bag to keep your feet warm. Or wrapped in towels, they can be used as foot warmers or body warmers while you read by flashlight.

These little ideas certainly aren't as good as having a heater or fireplace, but they're definitely better than nothing if a barbecue is all you have to work with.

INDIVIDUAL HEAT SOURCES

There are a few resources that could possibly provide heat for a single individual, though probably not for more than that. For example, butane backpacking heaters/stoves can provide varying degrees of heat for a single individual during an emergency. The candelier, described in chapter 26, is designed so that it will provide heat while it provides a cooking and lighting source. You could huddle up next to it like a tiny campfire. Sterno stoves (chapter 25, Emergency Cooking) could also be a source to at least warm your hands.

Keep in mind that if you are planning on using these smaller resources for heat, you'll need to set aside additional fuel. Combining a small heat source with the ideas presented in chapter 22, Staying Warm without a Furnace, can provide a practical and workable solution for an individual.

THINGS THAT DON'T WORK

This paragraph is to remind you that, while you can do a few little tricks with a charcoal barbecue to keep from freezing, you must not burn a charcoal fire in your house! You will die! Don't do it. Don't even think it. It's not an option. Just forget it. Not on your life. Get the point? A charcoal fire in the house is a really bad idea.

CHAPTER TWENTY-EIGHT

TRANSPORTATION: GETTING FROM HERE TO THERE

In a major emergency where power for a large area is down for more than a day or so, getting from point A to point B may be a real problem. Without power, the buses don't run, nor do the trains, planes, or even the automobiles! Without power, the pumps at the gas station won't be working. No gas, no go. When you've exhausted the gas in the gas tank, your car will simply hold down the driveway until the power is restored and the fuel stations are back in business. If the emergency is a destructive natural disaster, you may have to deal with damaged highways or severely obstructed roadways in addition to power outages. Getting gasoline trucks in to refill stations' tanks may be difficult or out of the question. It is entirely possible that you will not be able to rely on your car. You will need some temporary transportation.

A bicycle could save some wear and tear on your feet, plus take you farther than walking can, if the roads are not torn up. Biking is one thing you could do regularly that would improve your everyday life and simultaneously get you ready for hard times. However, if the sole purpose of your bike is to take up space in the rafters of your garage, you may have a problem when the time comes that you need it. It may not be in rideable condition after years of neglect. If you have a bike but don't use it often, put "bike upkeep" on your annual preparedness checklist. Take it down, pump up the tires, oil the chain and take it for a little spin around the block to make sure it works. Then when you need it, it will be ready. A tire-patch kit is a good thing to have with your emergency preparedness supplies too.

USE YOUR FEET

Your temporary transportation just might need to be your feet. This could be a rude awakening if you consider pushing the buttons on the remote control to be an aerobic exercise. I remember when I was in high school, seeing an educational film predicting the directions society, as a whole, was going. In the movie, a woman in her housecoat and curlers got into her station wagon, drove thirty feet down the street, put a letter in a mailbox, drove thirty feet back to her garage, and went indoors. We all laughed at the time because it was so absurd. Yet that's pretty much where society is today. We drive everywhere because it's not safe to walk; there's no time to walk because we're too busy; we're too tired to walk because we're too busy; the 1,200 places we need to go today are not close enough to walk to, and other valid and not-so-valid reasons. We're in the car so much we've basically forgotten that walking is a viable mode of transportation. My daughter has a response for the (frequent) times her children badger her for rides to

> After being refused a ride to a friend's house a block away, one teenaged daughter muttered angrily at her mother as she flounced out of the room, "I am not driving you to the rest home!"

absurdly close destinations (a block or two). She says, "Why? Are your legs painted on?"

In case your car is ever grounded, you should always keep on hand (or on foot) comfortable sturdy shoes in good repair, and socks without holes to prevent blisters. You may have to walk more or farther than you are used to doing to obtain the things you need. A good thing to stash in the cupboard is a package of moleskin to deal with potential blisters. If you're used to walking a lot now, not only are you doing your body good with the exercise, you're preparing for emergencies also. If not, do yourself a favor. Get off the couch and get some exercise. It's a great way to prepare for emergencies.

USE YOUR WHEELS

In many ways, children are more prepared for transportation emergencies than adults are. They use their little bodies every day, all day. They have more energy in their little fingers than most adults have in their entire bodies. (Youth is so wasted on the young!) And they are loaded with transportation options. If their legs can't get them where they want to go fast enough, they always have a set of wheels to take them there: their bike, their roller blades, their skateboard,

their scooter, and so on. For a child, getting there is still half the fun. If you aren't sure if you still have any muscles in your legs left, take your child's foot-propelled scooter out for a spin around the block. By the next day, you'll be very sure the muscles are still there as you rub them down with Bengay.

You also need to think about how you can carry commodities or groceries or water or whatever you need to transport from here to there. Wheels are again a great answer. Though we haven't had small children at home for many, many years, we still have always had a wagon. Its main function is to haul potted plants or fertilizer or grandchildren around the yard or neighborhood. Its equally important secondary function is as an essential piece of emergency preparedness equipment. A child's wagon, a stroller, a personal folding grocery cart, or a garden cart could all be invaluable. If nothing else were available, you could use a wheelbarrow or a rolling suitcase to carry buckets of water or other things wherever you needed them. If you can't find any wheels at all, you can put on a backpack and use your feet. Look around your house and see what you might use if your car were not an option. Think of at least one alternative that will work for you.

CHAPTER TWENTY-NINE

COMMUNICATIONS: "THIS IS A TEST . . ."

"This is a test . . . this is only a test. In case of an actual emergency, instructions would follow on this station. This has been a test of the Emergency Alert System." In case of the actual emergency, you need to know what the warning systems are in your area.

THE EMERGENCY ALERT SYSTEM

Usually during a crisis, instructions about what to do will come through the broadcast media (radio and television stations) via the Emergency Alert System. The Emergency Alert System replaced the Emergency Broadcast System, which was originally designed so the president could address the country in the event of a disaster, though it was never actually used for that purpose. Almost all radio and television broadcast stations and cable companies are required to carry EAS messages. These broadcast stations, especially those with emergency power generators and equipment, provide extensive information about local disaster conditions, warnings, what to do to handle specific problems, and how to locate missing family members. This system is used whether the crisis is restricted to one city or an entire region. The system is designed so that local city or county dispatchers contact the stations with specific crisis-related information, such as what areas or neighborhoods are isolated, what roads to use, where shelters are opening up, and so on. These broadcasts are where you will receive the most reliable information and directions.

Law enforcement agencies also use EAS to issue Amber Alerts, which allow officials to rapidly share information about abducted children with the public to increase the chances for a safe and prompt recovery.

The standardized Emergency Alert System operates throughout the nation.

COMMUNITY WARNING SYSTEMS

In some areas, a community warning system (horns or sirens) will sound in an emergency. These are usually tested from time to time, so you may already be familiar with their sound. If the siren goes off, you should immediately turn on your radio or television for instructions.

If the forthcoming emergency is a predictable natural disaster, such as a hurricane, flood, or tornado, the radio or television broadcaster may tell you there is a "watch." That means you will have some time to prepare for possible danger. If the station tells you that there is a "warning," disaster is imminent. In this case, follow the instructions that are being broadcast, and take shelter immediately.

OTHER WARNINGS

Another way you may learn about impending danger is from local authorities, such as the police, fire department, or National Guard. Within hours of the October 1989 Loma Prieta earthquake in California, police came through our neighborhood with bullhorns, telling us to shut off our gas and water lines due to cracked mains. And in 2005, when a train car began leaking toxic chemicals not far from a residential area in Utah, over 8,000 people were evacuated from their homes. Police and trained CERT volunteers went door-to-door telling people to get out. If you are warned by local authorities to take certain actions, you should follow their instructions explicitly and immediately.

YOU NEED A
BATTERY-POWERED RADIO!

In a crisis, a battery-powered radio may well be your lifeline. I realized firsthand how valuable a battery-powered radio was during the aftermath of the 7.2 Loma Prieta earthquake in northern California. The power was down all over and we had no idea how long it would be before the power would be restored or a phone would work. The rest of the nation saw the earthquake destruction before we ever did, since they had television. We only had our battery-powered radios and word-of-mouth. We were so grateful for those radios! They were our lifeline to the outside world and our security. We also learned very quickly to limit our listening time to conserve the batteries, even though it was tempting to just keep it on for the company. It would have been easy to run through our batteries in just a short span of time; in fact, many people did. After a day or so of continual usage, their radios were useless. Having spare batteries is a good idea, but using your radios conservatively is just as important.

There is a huge variety of portable radios available. The bigger the radio (and the more things it does besides just being a radio), the more batteries it will use for operation. For example, a medium-sized boom box may take eight or more D-cell batteries for a mere seven or eight operational hours. For emergency purposes, you would be better off buying a small, inexpensive handheld radio that operates on two AA batteries (or better yet, an emergency preparedness radio that operates on several power options, including batteries, AC/DC, solar power, or by hand-cranking or shaking).

I highly suggest that you have a radio (and batteries) specifically for emergencies, and that you keep it off-limits for everyday use. You may be tempted to get out the radio some weekend at home when you want some music while you putter in the garage. Don't do it. Resist the temptation to use this radio for leisure. You don't want to end up kicking yourself when you desperately need disaster information and can't find the radio, or your batteries are dead because you used them up listening to a baseball game while you washed the car one Saturday last year. Not only should you dedicate a radio to emergency use *only*, but also once an emergency occurs, you should limit this radio to obtaining information, not recreational listening. Remember that the main purpose of the radio is to provide information and instructions about an emergency. If you feel that listening to music would be a relaxing morale booster for you or a member of your family (a.k.a. teenagers), then you must include additional extra batteries for just this purpose. (That is, extra batteries for music, in addition to the mandatory extra batteries required for emergency use.) This is a good topic to discuss during a family meeting. Talk over ground rules and regulations about how often and how long the radios may be used for entertainment during an emergency situation. Since you won't know how long

A solar-powered battery charger is also a smart emergency preparedness purchase.

Remember the radio in your car or truck. It can serve as a source for emergency information in a pinch.

The following note was handed to me after a seminar in the Moses Lake, Washington, area. It was six weeks after the Mount St. Helens eruption. "We all thought the end of the world had come. We never dreamed of anything so ferocious in all of our lives. When the ash hit, we found one thing we never thought of—radio batteries. Not knowing what effect volcanic ash would have on electric transformers, we were told to have on hand a portable radio. The radio we had, but since it had a cord, we never provided batteries for it. Then we couldn't use the radio. We were too frightened to plug it in. We didn't know if the ash would cause an electrical short or a fire or what."

a disaster-caused power outage may last at the outset, you'll need to set an agreed-upon number of rationed hours of battery time each day. Perhaps your family members are responsible enough to receive their allotted number of batteries at the beginning and pace their individual use accordingly. For younger children, you might get creative and have "battery coupons" good for an hour of radio listening (or electronic-device playing) that you hand out as you see fit. Whatever you do, the point is, batteries don't last forever, and it's important that all family members know that when the entertainment batteries are gone, they're gone, and emergency radio batteries will not take their place!

TELEPHONES

There is no feeling quite like the aloneness that comes when you realize that, even though you may be in the middle of a city, you can't contact anyone. You can't pick up the phone and call Mom or your best friend. There is no power; there is no nightly news, no talk radio. The silence can be deafening!

We are a society completely dependent on our telephones. To live in a fast-paced society like ours, you have to be able to communicate quickly. Just think, a hundred years ago, if you wanted to talk to someone, you had to do it face-to-face. We progressed to a phone on a party line, to a phone attached to the wall, then to cordless phones around our houses, and now, with our cell phones, we can go anywhere and talk to anyone at any time (whether we ought to or not!). We think we are lost without our phones! But that's just what can happen in emergency situations. Phone wires go down, switch stations can be destroyed, transmitting and receiving cells damaged, and in an instant communications can be cut off completely. You can't even rely on e-mail or instant messaging because your computer requires electricity and a phone line to operate!

In a minor, local power outage, your cell phone may still work, though only until the battery runs out. (You may be able to eke out a few more hours if you have a car charger to recharge the phone on.) Every home should have at least one phone attached to the wall with a cord because, although your cordless phone will not work when the electricity is out, a corded phone usually still will. In northern California, in the energy crises of 1999 and 2000, rolling brownouts were a regular part of life. To conserve the

I live in Utah, and my son and daughter-in-law live in New Jersey. My son, a lawyer, works across the bay in New York. On September 11, 2001, I watched the terrorist strikes in horror with the rest of the country. I was especially terrified because I knew that my son's commuter train traveled directly under the World Trade Center every day at about the time of the disaster. I called my daughter-in-law, told her to turn on the television, and to find out if David was okay and let me know. While I waited anxiously for her to call me back, my phone rang and, thankfully, it was my son, on his cell phone. He said he'd been trapped in the subway in New York when his train stopped abruptly, but that he was okay. He couldn't get hold of his wife, though, and he wasn't sure what was going on. I was able to tell him about the terrorist attack and said I'd call Trisha and tell her he was okay. I called her back, and she was frantic because she couldn't get through to David, and didn't know if it was because the phone lines were jammed or because he was involved in the attack. I was able to reassure her as to his safety and whereabouts. That went on for the next two days. They couldn't call each other, but they could each get through to me, 2,000 miles away. It took David over twenty-four hours to get home, but at least his family knew that he was safe and working his way home as best as he could during that time.

—W. W., as told to S. S.

insufficient energy, specific areas were scheduled to be without power on specific days, at specific times, for a specific time length (usually three to four hours). This went on annoyingly for months (as utility bills soared up and up). When the power was off, cordless phones were useless, but corded phones and cell phones still worked.

In a major disaster, it's likely that none of your phones will work, cell phones included. Cell phones are still dependent on cells, stations usually situated on a mountain or hill in your general area that channel the cellular signals to satellites orbiting the earth. If the cells go down (as some did during the Loma Prieta), cell phones won't function. Storms or earthquakes easily disrupt regular telephone lines. And even if the phones work, during a major disaster, the trunk lines are often so inundated with calls that it can be impossible to get through. A general guideline during a major emergency is that you are not to use the phone except in a dire emergency, so the lines can be kept open for emergency workers.

FAMILY MESSAGING

A plan to communicate with your family during an emergency is a must! Keeping this in mind, as a family, designate both a local person and a long-distance person (outside your state) to call for family and individual updates. Oddly enough, it is sometimes easier to get through to a long-distance number than to a local number when the lines are jammed. If family members are separated in an emergency, they may not be able to get to each other or even contact each other, since local phone lines may be inundated,

even if they are only a few miles apart. However, it may still be possible to check in with Grandma in San Jose, or Uncle Fred in Des Moines. Grandma or Uncle Fred can keep track of who's safe and where they are, even if you can't get to them or contact them directly. At least you know they're okay. Grandma can also call the rest of the worried extended family spread across the country to let them know how you're doing, without overloading the phone system in your locality even more.

During an emergency warning, do not try to use your telephone to call the authorities just to verify the emergency or to obtain more information. Turn on your radio, remember? Tying up the phone lines might prevent emergency calls from being made. Use the phone only if you have to.

HAM ON YOUR PREPAREDNESS MENU

If you're looking for a fun hobby that would double as a valuable preparedness measure, check out ham radio. You can be in touch with people all over the world without relying on Ma Bell or any of her competitors for equipment or lines. For information on getting started, license requirements and how-tos, check your local library, the internet, or contact your city director of emergency services. Your chamber of commerce should be able to tell you where the local chapter of ham operators meets. Ham radio operators are in great demand during major crises! In fact in most emergencies, ham radio operators are an integral piece of the response plans for city and county emergency services.

CHAPTER THIRTY

SANITATION

One of the most unpleasant aspects of an emergency situation comes from the need to answer the call of Mother Nature. It doesn't matter one little bit if the plumbing system is out of order. When you've got to go, you've got to go.

Our city sewer systems are dependent on electricity and an intact system of underground pipes. If either of these systems malfunctions, so do your bathroom facilities. If the electricity is out just in your individual neighborhood, your plumbing is probably fine. But if the main city system is powerless, that's another story. The main pumps that keep the water running to your home require electricity to work. If the electricity doesn't flow, neither does the water. Backup generators can tide the power company over for a while, but not forever. Eventually, the system will shut down and that's the end of running water until electricity is restored. If, in the case of an earthquake or severe storm, any of the pipes between the water treatment plant and your home are broken, the water won't make it to your house and you'll be left high and dry.

Sanitation may be unpleasant to discuss, and it's certainly not a socially acceptable dinner-table topic,

but it needs to be covered, nonetheless. It's a very real problem to deal with during an extended disruption of services. In many countries suffering from serious natural disasters, we've seen the consequences of unsanitary conditions and polluted drinking water; it doesn't take long. The resulting dysentery and spread of epidemic diseases can be as disastrous as the original catastrophe.

Just because you are without power doesn't mean you are without options. Let's consider first the least objectionable situation: your sewer pipes are intact but the power is out for a while so the water won't flow.

USING GRAY WATER

One of the most common-sense solutions is to use gray water to create a "flush" for the toilet. Gray water is water that is not fit for drinking or food preparation. It's water that you have first used for personal hygiene or cleaning, and reserved to make your toilet system work. Or it could be collected rainwater. If the weather should be stormy you can collect rainwater or snow in buckets or pans and keep it in a larger trash can just for gray water. An entire gallon of water poured directly and quickly into the toilet bowl will enable your toilet to flush. Give it a try now, before there's a need to know how to do it. To simulate the conditions brought on by a lack of running water, turn the water off behind your toilet and flush it to get rid of the water in the tank. Then plunge out the water in the bowl. This is how your toilet would be if there wasn't any running water. Toss a square of toilet tissue in the bowl so you can see how this process works. Now, fill a gallon-size pitcher or bucket with water and dump it all at once into the bowl (not the tank). It should swirl your toilet tissue square right

> A person who went through a major Midwest flood told me that one of the greatest problems they had was sanitation. Accustomed to the convenience of modern facilities, no one had made any emergency provisions. It had a devastating effect on morale as conditions rapidly became deplorable.

on down. I found that half a gallon usually doesn't create enough pressure to make it work. It has to be a whole gallon or more. You can experiment to see the minimum amount of water your toilet requires to flush. This is a good thing to know before a disaster, in order to not waste precious gray water after a disaster, in case water should turn out to be a scarce and precious commodity. (Don't forget to turn the water to the toilet back on when you're through experimenting.)

We experienced two severe droughts during our years in California where strict water rationing was a reality. So was selective flushing. Selective flushing means that you don't flush the toilet every time you use it. You can make do with flushing only once or twice a day to conserve your gray water, depending on how many people are using the facilities. There is a common saying that I apologize for quoting here, but it's memorable and appropriate. "If it's yellow, let it mellow. If it's brown, flush it down." During those droughts, we learned to use gray water wisely. The idea of selective flushing is just as appropriate when there is absolutely no running water as when there is only severely drought-restricted water.

BROKEN PIPES COMPLICATE THINGS

If your sewer pipes are broken, or if there is no gray water available, then the situation becomes more complicated. Then you have to deal with the problems of safely disposing of human waste. It's not fun but it is a possibility, so it's best to know how to cope.

We'll assume that the sewer pipes are kaput, but your house is still standing and in fairly good condition. At this point you still have the bathroom itself, and you can still use the most obvious facility, your toilet that is already in place, just not in the usual way. The ingredients for success are already there; it just takes a little bit of creative thinking to make it work.

Your toilet becomes the basis for a permanent port-a-potty. You will also need the following basic sanitation supplies:

- Thirteen-gallon kitchen size or larger heavy-duty trash bags. (Oblong toilet bowls may need a larger-sized trash bag to fit around the circumference of the bowl.) Buy the heaviest-gauge bags you can find. "Mil" on the label means millimeter, and it refers to the thickness of the plastic. The larger the number, .5, .8, 1.3, and so on, the stronger the bag. This is not the place to be overly budget conscious. Avoid the cheap generic bags and buy the strongest bags available. You've seen the commercials where the frustrated homeowner is carrying out his full trash bag and it rips and garbage spills all over the floor? Think how much more unhappy you'll be if this trash bag rips and its contents spill all over the floor!

- Duct tape or other heavy tape that will stick to porcelain.

- Twist ties.

- An empty bucket with a handle.

- Household chlorine bleach or other sanitizing chemicals.

- Toilet paper.

- Latex or rubber gloves.

- Aerosol air freshener/room deodorizer (optional but desirable).

Start with an empty toilet bowl. If water is at a premium, dip all the water out of the tank that you can and reserve it for other uses. Then, flush the toilet to get rid of the rest of the water from the tank and plunge away any remaining water in the bowl. Lift the seat and lid so they're out of the way. Place the bottom of the opened trash bag into the toilet and stretch the top down and around the outside of the bowl. Tape it firmly in place. Close the seat. The seat will hold the weight of the person just like it regularly does, and the tape will hold the bags in place. (Tape the handle in place to keep someone from flushing the toilet out of habit.) After each use, pour a small amount of disinfectant into the bag. This will help avoid the spread of germs and disease. (See the following section on disinfectants.) You can pull another thirty-gallon plastic trash bag over the whole toilet bowl, seat, lid, and all, in between uses to help contain the smell and to keep insects out. After several uses, remove the tape and, while the bag is still in the toilet, twist the edges of the bag together and fasten it tightly with a twist tie. Put an empty bucket with a handle right next to the toilet and lift the used bag right into it. Then you can use the handle to carry it to a holding container outside your home. A holding container is any container with a tight-fitting lid, such as a garbage can or large bucket.

OPTIONS IF THE TOILET IS NOT AN OPTION

If your toilet is completely backed up to begin with, it is probably not worth trying to clean it out to use as a permanent port-a-potty. Sprinkle it with disinfectant, and cover it with a big trash bag to help contain the smell until the pipes are repaired. Then, use a five-gallon bucket instead of the toilet, following the same basic use and disinfection guidelines. Keep the plastic bag securely on the bucket, either with tape or large rubber bands. You can make a toilet seat out of two boards placed parallel to each other across the bucket (watch out for slivers), or you can use a regular toilet seat. Either take one off a household toilet temporarily, or keep an old one tucked away in your attic or garage just for this type of situation. Another option is a snap-on toilet seat and lid that is specifically designed to fit five-gallon poly buckets. Change the bag when it is about one-third full.

If you can't bear the thought of making your own toilet out of a bucket, you can instead buy an actual portable toilet just for this type of situation. They are the same basic thing as a homemade bucket potty but they may possibly be a little sturdier and better balanced. Look for them in the camping section of sporting goods stores or in emergency preparedness stores.

You'll want to check with your city officials to find out how to dispose of the waste you have stored in the holding containers. Often the local newscasts on the radio or television will have bulletins as to what each area is supposed to do. There may be vehicles scheduled to come around and pick up waste. Other cities will provide places to dispose of waste and you'll be advised which waste disposal site to use. If you don't receive instructions from the media, call your city for directions—providing you have a working telephone and transportation to take you to the indicated waste station.

If that doesn't work out, and if the crisis goes on for an extended period of time, you should bury human waste daily to avoid the spread of disease by rodents and insects. This is assuming, of course, you have unpaved yard area available that isn't frozen solid. Dig a hole at least two to three feet deep to prevent insect breeding and discourage animals from digging it up. The pit should be at least fifty feet away from your home or any well or water supply.

Apartment dwellers, people without any yard space, or people with solidly frozen ground don't have the option of burying waste in their yards. In this situation, you should have a number of waterproof containers on hand for emergency waste disposal. When a bucket is nearly full, tamp the lid down tightly and set it to the side where it won't be disturbed until power is restored and/or your city officials make other options available to you.

THE DIAPER DILEMMA

If you have a baby in your home, have a couple of weeks' worth of disposable diapers on hand all the time. Keep in mind how quickly babies grow and prepare for that contingency. For example, keep three or four packages of size small diapers on your shelf. When the baby is getting close to growing out of the small size, begin using up your stash of diapers by replacing a package of small diapers in the closet with a package of medium diapers each time you purchase a new bag of diapers. Then you'll always have the right size on hand for emergencies, without any extra expense. By the time the baby needs medium diapers, the small ones will all be used up. For sanitation purposes in emergencies, keep the used diapers in waterproof containers with tight-fitting lids until the emergency is over and you have a safe way to dispose of them.

If you run out of disposable diapers, you can fold a dishtowel into a triangle and pin it on with large safety pins the way they did in the old days (you know, ten to fifteen years ago). Cover them up with a pair of plastic pants. Prepare for this contingency by keeping several pairs of plastic pants (in various sizes) in the back of the baby's dresser drawer. If you don't have even a single pair of plastic pants, you can loosely wrap the dishtowel diaper with plastic wrap and tape it in place. Be extra cautious doing this though, because plastic and babies can be a lethal combination if you're not careful. (And if that doesn't work, you can simply lay the baby on thick towels or blankets, providing he's small enough to hold still.) Store the soiled dishtowel diapers in a waterproof container with a tight-fitting lid (in the same olden days, it was called a diaper pail) until water and power are restored and they can be soaked and washed with bleach.

DISINFECTANTS

It's very important to control germs in emergency situations. Common household chlorine bleach is one of the best and most readily available choices. Use a solution of one part liquid chlorine bleach to ten parts water, (approximately one cup bleach to one-half gallon of water.) Use bleach that contains at least five and one-quarter percent sodium hypochlorite, which is standard. You can also use "ultra" type bleaches, which are six percent sodium hypochlorite. Don't use dry or powdered bleach. It is caustic and not safe for this type of use. It doesn't take large amounts of disinfectant to do the job. Liquid disinfecting solutions are meant to be sprinkled on, not poured in with a bucket. A little bit goes a long way. You don't want to add a great deal of liquid to your portable toilet. (One half-cup to a cup is probably sufficient.)

Other portable toilet chemicals, both wet and dry, are available in recreational vehicle supply stores. These chemicals are designed specifically for toilets that aren't connected to a sewer system. You can also use HTH (calcium hypochlorite), which you can get in swimming pool supply stores. It is intended to be used in a solution, not dry. Follow the directions on the package to mix and store it. A word of caution: don't use calcium hypochlorite to disinfect drinking water. It kills all the beneficial bacteria in the intestinal tract as well as the damaging ones, causing mild diarrhea. You can purchase powdered, chlorinated lime in building supply stores (not quick lime, which is corrosive). You can sprinkle it on dry. Pine-Sol, Lysol, and ammonia are acceptable disinfectants, and even powdered laundry detergent or baking soda will work in a pinch, though they're not as effective as the other disinfectants mentioned.

Caution! Do not combine ammonia and bleach in any solution. Do not add both to the same bag, not even alternately. The combination of bleach and ammonia will cause toxic fumes. Some laundry detergents contain bleach, so read labels and pay attention. If you are using a laundry detergent with bleach as a disinfectant, you must not add ammonia of any sort to that bag.

TOILET PAPER—A PRIORITY

While we're talking about basic sanitation supplies, it's important to throw in a word or two about toilet paper. First and foremost, you ought to realize how valuable toilet paper is. It could be almost as important as any item you can think of. You've probably heard someone jokingly suggest that you use pages from catalogs or newspapers if you run out of toilet paper. Remember that this is just a joke. You don't want to really do that. The ink/print from the pages could cause sores and increase problems, let alone clog up any sewer lines that might be working. You really need toilet tissue. I suggest that you keep a supply on hand just for emergencies that no one is allowed to use for anything else (especially not for the favorite pastime of honoring someone's house, trees, and bushes with a twenty-four-roll salute in the middle of a dark night). To get an idea of what a supply of toilet tissue might need to be, tape a piece of paper on the wall near the back of the toilet for three to four weeks. Every time you replace a roll of toilet paper, mark it down. You'll probably be surprised how much you go through, especially since in most households, toilet paper is a multiuse item, used for everything from its intended purpose to runny noses to makeup removal.

KEEPING AHEAD OF GERMS

Sanitation entails more than just having bathroom facilities. You must take steps to keep ahead of the germs and disease that spread so easily under disaster conditions. For general cleaning in an emergency, you can keep the worst of the germs down if you make sure you always have an extra spray bottle of Pine-Sol, Formula 409, or other disinfectant in your cupboard. These would be particularly useful because they don't require any extra water but will clean

> We have friends who lived in Idaho during the Teton Dam break and the resulting floods. In some of the outlying areas, toilet paper was one of the most sought-after items, as neighbors shared supplies until somewhat-normal life was restored.

> *As I was writing this book, I wanted to get an accurate count on how much toilet paper a family of two would go through in a month's time. I kept forgetting to tape a piece of paper on the wall to check off whenever I got out a new roll. Instead, I just started stacking the empty rolls on the end of the bathtub. After a few weeks, Larry pointed at the growing pile of empty rolls and asked, "Is there some reason you're keeping empty toilet paper rolls?" I responded, "I'm counting exactly how much T.P. we use in a month. The rolls are that exact number." Larry looked at the pile, grunted non-commitally, and turned away to go down the hall. I heard his muttered comment anyway: "Only in our house. Only in our house." (It was seven rolls, by the way.)*

up most messes and kill disease-causing germs. Read the labels on your disinfectants. There is a difference between cleaning and sanitizing.

You may think I'm going a little overboard talking about housecleaning when the world is collapsing around you. I'm not advocating that your house should be ready for the white-glove test even in the aftermath of an earthquake. I'm just suggesting keeping the worst of the mess and germs cleared away. For example, what if someone is sick all over the floor? If you don't have much water, you could still do a good job of cleaning up if you had a roll of paper towels and a spray bottle of disinfectant. If some water is available, you can make your own sanitizing solution by mixing a teaspoon of liquid household bleach with a quart of water. This is good for wiping surfaces (floors, cribs, tables, and so on), as well as rinsing and sanitizing laundry in order to control disease. (Bleach will leave spots on fabric, so be careful.)

LAUNDRY

If your power has been out for a couple of weeks, it's likely that your laundry baskets are full to bursting. When there's not a clean sock left in the house and your jeans stand up by themselves, it's time to figure out how to get things washed without a washer. Or, you can subscribe to my granddaughter's roommates' washing theory at college: Buy enough clothes so that you don't have to worry about washing them until you go home for a weekend every other month.

If you don't have sixty pair of undies filling your drawers, you'll need to do some wash now and then, even if you don't have any power. If you have not thought about it in advance, you can still use what you already have on hand to clean your clothes. See chapter 31 for full details on doing laundry without power.

You'll find from the basic instructions in the next chapter that machineless laundry requires tubs full of water. That only works if you have water available. If the only water you have is for drinking and basic cleaning, you may just have to wear dirty clothes for a while. One thing you could do is to save up any dish-rinsing water for a couple of days until you have a panful, then use it to wash out underwear and socks. Boy Scouts have a lot of experience in surviving long periods of time with a minimum of clean clothes. Send a twelve-year-old to Scout Camp with three extra pair of underwear for a week, and he'll come home with everything else filthy, and three clean pair of underwear stuffed in the bottom of his backpack. If Boy Scouts can survive, so can you.

CHAPTER THIRTY-ONE

DOING THE LAUNDRY THE NONELECTRIC WAY

Having access to a washer and dryer or local Laundromat is so much a part of our lives that we take them for granted, always expecting them to perform when wash day arrives. For some, even washing out a pair of socks without the machine is a mystery. No one is happily planning to resort to primitive living conditions, but if the power should fail for more than a day or two, having clean socks could become a challenge. You still have a choice. Continue to wear the socks until they can walk around by themselves, or figure out how to wash them and a few other critical items by hand.

This will be one of those skills that you need to have to get you through. Should you be without power for a week or more, or face often intermittent power for days at a time when bad weather hits, it will be a skill you will be glad to have learned. This is especially true if in your household you have a person with special needs, such as an infant, someone who is chronically ill, or even the miserable possibility of having several household members down at the same time with the flu or nasty colds—and no working washing machine. The ability to have clean clothing or bedding could make the difference between lengthening the stay of germs or keeping ahead of them.

These basic instructions are based on a few assumptions, the first being that you have running water. If you don't, these directions will still work, only on an extremely limited basis. You'll have to save any and all gray water and use it for laundering only the most dire necessities. If your power is out, you may or may not have hot water. If you do, use it, because hot water cleans better than cold water, plus it's easier on your hands. If your water heater is

electric and the electricity is off, you'll only have cold water. If you have a gas stove, you may be able to heat pots of water a few at a time to warm your laundry water. If you don't have a gas stove, or if the gas is out too (and you don't have a camp stove and fuel), you're back to using plain old cold water.

Your kitchen sink is the most logical place to wash clothes by hand, as long as it has a tight-fitting drain plug. If it is a double sink, all the better. If it is not a double sink, you'll also need one or two very large bowls or tubs (like Rubbermaid or Sterilite, eighteen- to twenty-gallon tubs) to hold rinse water. It is possible to use your bathtub for a laundry-washing place and it seems a logical choice, but I don't recommend it primarily because it is really hard on your knees and back to kneel and lean and scrub for any length of time. It's far less painful to stand at your kitchen sink. That said, here is a list of supplies you'll need to do laundry by hand.

Bare-Bones-Basic Supplies and Equipment for Doing Wash by Hand

- Laundry detergent designed to be used in *cold* water
- A bar of hand soap
- A scrub brush, fingernail brush, or old toothbrush for scrubbing stains

Additional Supplies for People Who Want to Be Prepared

- Laundry soap designed for hand washing in cold water (Woolite, White King, Ivory, and so on)
- Fels-Naptha laundry soap bar or Ivory bar soap

- Washboard
- Latex kitchen gloves (to prevent chapped, sore hands)
- Hand lotion (for use after you've had your hands in cold, harsh soapy water for a while)
- Clothesline or rope, screw eyes, bolts
- Racks for drying
- Clothespins

PROCEDURE

You will need at least two tubs, large basins, or buckets, preferably three. Tub number one (possibly the sink) becomes the washtub. Tubs two and three hold rinse water. Fill the tubs no more than three-quarters of the way full to avoid slopping over the edges when you add or swish the clothes. You will not be emptying these tubs and refilling them with fresh water in between loads. The same water can/will be used for all the loads. Therefore, sort your clothes or socks as you normally would, and wash them from lightest color to darkest, and from cleanest to dirtiest (that is, underwear and light shirts first, then white socks, colored clothing, dark clothing and socks, heavy jeans and towels, and finish up with anything particularly dirty).

Add a small amount of soap to three to five gallons of wash water, approximately one to two tablespoons liquid, or one-eighth to one-quarter cup powdered laundry detergent, laundry soap, or for lack of anything else grated hand soap (grating enables the soap to dissolve in the water more easily). A word to the wise: use only a small amount of soap. It's very difficult to thoroughly rinse clothes when hand washing in cold water. Soap that is left in fabric can cause rashes, allergic reactions, and miserable itching. Don't use dry or liquid bleach for hand laundering. The added bleach might not get thoroughly mixed, or be too much bleach for the volume of water. This could permanently damage your clothing by bleaching out spots on the fabric. Besides, bleach is extremely harsh on your hands. If you have an article of clothing that requires bleaching, just wait until the power is back on.

THE ART OF LAUNDERING BY HAND

Washboards come in a variety of sizes from tiny, specifically made for small hand washes, to medium and large to use for a full-sized wash. They are made with a ridged surface of heavy glass or metal. The ridges are used for scrubbing dirt out of clothes. To wash, place the board on a slant into the tub of soapy water with the top and some of the ridges sticking above the edge of the tub and the bottom half of the ridges under the water. Place a few articles of clothing at a time into the tub. Hold on to the washboard with one hand. If you are right-handed, it works best to have the top of the washboard to the left side of the tub, and vice versa if you're left-handed. Place the wet articles, one at a time, onto the board. Fold the item up and over, so that you are using the article to scrub itself with. With a scrubbing motion, rub the article up and down multiple times across the ridges. Turn the article frequently so that you are not just scrubbing one side or one place. Be sure to scrub soiled areas, for example, collars, cuffs, and underarms of shirts, or the foot portion of socks. The more soil in the article, the more you need to scrub.

For particularly soiled areas, rub bar soap (preferably Fels-Naptha or Ivory) directly onto the piece of clothing with a rubbing motion up and down across the ridges of the board. The harder you press with the soap, the more soap will be forced into and onto the item. This may or may not be a good thing. Remember, when working with cold water it is harder to rinse the soap out of the fabric. Use your scrubbing brush, fingernail brush, or toothbrush to scrub these particularly dirty sections also. Most washboards are designed so that you can place the bar of soap on a small ledge at the top to keep it out of the water while you scrub. Soap dissolves in water, making the water soapier than you may want or need.

If you don't have a washboard, you're going to just scrub the clothing against itself. If you're using bar soap, rub the soap into the fabric just as if you were lathering a washcloth. If the soap or detergent is in the washing water, slosh the item through the water to ensure that the soap gets into the fabric. With different ends of the item in each hand, scrub or rub the article together. Transfer or change your handhold on the article several times, until the entire article has been scrubbed. Pay attention to the soiled areas as previously mentioned.

After washing, hold the item above the soapy water and wring out as much water as possible. The larger the item, the heavier it will be when full of water, and the harder to wring out. Wring tightly to squeeze out as much water as you can. (You can try convincing your teenage boys that this is a surefire weight-training exercise to improve their pecs and deltoids.) Then, place the item in the rinse water, swish the items back and forth to force the water to pass through the cloth, and wring it out again. You will probably want to repeat the process in the third tub to get out as much soap as possible.

You will quickly realize that if you are washing many items it won't take long before tubs number two and number three become soapy water. If there is ample water available you may wish to change your rinse water frequently. Or, if plenty of water is available and the weather is cooperative, you can carry all your freshly washed clothes out to the yard and rinse the soap out with a garden hose. If water is scarce, just rinse as best as you can. After rinsing, again wring out as much water as possible. The clothes will be very wet and very heavy compared to what you are used to from a washing machine.

After the white batch, you don't need to empty and refill your tubs. Just begin the next batch of laundry in the same washing water you previously used. When your soapy water becomes too dirty, and/or when all the laundry is done, use the gray water to water your plants. (No, the soap won't hurt them. During many years of drought in California, residents were advised to recycle their washing machine water by running a hose from the washing machine out to their lawns rather than letting it run down the drains. For several of those draught years, I watered my indoor plants with dishwater and none of them were ever worse for wear because of it.)

SANITIZING: EXTERMINATING THE GERMS

If someone in your household is ill, it may be necessary to sanitize clothing or bedding in order to control germs. Rinsing items in a mild bleach sanitizing solution is a good method to do this. It's probably not necessary to sanitize all the laundry, just a few pertinent items.

Mix a teaspoon of household bleach in a quart of water (four teaspoons per gallon). Prepare enough solution to cover the laundry items and soak the clothing or bedding in the solution for half an hour or so. You may wish to wear latex gloves to protect your hands when working with bleach. Then, wring out the sanitizing solution and proceed to wash and rinse the items as previously directed. If possible, dry your items in bright sunlight to kill even more germs. It goes without saying that you only want to use a bleach solution on white or bleachable clothing, and watch out for the clothing you are wearing when you use it. Bleach will ruin colored items.

DRYING CLOTHES WITHOUT A DRYER

Laundry will dry best, and fastest, if you have some sort of clothesline. If you want to be prepared, you can permanently install one and even use it occasionally for no reason other than the wonderfully fresh smell that you can only get from clothes dried outdoors in the sun.

PERMANENT CLOTHESLINES

Real clotheslines are not just any old piece of rope tied between two trees. They are usually heavy-duty, vinyl-covered wire, which is strong enough to support the weight of waterlogged laundry. You'll often find clotheslines strung between two T-shaped sturdy steel poles, or between a house and garage. It is also possible to install retractable clotheslines that you pull out and attach to a support whenever you need it, and when you're done, it retracts compactly so as to be out of the way.

There is another style of permanent clothesline system that is supported by a single steel post sunk in the ground. The clotheslines are usually stretched across and through metal pipes so that the lines form a close, compact square area instead of stretching across a yard or garage. Many fold down, similar to an umbrella, when they are not in use. Check your local hardware or home improvement stores to see all the different options you can choose for permanent clotheslines.

If you already have a clothesline, and it has been has been moldering outside in complete retirement, remember to use a wet soapy cloth to wipe off the grime before hanging anything on it.

PUTTING UP A TEMPORARY CLOTHESLINE

You may not want to be bothered with putting up a permanent clothesline on the off-chance you'll be doing a few loads of wash by hand someday when the power is out. That's perfectly okay but it would still be in your best interest to think your way through the potential problems of doing laundry without electricity and prepare with a few simple items that could make your life easier. If you're washing more than just a handful of socks and underwear, you'll still want a clothesline, albeit a temporary one. You'll need two supports, ten to thirty feet apart, to anchor your line. Two trees will work, or you could screw heavy-duty eyebolts into studs on opposite sides of a garage or carport. Or, you could use a strong fence post and a tetherball pole. Or, the swing set and the corner post from a covered patio. You get the idea. Any two stable supports will work, as long as they are a reasonable distance apart and at least five feet in the air. For the line itself, if you don't have authentic vinyl-covered wire, use nylon rope stretched as tightly as possible between your chosen end supports. Use cotton rope as a last resort. Cotton rope will absorb water and sag, allowing your clean laundry to drag on the floor or ground.

NO CLOTHESLINE IN SIGHT? HERE ARE A FEW MORE OPTIONS

There are a few more options to try if putting up a clothesline is just not going to work for you. An old-fashioned folding clothes rack works very well. There are wooden and vinyl ones available in some of the home product catalogs, home improvement stores, or hardware stores. When unfolded and put in place, these racks are approximately four and one-half feet high, three feet long, with about ten rungs to drape clothes on. These racks can be used outdoors, or they'll work indoors in small areas such as in a kitchen corner on the linoleum, or an apartment balcony or patio. A particularly good choice is to stand them in a bathtub—no drippy floor to clean up. Be sure the shower curtain is pulled back to allow as much airflow as possible. Be aware of how you layer the laundry on them. The bulkier, heavy items should go on the middle rungs or toward the bottom. If you have a fully loaded, top-heavy rack of wet laundry, a slight breeze or even its own weight will topple it. Clean wet laundry and a dirty ground or porch floor aren't a happy mix.

You can hang clothes on hangers and hang the hangers on door-frames in doorways. If you do this, leave plenty of room between the hangers to allow airflow so the clothes will dry. You can't wring out as much water by hand as the washing machine can (no matter how many bulging biceps you involve), so you'll have to deal with dripping as the clothes dry. Just keep this in mind and be prepared to mop it up or lay towels down to catch it so that the dripping water doesn't ruin your flooring. (Of course, then you have to hang those towels to dry! It never ends!)

Shower curtain rods work if the load is not too heavy. "If the load is not too heavy" needs to be emphasized. The majority of curtain rods are held in place by pressure. They will not sustain very much weight, but they'll accommodate a few lightweight things at a time. A simple solution is to fold items over hangers, spreading the articles out as flat as possible. Pinching clothespins will hold many small items on one hanger to increase the hanging capacity. Space the hangers out along the shower curtain rod so that the weight is distributed along the rod, not all in the middle or at one end.

You can always lay wet laundry over a porch, patio, or balcony railing. First, dip a cloth or sponge into the soapy wash water and wipe the dirt off of the railing. If you are higher than the ground floor, you may want to secure the sides of the items together below the top rail with a pinching clothespin to prevent them from blowing off. If the weather is damp and rainy, clothes that are doubled over a railing may mildew rather than dry. Pay attention and bring them inside rather than have them ruined. One possibility is to lay clothing items out to partially drip dry, then when most of the water has evaporated or dripped off and the items are not quite so heavy, bring them inside to continue drying. Now, hang the lighter clothes on hangers and put them on the shower curtain rod or on doorways where excessive dripping is no longer an issue.

Don't lay wet clothing over a wooden banister or railing, or over wooden chair backs! The water will ruin your woodwork. This is the voice of experience speaking.

Mesh racks that fit over a bathtub and are designed to dry sweaters will work as drying racks for a few items at a time. Two mesh racks will fit on one tub.

Laying laundry flat on something to dry (the floor, the counter, the sidewalk), as opposed to hanging it where it can have airflow, will work, but it is slower and less effective than hanging. When you lay out clothes, you must pay attention and turn the items over after a couple of hours so that the bottom layer will dry and not mildew. (Mildew stains are usually permanent.)

> *Of course, it figures that if you have no electricity to make the washer work, and the wrinkle-free cycle on the dryer isn't drying, you won't have to worry about your electric iron either. But then, in this day of permanent press, some people never do anyway. Not too long ago I was at my daughter's home. It came time to leave and I commented I really needed to get going since I had quite a bit of ironing to catch up on. My nearly teenage granddaughter looked at me with a puzzled expression and asked, "Grandma, what is ironing?"*

HANG OUT WITH A SYSTEM

There is a system to hanging out clothes that will help make them more presentable. This is assuming that if the washing machine doesn't have any power then the dryer and steam iron will not work either. Hang flat items like towels by using pinching clothespins, pinning them together at the corners, while stretching them tightly along the line. (The right corner of towel number one can overlap the left corner of towel number two and be held in place with the same clothespin. It takes fewer clothespins this way.) For shirts, blouses, T-shirts, and so on, hang them upside down. Pin the cuffs of long sleeves on the line instead of letting them hang down. Flatten out any wrinkles that you can with your hands, and the weight of the water will straighten the clothes a little more as they dry. Pants will dry fairly wearable if you will place the inside pant leg seams together and stretch out the cuffs so that they are tight and even. Hang the pants upside down by pinning the taut cuffs to the line. Pull the pockets out and stretch them to hang down flat to dry. Pull on the waistband of the pants (gently or they will come off of the line) to stretch the material and minimize the amount of wrinkles.

Line or air-dried laundry will feel stiff compared to tumble-dried. "Stiff as a board" describes line-dried laundry. However, there are benefits too. Many people with ready access to an electric dryer still hang towels and sheets out to dry because they smell so wonderfully fresh after a day on the line in the sun. And the clothes soften up in just minutes when you put them on, so it's not a major problem.

Now this may seem like much ado about nothing but if you must get through several weeks or so without the convenience of electricity, it doesn't hurt to know how keep ahead of the grime and maintain as much normalcy as possible in your appearance. (And remember, if a sock turns up missing, it's not the dryer's fault.)

CHAPTER THIRTY-TWO

FIRST AID OR WORST AID: YOU DO HAVE A CHOICE

If you want to be fully prepared to deal with wounds and injuries during an emergency, the best thing you can do is to spend eight years in medical school, with ten subsequent years' experience as an E.R. doctor. If you don't have eighteen years and $50,000 to devote to being ready for medical emergencies, you'll have to get by with learning some of the rudiments of first aid.

All of us know the first basic steps to treating a wound: (1) slap a Band-Aid on any source of blood, and (2) dial 911. That pretty much covers it. Or perhaps not. In all seriousness, first aid is a frightening subject, one most of us feel inadequate to deal with. We can cope with the everyday scrapes and stings and bruises, but what should we do if something goes really wrong and help isn't immediately available? A disturbing aspect of first aid is that you may need these skills and supplies at any time, not just in a large-scale emergency.

LEARN SKILLS NOW!

First aid is a subject that cannot be left to chance. You absolutely have to prepare in advance to treat injuries. That means not only gathering basic first aid supplies, but also learning the procedures for a few lifesaving techniques. For example, every man, woman, and child should know how to do the Heimlich maneuver to save a choking victim. It takes about two minutes to learn and can literally be a lifesaver. It doesn't require a local disaster or major catastrophe to need this action. A member of your family could choke over a bit of food at any time and die in front of your eyes before help has time to get to you. Or you could perform the Heimlich maneuver and pop out the food in just a few seconds. In this case,

everyone will take a big sigh of relief, and pretty soon conversation will begin again and the incident will be forgotten. The difference between life and death is two minutes of learning. Surely you can spend that much time to learn this lifesaving act.

Another thing every person should know is CPR (cardiopulmonary resuscitation). If someone in your family sticks a knife in the toaster tomorrow and is accidentally electrocuted, it's too late to begin learning how to save his life. You have to have the knowledge already, before the need arises. It's the same story with basic first aid skills. If someone is bleeding now, it's too late to run find the first aid book, turn to the bleeding chapter, and start learning the techniques of direct pressure, elevation, and pressure points and

Did you know that the only time you apply a tourniquet is as a very last resort, after you have tried everything else, and the victim is going to die soon because you can't stop the bleeding? Using a tourniquet will cause the victim to lose their limb below the point of the tourniquet. If they lose a limb but save their life, it's worth it. But if their life wasn't ever in question, using a tourniquet consigns them to living the rest of their life as an amputee for no reason. One man said that he had been a paramedic for thirteen years and had never needed to use a tourniquet yet.

tourniquets. By the time you finish reading the chapter, he'll be knocking on the Pearly Gates. To learn lifesaving first aid skills, contact the American Red Cross or your local fire station (the numbers are listed in the phone book or on your city's Web site). They offer classes on a regular basis on all sorts of first aid skills for a low fee or, in some cases, no fee. The life you save may be that of someone you love.

SUPPLIES ARE NECESSARY

Learning basic first aid skills now is the lion's share of being prepared for an emergency. But you aren't really prepared if you don't have some of the supplies necessary to treat wounds and illnesses. You can purchase ready-made first aid kits in most discount department stores, drugstores, or pharmacies, in about any size and complexity you want, from kits containing just the very basics to ones stocked with every size bandage known to man. Or, you can put together your own personalized kit containing just the things you are likely to use most. A rugged, lightweight container like a fishing tackle box, a toolbox, or a Tupperware-type container, are all good choices for keeping your supplies conveniently in one place. Make sure it is clearly marked and identifiable as a first aid kit. Keep a good first aid manual inside or fastened to your kit. A large, sturdy ziplock bag and several strips of heavy tape would do the trick. (A couple of good choices include current copies of the *Boy Scout Handbook, Boy Scout First Aid Merit Badge Handbook, Standard First Aid and Personal Safety* by the Red Cross, and *Reader's Digest First Aid*.)

Dust off the cobwebs and replace outdated items. First-aid kits and supplies don't last forever. Medicines expire, towelettes and swabs dry out, Band-Aids get used and not replaced. Keep on top of things by checking your first aid kit yearly to keep it freshly stocked and ready for use. (It's one more important thing to add to the to-do list for when the time changes, on your birthday month, or whenever.)

HAVE SUPPLIES ON HAND BEFORE THE NEED ARISES

Not only should you keep supplies on hand to treat wounds and injuries, but standard medications for illnesses also. You know you're most likely to need Rolaids or Tylenol in the middle of the night, rather than at a reasonable time in the day when you can run to the store to get it. It's another one of those Murphy's Law things. The idea behind first aid preparedness is to have what you need on hand before the need arises, particularly if you are in the position where you can't run to the store to get relief, like during an emergency.

I recently discovered that my "first aid shelf" definitely needs to contain more than a box of Band-Aids and a bottle of aspirin. In theory, I knew this, but I guess I'd just gotten a little lax in keeping my supplies up-to-date. When my husband unexpectedly needed an urgent and frightening operation, we were caught off guard. For the first few days at home after surgery, he required ointment, many bandages, and much patience and care. I quickly realized that I didn't have sufficient first aid supplies on the shelf, and I was forced to leave him alone at home, suffering and barely stable, while I hurried to the store to get the supplies he needed.

Granted, this was not the end of the world. He survived by himself for that half hour, and has since recovered, but it was enough to make me think. At that moment, I was worried and scared and upset, and the last thing I wanted to do was to go to the store. If I had been a little more prepared, it would have been one less stress on both of us during an extremely stressful time.

Taking that a step further, what would you do if a disaster occurred and you or a loved one was injured? If you could not get to help, and help could not get to you, could you care for injuries or illnesses on your own for a while? I'm not suggesting that you need to have supplies on hand for a portable operating room so you can remove your own appendix or perform brain surgery. I am recommending that you be able to care for likely needs such as allergies and upset stomachs, as well as have standard first aid supplies for the cuts, scrapes, and bruises you're likely to run into. Remember, when your child comes in with skinned elbows, the last thing you want to do is say, "Hold on and don't bleed on the rug while I run to the store for some ointment and Band-Aids, dear." You want to be ready now!

COMMON FIRST AID KIT SUPPLIES

Here are some of the most common supplies included in first aid kits. Of course, as with everything else in this book, you should adapt your list to your needs and situation. This list is just to get you thinking of your needs.

Bandages

- Sterile gauze pads (4 by 4 inches and other sizes)
- Rolled gauze (for holding dressings in place), various sizes
- Adhesive bandages (like Band-Aids), assorted sizes, including butterfly bandages and fingertip bandages
- Nonallergenic adhesive tape (for holding dressings and small splints)
- Elastic compression bandages (like Ace bandages)
- Knee, wrist, or ankle braces
- Triangle bandages
- Hot/cold compresses

Medications

- Analgesics
  - Aspirin (for pain, fever and also to give to heart attack victims while waiting for help to arrive)
  - Acetaminophen (such as Tylenol)
  - Ibuprofen (such as Advil)
- Throat lozenges
- Toothache remedies (such as eugenol or Anbesol)
- Antiseptics and topicals
  - Soap, liquid soap
  - Hydrogen peroxide
  - Rubbing alcohol
  - Triple antibiotic ointment (such as Neosporin)
  - Calamine lotion or hydrocortisone cream
  - Minor burn cream
- Antihistamine (such as Benadryl)
- Diarrhea medication (such as Imodium or Pepto-Bismol)
- Laxative (such as milk of magnesia)
- Antacid (such as Rolaids or Alka-Seltzer)
- Activated charcoal (for poisoning)
- Eyedrops

Tools and Other Items

- Sharp scissors
- Tweezers
- Nail clippers
- Thermometer
- Safety pins (various sizes)
- Matches (for sterilization)
- Needles
- Medicine dropper and spoon
- Cotton swabs, cotton balls
- Latex gloves
- Dust masks
- Antiseptic towelettes
- Chemical hot or cold packs

Special Individual Needs

- Baby/toddler needs
- Liquid pain reliever
- Teething ointment
- Diaper rash ointment
- Baby wipes with glycerin
- Oil/lotion
- Rubber syringe
- Current immunizations
- Prescription medications (talk to your doctor about obtaining an emergency supply in addition to your regular supply, and check with your pharmacist to determine shelf life and storage requirements)
- Compression socks or stockings
- Insulin
- Diabetic testing supplies

If you live alone and your medical condition requires life-sustaining medications, it's a good idea to post a large, bright note on your refrigerator or medicine cabinet stating the name, location, and dosage of each medication. In an emergency, anyone who comes to help you would be able to find these critical items immediately.

- Contact lens supplies
- Eyeglasses
- First aid book

Will your preparedness pantry hold supplies for first aid or worst aid? It's up to you to choose, and the time to choose is now. (I wonder if chocolate-covered raisins count as required prescriptions for stressful situations?)

CHAPTER THIRTY-THREE

PERSONAL CARE

If you've ever been camping or backpacking for a week or so, what's the first thing you do when you get home (besides unload the car, and sometimes even before that)? Head to the shower, of course. It is such a relief and a luxury to have that lovely hot water wash all the dirt and grime down the drain. It makes you feel like a new person. Cleanliness is a mark of a civilized society. We spend millions each year to be clean and smell good. We all know the important role being clean plays in good health and staying ahead of germs and disease. However, the psychological aspects of being able to stay clean during times of stress are just as important as the physical aspects.

PERSONAL CARE BOX

You'll generally have some personal hygiene items on hand if a crisis occurs because you use them every day. It is possible, however, that your major catastrophe will happen the day before your weekly trip to the store rather than the day after. So, if you're down to the last roll of toilet tissue in the house and your only soap is a sliver melting on the floor of the shower, you'd be in trouble. Personal care after a disaster is an eventuality you'll want to make plans for. For example, you could prepare a small personal care box (for each individual, or family-sized) containing a supply of essentials that you tape closed and store on the highest shelf in the closet so no one can touch it unless it's an emergency. In it you could have a tube of toothpaste, bar of soap, razor and shaving cream, bottle of shampoo, a few rolls of toilet tissue, feminine hygiene supplies, and so on. That way, if an emergency struck at an inconvenient time, your box would see you through for a little while, even if your cupboard were empty.

PERSONAL CLEANLINESS WITHOUT WATER

Some hygiene practices will have to be altered to allow for the exigencies of the emergency. If there's no water but the few gallons you have set aside for drinking, cleanliness is going to be totally different than what you're used to. Daily showers, long soaks in the tub, and squeaky-clean and conditioned hair may become a fond memory of the past and a luxury to look forward to.

Waterless hand sanitizer is a boon for emergency purposes. You can buy it in just about any store. Rub it on your hands like lotion and it kills germs without any need for rinsing. Another good idea is to keep a supply of baby wipes on hand. Baby wipes, moist towelettes, and body wipes are all basically the same thing. Baby wipes have glycerin for soft skin as an ingredient, and moist towelettes have alcohol for killing germs.

A friend of a friend went on tour with her singing group to some of the less tourist-oriented countries in Europe. She had heard that it wasn't safe to

---

Water Substitutes for Cleaning:

Rubbing Alcohol
Lotions containing alcohol
Shaving lotion
Face creams and lotions
Moist towelletes
Hand sanitizer

drink the water there, and she was worried that the water wouldn't even be safe to wash with. Instead of taking a chance, she stocked her suitcase with baby wipes. Each day she would give herself a wipe-down with her moist towelettes instead of risking a bath in allegedly polluted water. Besides keeping clean, she also saved on her perfume bill because everywhere she went a faint smell of lemon wafted around her. You may consider this going overboard, but it worked for her. In a pinch, it could work for you too.

It's amazing what you can do with a small cup or bowl of water when you put your mind to it. You can brush your teeth with a small cup of water. It really is possible to shave with just a cup of water. You could even take an entire sponge bath with a cup of water for washing and a cup for rinsing if you're careful.

It's crucial to keep your body, hands, and eating and cooking utensils clean. Contaminated water and food can lead to intestinal problems, and who needs diarrhea on top of all the other problems you'll be dealing with? The best advice is wash your hands, wash your hands, wash your hands! Be as fanatical about cleanliness as you can.

COMMON PERSONAL CARE ITEMS

Here's a list of common personal care items. Check through it (and add to it if something important to you is not listed) and think about each item in conjunction with a disaster situation. Do you have plenty on hand? Should you get a designated supply and put it away for an emergency? If it requires electricity, how will you get along without this? Can you use this without water, and if not, what options do you have? What is the minimum amount of water absolutely required to be able to use it?

Shampoo
Conditioner
Spray-on conditioner or detangler
Hair spray
Blow dryer
Comb/brush
Bar soap, liquid soap
Toothpaste
Mouthwash
Dental floss
Toothbrush
Razors, blades, disposable razors, shaving cream
Antiperspirant/deodorant
Hand lotion
Sunscreen/sunblock
Lip balm
Feminine sanitary supplies
Toilet tissue
Kleenex
Makeup (No joke. Some women would rather die than be caught without makeup.)
Baby/toddler needs
    Disposable diapers
    Diaper wipes
    Baby powder/lotion
Denture needs
Contact lens needs
Acne medication
Cotton swabs

Make plans now to be able to get or stay clean during stressful times. You'll be glad you did.

CHAPTER THIRTY-FOUR

MORALE BOOSTERS: GAMES AND GOODIES ARE ESSENTIAL INGREDIENTS

If you're confined to your home for an extended period of time due to a power failure, storm, or disaster situation, fear and confusion tend to give way before too long to frustration and boredom, especially for children. The immediate crisis may be over and the danger may be past but life is not back to normal yet, and may not be for quite some time yet. Mom and Dad might be tearing their hair out trying to clean up disaster messes, get things back to normal, and keep body and soul together. But for the little ones, all they know is that they are upset, they are tired, they are bored, and the TV doesn't work. When you toss into the mix frayed nerves and fear bubbling just under the surface, it's a situation ripe for emotional explosions.

Familiar situations tend to lessen sorrow and fear. They also soothe nerves strung out near to snapping. In the face of the tumult that's gone on around you, it's important that you be prepared to be happy and to maintain a good attitude. The underlying purpose for morale boosters is not just to entertain but to be able to consciously redirect thoughts, lift spirits, and create a positive mind-set. Of course, these suggestions and ideas are for the time frame after a crisis has passed. I'm not suggesting you gather your family together for a cheery cup of hot cocoa and a rousing game of Monopoly when tornados are still gobbling up mobile homes on all sides of your home. These are things to focus on after you and your family are safe, your neighbors are safe, and the cat is safe. These things are to help you through the days or weeks when life is not yet back to normal, while you are still without heat and power or access to the corner store.

In this chapter, I speak a lot about being prepared in order to comfort children. The well-being of children should naturally be a top priority of the adults entrusted with their care. However, children are not the only ones who become restless and anxious. Everyone does, regardless of age. If you don't have small children in your home, apply these concepts to your teenagers, to yourself, and to the other adults living with you. They will need the comfort just as much as any child. For many years when my children were younger, it was I, the mom, who needed the comforting. I was terrified of thunderstorms. When a particularly severe storm would come up, our family would head to the family room in the basement to play board games, where the kids would laugh and joke as we played to distract my attention from the tempest outside. My fear was real, but so was our ability to control it.

COPING WHEN LIFE IS TURNED UPSIDE DOWN

In planning ahead for the times when normal life may be turned inside out, realize that there are two sides to the "crisis repercussions" sword: (1) dealing with frightening and upsetting circumstances, and (2) dealing with the lack of normal, comfortable conditions. Many of today's generation have grown up glued to the television and the Nintendo. Mass media provides such effortless entertainment that many of our youth have forgotten how to entertain themselves. Employing a good imagination is a dying art. In a major power outage, many little media junkies (and our older media junkies as well) will be lost when they are deprived of their usual source of amusement. It may be an uphill job, but you need to be prepared to keep yourself, as well as your family, busy without TV, computers, or battery-operated toys. (See chapter

24 for some ideas on battery rationing for handheld entertainment devices.) With the electricity out, be ready to help each other through the TV withdrawal period. I'm serious. Television is addicting, and if it's suddenly eliminated, you may have to deal with some really grouchy people until they get past the need to "relax" in front of the tube. Be patient and be prepared with alternatives.

STOCK A CUPBOARD

You need to stock a cupboard with games and goodies. Games, puzzles, books to read or reread, craft supplies, coloring books and crayons for young and not-so-young alike, and inspirational materials could prove to be very calming. These kinds of preparedness items are another way to build confidence and a sense of security. They can help make the long, dull days and dark nights a whole lot more bearable. You'll want to be prepared with a variety of activities. If a longer time of waiting must be endured, you'll value the opportunity to change activities,

especially if you are confined indoors.

You may find out how much fun it is to spend time with your family. Sometimes we get so busy that we don't have time to stop and enjoy being together. It might take being trapped in our homes by a week-long ice storm to help us rediscover the simple pleasures of a game of Scrabble or Uno, the enjoyment that comes from working a 1,000-piece puzzle, and the personal interaction that is a natural by-product of spending time together.

Without TV or computer games to fall back on, children may discover that they do have imaginations after all; they've just been dormant. Think about what your children's strengths are and prepare activities that accentuate those strengths. If your children like to draw, have drawing materials. If play-acting is fun for them, keep books of easy plays, or fun stories they can act out. Add a box of dress-up clothes and props from around the house, like a fuzzy bathrobe, a saucepan "helmet," and wooden spoons as swords, scepters, or magic wands, and the fun will be automatic. If they

Do you have a Scrabble game but your kids think the game is too slow and boring to play? Try our family's made-up version that we call Turbo-Scrabble. Turn all the tiles facedown in the center of the table and everyone takes seven Scrabble tiles to begin with. Someone says, "Go!" Each person turns over his tiles, and begins to make up his own Scrabble game right on the table (You don't use the official Scrabble board.) You use your tiles in the typical down-and-across crossword fashion, arranging and rearranging the tiles in words until you've used up all the tiles. The first person to use up all their tiles shouts, "Go." Then everyone takes another tile and goes on arranging and rearranging their own tiles in front of them. When someone shouts "Go!" you must take a tile whether your previous tiles are neatly organized into a finished crossword arrangement or whether you're stuck trying to figure out how to use an X, J, and K with only one vowel. Play continues until the last tile is taken and one player finishes making all his letter tiles into words. Then he shouts, "Go—thirty seconds!" Everyone else has thirty seconds to frantically get any of his remaining tiles organized into proper crossword arrangement. At the end of the thirty seconds, each person tallies his points. Any letter tiles successfully used in words count as points for you (only count them once, even if they are used in more than one word), and any remaining unused tiles count as points against you. (Use the point value printed on each tile.) Everybody loves this game. It's fast, requires just a little brainwork and a little luck, and any number of people can play.

like to write stories, be ready with ideas to encourage that interest. A fun idea for budding writers is to write words on slips of paper (dog, run, swamp, pillow, sandwich, and so on) and drop them in a hat or bowl. Have your child draw out four to six words, and they have to make up a story that uses all those words.

My family loves to play cards. We "collect" different games that can be played with just a deck or two of cards. We know dozens, and have probably forgotten more than we remember. If you're stuck at home and time is hanging heavy on your hands, learn to play different card games. If you keep a few decks of cards in your game drawer and *Hoyle's Book of Games* on your bookshelf, you'll be set for hours and hours. If you're by yourself, you're still in good shape because there are a gazillion different ways to play Solitaire. (Or, you could always build card houses!)

You may say you have all these items already. That's good, they will certainly come in handy should hard times come (though only if your games still have all their critical parts and pieces!). But I suggest that you put in your preparedness pantry something new. Have something special to bring out as a surprise. The novelty of the surprise will help ease the tension of a tough situation. Something as simple as a new puzzle or new set of colored pencils can be great for lifting sagging spirits.

WRITE YOUR EXPERIENCES

A fun and practical activity during those trying times would be for everyone in the household to keep a journal of their thoughts and reactions to the current crisis. Fortunately, disasters don't last forever and years later you'll be glad to have documented the experience and everyone's thoughts and feelings about it. For a child too young to write, have a big brother or sister or mom or dad be their secretary. The child can dictate his thoughts and the elder can write them down for him. Don't forget your camera; photos can provide interesting memories of cooking by lamplight and other emergency adventures. Our pictures of the wreckage in our home after the Loma Prieta earthquake are priceless. We look at them now and just shake our heads in wonder at the awesome destructive power we witnessed and survived.

WHO'S GOT THE GOODIES?

Most people eat not just to supply their bodies with nutrients and energy but also because eating is pleasurable. We derive a great deal of enjoyment from food, both physically and psychologically. When something good happens, we celebrate with food. When we want to show people we care for them, we often say it with food. When we are depressed, we turn for comfort to food.

When stressful times last for more than a day or two, it's especially important that you be able to have a treat. It's great to have food to satisfy your hunger, and all the things you learned about in the Makeshift Meals, chapter 21, about food for emergencies are absolutely true. But face it. When you're scared, frustrated and worried, a can of cold SpaghettiOs just

---

Finger Paint
Soak 1 envelope unflavored gelatin in ¼ cup water. Then, combine ½ cup cornstarch and 3 Tablespoons sugar. Then gradually add 2 cups water. Cook slowly over low heat, stirring constantly, about 5 minutes. Remove from heat and add gelatin mixture. Divide into containers and add a drop or two of liquid dish detergent. Then stir in food coloring. (It may be worth it to use a few minutes' worth of fuel from your emergency supply to make this.)

Play Clay
Mix 2 cups flour and 1 cup salt. Then stir in ½ cup water and 1 teaspoon vinegar. Knead until soft, divide into portions, and knead food coloring into each. (Keeps indefinitely in the refrigerator.)

doesn't fill the bill as a comfort food. You want something that will take your mind off your misery, even if only for a minute. You want something familiar that says to your mind, "It's going to be okay. Just hang on." You want a treat!

You may have noticed the word chocolate has popped up several times in this book. I joke a lot about chocolate but don't get me wrong. In this chapter, the principle of having a treat to rely on is important, be it chocolate or anything else you normally turn to for comfort. So here are a few ideas to get you thinking. You'll need to personalize them to fit your tastes and needs.

Popcorn could almost be considered one of the staples of any preparedness program. You'll need to have regular popcorn in your pantry, since the microwave style won't work without power. You know, some popcorn aficionados aren't even aware that people were eating popcorn for centuries before the microwave version was invented. You pop it on a stove or camp stove in a frying pan or over a fire in an old-fashioned popcorn popper. Learning to use a regular frying pan to pop popcorn so the corn is edible and not burnt can be an experience all by itself. The trick is to use oil, a lid, and never stop shaking the pan!

Look now for a few recipes for no-bake treats, and stock the supplies for them.

SHELF LIFE FOR TREATS

Some treats can be stored on a short long-term basis (providing, of course, that they are hidden away and no one knows they are there). Chocolate candy, granola bars, fruit leather, and more will all last for six months to a year under reasonable conditions. Mark a date to buy more on your calendar six months or a year from when you first buy your treats; then haul out the past year's goodies and have a little party, courtesy of your emergency preparedness program. For example, you can store pretzels in an airtight can or jar and they will stay fresh for about six months. Roasted nuts in unopened cans or jars from the store are good for three to six months. Hot chocolate mix keeps easily on a shelf, and so does instant pudding. (You may need to make it with reconstituted canned or dry milk.) Chocolate candy bars, M&M's, and other chocolate candies (without nuts)

My experience happened when I was a newlywed living in Hawaii. A hurricane came through the islands and we were left without water for twenty-four hours and without electricity for a week. At the beginning of the storm, I filled the bathtub up with water. This helped with flushing the toilet and drinking and cooking water the next day. My husband had brought to the marriage a very small backpacking-camping stove that we used to cook on for the first day. However, a family from my husband's hometown was visiting the islands at that time. They came to visit us after the storm. Upon noticing our plight, they went and bought us a two-burner Coleman camp stove as a late wedding gift—probably one of the most useful wedding gifts we received. Eventually, the university provided our on-campus apartment building with a refrigerated truck that we were only allowed access to twice daily. Honestly, our biggest problem was boredom. Because of the storm, the beaches were closed and uninhabitable because of debris and dying fish, school was cancelled for the week because of the lack of electricity, and we didn't own a car. We were lucky to be young marrieds, and we mostly hung out with our other newly married friends and played a lot of cards and made no-bake cookies! The Coleman stove got a lot of use by us and others that needed to cook the meat in their refrigerators. It was more of an adventure than a hardship.
—Kirsten E., Baltimore, Md.

will technically stay fresh for three to six months or more in a cool, dry place. I say "technically" because we were never actually able to test this theory at our house when our kids lived at home. As soon as they were spotted, they were gone. If your family is the same, you may have to get sneaky about storing treats for an emergency. Go to the store and buy a box of frozen codfish filets or something equally nontempting. Use up the actual food and then use the box to keep those goodies in. On the shelf, a dry oatmeal carton ought to do the trick if a brown paper bag is too obvious.

There are a few people in this world who have completely eschewed sugar and junk food in favor of more healthful diet. I admire their good sense and their willpower. Even these people have their comfort foods, though. I have a vegetarian friend who is no more interested in eating sugary foods than in chewing on road tar but she still likes food, and she likes to have treats. Her favorite snack food is freeze-dried corn and peas. If traditional treats don't work for you,

figure out what it is that you eat when you are feeling down and then stock up on that food.

I like to emphasize good nutrition, even in my snacking. I make sure all our food choices are based on the four basic food groups: chocolate cake, chocolate-covered raisins, chocolate-covered peanuts, and fudge.

No-Bake Cookies
2 cups sugar
½ cup cocoa
½ cup milk
1 cube butter or margarine
Bring above ingredients to a boil in a large saucepan. Boil two minutes, stirring constantly. Stir in:
3 cups oats
1 teaspoon vanilla
Mix and drop by tablespoons onto waxed paper. Let cool.

CHAPTER THIRTY-FIVE

IF YOUR FAMILY IS SEPARATED DURING AN EMERGENCY

One of every parent's fears is that an emergency will occur while they are separated from their children and they won't be able to get to them. It's built into our DNA to care for and protect our children. The same thoughts apply if we have a handicapped member of our family or elderly parents in our care. We are the caregivers and we are responsible. The thought that they could be in need and we couldn't help them is terrifying. Unfortunately, it is a real possibility. There are no guarantees that families will be safely together in times of disaster, so you must do what you can to protect your children/family member by preparing, practicing, and putting an emergency plan into place now. The key word is *now*.

PREPARING

Most elementary-school-age and older children spend some time alone at home. Some are latchkey children who care for themselves an hour or two every day after school until their parents arrive home from work. Others are alone only occasionally while Mom runs to the store for a few ingredients for tonight's dinner. Either way, it is feasible that an emergency could occur during those minutes or hours of separation. Your first line of defense is to physically make your home as safe as possible. Have fire extinguishers and smoke detectors in place. Make sure all exits in every room are clear and uncluttered at all times. In apartment complexes, make sure all family members know all the ways out. If you live in an earthquake-prone area, bolt down or otherwise secure heavy pieces of freestanding furniture and potential hazards such as large mirrors or pictures as much as possible. Show your children the safety practices you have put in place and make sure they know you are doing all you possibly can to keep your family safe at all times.

Make sure any children who are old enough are familiar with ways to protect themselves in an emergency. They should know, room by room, where to take shelter and how to protect their heads from falling debris. They should know where you keep emergency supplies: flashlights, batteries, water, first aid kit, and so on. They should know your agreed-upon Care-in-a-Crisis procedures (see chapter 36) and where they should go in the event of an emergency when they are home alone. Even if an older sibling is usually responsible until a parent gets home from work, situations change drastically in an emergency and it should be mandatory to take younger brothers and sisters to a designated neighbor's home until a responsible adult arrives. Warn your children that it may take you several hours or longer to get home after a disaster, but reassure them of your love and that you will be doing everything possible to get to them.

HAVE A PLAN

Since you can't really simulate an earthquake, flood, hurricane, or the trauma necessitating a possible evacuation, reading and talking about another's experiences and deciding what you would do in a similar experience is the next best thing. Gather your family together and focus on those emergencies most likely to occur in your area. Go through a few trial runs to make sure everyone knows how to act in different emergencies and what their responsibilities are. What if a disaster occurs in the nighttime? What if the family is separated when the crisis occurs? Who will get the little ones from school? What if Mom or

Dad can't get home for a long time? Where do we keep the flashlights and emergency supplies? The list to be discussed can go on and on.

NUMBERS TO KNOW

Every member of the family should know by memory the names and phone numbers of the parents' places of work. Even little children should know the exact names. Don't assume that because you know it, see it, write it, and live with a business every day, your children are equally familiar with the correct name of your work. "Kartchner, Barrington, and Wilberforce, Inc." may just be "Mom's law firm" or "Dad's office" to a child. As far as the phone number goes, memorizing the home phone number and the phone numbers of Mom's and Dad's works are crucial before any kind of emergency. And just as a brief reminder, speed-dial numbers don't count. Once I asked a neighbor's child what his dad's phone number at work was and he responded, "Two-two." That's only going to work if your child is calling from his home phone.

Just in case a child is anxious about remembering these crucial numbers, you can ease his anxiety by posting them where he can find them and grab them in a hurry. Print the phone numbers and addresses on a sturdy piece of cardstock, laminate it if possible for extra sturdiness, and tape or pin it inside a cupboard door at a level where all who are old enough to use a phone can reach it. If the child has to leave in a hurry, he can grab the list on his way out. You might want a close neighbor to know where this list is or give her a copy of it. These will be just a few critical numbers, not the calling tree used for neighborhood barbecues. Memorizing is better in the long run, but these simple actions can help relieve anxiety in little ones for now (and even for older ones whose memories may not be as sharp as they used to be).

They need to remember one more phone number. Choose a friend or family member who lives well away from your area (preferably in another state) and designate him as your check-in person. If your family is separated or evacuated because of a major disaster such as an earthquake, it's possible you may not be able to reach your home or designated gathering spot for quite some time. In such a situation, local phone lines may be jammed or down, but you may be able to make a long-distance call. Family members should

all know that they are to call the designated check-in person as soon as possible, and the check-in person will coordinate and keep track of where everyone is and how they are. It may still be hours or days before you can get your family together but you won't spend that whole time sick with worry about them.

It's a good idea to write these names and numbers on a business-sized card to carry in a purse, wallet, or school backpack, or load them into a Palm Pilot or cell phone memory also. But it's easy to lose a purse or a Palm Pilot in an emergency, so I emphasize the importance of memorizing important numbers. You may lose your purse, but hopefully you won't lose your mind.

ICE (in case of emergency) is a relatively new but great idea, conceived by East Anglian Ambulance Service paramedic, Bob Brotchie, in 2005. The idea spread rapidly throughout the world after the terrorist attacks in London. Mobile phone users are encouraged to enter a number into their phone's memory with the acronym "ICE," with the contact person's name and number. Since a majority of people now carry cell phones, in the event of an emergency, paramedics or police can quickly find the number and use it to reach a relative or friend who could provide information, including details of any medical conditions, which could be vital in a life-or-death situation. Mr. Brotchie said, "I was reflecting on some of the calls I've attended at the roadside where I had to look through the mobile phone contacts, struggling for information on a shocked or injured person. . . . With ICE, we'd know immediately who to contact and what number to ring."[1] To put ICE in your phone, select a new contact in your phone book and enter the word *ICE* and the name and number of

> *You should also put a label on or near your phone with the new national toll-free number for poison control: 800–222–1222. A phone call here will connect you to your regional poison control center where trained operators can help you with any poisoning emergencies anytime, day or night.*

the person you want to be contacted.

It's also a good idea to tape a label on your home telephone with "911," or the emergency number to call in your area, in plain view. Even very young children can learn how to respond in an emergency.

WORK TOGETHER WITH OTHERS

Because you may not be immediately available to meet your child's needs and calm his fears, you need to organize your neighborhood to support each other in the event of a disaster. Care-in-a-Crisis is a simple, effective way to organize a network of families or neighbors and assign actions and responsibilities before a need arises. It is designed to provide the support and extra hands so necessary in a crisis. Banding together can be much more effective and efficient if you are organized. Work together with your neighbors to make sure everyone's needs are met. Be sure that someone will check on your children and be prepared to take charge of them should you be unable to get to them right away. (You should be prepared to do the same for others in your neighborhood should you be the one at home.) Discuss with your children who will pick them up from school in the event of an emergency and who will care for them until you get home. Work out a message system (for example, notes on the kitchen table or front door) so you can find and reunite family members as soon as possible. Find out what plans your schools and daycare centers have for dealing with disasters and tell your children about those plans. Knowledge and practice of emergency procedures will not cause concern for children. Rather, it will empower your children to react appropriately and with assurance in a disaster.

PRACTICE

Knowledge is power, even for children. The more they know, the more control they will feel over their situation. Practice sessions could prove to be priceless preparation in case an emergency ever occurred. You are more likely to keep your head about you in a strange, frightening situation if you have planned, imagined, and practiced possible responses beforehand, even if the practice is full of giggles and eye-rolling. If it doesn't go as well as planned, what counts is that it goes!

Gather your family together and have a Preparedness Picnic or a No-Fear Feast. As you eat, discuss preparedness plans. Talk about how to look out for each other while you digest your potato salad and watermelon. Instead of playing a relaxing game of Monopoly or Old Maid, practice taking screens out of windows as part of an escape route, or learn to light a lantern or work a fire extinguisher. Relaxing may be enjoyable but preparedness planning will pay off! Being separated during an emergency is a frightening thought. Having a plan before it happens can help ease those fears, both for you and your children.

Notes
1. www.eastanglianambulance.com

CHAPTER THIRTY-SIX

NEIGHBORHOOD CARE-IN-A-CRISIS

There is always a chance that your neighborhood will someday deal with a major crisis. It only makes sense for neighbors to band together and prepare for it in advance. What you need is a simple plan, one that can be implemented now, so that survival does not depend on mere chance. It should be a plan that cooperates, rather than competes, with your city or county emergency plans.

Care-in-a-Crisis is a simple, effective way to organize a network of families or neighbors and assign actions and responsibilities before a need arises. It is designed to provide the support and extra hands so necessary in a crisis. By now you understand the likelihood of being without communications and outside help during and after an emergency. This means you and your close neighbors will probably be dependent on yourselves and on each another. Banding together can be much more effective and efficient if you are organized. This is particularly important when so many families have only one parent trying to do the work of two, or where both parents work, or, in an aging population, where senior citizens live alone. The confusion immediately following the Loma Prieta earthquake illuminated the need to know and care for the needs of others around us. In a community completely dependent on the daily commute, commuting was impossible. Phone lines were down. Families were separated and stranded. Latchkey children were alone and afraid. I spoke with one woman who related how frantic she was. She and her husband commuted separately to Bay Area jobs from their home in Manteca, more than an hour's drive away. In the immediate aftermath of the earthquake, they could not get home to, nor get hold of, their three children, ages six, nine, and thirteen, for two days. When she finally made it home, she discovered, to her infinite relief, that neighbors had taken her children into their home for those days.

HAVE A MEETING—MAKE YOUR PLANS

The first step toward watching out for each other is to become familiar with the detailed planning pages, Care-in-a-Crisis Plan and the Family Information worksheet, which follow. They are the backbone of the Care-in-a-Crisis program. Decide which individuals or families to team up with and invite them to meet to discuss the program. Logically, these people will be your close neighbors. You may join forces with three or four other families who live in close proximity to you or you may include your entire block or neighborhood. Maybe you'll want to collaborate with your entire apartment building, or maybe just the families on your immediate floor. There's a lot to be said for uniting in a large group (strength in numbers, you know) but the logistics may be easier to manage on a more intimate scale. It's up to you.

When you meet, give each person or family a copy of the form entitled "Family Information." Each one should fill out this form and then give the other participating neighbors a copy of it. Next, give each family a copy of the form entitled "Care-in-a-Crisis Plan." Fill out these forms together during your meeting. If necessary, have more than one meeting and discuss who will do what in every conceivable emergency situation. Then, write the decisions on your planning forms. Emphasize that no one can afford to take anything for granted. Try to plan for every contingency in specific detail. Consider carefully what private information you will share and with whom. Some people may not want their work phone numbers or daily schedules handed out indiscriminately, or they may have strict family rules about whose homes their children may enter and so on. Work with these considerations until everyone feels comfortable with the decisions. After your plans are in order, calendar annual or semiannual meetings for updates and revisions.

Be sure to share your decisions with close friends or relatives who do not live in your area so that in an emergency they will know whom to contact, and they will also not feel that they have to endanger their own lives by coming to rescue you. In addition, keep copies of your plans by your telephone and inform such people as babysitters, daycare personnel, and nannies about your plans. It would be a good thing to include the names of your participating families on school records as individuals who have permission to pick up your children in an emergency. Most schools will not release children to anyone without specific written authorization in their files.

As you make your plans, include neighbors who live alone, have special health problems. or may be physically impaired. Involve them in the planning meetings to evaluate how to meet their needs, and by the same token, to see how they can serve as well.

WHAT YOU CAN DO TO HELP

Not everyone will want to be actively involved in a Care-in-a-Crisis plan. You may not have the

---

Susan R. of Salt Lake City, Utah, had great success with her neighborhood planning meeting. She and a friend passed out flyers, got permission from the police to close off a block of their street, set up chairs, and had an old-fashioned street meeting. By having everyone gather to hear the information at one time, the entire neighborhood was quickly organized and enthused.

---

opportunity to organize your neighbors as fully as you'd like. That doesn't mean that you can't look out for each other anyway. If you are prepared before a crisis occurs, you may be the only one in the neighborhood who is actually able to help the less fortunate. Here are some things you can do:

- Offer reassurance, security, comfort.
- Take stranded children into your home. Secure a note in a prominent place in their home telling where the children are and with whom. Keep the children with you until their parents or responsible family member comes to retrieve them.
- Take an elderly person into your home. Keep the person with you until a family member is able to come for him or until it's safe and secure for him to return home alone.
- Look after a senior citizen or physically challenged person who might be living alone near you. Offer assistance as needed.
- Help provide transportation to a shelter in an evacuation situation.
- Help another family with children.
- Help another family with an invalid or elderly person.
- Make sure all neighbors are all right and give assistance and comfort where needed.

A TWOFOLD PROGRAM

The Care-in-a-Crisis program is twofold. It not only assures others of your help but you, in turn, have someone else to count on when disasters strikes. Naturally, you will take care of your own family's needs first. But at the same time, if a program is planned, practical, and practiced, you will be in a position to help someone else and do good to those around you, even when you are afraid.

Chapter 45 will explain how to extend the Care-in-a-Crisis concept to an evacuation situation.

Care-in-a-Crisis Plan

Family I am responsible for:		Name	Address	Phone Number
	Cell phone	Work address	Work phone	General hours
Father				
Mother				
Child's Name				
Child's Name				
Child's Name				
Child's Name				

My specific assignments, during and after an emergency (for this family):	

The out-of-area contact for this family:	Name	Phone	Relationship

Family I am responsible for:		Name	Address	Phone Number
	Cell phone	Work address	Work phone	General hours
Father				
Mother				
Child's Name				
Child's Name				
Child's Name				
Child's Name				

My specific assignments, during and after an emergency (for this family):	

The out-of-area contact for this family:	Name	Phone	Relationship

Person responsible to help my family:	Name	Address	Phone Number
Their specific assignments during and after an emergency:			
My other neighborhood assignments:			
Tools, skills, and abilities I have that will benefit others in an emergency:			

Family Information

Description of Family Members

Name	Birthdate	Height/Weight	Coloring	Hair Color	Eye Color	Distinguishing Marks	Special Needs

Schedule of Family Members

Name	Cell Phone	Regular Activity (work, day care, school)	Address	Phone	Approximate Hours

Our family's emergency meeting place (nearby but not at home): _____

_____

Our family's out-of-area contact (name, phone, relationship): _____

_____

Special needs to be aware of: _____

_____

Person or family assigned to look out for our family in an emergency: _____

_____

Person(s) or family(ies) our family is assigned to look out for in an emergency: _____

_____

PRINCIPLES FOR EMERGENCY EVACUATIONS

CHAPTER THIRTY-SEVEN

IT'S TIME TO PLAN. . . NOT PANIC

Disasters happen, maybe even to you (even though we all think that disasters are what happen to other people, not us). The fact is, sooner or later you may be forced to leave your home, even if only briefly, because of some kind of crisis. Earthquakes, tornadoes, fires, floods, and hurricanes can occur almost anywhere and at any time. To the natural disasters we can add a long list of man-made problems: explosions, leakage of hazardous chemicals or radioactive waste, terrorism, and more. Perhaps not everyone will be forced to flee from their homes, but it is more common than you think. Disasters are increasing, not decreasing, throughout the world. Shouldn't you be prepared so that if you have to leave your home, even if only for a few hours, you can do so with a minimum of discomfort?

You must be able to build a "home away from home" from the equipment and supplies in your kit. Proper planning can provide relative protection and even some comfort. The normalcy created by having a tent to pitch, a lantern to light, and a card game to occupy your mind may not take away all the fear and worry but it certainly will provide a glimmer of security in the mire of chaos.

> [Natural disasters] are all around us and seem to be increasing in frequency and intensity. For example, the list of major earthquakes in The World Almanac and Book of Facts, 2004 shows twice as many earthquakes in the decades of the 1980s and 1990s as in the two preceding decades (pp. 188–90). It also shows further sharp increases in the first several years of this century. The list of notable floods and tidal waves and the list of hurricanes, typhoons, and blizzards worldwide show similar increases in recent years. Increases by comparison with 50 years ago can be dismissed as changes in reporting criteria, but the accelerating pattern of natural disasters in the last few decades is ominous.
>
> —Dallin H. Oaks, "Preparation for the Second Coming," Ensign, May 2004, 8

> "Train crash kills 8; Chlorine cloud hangs over town," screamed the headlines. On January 6, 2005, a freight train carrying chlorine gas struck a packed passenger train, killing nine people and injuring more than 240 others. A cloud of poisonous chlorine gas rolled slowly through the neighborhood, seeping into houses through heating vents and cracks. Because they were unable to contain the deadly gas, authorities ordered 5,400 people within a mile of the crash to evacuate. Ten days later, more than 1,300 people were still displaced.

As reported in the *Ladies' Home Journal*, November 1993 "Apart from financial costs, a disaster takes its toll on victims emotionally, and children are the most likely to be traumatized." The stress is very real as well for adults. You possess the ability to lessen at least some of that emotional trauma and stress, by planning, projecting, and providing now. So just do it!

If you are forced out of your home and immediate area, it will be due, in most instances, to a life-threatening situation. Once you have been evacuated, you will not be allowed to cross back through the police lines until the evacuated area has been declared safe by the authorities. This could be a few hours, days, or even weeks.

LAG TIME: A CRITICAL FACTOR

The villain of disasters that are severe enough to cause evacuation is lag time. This is the period between the actual occurrence of the emergency and when organized help arrives. Most people evacuated from their homes don't expect to be away for more than one day. This is a serious misconception. Many evacuation periods last several days or more. For the first hours—or even days—of an evacuation, you may be on your own to provide food, clothing, and other supplies for yourself and family until help arrives.

Research has shown that in very serious situations, lag time is at least seventy-two hours. It could easily take two to three days or longer to get evacuation shelters up and running. During those three days, evacuees could be faced with living in fairly primitive conditions. There may be no clean water, heat, lights, toilet facilities, or shelter. The longer the lag time, the more the problems. The more severe the crisis, the more intense the problems associated with lag time will be. While discussing this situation with me, the director of one of the Utah Chapters of the Red Cross commented, "Lag time is not given the emphasis that it should be given. It is one of the most critical factors during an evacuation, yet most people don't even recognize it, let alone prepare for it."

Remember, the disaster has to take place first. Then lag time begins! Then the procedure of government officials touring, deciding, and declaring whether or not a state of emergency should be declared begins. At that point, orders can be issued to bring in additional help. Till then, you're on your own.

After the October 1989 7.2 Loma Prieta earthquake in California, I was shocked at the feeling of helplessness and being alone that immediately descended, even in a city of hundreds of thousands. Our battery-powered radio was our only contact with the outside world, and over and over the broadcasters intoned, "You will need to take care of yourself for the next several days."

Preparation for lag time is a must! Most evacuees have not prepared at all. They simply lock their doors behind them and leave. They survive the displacement but they enjoy little dignity or comfort during the experience. When people have prepared for evacuation, they have far fewer problems than they would have had otherwise. They are somewhat comfortable, have activities to occupy their time, are less concerned about unfinished business, and are less likely to have problems at a shelter.

The entire Des Moines area had come to a virtual standstill. People were using boats to travel down the streets. Houses and stores were waterlogged and inaccessible. . . . Water covered our neighborhood for three weeks. . . . A disaster like this makes you realize how vulnerable you really are, . . . So many people don't understand what it's like to lose everything, including your security.

—"Diary of a Disaster," *Ladies Home Journal*, November 1993

During the Oakland firestorm, we saw the fires from our home and considered carefully what we would be able to take with us if we had to evacuate. It helped us realize that storing a lot of food at home isn't enough. Some sustenance needs to be available to be mobile.

—J. P., Alameda, Calif.

ANALYZE THE RISKS

Analyze the risks in your area. Assess the likelihood of a man-made disaster in your own neighborhood. As you become aware of the problems that could occur, the chance that you could be forced to evacuate your home will be brought more clearly into focus. When you combine these problems with the possibility of natural disasters, you'll understand why you need to prepare an individual evacuation plan and kit. The more detailed your research, the better prepared you will be. Go out into your neighborhood to see what is there. Don't just go on a virtual tour in your mind. Go on an actual tour. Memory may not be completely reliable and changes occur constantly around us. Familiarity allows you to gaze at a scene without recognizing the details of what you are looking at. What around your home could happen that could force you out? Look at businesses, such as a common gas station or paint store, with a different perspective. If that paint store caught fire, would toxic fumes engulf the whole area? Keep in mind this is planning, not panicking. It is simply having the foresight to assess a potential problem and deal with it!

Five-Mile Rule

The area that can directly affect you is usually within a five-mile radius of your home. (Of course, Mother Nature cannot be confined to an area.) Determine the proximity of freeways, railroads, and factories to your home. What kind of freight is shipped near you? What kinds of factories are there? Think of the specific problems they could cause. For example, are you aware that toxic materials are often transported by truck? If a spill or leak occurs on a nearby highway, you could be evacuated. Railroads also carry substances that could be threatening. Are there tracks near your home? Are you in the flood path if a dam or levy should break? Would your geographical terrain ease or aggravate possible problems? Once you have appraised your danger zone, you should be able to analyze the perils that would have the greatest effect on you.

PREPARATIONS MUST INCLUDE PRACTICE

While you develop all of the facets of a sound emergency evacuation plan, build practice into it. The main reason for planning, studying, and practicing is that you are more likely to keep your head about you when the real thing happens if you've thought through the steps for dealing with a possible evacuation in advance. Those drills at home could prove to be priceless.

LOCATE YOUR EVACUATION SHELTER

Some people may never need to stay in an evacuation shelter, even if they are forced from their home. If you are lucky enough to have friends or family living nearby yet not in your immediate area, you can make arrangements to stay with them in case your home might be rendered uninhabitable for several days or weeks. If staying with a friend or relative is not a possibility, then your most likely option will be a community evacuation shelter. Preparing to survive in the wilderness is not necessary. You will not be the Von Trapp family, escaping over the Austrian Alps with only the clothes on your back and a song on your lips. In today's world, schools, churches, National Guard armories, and other large public buildings with large recreation rooms and kitchen facilities are used to house evacuees. An earthquake or major disaster could cause a possible exception, where buildings that would normally be used in your immediate neighborhood to shelter disaster victims would be considered unsafe. Evacuees would then need to stay in tents or makeshift shelters outside. In these instances, the National Guard generally sets up large community tents for public use as soon as it is possible, and other shelters are opened in close-by neighborhoods.

After an emergency occurs, a designated person at the city's Emergency Operations Center calls the Red Cross. The Red Cross then determines where the service center or shelter will be set up. For example, a toxic leak from a train car on a railroad spur forced a neighborhood evacuation in Salt Lake City in 2005. The Red Cross was called and before many hours had passed, service centers were set up in two churches outside the evacuation area.

In order to eliminate guesswork and confusion at the time of evacuation, buy or draw a large map of your area. Using the results and information from your completed Neighborhood Evaluation form, mark the routes to several of the buildings that you have determined are the most logical evacuation centers. Be sure to record street address numbers. A few practice runs now are essential to creating calm when a crisis comes. Keep this map with your 72-hour evacuation kit.

And for those skeptics who ask, "What if I go to all of the effort to create an emergency kit and nothing ever happens?" I say, "Lucky you." Call it a security blanket in a box. Be ever so grateful if you never have to use it. However, it only takes once . . .

Start now to get ready. In a crisis, any preparation, even minimal preparation, would be far superior to having none at all to rely on. Who knows when an emergency will come knocking at your door? When it does, don't be caught unprepared! By acting now to be ready for an evacuation, you will not only survive, but survive with dignity, confidence, and even some comfort.

CHAPTER THIRTY-EIGHT

CREATE A KIT: YOUR MINI HOME AWAY FROM HOME

The first and most important thing to do in preparing for an evacuation is to assemble a 72-hour emergency kit for each member of your family. The emergency kits should contain basically what you will need to survive for a minimum of seventy-two hours, including food, clothing, and everything else. These kits must be ready and accessible before an evacuation order comes, and how well you prepare them will determine how well you survive a crisis and with what degree of dignity and confidence. If you are forced to evacuate, your kit becomes your "mini home away from home."

ALL KITS ARE NOT CREATED EQUAL

The ideal portable evacuation kit, in many people's opinion, has four wheels, a well-stocked fridge, and a generator. It is commonly called a motor home, rather than an evacuation kit. This would indeed be a comfortable and secure solution, meeting all the requirements for an evacuation situation (shelter, heat, light, food, and so on), unless, of course, you should have to walk out. In that case it would be a little heavy to carry. Should you own a motor home or recreational vehicle, keep it stocked with evacuation preparedness in mind. Most of us, however, don't own a motor home, so we have to look to other alternatives.

LIMITED SPACE: A KEY FACTOR

One of the major differences that sets evacuation preparedness apart from the other preparedness categories is the extreme limitation of space. Everything you need to survive for three days must be organized and squeezed into a portable container small enough

for you to carry. "Portable" and "small enough to carry" are the operative words. You need to choose a container big enough to hold all you need but small enough to move easily. All subsequent decisions will be based on the kind and size of container you choose. All food, equipment, and supplies must now fit within the strict limitations of space determined by that container (or containers, if you are capable and prepared to transport more than one). It should be rugged enough to withstand rough handling and adverse conditions. It should have sturdy handles. Preferably, it should be waterproof. However, don't wait to start assembling your kit until you have the perfect container. Begin now with whatever you have, polyethylene buckets with tight-fitting lids, suitcases, or even cardboard boxes. Even though it might not meet the ideal requirements, this is one instance where something is much better than nothing. Start now, and improve and upgrade your kit container later.

No single type of container will meet all the needs of everyone. Try to use containers that are best suited to each individual's capabilities or limitations. Your completed kit will probably end up consisting of two units: one for food, supplies, and equipment, and the second for water. Take into account each person's particular needs, such as age, size, health, and strength. Consider carefully how much each kit will weigh when filled, and whether or not the person will be able to carry it without too much trouble. You never know how far or how long a kit might have to be carried. For example, a backpack on a frame might suit a strong teenage boy, while a sturdy suitcase with a secure handle and wheels would be a more practical solution for a grandmother in her eighties.

Don't try to cram supplies for your entire family

into one large container. If you do, you won't be able to move it when a critical situation arises. It's not called a 72-hour kit because it takes you seventy-two hours to get it out of the house and into your car! The contents of a 72-hour kit should be limited to the needs of just one person.

UPGRADING IS AN OPTION

When choosing a container for your evacuation kit, don't worry that you're going to do it wrong and you'll be stuck with your bad choice forever. You can always change your mind and choose a different or better option. I've upgraded and changed our containers several times. I'm always on the lookout for new ideas that improve on what I have. Maybe it will be something easier to handle, or something with a different design that has more space yet is still compact, or maybe just something that is better quality. Seventy-two-hour kits are not store-and-forget items; you'll need to update them and replace perishable items regularly. That's a good time to upgrade to a new container if you need/want to.

CONTAINER OPTIONS

The following options could be used effectively for your emergency kits. I have graded them according to how practically suited they are for the purpose of a 72-hour evacuation kit.

Recommended: Very well suited for this purpose.

Good: This will function acceptably.

So-so: You can make do with this, but another container would probably be better. Plan to upgrade as soon as you can.

Not recommended: This does not suit the purpose.

Polyethylene Buckets: Recommended

Polyethylene Buckets-Recommended. Polyethylene buckets are at the top of my "Best Choice" list for use as 72-hour kits. Six-gallon buckets (fifteen inches high with a diameter of twelve inches) with sturdy handles and snug-fitting, flanged lids are almost perfect. They are large enough to contain all the essential items for one adult; they stack well and are usually reasonably priced. They are waterproof and are versatile enough once at a shelter to also carry water or to be used for a seat, washbasin, or even as a toilet, if the need should arise. For these reasons, I strongly recommend that each family have at least one bucket,

even if you choose to go with other types of containers for your main evacuation kits.

Most places (hardware stores, emergency preparedness outlets, and so on) that stock these buckets also carry a resin-type bucket wrench which will quickly and efficiently open the lids. Poly buckets can be very difficult, though not impossible, to open without one. Lash the wrench securely to the handle of one of your buckets, or tape it to the outside. (Just a note, don't pack your wrench inside the bucket with the rest of your supplies. That pretty much defeats the purpose of having it.)

Too difficult to carry? Creative thinking will help you find solutions. Use a bungee cord to tie a bucket container onto a wheeled suitcase tote for easier mobility. A lightweight, folding hand truck with your container or containers would make moving them a snap. For more ideas, see chapter 46, Guidelines to an Emergency Evacuation.

You can find used buckets at bakeries, doughnut shops, and delis and at comparable sections in supermarkets. These originally contained baking mixes, frosting, pickles, or the like. These outlets often will save the buckets for you if you ask. Some will give them to you for free; others will charge a nominal

I started my first emergency kit in a large wooden footlocker, complete with heavy rope handles and a metal hasp. I regularly accumulated supplies in this box, and from time to time I would lift the lid and gaze at the contents, enjoying the feeling of security it gave me. Then, one day, we decided to have an evacuation drill. When it came time to move the footlocker, I couldn't even budge it. In fact, it was so heavy that I probably couldn't have moved it even if it had been on wheels. We quickly learned that we needed to have smaller, separate containers for each member of our family, rather than one large group unit.

fee. Be sure to get ones with lids that fit tightly. Used buckets work just as well as new ones, though you may need to scrub them and/or soak them for a while to get rid of residual smells. It's not so bad if your buckets smell like chocolate or cherries, but having all your supplies take on the aroma of pickles or jalapeno peppers isn't quite as acceptable.

Plastic Storage Tubs: Recommended

The ten- or twenty-gallon plastic, rectangular storage tubs with carrying handles molded into the sides are excellent container choices. You'll find them in the housewares, or closet-organizer sections of most hardware and discount department stores. Select the kind that have snug fitting, snap-lock lids that tend to make them water resistant. Don't use tubs much larger than eighteen to twenty gallons because they will begin to weigh too much to be portable. Tubs stack well, and could be utilized in many useful ways at a shelter, including carrying water, though it probably would be more difficult than in a bucket. (Put the lid on to avoid splashing water.) Some larger storage boxes have built-in wheels. Wheels could be very helpful, but don't get carried away and buy a container big enough to hold a live ox just because it has wheels. It would still be too heavy when full. Remember, you'll have to lift that box into and out of your car, and possibly carry it up stairs or over rough ground.

Backpacks: Recommended to Good, Depending on the Quality of the Pack

Backpacks can be excellent containers for emergency kits. I highly recommend sturdily made camping or backpacking packs on frames that have been created to withstand the rigors of bad weather and rough handling. By design, they are easy to carry, and most are water-repellent. (Note that this is not the same as being waterproof.) If you use a back-pack with a backpacking frame you could expand your kit capacity by including a sleeping bag or bedroll, along with additional lightweight equipment like backpacking tents, stoves, lanterns, and so on. Keep in mind, however, that a fully loaded backpack can weigh upwards of sixty or seventy pounds, much more than an average person can or ought to carry. Just because there are pockets and tie-downs everywhere doesn't mean you have to stuff them full (unless it's with waterproof bags of chocolate). Keep your supplies lightweight. A backpack shouldn't weigh more than about 25 percent of the weight of the person carrying it. Backpacking backpacks are not suitable for small children or elderly people, though they can usually manage lightly packed school-type backpacks more readily than many other container choices.

School-type backpacks may or may not be recommended, depending on the design. The features that would deny them a high recommendation are their smaller size, zippers that open too widely, and poor-quality construction. Some backpacks just don't have the capacity to hold all the supplies a good evacuation kit will require. On the other hand, I've seen some that will hold forty pounds of textbooks, a jacket, sack lunch and school supplies, and still have room for art projects and show-and-tell items. These kinds may be plenty large enough, especially when you consider all the pockets on every surface. Some even have wheels and handles. To get all those books in and out, manufacturers often put zippers that stretch from one bottom corner up and around and down to the opposite bottom corner. This is good for books, but it's not so good for evacuation kits because all your supplies will fall out anytime you open it up. To get around this problem, you can fasten big, sturdy safety pins over the zipper teeth near the top of the backpack as zipper stops. Make sure a school-type backpack is well built, made of quality materials, with sewn—not glued—seams, and that it can be securely closed. If it meets these conditions then I can recommend it. If not, use it to get started and upgrade later.

Backpacks and backpack units hang more easily than they stack. For example, sturdy hooks in a mud-room or garage are useful for keeping them accessible yet out of the way,

Duffel Bags: Good

Heavy-duty, shoulder-strap-style duffel bags or gym bags make fairly good emergency-kit containers. Some are water-repellent and usually they are quite sturdy. Many have wheels and a handle, as well as quality zippers and multiple compartments. I can give these a "recommended" grade. I don't recommend the drawstring-style bags like students use to bring their laundry home from college, as they can be cumbersome and difficult to carry.

Luggage: Good to Recommended

Cloth/material would be the type least recommended. Check out the luggage section in a good discount department store. You'll find suitcases and baggage in all sorts of sizes and for all sorts of purposes, most of which adapt very well for use as an evacuation kit. Keep in mind, though, that if you fill a giant suitcase to the brim, it will be too heavy for most people to carry. Just because you can choose the largest suitcase known to man, and just because you can stuff it to near-exploding with supplies, does not mean you should. Remember, lightweight and portable are the keys. Wheels are very helpful. On any suitcase, make sure that the handles are secure. If the strength of the locking mechanism is questionable, strapping or tying the suitcase closed increases the stability. On the other hand, it also makes it more difficult to update each year. Most suitcases are not water-repellent or waterproof. Use heavy untreated trash bags inside the suitcase to keep the items protected from water.

Wheeled carry-on cases with retractable handles are generally a really good size as a 72-hour kit. Sometimes these are called travelers. They're usually big enough (when fully expanded) to carry all your supplies, yet not so heavy that you can't lift them. I recommend them.

Tote Bags: So-So

Tote bags can be used for emergency kits if they can be closed securely, although they are usually not very sturdy and the short handles make them difficult to carry. One of the main drawbacks is that they're usually just too small. If you use a tote bag, make sure that the handles are securely fastened to the bag.

Produce Box: So-So

A sturdy, waxed produce box with handle holes can be used as a makeshift kit container. It's adequate

to start with, but you should replace it with a better choice as soon as possible. Boxes are on the list only because they are a great choice if you want to start your evacuation kit right this minute. Boxes are affordable and available. Other than that, they're not so great. Cardboard boxes are not waterproof at all. If one gets wet, it may fall apart. It will help provide some protection against water if you place the contents of your kit in a heavy-duty, plastic trash bag inside the box and then put the whole box into another trash bag. Strapping or tying would increase the stability of the box, and the tape or rope could function as a handle if you fasten it that way.

Trunks, Footlockers, and Ammunition Boxes: Not Recommended

I can't recommend using these for emergency kits. They are much too heavy and unmanageable for one person, or even two, to move.

Garbage Cans: Not Recommended

Metal, plastic, or rubber garbage cans don't make good emergency kit containers. They are much too heavy and unwieldy when filled, even if they have wheels. I know many people have recommended using them, but a thirty-gallon can full of supplies

> We are a senior couple. Both of us have back problems. We resolved our 72-hour kit dilemma with suitcases that have expanding handles and extra-sturdy wheels. The key stays on our key ring.
>
> —M. J., Sandy, Utah

> During a mock disaster and evacuation drill in the summer of 1985 the following "garbage can incident" was reported by a Red Cross director in Provo, Utah. The mock evacuation center was established.
> As the drill progressed, it was brought to the attention of the authorities that an elderly, disabled lady who lived across the street from the command center, required help to evacuate. Three male volunteers were sent to "rescue" her. It took several more volunteers to bring out her evacuation kit. Their response was, "It weighed a ton!" "It" was a thirty-gallon garbage can, filled to the brim!

can weigh upwards of 200 pounds and require a hand truck and a moving crew to move. Another problem with using a garbage can as a kit container is getting to the supplies at the bottom of the can once at a shelter, if you manage to get the can there in the first place. The can would be very difficult, if not impossible, to get into a car.

FAMILY OPTIONS

In assembling kits for a family or multi member household, a combination of units may better suit your needs than individual kits. Make individual kits for each separate family member, including the personal items and supplies every person should have: clothing, a blanket, flashlight and batteries, morale boosters, personal hygiene supplies. Then, create food kits for the whole family in one or two buckets, including whatever fuel options and utensils you'll need to prepare and eat those food choices. This will allow for a greater quantity of food. In a parent's kit or additional container, include other essentials such as the battery-powered radio for the group, a small tent, family first aid supplies, spare batteries, and the other necessary communal items. Adapt and adjust your kits as your family grows and changes.

BEWARE OF RUMORS

Emergency preparations can easily be driven by rumor, fads, or panic. Before you let yourself get all stirred up, use your head and think! I heard one the other day: "Never use a bucket as a kit if you have small children because you can't carry a bucket and carry your child—you'll have to leave one or the other behind." Talk about absurd! Firstly, if your kits are ready and waiting to be grabbed in an emergency, you'll have plenty of time to put both your kit and your kid in the car, or in the stroller, or the wagon, or on whatever mode of transportation you've already decided on. Secondly, it should be obvious from my recommendations above that buckets make much better containers than many other options. In "personal preparedness," the operative word is *personal* (unless of course you're making a different point, and then the operative word is *preparedness*). You choose what container—of all the good choices—will best fit your needs and you find the ways to make it work. (It sounded to me like someone had something to sell—and it wasn't a bucket!) Before you jump on any

faddish bandwagon, think it through first and then sensibly make up your own mind.

KEEP YOUR KITS ACCESSIBLE

A kit is useless unless you can get to it! Find an unobtrusive yet convenient spot to keep your kits where you can grab them at a moment's notice. Assess your home or apartment from a structural standpoint. The storage area should be as sturdy as possible. For example, a closet is a good selection in an earthquake-prone area because of the support of the wall studs. Our family's kits are in buckets stacked in a closet near our front door. One family I know has their kits in backpacks, which hang on hooks near their back door. A widowed senior citizen in my neighborhood keeps her suitcase kit in a small space at the end of a kitchen cupboard. Still another family adjusted the rod and shelf in a family room closet. All of their kits fit in one end of that closet. An alternative location for your kits might be outside of your living quarters, perhaps neatly stacked in the garage, near to but unencumbered by a door. A weatherproof utility shed on your property would work also. Lots of options will do, just

On a wet, blustery winter night in 1984 some friends of ours heard sirens. Suddenly, a policeman pounded on their door. "You have just five minutes to get out," he said. "There is a fire in the chemical plant just west of here. Grab your family and leave." Acrid smoke was already beginning to fill the air. They wanted to take their emergency kits, which were stored under the stairs in the basement. Unfortunately, they quickly discovered other objects had gotten piled on top and in front of the kits. They couldn't take the time required to dig the kits out. Ultimately, they picked up their children, wrapped them in quilts, jumped in the car, and drove off.

as long as you are likely to be able to get to them in a hurry and go!

LABEL YOUR KITS

Be sure to label your kits with your name (or first initial and last name) and phone number. (Don't use your address, for security purposes.) Use indelible marking pens and make the writing as bright, permanent, and easily identifiable as possible. This will help you to keep track of your kits in an evacuation center where there may be a great deal of confusion and someone else could have a kit similar to yours. (One poly bucket looks very much like any other.) You might even decorate your kits for easy identification. This could also help brighten a dreary evacuation center. You may wish to use a slogan, such as "When you get to the end of your rope, tie a knot and hang on." Don't underestimate the positive psychological influence this can have on you and others. Label the items in your kit as well. A lot of people besides you may own cheap plastic flashlights or Sony portable radios. In the long run, it could prevent confusion and loss of property in a crowded shelter.

WHAT IF SOMEONE IS AWAY FROM HOME?

There's always the chance that one or two people may be the only ones at home when a crisis occurs. It will be their responsibility to get the kits out and to the evacuation center (or to a predetermined family meeting place). If someone is away from home when

*Uplifting Quote Ideas
to Brighten Your Kit:*

- *This too shall pass.*
- *My other evacuation kit is a Winnebago.*
- *No one ever said it was going to be easy but this is ridiculous!*
- *Have bucket, will travel.*
- *I'm just here for the food.*
- *You know, Toto, I don't think we're in Kansas anymore.*
- *The sun will come out tomorrow.*

you are evacuated, take his or her kit(s) with you. As soon as humanly possible, separated family members will be reunited, with the help of the authorities, friends, and neighbors. At that point, the missing family members will need their kits for the rest of their stay in the shelter. In a situation with latchkey children, it is critical to work this problem through before the need arises. Chapter 35 has more ideas for coping with emergencies when your family is separated.

THE DON'T-FORGET LIST

A "don't forget" list should be a permanent part of your kit container. Include on it items you must remember to take with you but are using each day so that they can't be put into your kit now, such as eyeglasses, prescription medicines, shoes, or special needs. Solidly tape it to the lid or the side with duct tape, strapping tape, or some other tape that does not readily peel off or lose its adhesiveness with time or humidity. In extreme trauma you can even forget your own name. Writing down such things as "keys" and "wallet" may seem extreme now, but should the occasion arise, such a list could prove to be a lifesaver. Write down the location of the items as well so that you will be able to find them immediately, or so that if someone outside your family is helping you evacuate, they will be able to quickly find them. If your kit is already assembled and waiting, you will usually have time to quickly gather these few critical items.

CREATE A CAR KIT

In today's commuting lifestyle, many of us spend a great deal of time in automobiles or at work away from home. The reason to have a kit in your car is so that if you should ever be stranded you would not be helpless. It wouldn't even have to be a major disaster. In a land laced by freeways and belt routes and plagued with traffic congestion, it can be a commonplace occurrence to be caught in the gridlock, sometimes for hours at a time. Anyone traveling any distance, especially with children, should always place a top priority on a car kit. This type of kit is in addition to any emergency tool or equipment kit you choose to keep in the trunk.

I recommended that the kit container for your car be a backpack so that, regardless of the circumstances, you are able to care for yourself and walk, with supplies that will sustain you. The scope of a car kit is smaller than that of a 72-hour evacuation kit. Weather and seasonal changes will affect the kind of food as well as emergency clothing that you include. For example, in areas with extremely cold winters where you might actually be trapped in your car, consider including a heat source, such as chemical hand/foot warmers, and/or canned fuel and a backpacking stove, along with envelopes of instant soup or hot cocoa. (Not for use inside the car, of course. Put it on the ground outside, or on the hood of the car.) In hot climates you'd need to include more water. The fluctuating temperatures in a car's trunk will cause anything perishable to deteriorate faster than in a kit kept in a home. You'll need to change them out on a regular basis. Foods containing chocolate or other ingredients that melt easily are obviously not good choices. (Darn!)

Determining how many people are in the car most of the time will help you determine the contents and amount of supplies in your car kit. A few items to consider are:

- Water
- Sturdy walking shoes and socks
- Poncho
- Small first aid kit
- Facial tissue
- Moist towelettes
- Flashlight with extra batteries
- Energy foods or bars
- Trail mix
- Ready-to-eat canned food—include a can opener (or choose pop-top cans) and spoon

> *I always keep plenty of things in my trunk of my car for all emergency situations (blanket, food, water, children's activities, etc.). I have needed to use these items on many occasions, and they provide peace of mind. Especially with children. I am a nanny and I always know if I were stuck, I'd be as prepared as possible.*
> —Jamie B., Santa Clara, Calif.

- Small battery-powered radio with extra batteries
- Space blanket/fleece throw
- Small bottle of aspirin or pain reliever
- Small pad of paper and pencil—to be able to leave a note on the car, where you have gone, along with the date and time
- Small journal and pen
- Charger for your cell phone
- Small folding umbrella

MINI-DESK PACK

The probability of facing an evacuation while at your workplace is as great as at home. Should the crisis be of major proportions, you may be required to walk out, especially if you rely on public transportation to get to and from work. After the 1989 Loma Prieta earthquake in California, commuters in San Francisco were literally stranded in the city. The bridges were shut down until safety engineers could determine whether they were safe, and the only land routes out of the city were in the south, and the roads were damaged or gridlocked. With no communications and chaos all around, people had no idea how long it would be until things got back to normal. Some people opted to wait it out in the city, sleeping in their cars; others chose to walk on back roads and try to make it back to their families on foot, or as best they could. Do you have a locker or desk drawer where it would be permissible to maintain a small emergency kit? This could prove to be critical if you are diabetic or hypoglycemic. Many large companies encourage and assist employees to have a plan in place in case of emergencies, including individual evacuation kits. (Don't use this kit as a replacement on the days you forget your lunch!) A school-type backpack or small duffle bag is a good kit option. I suggest that you include a good pair of walking shoes and heavy socks in this emergency kit in case you need to make your way home on foot (providing you live within a dozen or so miles from your work), or make your way to a distant spot where public transportation may be working. This is especially important for women who usually wear high heels to work.

The list of suggested items for a car kit is also a good suggestion list for an at-work kit.

AT SCHOOL

Contact other parents and get involved with your PTA or P.T.O. to insure as much security as possible for children while they are at school. For example, I know of several schools in Utah and in California that have similar emergency preparedness plans for their children. These schools send home a simple list of items to be included in a mini-emergency pack for each child (suggestions include practical foods such as granola bars or energy bars and a space blanket). This list is one of the first things sent home at the beginning of each year, along with a Ziplock bag with the child's name on it. The schools then collect these mini-packs and put them into a container that is sealed and tucked in a corner of each classroom. Each class also has a flashlight that hangs on a hook and a backpack full of first aid supplies so the teacher can grab it in a rush, if needed. The faculty is assigned different responsibilities and they have drills. Another school reported that parents also included in the child's mini-pack a picture of the parents and/or family and a short, encouraging letter. These were returned sealed with the mini-pack. to be opened only if needed. In my granddaughter's school, they have a read-a-thon the last week of school, and the children get to eat the contents of their emergency kits for their treats as they read. Other schools send the packs home with the child at the end of the school year. One word of caution is to make sure parents understand the foods are to be nonperishable. One school reported a strong odor that caused a small crisis in one classroom until the source could be tracked down. It turned out to be some very perishable food in one of the children's kits.

For older children in junior high and high school, where the students are more independent, a small kit in any number of unobtrusive containers could remain undetected even when a locker door was open. No-snitch rules must apply to the food in the kit, but that's no guarantee that snitching won't happen. You may have to send replacements several times a year for your peace of mind.

Many schools and school districts have very detailed plans for dealing with emergencies of all sorts, including how to get children home or what to do with them if going home isn't an option. Call your local principal or district office to see what plans they have in place. It will either relieve your mind to know their plans or galvanize you to action if your school has not taken any steps for preparedness.

DO YOU HAVE PETS?

If you have pets, take as many precautions as possible to ensure their survival. As part of your planning sessions, write a list of pet to-dos and must-haves. As a general rule, pets are not allowed inside shelters (excluding service animals) due to health regulations. If you plan on taking your pet with you and keeping it outside the shelter, you will need to have a 72-hour pet kit, consisting of food, water, leashes, kennel or cage, and some plans as to how to take care of droppings. Consider taking a tent along to the shelter. If necessary, you could stay in it outside the shelter with your animals. Don't simply turn your animals loose, thinking they can fend for themselves. In cases of disasters such as earthquakes or hurricanes, roving animals may be destroyed in order to prevent more problems and the spread of disease.

CHAPTER THIRTY-NINE

MEALS FROM A KIT

During an evacuation period eating the right types of foods is critical. A stressful situation demands more energy than normal, which is why foods high in calories are recommended for survival. Practical advanced preparation can insure a relatively good balance of nutrition along with the necessary high calories.

People can live for many days—even weeks—without food if they have water to drink. However, most of us are accustomed to regular meals and plenty of food. To suddenly cut from three full meals plus snacks each day to just a food bar or two would be torture. Even if that food bar is chock full of 200 percent of your recommended daily allowances of every vitamin and mineral under the sun, an eight-ounce bar twice a day is not going to fill you up and make you feel satisfied. Along with hunger comes headaches, weakness, and irritability. There is no need to add the misery of hunger to the stress of the evacuation situation. The emergency itself will be enough to deal with.

Eating a meal does much more than just fill your stomach. As I mentioned back in chapter 24, Makeshift Meals, besides providing nourishment, the eating of meals during an emergency has a positive psychological effect. It brings some order to otherwise chaotic times and it helps people feel as if they have some control during difficult situations.

SPECIAL DIETARY CONCERNS

Food will eventually be provided in evacuation centers during an emergency. However, lag time is the problem during a crisis. Days may pass before the courtesy kitchen can be brought in, set up, and begin to function. That is why you have an evacuation kit in the first place—to deal with lag time.

Without it, without proper provisions, chaos that normally could be coped with will be a nightmare for anyone. For those with special dietary needs, it will be even worse. It is imperative that you plan ahead with special attention if you or someone in your care has unusual dietary requirements. Not only will you have to provide the special food or supplies during lag time, but perhaps even longer. Individuals, canneries, and restaurants usually donate food to evacuation centers, and you may have only two choices: take it or leave it. Even if lag time were eliminated altogether and food was available immediately, there may still be problems for diabetics, hypoglycemics, and others with dietary restrictions. There are usually no options for eliminating sugar, salt, or other additives from your diet. Those with severe food allergies cannot take the chance of eating from a totally public food line. I am severely allergic to nuts. If someone even cut a bologna sandwich in half with a knife that had previously been used to make a peanut butter sandwich, it could be deadly for me. I have to provide more food for myself in my emergency kit than most people because it may be too risky to eat food that I am not completely sure is safe for me.

In preparing your evacuation kits, give special attention to the dietary needs of invalids, the elderly, diabetics, hypoglycemics, people with severe allergies, and those on no- and low-sodium diets. If someone you love has a crucial dietary condition, prepare now, and prepare for a longer period of time than you would otherwise need to do.

FOOD FOR A BABY OR TODDLER

Infants and small children may not be able to eat unfamiliar food in a shelter situation. I have discussed these situations with several Red Cross directors and each has emphasized that one of the greatest problems, in a major crisis involving several days and many people, is trying to feed babies and small children. Unfamiliar food is very difficult on their tiny systems. If you have a baby or toddler, you will need to provide for his special needs. If your baby is eating solid foods but not all the regular foods an adult eats, you will need to include some kind of baby food. The drawbacks to baby food in jars are the weight and the glass. You can deal with the glass by making sure the jars are padded and protected from breakage, or choose the kind in the plastic containers. Instant dry foods such as cereal, fruits, and vegetables are all available without the disadvantages of glass jars. These must be reconstituted with water, but even cold water would do in a pinch. Whatever you use, be sure that they are foods your child has eaten before and likes. You could also include bottled juices and aseptic milk if your child is used to having a bottle throughout the day.

Nursing mothers should consider the possibility that, because of the stress brought on by the emergency, they might not be able to produce enough milk for their babies. If you are a nursing mother (or soon-to-be-nursing mother), you should include some liquid formula in your kit in case you are unable to nurse. Even though powdered formula weighs less, you may not be able to use it if water is not available. Think about including both liquid and powdered formula in your kit. Don't forget baby bottles and nipples.

KIT FOOD BASICS

Because food will comprise the bulk of your kit, carefully planning which foods you will take and how much is very important. Balanced meals are not the main concern in this instance. Good nutrition along with high calories are what to look for. Many of the nutritious staple items you already have in your home, such as flour, grains, beans, and pasta absolutely will not function in an emergency kit. They are bulky and require too much preparation. Foods that are lightweight, compact, and that require no refrigeration, preparation, or cooking fit the bill best.

The type, style, and packaging of foods that you choose to put in your kit will determine the kind of utensils and equipment required. For example, compare the differences between regular cans of pork and beans and granola bars. With the pork and beans, you must also pack a can opener, spoon, possibly a bowl to eat from, and ideally, a pan to heat them in. This is not necessarily bad, just heavy. With a granola bar, all you need to pack is the granola bar, though it may not be as satisfying to eat. Food form alone will determine a major portion of the bulk and weight of your kit. Remember, a little weight can add up quickly, as well as take up much of the limited space in your container.

FOODS SUITABLE FOR EVACUATION KITS

You will be surprised at the wide variety of foods that are suitable for emergency kits. The majority of them are available at your local supermarkets. Others may be available at sporting goods outlets or health food stores. Remember though, an evacuation shelter is not a good place to try new, unusual foods. When possible, stick to simple foods and tastes that you are accustomed to. Consider a combination of the following suggested foods to meet your needs:

Stress Food

Foods such as hard candy, energy bars, and sugared dry cereal are known as stress foods. These are a necessity in a 72-hour kit. In stressful situations, people require an increased caloric intake to meet the extraordinary demands for energy. Stress foods meet the requirements for survival, not for a balanced diet. They are small and compact and should be liberally tucked into little spaces throughout your evacuation kit. They also help boost morale. If you can't eat sugar because of dietary restrictions, try the diabetic candies made with artificial sweeteners.

Compressed Food Bars

Compressed food bars, such as power bars, granola bars, and trail bars, are excellent for use in emergency kits. They are small, store well, are lightweight, taste good, and are fairly nutritious and high in calories.

Survival Drink Mix

These drink mixes are a blend of proteins, vitamins, and minerals, which need to be mixed with liquid. Available at emergency preparedness outlets, this type of mix is a fine choice as part of the emergency food in your kit. Don't count on it to be the only thing you include, though. You'll need solid food also. Remember, you'll have to include extra water to mix it with. Try it first to see if you like it.

Trail Mix

Trail mixes are mixtures of grains, cereal flakes, nuts, seeds, dried fruits, and other similar food. They taste good and are high in calories and nutrition. The drawback is that they don't store very well. After a few months they can become rancid, especially if stored in a hot location. If you use trail mix, trade out the old for new several times a year.

Dried Foods

Dried foods, especially meat (jerky) and fruit, are fine for 72-hour kits. They taste good, are nutritious, and are satisfying. One problem with salted jerky is that it may make you thirsty. You may need to carry more water to compensate. Remember that dried food is not the same as dehydrated food, which is not recommended.

Freeze-Dried Foods

Freeze-dried foods are excellent additions to 72-hour kits. You may be familiar with these as backpacking foods found in sporting goods stores. Many are available in supermarkets, as well. They are lightweight, tasty, and store well, but water is needed for their reconstitution. If necessary, they can be reconstituted with cold water. Some freeze-dried foods come in larger No. 2 cans. If these cans are too large and bulky for your particular kit, you can repackage the food into something smaller, like Ziplock bags or small Tupperware-type containers.

Instant Soups

Envelopes of instant soups are compact and excellent for 72-hour kits. They provide nourishment and, if necessary, could be fixed in a cup of cold water.

Instant Meals

Instant meals as cups of noodles, cups of casserole, and so on are usually freeze-dried (ergo, very lightweight), and will reconstitute immediately with hot or cold water. They are an excellent consideration for 72-hour kits.

Shelf-Stable Foods

Shelf-stable refers to retort processing, which stabilizes the food so that it requires no refrigeration. Shelf-stable foods usually are packaged in plastic pouches. Many of them are marketed as microwave meals, similar to frozen TV dinners, but found on the shelf in the supermarket instead of the freezer case. The small plastic containers of ready-to-eat stew, pastas, and soups are a very good choice for kits. They are designed for microwaves but if necessary they could be eaten cold since they are already processed. You can find shelf-stable lunch meals like tuna, ham, and chicken salad also. These kinds of meals make it easy to have high-quality protein in your 72-hour kit meals. For better space efficiency in your kit, consider discarding the outer cardboard packaging.

MREs (Meals Ready to Eat)

The current version of army C rations, MREs are the shelf-stable foods designed for the armed services. Most come as single servings in a multilayered foil/plastic pouch. However, if you consider using MREs, try several first, particularly if they are of the armed services variety. Some are good; some might make going hungry seem like the lesser of two evils. MREs usually are available at emergency preparedness outlets, sporting goods stores, and surplus outlets. Use caution if you find cases of MREs on sale; the prices may be good but you may end up with seventy-two or more of the same meal. That could get old really fast.

MRE-heater bags are also available. They somewhat resemble a plastic mailing envelope. A cardboard heater in the bottom is chemically activated when water is added; therefore you need to have additional water with your kits to make them work. Space may be an issue, since each heater can only be used once. They become very hot, so children should not be allowed to use them without supervision.

Instant Cereals (Instant Breakfasts)

The variety of instant cereal packets (like instant oatmeal) and instant breakfasts available are a boon to evacuation kits. They provide good food value and could be eaten cold (or even dry) if necessary. Consider including small packets of dry instant milk, which could be used with cereal or to fortify other foods for added nutrition, or could be used alone. Put serving-size portions in resealable zipper bags for individual use. Just add water to the zipper bag, seal it tightly, and shake to reconstitute the milk right in the bag.

Snack-Sized or Single-Serving Canned Goods

Pull-top, snack-sized canned goods are worthy choices for evacuation kits. Such items as gelatins, fruit cups, puddings, and tapioca provide food value, familiar taste, and bulk to your diet, with variety to boot. The smallest-sized cans of items such as corned beef, deviled ham, Vienna sausages, and luncheon meat also fit 72-hour kit parameters. Soups, pork and beans, vegetables, and fruits are all available in single-serving size with pop-tops. Since these foods are already processed, they could be eaten cold if necessary. A can opener may be required if the cans don't have pop-tops. Weight and bulk will be the problem with canned goods. Consider using small canned items in conjunction with other, lighter types of food in your kit.

Liquid Dietary Supplements

Liquid dietary supplements, such as Ensure and similar single-serving dietary supplements, often recommended by doctors for older patients, are a source of nutrition in a can, and not just for seniors. They could be considered a good option for an evacuation kit, though you'll still want some solid food to round out your meals. They feature pop-top openings, which is a plus. Weight might be a problem.

Snack Foods

Some small, packaged snack foods are just the right size and weight for evacuation kits. Snack-pack cheese and crackers or peanut butter and crackers, roasted nuts in cellophane or foil packages, fruit snacks, or small variety-pack dry or sugared cereals are a few examples. Some tend to have a short shelf life (like nuts), so you'll need to be aware of this and trade them out fairly often. Because of their flimsy packaging, be careful how you stuff these foods in your kits. You could end up with crumbs and mush instead of crackers and cheese.

Canned Goods

I mention canned goods with some reservations. Though they are familiar and tasty and come in a huge variety, they are also heavy and bulky. They have a place in evacuation kits as a supplement to other lighter-weight foods. A can of ready-to-eat soup or baked beans (eaten cold or hot) would be an appropriate, filling meal, complemented by granola bars and crackers. Just be sure to limit them to a few to keep the evacuation kit as light as possible. You don't want to add a hernia to the disaster. Don't forget to include a can opener.

Drink Mixes

Drink mixes add variety to a 72-hour kit. Try such items as hot chocolate mix, presweetened powdered fruit drinks, and herbal teas. These usually come in small, individual envelopes, so they fit easily in a kit. You'll have to carry additional water, of course.

Liquid Beverages

Juices, juice drinks, and milk are available in aseptic packaging. Often referred to as "soft cans," they come with a straw and require no refrigeration. CapriSun pouches are an example. These are perfect for use in emergency kits. (Pouches may be easier to fit into a kit than boxes, if you have a choice.) Juice is also available in small cans that open with a pull-tab.

A SEVENTY-TWO-HOUR MENU

Following are sample menus that could get one person through a seventy-two-hour emergency. Although lacking the bulk of usual meals, they contain a good variety of food with sufficient calories and are fairly inexpensive. Note that although water is not shown on this menu, it is vitally important and you must have it in addition to your food. Also note the difference in weight between the two sample menus.

SUGGESTED 72-HOUR SUPERMARKET FOOD MENUS

Sample #1

Item	Weight	Extra water required?	Calories per day	Amount for hours	Cost for hours ($)•
Pop-Tarts	11 oz	NO	420	6	1.79
Granola Bars	3 oz	NO	120	3	.78*
Cereal Bars	3.75 oz	NO	180	3	1.41*
Cup of Noodles	6.75 oz	YES	290	3	1.77
Banana Chips	5 oz	NO	750	3	4.47
Pork and Beans	8 oz	NO	240	3	2.37
Sunflower Seeds	3.25 oz	NO	170	3	1.47
Cracker Jack	3.75 oz	NO	120	3	1.19
TOTAL	44.5 oz (2¾ lbs)		2290		$15.15

Sample #2

Item	Weight	Extra water required?	Calories per day	Amount for hours	Cost for hours ($)•
Instant Oatmeal	4.5 oz	YES	150	3	$ .87*
Milk, Aseptic	24 oz	NO	120	3	1.09
Fruit Cup	13.5 oz	NO	60	3	1.50*
Peanuts	9 oz	NO	585	9 oz	1.12
Ramen Noodles	9 oz	YES	400	3	.75
Pudding	12 oz	NO	160	3	1.10*
Lasagna MRE	30 oz	NO	350	3	5.96
Fruit Roll-Up	1.5 oz	NO	50	3	.84*
Cereal Bar	3.75 oz	NO	180	3	1.42*
TOTAL	107.5 oz (6¾ lbs)		2055		$14.65

•Prices were accurate at the time of the survey in and are listed as examples only.
† Full box not required, price prorated.

SUPERMARKET SUCCESS WITH 72-HOUR FOODS

The following foods are listed to give you an immediate overview of some of the items that are readily available on supermarket shelves, their weight, calories, and approximate cost.

CANNED FOODS

Item	Weight (oz)	Calories	Cost ($)
Tuna	6¼ oz	195	$ .79
Corned Beef *Hormel*	12 oz	720	2.09
Deviled Ham	2½ oz	—	.98
Vienna Sausages *Libby*	5 oz	180	.59
Spam	7 oz	1020	1.39
Pork and Beans *Van de Camp*	8 oz	60/2 oz	.79
SpaghettiOs	15 oz	160/7½ oz	.59
Chili con Carne w/ Beans	15 oz	240/7½ oz	.99
Pudding *Snack Pak*	16 oz/4	160	1.49
Peaches *Del Monte*	8½ oz	100/4¼ oz	.75
Jell-O Cups	14 oz/4	100	1.19
Applesauce *Musselman's*	24 oz/6	80	1.88
Soup *Hormel*	7½ oz	110	.98
Lasagna *Top Shelf*	10 oz	350	1.98
Beef Stew *Nalley*	7½ oz	—	1.09

CEREALS

Item	Weight (oz)	Calories	Cost ($)
Granola Bars *Quaker Chewy*	10 oz/10	120/1	$2.59
Granola Bars *Nature Valley*	10 oz/12	120/1	2.39
Cereal Bars *NutriGrain*	10.4 oz/8	140/1	2.85
Cereal Bars *Kudos*	7.5 oz/6	180/1	2.85
Box Cereals *Snack Size*	10 boxes	100-210	3.29

	Weight (oz)	Calories	Cost ($)
Instant Oatmeal *Quaker*	15 oz/10	150/1	2.89
Cream of Wheat, instant	12.5 oz/10	130/1	2.89
Baby Cereal *Gerber*, trial	6 oz/6	50/½ oz	1.45
Granola *American Mills*	64 oz	100/½ cup	5.98
Trail Mix	bulk	1 50/oz	lb 2.99
Cracker Jack	3¾ oz/3	120/oz	1.19
Pop-Tarts	11 oz/6	210/1	1.79
Peanuts, salted	bulk	585/3 oz	lb 1.98
Peanuts, pull-top can, *Planters*	6½ oz	170/oz	1.59
Sunflower seeds shelled, Fisher's	3¼ oz	170/oz	.49

INSTANT MEALS

Item	Weight (oz)	Calories	Cost ($)
Cup of Noodles *Nissin*	2¼ oz	290	$ .59
Top Ramen *Nissin*	3 oz	200/1½ oz	.25
Cup-a-Soup *Lipton*	2.1 oz /4	50/1	1.17
Noodle Soup *Campbell's*	1.33 oz	140	. 69

DRIED, NOT DEHYDRATED

Item	Weight (oz)	Calories	Cost ($)
Banana Chips *Mariani*	5 oz	150/ oz	$1.49
Pears *Mariani*	8 oz	150/2 oz	2.98
Apple Rings	6 oz	150/¼ cup	2.49
Raisins, canned *Sun-Maid*	24 oz	250/½ oz	2.49
Beef Jerky *Smoky Mountain*	1 oz	80	1.69

STRESS FOODS			
Item	Weight (oz)	Calories	Cost ($)
Peppermint Candy *Brach's*	bulk	—	$ lb 1.49
Chocolate-Covered Peanuts	bulk	—	lb 2.99

LIQUIDS			
Item	Weight (oz)	Calories	Cost ($)
Capri Sun Juice, foil packets	67 oz/10	—	$2.79
Juice *Squeeze-It*	40 oz/6	110/1	2.79
Pineapple *Dole*	36 oz/16	100/1	1.99
Juicy Juice *Libby*	24 oz/3	130/1	1.29
Milk, Aseptic Boxes	24 oz/3	120/1	1.09
Instant Breakfast *Carnation*	10 oz	220	1.09

MISCELLANEOUS			
Item	Weight (oz)	Calories	Cost ($)
Peanut Butter *Skippy*	12 oz	58⅓ oz	$1.98
Apple Jelly	10 oz	—	1.29
Cheese and Crackers *Handi-Snack*	1.1 oz	—	.39
Cheese and Pretzels *Handi-Snack*	1.02 oz	—	.39
Fruit Roll-Ups *Betty Crocker*	4 oz/8	50/1 each	2.29
Instant Breakfast, add milk *Carnation*	12.6 oz/10	130/ without milk	3.79

Prices were accurate at the time of the survey in and are listed as examples only.

FOODS NOT SUITABLE FOR EVACUATION KITS

Because 72-hour kits have such rigid parameters for space and weight, there are many types of food that are just not suitable at all for inclusion. These include the following:

Commercially Dehydrated Foods

Even though these are excellent products for long-term preparedness and worst-case scenarios, they are not appropriate for seventy-two-hour preparedness. These foods cannot be eaten as if they were dried foods. This could cause stomach problems. They must be reconstituted, which requires a great deal of hot water and extensive soaking or cooking. They would be very difficult to prepare properly in an evacuation situation.

Bottled Foods

Bottled foods in glass jars are too heavy and take up too much space to make them practical for emergency kits. Also, bottles break easily.

Commercially Canned Foods

You may remember seeing canned goods listed in the "approved types of food" list. They are, and they aren't. Other than the small-sized canned goods previously discussed, commercially canned foods in general weigh too much and take up too much space. One government agency published a list of canned goods that they felt should be put in an evacuation kit. For two people, the weight of the cans of food alone was fifty-five pounds! This is just not practical. Canned goods would not be a bad choice if they were limited to only a few cans in each kit to give normalcy to your evacuation menus. Because they are so common, you might use canned goods to get started on your kits, but if you do, you'll probably want to replace the majority of them with lighter foods as soon as possible. Don't forget the can opener.

Grains and Beans

Under no circumstances should you include dry grains, beans, or pasta in your evacuation kit. These foods are completely inappropriate due to the time-consuming, and heat- and water-demanding processes required to make them edible. You will not be cooking anything from scratch in an evacuation shelter. Can you just imagine the scene? "Mom, I'm hungry!" "Not a problem, dear. I just put the beans on to soak. By tomorrow morning, I can cook them on the sterno stove, and we'll have a good lunch in about eighteen hours."

CONTAINERS, UTENSILS, AND EQUIPMENT

You will probably need to include some kind of utensils or other equipment in your kits, depending on the type of food you pack. Try to use as few as possible, because they add weight and take up space that could otherwise be used for food. The kinds of food you choose will directly affect the equipment or utensils you'll need. If something needs to be heated, you'll need a pan and spoon. Some food needs to be put in a bowl, on a plate, or eaten with a fork or spoon. Everyone should have a cup, at least. Review the food you are putting in your kit and determine what you'll need to fix or eat it. Heavyweight plastic untensils are lighter than metal forks and spoons but not as durable. The same is true of bowls, cups, and plates. The sturdy disposable plastic variety is lighter but the regular items will last longer. You decide. I'm not recommending that you pack enough plastic ware to throw out your utensils after each meal; that would take much too much space. With care, one set of heavy-duty plastic ware could conceivably last seventy-two hours or longer. Possibly. Another, less-breakable idea is to use camping nested utensils. A metal multiuse Sierra cup could function as a cup, bowl, plate and even minisaucepan, though not all at the same time. (Since they nest together, you could include several in a kit.) An aluminum pie pan would also suffice as a plate/bowl.

Some of your food may need to be transferred from its original packaging into small containers more suited to your 72-hour kit. Small Rubbermaid- or Tupperware-type products with tight-fitting lids are ideal. You can also use small plastic freezer containers. Heavy-gauge sandwich or freezer bags could

work, though they're not the best, since mice, moths, and weevil can get into them, or the product in them could easily be smashed. Aluminum foil and paper bags are poor choices for holding kit food because they are just too flimsy.

STOVE OPTIONS

Some of the food you choose to put in your kit may require heating to make it edible or tolerable. Obviously, you can't have hot chocolate without the hot. In that case, you have to provide a source to do that. It's important to note, though, that open flames of any size or configuration may not be allowed inside an evacuation shelter. Before you strike a single match, you'll want to check the regulations for the building. If you have the option, you could take a stove outside to heat your hot chocolate.

That said, there are many stove options that fit the size and weight restrictions of emergency kits. The extremely small winged-tab or folding stoves that use heat tabs for fuel are well suited for this purpose. Two heat tabs on top of each other in a winged stove will heat a cup of water to boiling in a short amount of time: five or six minutes. Canned Heat and the accompanying folding Sterno stoves are good choices. Small backpacking stoves that use canisters of fuel also work although they may weigh more and take up more space. (Not necessarily, though; you can find some pretty small, lightweight stoves on the market. The weight is in the fuel canister, more than the stove.) If you don't have any food in your emergency kit that needs to be heated, you can dispense with a stove and fuel altogether. However, warm food can go a long way to calming down frightened, worried people. You may wish to include a small cooking source and the food supplies for warm drinks or soup just for the soothing influence they can have. For a more detailed description of these types of stoves and fuel see chapters twenty-four and twenty-five.

EQUIPMENT SUGGESTIONS

Here are some equipment and utensils to consider for your kit. You may not need all of these things or you may need more than you see listed here. Use this list to jog your mind as to your needs.

- Small cooking pots
- Spoons, forks, and knives (some plastic, some metal)

- Nesting, camp-style knife, fork, and spoon sets
- Sierra cups (metal camping/backpacking cups that you can heat food in and/or drink from)
- Small, trial-size bottle of dish soap
- A hot pad
- One or more wash cloths, which can serve as washcloth, towel, or hot pad
- Can opener (the small GI-type is good)
- Matches in a waterproof container
- Small backpacking stove with fuel canister
- Canned solid fuel (such as Sterno) and folding stove
- Heat tablets and winged-tab stove or folding stove

PRACTICE SESSIONS

Before a critical situation forces you from home, it is important to practice preparing and eating meals from the kind of food you have included in your evacuation kits. It's important to discover if a "meal" consisting solely of kit foods like a granola bar, a couple of graham crackers, half a cup of raisins, and a hot drink from a mix will be sufficient. After you find out what normally hot food tastes like when prepared with cold water, you may make room in your kit for a cooking source. Or you may find foods generally eaten hot are not so bad when eaten cold. A food-practice session might seem more real if you hold it outside your home. (Make a rule that no one can go inside and eat more after the practice session. That defeats the experiment.) As your family eats, you will quickly learn what tastes good and what doesn't, and what works and what doesn't. This will help you make adjustments in what you include or delete from your kits.

If you are including a small folding stove in your kits, try cooking a meal on it. This will help you learn how to use the stove before you have to in an emergency. Every member of your family should be taught safety precautions in using the stove. For example, the instant a lit match touches a heat tab, the tab will ignite, although you may not be able to see it burning. A person not aware of this could easily be burned.

Another note from my experiences: For several weeks after the 1989 Loma Prieta earthquake in California, I was a guest on many radio talk shows. One of the questions I was asked, almost without fail, was, "Barbara, you supposedly were prepared; did you learn anything? Did your kits provide adequately for you?" Yes, I learned something. Even though we did not have to live out of our kits during the aftermath, I gave them a great deal of thought and deliberation, since at any minute during those first harrowing days, I may have needed to grab them and get out. After a few weeks passed and I got ready to put the kits away in the closet, I concluded that the meager quantities of food I had in our kits would have been just survival amounts. What was needed was more: more food, more water, more bulk and normalcy. Since there are only two members in my household now, I immediately began a third unit, a bucket that contains as much "regular" food as I could get into it and still carry it—items such as snack-pack fruits and puddings, cups of casseroles (freeze-dried meals), cups of soups, and so on. Still lightweight, still compact, but more.

A major problem, in my opinion, with most commercial kits is that the quality and quantity of the "bulk" in foods is lacking. Even though they provide sufficient calories, three survival bars as your "complete food supply for three days" does not qualify as adequate. If you have purchased your kit ready-made, it is critical that you realistically consider how "meals" are defined in your kit. Augment any insufficient food supplies with more, more, and more. You won't be sorry.

CHAPTER FORTY

WATER: A CRITICAL KIT COMPONENT

During an evacuation, water may or may not be available. The greater the severity of the crisis, the greater the probability that normal water supplies will be interrupted. Usually there will be water at an evacuation shelter but you can't be certain. In a widespread emergency, the water supplying the evacuation center may be as compromised as that of the surrounding area. Community water supplies may have become polluted, a common occurrence after a major earthquake or storm. If electrical power is out, the pumps that ordinarily bring water through the system may not be working. It may take a while to bring in large water trucks. Lag time will be a critical factor in how much and how soon water is available. After the Mexico City earthquake of 1985 it took two days to get water into some areas. It is crucial that you take water along with the rest of your emergency kit to enable you to cope without a normal water supply during lag time in an evacuation area. You need to provide a sufficient amount for yourself and your family to last until a water supply can be established.

The minimum requirement for drinking water is six quarts per person for seventy-two hours. This much water weighs twelve pounds. Other needs, such as brushing teeth and preparing foods, usually require an additional two quarts per day.

Some people naturally will require more than the minimum—teenagers, for example, or nursing mothers. What about the kinds of food in your kit? Have you included food that will require water for preparation? If many of your foods are dried, salty, or spicy, or if they require water for preparation, you will need to pack more water to compensate.

If you have included aseptically packaged juices or milk ("soft cans") or bottled water or juices in your kit, these will reduce the amount of water you need to carry in your water unit. On the other hand, liquid containers inside a kit use the space that might otherwise be filled with food or other essentials. Prioritize carefully.

How much you should carry is going to realistically be superseded by how much you can carry. I recommend that you fill some jugs or bottles and practice carrying them to your car, or down the stairs, or to the neighbor's house across the street. It may seem silly now but I have had many people report that they just did not realize how heavy a bottle of water could be, nor how it seems to increase in weight the further it's carried.

I strongly recommend that you resolve the water/weight dilemma now. One solution is to start a serious regimen of weight training today. With nineteen-inch biceps and a physique like Arnold Schwarzenegger, a couple of five-gallon jugs of water will be child's play. If you can't make time in your schedule for that, then a good idea is to have some mode of transporting containers, such as a luggage tote or a hand truck. You could attach small water bottles to belts for easier

> In the aftermath of the Northridge quake, people standing in line at the water trucks related how they had had water stored for just such an emergency. But in the shock and trauma of the situation they drank up their entire supply within just a few hours.

carrying. Nylon rope could be used to lash several containers together, creating a handle, or you could tie containers to a polyethylene bucket or backpack. You could also fashion a yoke to wear over your shoulders for carrying water bottles. You can purchase straps that fasten onto the necks of two-liter soda bottles and can be slung over your shoulder like a purse. Or, place bottles in a sturdy canvas shopping tote for carrying. Or, carry your water containers in a school-type backpack if your kit is a hand-carried one.

WATER-CONTAINER OPTIONS

Many kinds of containers can be used to carry water. Whatever you use, make sure it is clean, has a tight-fitting lid, and has been designed for food or water. The following are a few options:

Canteens and Flasks

Canteens and backpacking flasks, which usually come with either a strap for carrying or hook onto a belt, are good choices. One disadvantage is that they only hold a small amount of water.

Commercially Bottled Water

One advantage of commercially bottled water is that the containers are sealed. Bacteria growth would not be a problem, nor would you need to frequently check and change the water.

Commercial Water Pouches

Emergency preparedness stores, army/navy stores, and sporting goods stores sell individual four- to eight-ounce pouches of water that could be used in conjunction with a 72-hour kit. One disadvantage is that the pouches are neither large nor refillable. You could include several of these inside your kit, in conjunction with more, larger containers carried separately.

The 1994 Northridge, California, earthquake received a lot of media coverage. One of the more shocking reports was of the sale of a single cup of water for one dollar! That should motivate you go run out and get your water supplies!

Water Bottles

Two-, four-, or six-quart water bottles with tight-fitting lids, such as the Rubbermaid ones found in housewares departments, will work with an evacuation kit. You would have to devise a handle or a way to carry them.

Water Jugs

Sturdy plastic water jugs with handles, with or without spigots, are excellent choices to use as water units. They usually have a two-and-one-half- or a five-gallon capacity. A five-gallon jug weighs forty pounds when full, so you'll have to plan in advance how to transport it.

Picnic or Camping Insulated Jugs

You may already have a two- or five-gallon insulated jug on hand for taking on picnics or camping. Most have tight-fitting lids and handles. Many have spigots. These will work fine. Keep them full on the shelves when you're not picnicking, and you're set.

Plastic Soda Bottles or Juice Bottles, but Not Milk Jugs

To use these kinds of containers for water, wash and rinse them thoroughly. If you can smell the former product or soap when the containers are dry, it will affect the taste of the water. Wash and rinse again until no smell remains. Use only heavy-duty plastic bottles. Lightweight plastic, like you'd find in a milk bottle will not hold up more than a couple of months. Then they will disintegrate and your water will drain out, leaving you with nothing when you need it most. Plus, this type of plastic can harbor germs even after you think you've rinsed it thoroughly.

BE ABLE TO CARRY WATER AT THE CENTER

Once the water supply is established at the evacuation center, you will probably need a container to carry water from a main source (such as a truck) to your personal or family area. Even if you are relocated into an evacuation shelter, it may still be necessary to carry water to your area, even if the water is still running in the faucets.

The importance of having a suitable container for carrying water was reinforced as news broadcasters focused on human struggles during the aftermath of hurricanes Andrew in Florida and Iniki in Kauai, and the earthquakes in California. People were shown standing in long lines at the water trucks. You could see every container imaginable in their hands for carrying water, from soda pop bottles to ice cream buckets, from empty bleach bottles to picnic thermoses.

Buckets

A six-gallon-bucket kit container can do double duty as a water container. When you pack your kit, tuck in one or two heavy-duty garbage bags to hold your supplies while you use the bucket to carry water or as a washbasin.

Rubber or Plastic Storage Tubs

If you have selected fifteen- or twenty-gallon rubber or plastic rectangular storage tubs as your kit container, these could also be used to carry water. It would probably be more challenging than using a bucket with a handle but not impossible. Putting the lids on them would keep the water from splashing on you or the ground as you walk. Tubs also can be used as washbasins.

Collapsible Water Jugs

Collapsible water jugs with handles and spigots are usually available wherever sporting goods are sold. When empty, these two-and-a-half- or five-gallon containers collapse flat to fit inside some kits, or they could be fastened to backpacking frames. They could be tied to a bucket handle or carried inside a canvas tote with the lag time water supply.

Collapsible Buckets

Small, collapsible canvas or plastic backpacking buckets hold about a gallon of water. They are flat when empty but constructed to twist or pop open. A wire frame supports the walls sufficiently so that a full bucket will stand by itself on the ground or table.

Canteens, Flasks

Small water bottles or canteens are appropriate for your lag time water unit, but at a center where water is being provided, they are ineffectual for carrying adequate amounts from a main source to your personal area. Though better than nothing at all, you could end up being very frustrated if you have

to stand in line for hours to get a cup of water at a time. It's better to plan ahead with one of the above options for carrying quantities of water at a shelter, even if you use canteens or the like to carry your lag time water supply in.

FILLING YOUR OWN CONTAINERS

It isn't necessary to buy commercially bottled and sealed water. You can fill your own containers for free (or as close to as doesn't matter) in your own sink, and the water is just as good. The trick is to start with clean water and clean containers, and then fill the containers all the way to the top until the water overflows. Don't put the lid on if the inside of the container is covered with air bubbles. Gently tap on the sides of the container or bounce the container on the counter or floor to cause the bubbles to come to the surface. When the bubbles are gone, top it off with more water, eliminating all the air possible. Then, put the lid on securely. This will help reduce the growth of bacteria. Of course, if there is a chance that your water will freeze during storage, you will have to allow some space for the water to expand. Otherwise, your containers could break and leak, ruining the contents of your kits. In this case, just plan to replace your water supply at least annually.

The water from the tap that you fill your containers with is safe to drink. It does not need to be treated or purified. Keep the containers in as dark and cool a place as possible, along with the other kit units, and change your water at least every year or so. Check periodically to see if it has become cloudy or developed any other problems. You only need to treat your water with bleach or other water purification methods if you suspect a problem. If you haven't changed out your water in twenty-five years and there are frogs swimming in it, you have a problem and purification is probably in order.

PURIFYING WATER

Even though we discussed water purification in chapter 15 it's a little different in an evacuation situation. It is always possible that your water supply will be compromised between the time you store it and the time you need it. If your water is cloudy or polluted, it should be purified before use. If the water is clear but you are not sure whether it is safe or not, purify it anyway. It could contain bacteria, and it is better to be safe than sorry. The following instructions are included so that if you know there's a problem, or if you even suspect the available water is unsafe to drink, you'll have the knowledge and means of purifying it.

You should have the following water purification supplies in your emergency kits:

- A collapsible bucket (if your kits are not in polyethylene buckets) or sturdy plastic bags, such as a gallon-size Ziplock bag. (Use only food-grade plastic bags. Colored or treated trash bags will not do, nor will bread sacks or very thin plastic bags.)
- A small pan or large Sierra cup in which to boil water.
- Cheesecloth or other cloth for straining impurities from water.
- Heat tabs and stove, or other heat source.
- Water purification tablets or tincture of iodine. (Although household bleach is usually recommended to use in purifying water, it has been intentionally omitted here because of the difficulty in keeping or transporting it in a kit container.)

HOW TO PURIFY WATER

If the water is especially dirty, strain it through a cloth to remove debris and dirt. Then, boil it for five minutes at a rolling boil to kill bacteria. This is the safest way to purify water. Note that the water has to be boiling before you start counting off the five minutes. That could take anywhere from five to twenty additional minutes, depending on your altitude. Be sure to take into account the high rate of evaporation at the boiling point and increase the amount you boil. Otherwise, the water could boil away, leaving less than the amount you intended. (Using a lid, or covering the pan with aluminum foil will help, if you have either of them in your kit.) Clearly, boiling as a method of purification is only appropriate when you have an abundance of water to start with. Boiled water will taste better if you pour it from one container to another a few times to put oxygen back into it. This is also true of water that has simply been stored for some time.

To use water purification tablets, follow the instructions on the package. Usually, four tablets per gallon are sufficient. Use twelve drops of tincture of iodine. Mix the tablets or iodine thoroughly into the water and let it stand for several minutes. If the water is cloudy, double the number of tablets or drops of iodine. The water will taste better if you let it stand for a little while before drinking it.

DEHYDRATED WATER?

Sufficient water is an absolute necessity. If you could obtain water in tablet form that instantly reconstituted when you dropped it into a container, it would solve many problems. The difficulty is that the label would read, "To reconstitute, just add water." Unfortunately, dehydrated water tablets aren't available; therefore, you have to look for other solutions to the problem.

CHAPTER FORTY-ONE

SHELTER, LIGHT, AND A SECURITY BLANKET

When the siren has sounded, it's too late to figure out how you will be sheltered from the stormy elements until help arrives. You must be able to build your home away from home from the equipment and supplies in your kit. Proper planning can provide relative protection and even some comfort. The normalcy created by having a tent to pitch, a lantern to light, and a card game to occupy your mind may not banish all the fear and worry but it certainly will provide a glimmer of security in the mire of chaos.

ADJUST YOUR MIND-SET—THINK SMALL

The equipment required to shelter you and keep you as warm and dry as desired could easily take up a small room, not just a small evacuation kit. You have to adjust your mind-set to think small, compact, lightweight. Catch the vision of how backpacking equipment can fill a unique niche here. By nature, backpacking equipment is as light and small as possible so it can be carried comfortably over long distances and rough terrain. That makes it ideal for an evacuation kit. In fact, there are a great many similarities between backpacking and being evacuated. In each instance, you have to be prepared to care for yourself completely with only what you can carry with you in a small container. The main difference is that the one is done by choice for fun, the other by force for survival.

SHELTER—PICK UP YOUR HOUSE AND GO

While it is true an evacuation center will provide a roof over your head, it is also true it may not provide much, if any, privacy. Most of us would feel very uncomfortable to have to be on display all the time. You can help yourself avoid that exposed feeling by taking some privacy with you. A small, lightweight tent provides dual-purpose protection. It gives you refuge from the elements if you choose not to take shelter in the community building provided by emergency services, or if you can't find the evacuation center for some reason and you end up in a park or a football field. Even at a community shelter, some people may feel more comfortable in a private tent outside on the grounds, where they still have access to the food, water, and bathroom facilities of the shelter, but are without the crowds. One firefighter reported that in the aftermath of the 1994 Los Angeles quake, many people were so frightened that they could not remain inside the shelters or even in homes that were safe. As the ground continued its unrelenting shaking, they persisted in remaining outside—and unsheltered.

The second purpose for a tent can be to provide a privacy barrier inside the shelter once there. Inside an evacuation shelter (usually a school, church, or other spacious building), you will probably be in a large room shared by many other people—not a very comfortable or private place. In this instance, a tent shifts its purpose from protecting you from the elements outside to providing you with some privacy inside. Now, this won't work if the shelter is bursting at the seams with people; there would not be room to put up a personal tent indoors. However, if it were not terribly crowded, you would welcome the chance for a little space to yourself.

Here are some of the tent/privacy options available:

Tents in General

Tents are great for evacuation kits, with some naturally being more appropriate than others. If you intend to use your tent for privacy inside a building, the only kinds that will work are pop-tents, or other small freestanding tents that do not require staking. (As a general rule, most places frown on people pounding tent stakes into their floors, even in an emergency.)

If you have camping equipment in your attic or garage that hasn't seen the light of day in a decade or more, your tent is probably an old-fashioned one that needs to be staked into the ground to maintain its shape. It would be unfortunate if you were to plan on using your tent only to discover at a crucial moment that it won't work.

Tube Tents

Usually constructed of heavy plastic, these are relatively inexpensive and can be purchased wherever sporting goods are sold. They are compact enough to fit inside most kit containers. They consist of simply a tube of plastic (usually bright orange). To give it its tent shape, you stretch a rope through the tube and tie the rope ends to trees or posts (or doorknobs or whatever you can find indoors) to form the peak of the tent. Next, you pull the sides out as far as they'll go and hold them down with rocks or books or other heavy objects. Tube tents are very primitive, and they'll only provide limited space for one or two people. As you can tell, it may be difficult to use them if you don't have access to stationary objects to fasten the rope ends to. Tube tents could also be used as a privacy barrier, like a tarp, without opening them up or climbing inside them. You would still have to come up with some sort of creative solution to tie the rope ends to, other than having people hold them up.

Backpacking Tents

Backpacking tents are usually very compact and lightweight, often weighing only four to five pounds. Many varieties would fit inside a large evacuation kit or on a backpacking frame and are highly recommended for 72-hour kits. They usually are only large enough for one or two people.

Small Tents

Small tents range in size and description from a two-person, rectangular tent, to a two- or three-person, pop-up, round-dome tent. These work very well as long as you plan for a way to carry them. Some fasten easily to a backpacking frame. Some have cloth cases with straps that would let you sling them on your shoulder. If nothing else, you could jury-rig a handle out of duct tape or rope on the box the tent came in.

Regular Tents

If you have tents that you use for camping, you may be able to use them during an evacuation if you have the means to quickly transport them, as well as the ability to carry them if necessary. The obvious disadvantages are the bulk and weight. Regular-sized tents are probably too big to be allowed in an evacuation center, though they may be able to be set up outside.

Tarps or Ground Covers

One or more nylon or heavy plastic tarps or ground covers can be folded flat to fit in or fasten

> *Scoutmaster Larry went camping with a group of Boy Scouts one weekend. A sudden summer storm blew up in the middle of the night, drenching everyone and everything. Only one boy had brought a tube tent. All the others were sleeping under the stars. At the first drops of rain, the camp erupted in a wild melee of activity as the leaders raced for the car to stay dry and the boys (all ten of them!) dove for shelter in the one tube tent. It was almost like a cartoon, with legs and arms sticking out both ends and constant hollering and yelling and waves of motion going on as boys crawled all over each other trying to get out of the rain and get comfortable. As for Larry, at the first threat of rain, he carried his air mattress and sleeping bag down to the large privy (smelly but not horrendous), down on the cement floor, and got the only good night's sleep had in camp that trip.*

onto a kit. (Thin plastic painting drop cloths don't qualify.) These could be fashioned into a simple tent in the same manner a tube tent is set up, or strung up as "walls" indoors. (Don't forget to include rope in your kit!) Outdoors, a tarp wouldn't provide much protection from the elements during bad weather, though one could be stretched overhead as a sunshade or tent if the weather was good. Shade could prove invaluable if a crisis occurred during a heat wave. Tarps can be very useful, serve a multitude of purposes, and take up less space than a full-fledged tent. Just know how to use them before a need arises.

BLANKETS: A CRITICAL COMPONENT

A critical part of your 72-hour kits will be some kind of blanket for each member of your family. Besides providing warmth, blankets give a feeling of security. A blanket can also be used as a screen to provide some measure of privacy in a crowded area. Blankets are especially important if you live in a locale known for inclement weather. The major problem with most blankets is how to get them to fit inside a kit. If you are using a backpack frame, you can wrap one as securely as possible in plastic and carry it as you would a bedroll or sleeping bag. If you are using a bucket and you just can't squeeze the blanket inside, protect your blanket from water as much as possible in a plastic trash bag, then wrap and fasten it securely around the outside of the container (duct tape—the handyman's favorite tool!). As soon as possible obtain a blanket that fits inside with all other items in order to keep your 72-hour kit compact and manageable.

However, you have to make a choice. Although it's nice to have everything neatly contained in the evacuation kit, you may decide you'd rather have a warm blanket or sleeping bag at a shelter, even if it means having one more thing to carry. In this case, find a small tote bag/duffle bag/stuff sack to carry your blanket in and figure out how you're going to carry it along with your kit. You'll still want it to be as small and lightweight as possible.

SOME BLANKET ALTERNATIVES

Use the following list of blanket alternatives to help you determine what you have on hand that will work for now, and what to plan to acquire. In the descriptions, you can translate "bulky" to mean "won't fit in a bucket or backpack and still allow room for anything else."

Virgin Acrylic Blankets

Virgin acrylic blankets are very warm, have many of the advantages of wool, and yet are lightweight and "squishable." A twin-size blanket will fit or squish nicely into a six-gallon bucket with all the other supplies. These blankets also dry quickly. This is probably the best type of blanket for an evacuation kit. Many times, lap robes or car blankets found in discount drug or department stores are made of virgin acrylic.

Fleece Throws

You can find fleece throws just about everywhere, in discount department stores, drugstores, and even in grocery stores. The throws are usually square, approximately 50 by 50 feet and very affordable. They can easily squish into a kit. Best of all, they dry quickly yet will keep you warm when wet.

Wool Blankets

Wool blankets are very warm, even when wet. However, they are very bulky, weigh a lot, and take a long time to dry. The older 100 percent wool blankets are stiff and nearly impossible to fold down into anything remotely resembling compact. Newer, part-wool blankets would be more appropriate, though probably still not your best choice.

Thermal Blankets

Thermal blankets are warm but fairly bulky. They dry quickly because of their open-weave design.

Polyester/Acrylic Blankets

Polyester/acrylic blankets are fairly warm but not as warm as some other blankets. They are also fairly heavy and bulky. However, they are probably the least expensive of all blankets.

Quilts and Comforters

Quilts and comforters are very warm but weigh a lot, are bulky, and take a long time to dry. Use these if they're the only thing you have but plan on upgrading to a better choice as soon as possible.

Cotton/Polyester Sleeping Bags

Sleeping bags are very warm and many are water-repellent. If you use a backpack with a frame, you can easily carry a sleeping bag. The bags are bulky, though, and do not dry quickly. The cute sleepover bags designed for children are not in the same category as sturdy camping sleeping bags constructed for warmth. On the other hand, they are also a lot smaller.

Down Backpacking Sleeping Bags

Most down backpacking sleeping bags are extremely warm and waterproof and are usually lightweight, though possibly bulky. They do not dry quickly. They usually squish into a stuff sack, and are, by design, ideally suited to a backpack frame. The stuff sack could possibly be attached to a bucket if needed.

Space Blankets

Measuring 56 by 84 inches, these "blankets" look as if they are made out of aluminum foil. They are compact, lightweight, inexpensive, and readily available where sporting goods or emergency preparedness supplies are sold. They were developed for the space program and function by reflecting body heat. Every kit should contain one or more. One downside is that they do not have the softness or feel of a real blanket, so you don't get the same psychological comfort from them. You get the best of both worlds if you combine a space blanket with a regular blanket or throw. Put the "real" blanket next to your skin (for the psychological comfort) and put the space blanket on over it (for the reflective, warming properties). To provide the maximum amount of warmth, I recommend that every kit include the combination of a space blanket with another blanket.

Emergency Blankets

A variety of compact and lightweight emergency blankets is available. One example is a 5-by-7-foot all-season blanket made of multilayered plastic, fabric, and aluminum, weighing about twelve ounces. This type of blanket also functions by reflecting body heat. They are a good choice, even if used alone, and even better if used in conjunction with a "real" blanket. They are generally affordably priced.

Disposable Emergency Blanket

Used by medical professionals, this lightweight, compact "blanket" is a disposable paper product. They don't have the warmth factor of a regular blanket. They are not recommended for use in a 72-hour kit because they don't hold up under normal use, let alone inclement weather.

Baby Blankets

Large or crib-size baby blankets are warm, though much smaller than regular blankets. They could probably fit inside some kit containers. If used for an adult, they would offer some skimpy coverage and warmth. You'll probably want to replace them with a better (that is, larger) option, if possible.

Blankets Cut in Half, or Blanket Material Remnants

Cutting a blanket in half will yield a blanket big enough to wrap around you (provided you don't thrash around too much when you're sleeping), yet small enough to fit inside an evacuation kit. It will still be bulky, but only half as much as a full-sized blanket.

CAN YOU FIT A CAMPFIRE IN YOUR POCKET?

Usually, it is not practical to carry a source just for heat in an evacuation kit. This could be a real problem, however, if you live in an area known for bad weather. Since preparing for lag time means you must care for yourself completely for seventy-two hours, you'll need some way to stay warm in cold and/or wet weather. It goes without saying that any heat source would have to be small and lightweight. If you have a cooking source in your kit, it can double as a tiny heater. Small folding stoves give off some heat, enough to warm your hands at least. Backpacking and mountain-climbing heat sources are available if you're willing and able to carry the extra weight of the heat source and the fuel. Keep in mind that it's unlikely that you will be able to use any equipment that has a flame in a shelter. But then, you probably wouldn't need a heat source if you're already safely sheltered in an evacuation center.

Chemical hand and foot warmers do a good job of providing heat. Squeezing them activates the chemicals, and they will produce heat for about eight to twelve hours. Since they're small enough to fit in your shoe or pocket, they're a good option for emergency kits. Plan on including several in each kit (enough to last seventy-two hours, preferably).

It's possible that Mother Nature and the power company may conspire to make shelter conditions as cold as possible. If there isn't any heat in your shelter (unlikely, but possible), or if you have only a tent to protect you from the elements, you still have a trick or two to pull out of your evacuation kit. We discussed the concept of layering clothing for warmth extensively in chapter 22. The idea works here as well, even though all you have to work with is what's inside your kit. (If you live in a potentially cold area you'd be wise to cram a hat, an extra pair of socks, and a pair of one-size-fits-all stretch gloves in your kits.) Begin with all the dry clothes you have, add your coat, wrap your space blanket over that (keep several large safety pins in your kit just for this purpose), and top it all with your poncho. Keep your head covered and do your best to stay dry. It's not as good as cranking up the thermostat but if it's the best you can do, it's a lot better than nothing.

SHED A LITTLE LIGHT

Every person should have his own source of light in an emergency. Light is a source of emotional security as well as safety. It means you can carry on, in some measure, with the things that must be done: fixing food, comforting family members, making sense of the mess, and on and on. The flame factor is a huge issue in an evacuation situation. Think twice before choosing any items that could pose a fire hazard. It goes without saying that the use of any equipment with an open flame, such as a lantern or candle, requires close adult supervision and safety precautions. Practice sessions and firm discipline should be mandatory.

Following are some of the lighting options available.

Flashlights

Every kit should contain a working flashlight. If, for some reason, you can't or don't take refuge in an evacuation shelter, your flashlights may be your only source of light in an unnaturally dark night. If you do end up in a shelter, a flashlight will come in very handy if your child needs to make a pit stop in the middle of the night and needs to find his way through a maze of bedding, piles of belongings, and sleeping people. Standard battery-operated flashlights are excellent sources of light. They are safe, and with new batteries and bulb, provide about seven hours of light, more or less. Alkaline batteries and krypton bulbs last longer. Include an extra set of batteries with each flashlight. The relatively new shake-and-charge" flashlights with LED bulbs may be even a better choice. Check out a few and see.

Flashlights come in all sizes from tiny to industrial-strength jumbo size. The smaller the better, as far as weight is concerned. But larger heavy-duty waterproof flashlights can also fill the bill for a 72-hour kit. These larger flashlights provide more light but they add weight and bulk as well. I'd suggest that before you buy a bigger flashlight, you look instead at buying a better flashlight. Even very small flashlights can put out powerful beams of light if they have quality construction and krypton or halogen bulbs. etc. Even if you have another light source in your kit, you should still have a flashlight and it should be packed on the very top. You may need it to locate other items.

Emergency Candles

I mention candles here with grave reservations. Technically, small utility or camping candles may be used in emergency kits, but they are so dangerous in a crowded area that I hesitate to mention them. I can't recommend them. If you have little children, skip the candles altogether and go with a safer light source. If you don't have children, there are a few candle options that may work. Keep in mind that candles and open flames will probably not be allowed in your evacuation center due to liability and fire risks. I know in my church building (which is designated as a potential evacuation shelter), candles or open flames are never allowed under any conditions. In chaotic emergency circumstances, those rules would be doubly enforced.

Knowing that, here are some candle choices, if you're determined to go with candles. Small tub candles are designed for emergencies or camping, and usually come in packages of six. They fit in small candle lanterns. Survival candles in a can, with one to three wicks, can function as a light source and for warming food. Some have a burning time of fifty hours or more. Long-burning emergency candles, approximately one and one-half inches in diameter, come with metal holders. If you are going to use candles, you would be wise to put them in candle lanterns, which will help solidly support the candles. Or small, solid candleholders may be used for the same purpose. Do not use dinner candles! They are not stable, burn too quickly, and are too drippy. I don't recommend decorative candles either. Aromatherapy advantages aside, they neither give off as much light nor last as long as emergency candles, which are designed specifically for emergency usage.

Backpacking Lanterns

This size is the only canister-fuel lantern to be used for a 72-hour kit. Backpacking lanterns are small and lightweight. Some are collapsible. Factor in the weight and bulk of the fuel canister as well as the lantern. Don't forget matches.

Backpacking Fluorescent Lanterns

Fluorescent lanterns use batteries and usually burn brighter and longer than a regular flashlight. Some are small enough to use in evacuation kits, though not all. If you create family-style kits consisting of several communal units, a fluorescent lantern is a good choice to stash in one of the units.

Cyalume Light Sticks

A light stick is a plastic tube filled with a chemical substance that glows when the tube is sharply bent to activate the chemicals. Most light sticks are small and lightweight and last varying amounts of time from thirty minutes up to twelve hours. The light is not extremely bright, and once the stick is lit, it can't be turned off. It will continue to glow until it is used up. They can't be used again. Each person would need quite a few of them. They are not recommended as the only source of light for a 72-hour kit but they could prove to be a good thing to have in addition to other sources. They could be used as night lights to provide security for adults and children alike. They aren't bright enough to keep neighboring evacuees awake but they are bright enough for you to see your kit, as well as your kids.

YOUR EVACUATION "WARDROBE"

Past experience with crises indicates that a complete change of clothing, from the skin out, is essential for any three-day kit. The basic purpose of your evacuation "wardrobe" is so that if you become soaked or contaminated in any way during the evacuation/rescue process, you will be assured of immediately having clothing to change into. It's unlikely that the volunteer organizations with their boxes and racks will be at the site immediately, and may not be for several days.

The second reason is if you did not need your "wardrobe" on arrival at the shelter area, but have to remain several days, it will be good to have a change of clothing. Dirt, dust, grime, and more are basic torments during lag time and the aftermath of disasters. Clean clothes could be a real pick-me-up.

On a smaller, yet just as viable scale, a toxic spill, forest fire, or similar incident could quickly force you out of your home in the middle of the night in pajamas or less. Even for a few hours or one day it would be nice to have clothing to wear. And still another reason, allergies to wool or other fibers could cause problems if you had to rely solely on donated clothing.

You can probably use clothing that you already have on hand, but you should make sure that it is good, sturdy clothing rather than lightweight, flimsy, or worn-out clothing. Don't worry much about designer labels, color coordination, or style. If you can find a few spare crevices in your kits, squeeze in extra undergarments and socks, especially for children. The object is to keep your body warm, protected, and dry. Remember that you may be exposed to the elements and to the public, and you will probably be engaged in helping people and in doing hard work. Your clothes will need to withstand the strain. On the other hand, since you will be exposed to the elements and the public, the clothes you put in your kit should not be Salvation Army rejects either. When my daughter and her husband were starving students in college, they put together their first evacuation kits. She included in her kits the most despised hand-me-down clothing they had, since that was all they could spare. A few years later when they updated their kits, she was appalled at what she had stuck in there: maroon pants with holes in the knees, an orange shirt, and pink-striped socks. She claimed she would rather have frozen to death than worn in public the outfit she had tucked away. So, while you don't need to worry about designer labels in your evacuation kit, consider that you may actually have to put on what you put away, and plan accordingly.

Unfortunately, the wardrobe in your bucket or backpack is not a store-and-forget thing. No, you don't have to have this year's styles, but you have to have this year's size! Whether you or your family members have grown up or out or both, the clothes still need to fit. Check them annually and replace as you need to.

Depending on your climate, it's not a bad idea to have one set of clothing for summer and one for winter, and put the appropriate set into your 72-hour kits when the seasons change. Mark your calendar with a reminder. And when the new calendar comes out, mark it again.

There isn't room in a kit for heavy winter coats, hats, and gloves, but in an evacuation, if your kit is ready, there is usually time to grab them on the way out the door. (Put them on your "don't forget" list.)

The wrong kind of clothing in weather extremes will compound already-severe problems. Lightweight, thin summer clothes in the dead of winter could pose a serious hypothermia risk. Heavy woolen pants and sweaters in the middle of a heat wave would be just as miserable, with heatstroke as a potential side effect. This point must be taken seriously, especially if you are dealing with babies, the elderly, or the ill.

Remember to take individual needs into consideration. For example, support hose are a necessity for many people. Don't forget such things as neck braces the scarf that prevents chafing, dentures, glasses, contact lens requirements, or arch supports.

A pair of sturdy shoes is another critical item. If you don't include a pair in the kit, they must be placed at the top of the "don't forget" list, with their location jotted down as well.

One item of clothing that should be in every kit is a poncho. Ponchos are generally made of heavy vinyl or plastic and resemble a cape with a hood. They are versatile enough to give protection from the weather, provide shade on a hot day, and can increase your ability to stay warm. If you had to, you could make a pocket of personal privacy by snapping up the sides and changing into dry clothes underneath the poncho, providing, of course, that your poncho isn't made of clear plastic. They are available in adult and children's sizes. Pack ponchos at the top of all kits.

If your container choice is not waterproof, use large Ziplock bags to protect clothing items, as well as anything else that isn't water resistant. Press out all the air possible. Or, you could line the kit with sturdy garbage bags before filling it.

CLOTHES FOR A BABY OR TODDLER

In providing clothes for a baby or toddler, think large. Six months from now, your child will have grown a great deal. The clothing you include in this kit should account for that. A medium-weight stretchable terry cloth playsuit is a good option, and it wouldn't matter if it were quite a bit too large. T-shirts and socks are a must! You can always remove a baby's clothing if it becomes too warm. Put shoes on the "don't forget" list. Even if your baby is not walking now, she probably will be within a year. Also, check your child's kit frequently to make sure that he has not outgrown the clothing in it and that the other items in the kit will still meet all his needs.

Be sure to keep a large package (with a handle) of disposable diapers on hand. Cloth diapers will not do because you will have no practical way to wash or store them once they have been used. Don't bother to repack diapers into a kit; you'll need too many and they are too bulky. Just keep a package next to your kit. (Update for size frequently.) A good thing to include in a baby's kit is a package of premoistened baby wipes. They can be used on both ends of the baby.

The kit for a baby or small child will need more consistent review and evaluation than any other.

I taught a workshop for a group of women in a small town in Utah on 72-hour kits. A good friend of mine belonged to the group. Since she knew I was coming, she decided she had better update her children's evacuation kits before I came. It was a good thing she did. Her seven-year-old's kit contained Huggies and Onesies!

Rapid growth, dietary changes, and other continually changing requirements make a baby's kit one of the most difficult to assemble. Another option would be to methodically create a small child's 72-hour kit on paper. It is essential that you complete this "paper kit" while you have a clear mind and can reason out the items that will be needed. During an emergency, you could have difficulty remembering such details, particularly if you have more than one small child. If your child has a special blanket or favorite teddy bear, be sure to include it on the list. For the child, that toy or blanket, no matter how ragged it is, probably ranks in priority with someone else's prescription medicine. If everyone else's kit is ready, you will probably have time to gather a baby's kit by following your list. Of course, it's only logical to have a container already prepared with as many basics and spare items as possible. Periodically review and update your "paper kit." Make sure you keep it and its container with your other 72-hour kits.

CHAPTER FORTY-TWO

SHORT-TERM SANITATION, HYGIENE, AND FIRST AID

In the realm of personal preparedness, perhaps two of the most overlooked and underestimated problems during an evacuation are sanitation and hygiene. Once a shelter is designated and functioning, it will have restroom facilities unless the water and power supplies are cut off. In that case, portable chemical toilets will be brought in but that takes time. During lag time you must be able to cope with the situation! It's not like mowing the lawn or doing laundry; you can't put off the call of nature until a more convenient time. You will need to have other arrangements in place to get you through until a more permanent solution to the potty problem is provided.

Insuring that you have at least rudimentary toilet facilities is especially important during an unsettled shelter situation because stress, a change of diet, lack of privacy, and loss of security can compound to cause unpleasantly upset digestive systems. Good judgment, a sense of humor, and—most of all—advance preparation will help you get through some of these problems.

SHORT-TERM SANITATION

One important reason to use a polyethylene bucket for at least one of your 72-hour kits is that it can be used as a makeshift toilet. (Backpacks and collapsible buckets just will not work in this instance!) I explained how to make a portable privy in chapter 30 but to save you all the work of turning the pages back to reread that, I'll summarize it again here.

To create a portable potty you will need the following supplies:

- One or two large (thirty-gallon or larger), sturdy garbage bags to hold your emergency kit supplies while your bucket is otherwise occupied. I like the drawstring type so you can immediately cinch the bag shut to keep your supplies from spilling out.
- A roll of toilet paper per person, or packets of facial tissue (smashed flat to fit into your kit).
- Some sturdy, extra-heavy-duty trash bags (thirty-gallon or larger) with ties. (Fold down, press out all the air, and roll tightly, then fasten with the following rubber bands to fit in your kit.)
- Large rubber bands, at least a quarter-inch wide, large enough in circumference to fit around the top of the bucket and strong enough to hold the heavy plastic bags in place.
- Disinfectant, preferably dry, such as the portable-toilet chemicals available in recreational vehicle supply stores, or powdered, chlorinated lime, which you can find in building supply stores. If you can't get these, include a small bottle of chlorine bleach, Lysol, or other household disinfectant. I discourage these just because it's so easy for a bottle to break or leak and ruin everything in your kit. (For use, dilute to one part bleach to ten parts water in your collapsible bucket.)
- Very small bottle of dish soap to be able to clean your bucket when water is available.

Here's what you do. Insert a garbage sack into the empty bucket with the edge folded down over the top of the bucket. Secure it in place with a large rubber band. (Duct tape would work too.) After using this toilet, sprinkle a small amount of disinfectant into the bag and cover the bucket with its lid. This toilet can be used several times before replacing the bag. To dispose of the waste, remove the rubber band, twist the bag closed, and secure it tightly with a wire twist tie. An official at the evacuation center can tell you where to dispose of the bag. Carry it in the bucket to the disposal site before removing the bag of waste to avoid having the bag break and make a terrible mess on the way to the disposal site.

Don't make a seat by cutting a hole in the lid of your bucket. You will need the lid intact to cover the bucket in between uses, plus later you'll need it as the lid for your 72-hour-kit container again.

If necessary, you can obtain some privacy while using this toilet by having someone hold a blanket or tarp in front of it, or by suspending a blanket on a rope in front of it. Put the bucket next to a wall or in a corner if possible. The wall will help you keep your balance, since perching on a portable bucket toilet isn't something we all do on a regular basis.

While you're safe in the comfort and privacy of your own home, give each member of your family the chance to practice sitting on the makeshift toilet. It's important that everyone understands how to do it and the balance required, even if they feel ridiculous. Falling over in your living room while perched on an empty bucket can be funny. Falling over in a shelter would be mortifying.

> *At a follow-up session for one of my workshops, a senior citizen returned to relate her solution for a portable potty. Following our class, she purchased her bucket and then proceeded to the local thrift shop. There, she purchased a wooden toilet seat, took it home, sanded and tole-painted it. She then securely lashed it to her bucket. She proclaimed, "If I ever have to be evacuated, I'll go in style and with class."*

PERSONAL HYGIENE IS MORE THAN A BAR OF SOAP

It's likely that circumstances will be less than ideal in order to force you from your home. The cause could be earthquake-related or due to a raging forest fire, as happened to thousands of evacuated families during the Colorado wildfires in 2002. Possibly flooding or toxic chemicals in the air will be the catalyst. With very few exceptions, all the causes will require a common response: getting safe, getting settled, and then getting clean.

During an evacuation you may be exposed to all manner of filth: mud, soot, sewage, dirt, chemical fallout, dust, grime. You will desperately want to be able to clean up as soon as possible. Of course, you can survive without a daily bath (ask any child), but for the sake of your health and physical and emotional well-being, you need to be able to get clean. Unrelieved filth can quickly cause sores and irritation, not to mention the spread of germs. Good hygiene is a must in a shelter situation. Doing such routine things as brushing your teeth or washing your face also brings some order to the day, and many times has the healthy and soothing effect of relative normalcy. (In the olden days, moms used to say, "Go wash your face and you'll feel better," and that was for everything from a scraped knee to a broken heart. Mothers were using good psychology back before they knew psychology even existed.)

Trial- or travel-sized health and hygiene products are the best choice for 72-hour kits. Here are some personal hygiene items to consider.

> A bar of soap
> Shampoo
> Toothbrush (travel style)
> Toothpaste
> Small mirror
> Comb and brush
> Lip balm
> Hand lotion
> Washcloth/small towel
> Disposable razors/shaving gear
> Premoistened towelettes
> Deodorant
> Feminine hygiene supplies
> Denture or contact lens requirements
> Baby/toddler needs (oil, powder, shampoo, and so on)

FIRST AID OR WORST AID— YOU DO HAVE A CHOICE

A small and simple first aid kit should be mandatory in any 72-hour kit. The intent is to deal with minor injuries and ailments, which could otherwise become serious if left untreated for a few days, or which just cause unnecessary misery. Be sure that your kit contains a first aid manual and read it before you pack it away. Know what supplies are in your first aid kit and how to use them.

A small commercial first aid kit is perfectly acceptable, or if you would rather create your own kit, here are some standard suggestions about what to put in it. You can contact your pharmacist or the Red Cross for suggestions if you wish to assemble more advanced first aid supplies. Keep in mind the problems particular to your family, such as severe allergies, and include the solutions to those situations in your kits.

Aspirin, acetaminophen, (Tylenol), or ibuprofen (such as Advil)

Antiseptic cotton balls or swabs

Burn ointment

Triple antibiotic ointment (such as Polysporin)

Adhesive-strip bandages (such as Band-Aids)

Allergy tablets, antihistamine (such as Benadryl)

Gauze

Needle

Matches (for sterilizing)

Elastic rolled bandages (such as Ace bandages)

Sterile bandages

Small scissors

Tube of petroleum jelly

Tweezers

Adhesive tape

Antacid

Sunscreen

Liquid pain reliever (babies)

Teething ointment (babies)

Diaper rash ointment

Baby oil/lotion

Fingernail clippers

According to the director of the Red Cross in Provo, Utah, a main problem in shelter situations is trying to help the people who arrive at evacuation centers without the prescription medicines they need. If you require prescription medicine, save yourself future problems by planning ahead now! If at all possible to safely do so, keep a prescription with your kit. Ask your doctor or pharmacist for specific instructions about how to do so. Make sure all medications and their locations, as well as other specific individual needs, are clearly listed on the "don't forget" list.

CHAPTER FORTY-THREE

IMPORTANT MISCELLANEOUS ITEMS

During the summer of 1984, a fast-moving canyon fire forced residents of Malibu, California, to evacuate. According to one newspaper account, a well-known Hollywood personality ran frantically from room to room trying to decide what to take with her. She had only forty-five minutes to decide. Unfortunately, she had made no preparations for such an emergency. First, she gathered her valuable paintings into the middle of her living room but then she remembered other valuables and went to get them. The chaotic sorting and gathering continued and the forty-five minutes passed too quickly. Finally, she was forced to leave her home without taking anything.

You should decide now—before a disaster—what you would do with your treasures in case of an emergency. You may save valuables that would otherwise be lost forever due to panic and indecision.

Sometimes the warning to evacuate may come with a little bit of notice attached to it. You may be told you have half an hour or an hour to get ready before you have to get out. If you're prepared, this kind of warning could make all the difference in the world. I suggest that you take a long, hard look at your home today and decide what is really important to you (besides your life and your family, I mean). Some things are just possessions and wouldn't be a tremendous loss if they were destroyed. (I have a neighbor who laughingly stated one time that in case their house ever caught fire, she had forbidden her husband to call the fire department until she had shoved all her living room furniture into the blaze.) The loss of other things would just break your heart. If your kits are ready to be loaded into your car in a matter of minutes and your survival is taken care of, the rest of that warning time can be spent saving the material things that matter most to you. Perhaps it is the painting your grandmother did as a child. Or your photo albums. Or the box of Christmas ornaments you've collected from all over the world. Or your children's baby books. Decide today what matters most to you, in what order of priority, write it down, and tape that list on your bucket also. It could be the difference between insurance-adjuster inconvenience and heartbreak.

THE QUESTION OF IMPORTANT DOCUMENTS

Every individual or family has important documents that need to be preserved. These include deeds, wills, insurance policies, birth, marriage, and death certificates, and so on. For many, it is difficult to find a particular document even during normal times. It would be almost impossible to gather up all your important papers in an emergency. Also, many people have more than enough important papers to fill an entire emergency kit by themselves. (My mother's family history alone would fill a small semitruck.) There is little semblance of order during an evacuation. In the confusion and possibility of relocation, there is a good chance papers could be lost or inadvertently taken. The possibility of loss or destruction increases with the severity and length of the crisis. A public evacuation shelter or tube tent is obviously not a secure place to keep important documents.

One of the following suggestions, or a combination of several, may provide a solution to protecting your documents. Some of these documents could be required to insure your rights, to prove ownership, and to file claims in case your home is destroyed. Be sure to check your papers regularly to make sure that they are always up to date.

Following is a list of documents that you may need to protect:

- Social Security cards and records
- Deeds
- Insurance policies and numbers
- Stocks, bonds, and mutual funds
- Wills/trusts
- Savings—and checking account—numbers and locations
- Credit card numbers and companies
- Passports
- Immunization records
- Vital records: birth, marriage, and death
- Inventory of household goods
- Financial records
- Personal and family records, certificates

One of the best ways to protect your important documents is to make several good copies of them. Have these copies notarized, if it will make them more valid in your area. Put the originals in a safe-deposit box at your bank. (How close to your home is the bank?) Keep a file of the copies at home, as secure as possible. Then give a set of copies, in a clearly marked, sealed envelope, to a trusted friend or relative who lives outside your area.

Another procedure is to make a list on one sheet of paper of all of your policy numbers and agents' names and phone numbers, with a short, concise, descriptive note or two. List checking, savings, and credit union account numbers, including names, addresses, and phone numbers of the institution where the account is located. Write down all pertinent names and phone numbers. If the list is extensive, write it on legal-sized or 8½-by-11-inch paper; with a computer or at a copy center it can be reduced to fit a smaller sheet of paper. Send one copy to the friend or relative who is out of your area. Laminate a second copy. Tape this waterproof, sturdy copy to the inside of your kit. It should fit snugly up against the side. Make sure it can't be read through the side of the container.

Or assemble all your documents into one heavy-duty, waterproof container, such as a locking metal file box with a handle. Consider it an additional evacuation-kit unit. If you are able to use your car to get to the evacuation center, keep it locked in your trunk. Decide beforehand what the alternative plan for your documents unit will be if, in order to evacuate, you must walk out of your neighborhood. Determine whether or not it would be feasible to carry it with you, and all which that might entail.

Remember also, that you may be required to baby-sit your document container at a shelter, keeping a constant close eye on it to avoid theft. Depending on the emergency that drove you from your home in the first place (for example, a chemical spill or structural damage due to natural disasters), it may be safer to leave this container locked in your house. If the information is in danger of being destroyed due to the emergency (for example, imminent flooding, mudslides, or fires), you'll want to take it with you and look after it carefully.

Current technology could provide valuable protection against the loss of critical information. You could always scan a copy of anything valuable and burn it to a CD. This would work for family histories, photographs, scrapbook pages, marriage certificates, legal papers, even small paintings and the like. The CDs can hold an astonishing amount of data and are small enough to fit easily into an evacuation kit. (You can also give a copy to a family member who lives in another area or state.) The originals may be destroyed in a fire or flood, but you'd have a good backup copy, which may be just as good, or at least some consolation. This is a good option if you have a home-based business. Make a backup of all your financial records or inventory or whatever on a weekly basis. Put "business backups" on your "don't forget" list and grab them on your way out. Then the most you would lose would be a week's worth of data. It could be the difference between inconvenience and bankruptcy.

MONEY

A trip to an evacuation shelter is not going to be a shopping expedition, but common sense tells you that even during a crisis you may need some money for such small things as telephone calls or some gas. Don't forget to take your wallet or purse as you walk out the door. Write them on your "don't forget" list, even though, in normal times, that's usually one of the first things you pick up. (Evacuations are not normal times!) Your checkbook and emergency credit card should allow you to make larger purchases if you need to. One suggestion is to keep a pack of blank checks and blank register near the bottom of your kit, along with a ballpoint pen. A debit card isn't as good as a checkbook because if the electricity is down, you can swipe your card all day and it won't do any good.

It would be foolish to try to carry large amounts of money, jewelry, or other valuables with you to an evacuation area. They could easily be lost or disappear. Let common sense be your guide.

An unfortunate example of what the cost of simple things could be during a crisis occurred in Los Angeles. During lag time and the aftermath of the Northridge quake, victims were reportedly charged $1 for one cup of water, while the cost of batteries escalated to an astronomical $12.

YOU NEED A BATTERY-POWERED RADIO

A battery-powered radio is a critical kit component. Every adult emergency kit should include a portable, working, battery-powered radio with an extra set of fresh batteries. This is an absolute necessity. Keep the radios near the top of your kits so that they will be readily accessible. Since the duration of an evacuation cannot be determined ahead of time, the spare batteries are mandatory, not optional. After the Loma Prieta earthquake, many people reported that their radios worked for only a short time. They had failed to replace the batteries and had no spares.

MORALE BOOSTERS

In times of trouble it pays to be prepared to brighten the mood. Discouragement and depression are abundant in the immediate aftermath of serious trouble. There may be hours or days where there is nothing to do but wait. Children are not the only ones to become restless and anxious. Everyone does. The longer the duration, the more difficult the waiting.

If possible, provide the means to boost morale and make enduring more bearable. Tuck small, lightweight morale boosters into your kit. Some items to include are:

- Small, flat games
- Decks of cards/card games
- Purse/pocket-size puzzle books, with a pencil attached

- Small/pocket-size books of word games, and a pencil (preteens love Mad-Libs)
- Crayons
- Travel-size games
- Paperback books
- Pencil and small tablet of paper
- Small sets of scriptures/other inspirational books
- Small needlework items (include on your "don't forget" list)

However, if space is critical and you just can't find three square inches to include all the morale boosters you'd like, you can still be prepared to lift spirits and relieve boredom. Check out library books that teach simple, fun activities *now*. Prepare a list of these and other old-fashioned family favorites that suit the ages of the individuals you are preparing for. A laminated list of a few concise game reminders and how to play them won't take up much room but it could prove to be a storehouse of nerve-soothing remedies during a stressful time. It will allow you to help others as well. In other words, if physical space is lacking in your kit, prepare yourself mentally.

DON'T FORGET THE TEDDY BEAR

If at all possible, provide a small and squishable stuffed animal in your evacuation kits. It does not necessarily have to be for a small child; it represents comfort and security for almost everyone. (I have one in my kit.)

A very vivid image remains in my mind. Immediately after the Northridge, Los Angeles quake, the news crews showed what appeared to be a college-aged girl. In a daze, she was going through the rubble of what was left of her apartment. She tightly clutched a teddy bear. Several days later she was in the camera focus again—still clutching that bear.

If your child, or anyone else in the family has a favorite stuffed animal that they cannot exist without, put it on the "don't forget" list. I recall another news clip from the aftermath of the Northridge quake. This time the news crews focused on an anxious mother and a compassionate firefighter going through the rubble of another apartment building. The woman explained that her two-year-old son had not been able to sleep the past several nights without a specific white bear. A few minutes later the firefighter uncovered the prize—a no-longer-white teddy bear. The mother, with tears in her eyes, said, "He may not have his bed but he'll be able to sleep now."

A CHOCOLATE KISS MIGHT HELP THE PAIN GO AWAY

Being able to have a snack or treat could be just the thing to turn the tide on some otherwise miserable days. Include candy or treats that can double as stress foods. Things like wrapped hard candies or sticks of gum (sugarless if there are dietary restrictions) might be scattered throughout the kit to fill in small spaces. There won't be room for large quantities of treats in an evacuation kit, so you'll have to remember to parcel it out slowly when the time comes at a shelter. You may need to issue dire warnings of severe bodily harm if anyone should be tempted to snitch the goodies out of the kits during nonemergency times!

OTHER ITEMS

There are other items that you may want to include in your kits, or in the case of multiple-unit kits, in a parent's kit. All of these could prove to be very useful in many ways and in many different situations:

- Pocketknife
- One hundred feet of one-eighth-inch nylon rope
- Pocket-size sewing kit
- Assorted safety pins
- Plastic thirty-three-gallon garbage bags (can be used as a poncho, a ground cloth, a garbage container, and so on; use caution around children)
- Duct tape (instead of putting the large roll in, wrap ten-foot lengths around a pencil or dowel)
- Small scissors
- Small windup clock
- Small tools (screwdriver, pliers, hammer)
- Dust mask
- Whistle (to gain attention to get help, not to be used as a toy)
- Crowbar (to be kept close by kits, but not necessarily in them)

CHAPTER FORTY-FOUR

GETTING IT TOGETHER AND KEEPING IT TOGETHER

So, you know what the dangers and risks in an evacuation are. You know what you can do about them. You know the different things you need to gather together. It's time to move beyond knowing and into doing. Getting started is usually the hardest part. But before you head to the cupboard for the flashlight, or to the store for the granola bars, get out your pencil and do your homework first. Here's where you figure out exactly what you need to do. It's important enough to emphasize again—begin with what you have! You can always improve your kit later but any preparation is better than none.

PLANNING YOUR KITS

Use a notebook to plan which food and equipment to gather or buy for your kits. Keep a record of the items you buy so you don't waste money buying duplicate items. Use your notes as a reference to help you adjust and update your kits until they are exactly what you need. Involve everyone in your family in the planning, purchasing, and putting-together process. This will help them to become familiar with the contents of their kit and to better understand how to cope with an evacuation. It also provides teaching moments to discuss how important it is that the materials in the kits stay there. For example, even though a kit may contain snack items, they are not to be eaten unless you're in an evacuation shelter with an emergency impacting your previous several hours.

If you can't afford to purchase all of the items now, spread the project of buying supplies over several paydays. Map out a buying system to assure meeting your goal. One suggestion is to set aside a specific dollar amount each payday to be used to purchase 72-hour kit supplies.

I recommend that your foods and menus be plotted with a strategy in mind. Begin with evacuation bare-bones basics, such as stress foods and compact energy bars. Purchase a variety of these foods rather than spending the whole amount on one food item. Then systematically add to them, eventually adding in other food groups. This way, should you need to use the kit before you have been able to totally stock it, your most important evacuation nutritional needs are still met.

Purchase any equipment or supplies in the same manner. Your notes and planning pages will help you plot what your priorities are. If you are planning more than one kit, it can sometimes seem overwhelming. Begin with some of the small essentials, such as flashlights and ponchos, and work up to a completed kit.

ASSEMBLY TIPS

In order to make all the paraphernalia fit compactly into one relatively small container, you may have to adjust your thinking. The packing will not be accomplished by neat layering. Key words are cram, squash, push, squish, squeeze, and stuff. The goal is to fill every niche, space, and spot.

Take food, boxes, and other packages apart. For example, granola bars usually are individually wrapped. You can get more into the kit container by putting the bars in individually, here and there, than by leaving them in the bulky square box.

Tightly roll a squishable blanket with the towel and washcloth. Slip several sturdy rubber bands around each end to hold it together. If your kit container is a bucket, place the roll in the center and tightly build around it. As other items are added, continue to push the blanket down. If a backpack and frame are your kit, roll the towel and washcloth in the bedroll or sleeping bag to allow more space in the kit container itself. If the bedroll is waterproof, clothing could be rolled inside of it as well.

WHAT TO PACK ON TOP

To insure your safety and security, there are several items that need to be at the top of each kit, or if you are using a backpack as a container, in one specific and easily accessible pocket. They are: a battery-powered radio and batteries, the flashlight with batteries, a poncho, essential prescription medication, and a small container with small change for emergency phone calls. Also, anything fragile or breakable, such as eyeglasses or contacts, must be kept on the top, protected if possible.

ONCE THEY'RE ASSEMBLED, MAINTAIN THEM

Once it is completed, don't allow the purpose of your 72-hour kit to be defeated. The supplies in the kit must remain intact. Don't rob the kit of its food or batteries or any other items with the promise that you will replace them as soon as possible.

The number-one priority in determining where to keep your assembled kits is accessibility. You must be able to grab them at a moment's notice and leave. That means nothing stacked or piled on top of them and nothing stacked or piled in front of them. The second priority is to protect them from the things that cause rapid deterioration, such as humidity, heat, and pests. (We've already discussed snack-seeking humans.) Your kits need to be kept in a place as dark, dry, and cool as possible. If possible, do not stack them directly on a concrete floor. Concrete "sweats" and promotes the growth of mold and mildew.

MARK YOUR CALENDAR AND SCHEDULE CHECKUPS

Unfortunately, you can't set your kits in their designated place and forget about them until a siren

The number-one priority in determining where to keep your assembled kits is accessibility.

wails. They have to be consistently and regularly updated. One time we neglected our kits for nearly four years, due to one thing after another, including a cross-country move and a year of serious health problems. I had experimented with adding a second unit to my 72-hour kit that was simply additional food. This bucket originally was filled with pop-top cans of fruit, aseptically packaged drinks, and other ready-to-eat canned foods and packaged meals. The idea is a good one but only if the foods are rotated and replaced every year. After four years of complete neglect, I only had a bucket of rust and slop left. The cans had rusted completely through and the food was spoiled to the point where you could no longer determine what it had been. I had to throw the whole thing away, including the bucket. If I had needed to use my kits for an emergency situation, I would have been in bad shape. Look at maintaining your kits as a rewarding challenge. Update and check your entire kit every single year. (If your climate is hot and humid, you may want to schedule checkups more frequently than is necessary in a more temperate climate.) Systematically check them to make sure they will function when you need them. Mark the calendar. Make it a family activity.

CHECKUP GUIDELINES

To do this properly, you will need to empty out the entire kit and repack it. Allow time to complete the project; it will probably take more than an hour.

1. Check the entire kit to make sure bugs or mice have not invaded and taken up residency.

2. Check all clothing to make sure it still fits. Growing children require constant clothing updates. Many adults do not remain the same size either (sad but true). Check clothing for evidence of bugs. Weevil, silverfish, and mealy moths will destroy clothing as well as food. Change the clothing weight from summer to winter or vise versa, if necessary. It may be easier to maintain one set of clothing, which will work as long as you plan for and understand the principle of layering for warmth. Usually you'll want to wash any clothing, towels, and blankets from the kits because being stuffed together with the other supplies in a closed container can give everything an odd odor. Make sure they are completely dry before replacing them in the kit.

3. Change out all the food in your kit, including juice. Even if bugs are not a problem, that food is a year old and time, heat, and humidity will have taken their toll. If you have a baby or toddler kit, you'll need to adjust just about everything in it: food, clothing, the works. Try to adjust for teenager food requirements (usually that means *more!*) The food should still be good, so have a party and eat it up.

4. Check your water containers. Commercial water containers (including aseptic or soft cans), if still sealed, should be fine. For containers you filled yourself, if the water is completely clear, it's probably fine. If there appear to be any problems, change the water. See chapter 20 for instructions on filling water containers.

5. All batteries should be changed at least once a year. The ones in your kit should still work. (It's only been a year since you replaced them, right?) Put the old kit batteries in a household battery box for non-emergency-use flashlights or battery-operated appliances. Put fresh batteries and spares in your kit. Keep batteries in their original containers; they'll last longer and it's safer.

6. If a bedroll or sleeping bag has been kept lashed to a frame, check it for bugs or mice. Unzip it, open it all the way out, and check creases and corners.

7. Evaluate the "don't forget" list. What should be added or deleted

8. Assess your "important document" list for additions or deletions of policy numbers or pertinent phone numbers.

9. Evaluate all car kits or office kits for any updating necessary.

10. Mark your calendar now for the next kit checkup.

CHAPTER FORTY-FIVE

CARE-IN-A-CRISIS EVACUATION PLANS

The possibility exists that your neighborhood will someday be faced with a crisis that will force you from your home. For the most peace of mind, you'll want to prepare for it in advance with Care-in-a-Crisis evacuation plans, similar to the Care-in-a-Crisis plans you've already made, only expanded to cover evacuation contingencies.

EVACUATION LINE

One point that few people fully grasp about evacuations is that once the police or fire department establishes the perimeter of an evacuation, you cannot cross that line to go back into the evacuation area. Should your home be in such an area, you may not cross back into the area, not even to help your children get out. Once out, you will not be allowed

In the spring of 1985 a gas leak in Salt Lake City, Utah, forced the evacuation of a ten-block area. The late night news was carrying the story live. News cameras were on the scene and the first thing viewers saw was a woman trying to enter the evacuation area. Police officers held her back as she explained in anguish, "I have to get through! I left my children alone while I went to the store. The oldest one is only ten. I must get home!" Calmly, yet firmly, the policemen told her she could not cross the evacuation line. She had no choice but to turn around.

to go back to retrieve a treasure or an evacuation kit. If you don't know where all your family members are, you must still get out. All others have to stay out.

I think people are confused on this point by the media coverage of the East Coast hurricanes in the last few years. Evacuation orders go out, yet you see stories all the time of the people (including news crews!) who decide to take a chance and ride out the storms in their homes. This is not the same as local police- or fire-department-mandated evacuations. In these, you do not have a choice whether to stay or go. You absolutely must go. Not only is your safety on the line but also the safety of the police or rescue workers who would have to track you down. I have two examples of why this is so. The first story occurred in a neighborhood adjacent to mine. A square-mile area of homes was evacuated in the middle of the night due to a domestic dispute. A man with a gun was threatening his wife. The police were called in and it turned into a hostage situation. The police determined that the gun the man had was an extremely powerful rifle capable of shooting a half-mile and powerful enough to shoot through walls. With the SWAT team there with their rifles and a crazed armed man, it would have been extremely dangerous for anyone to have been in the area. They could have been shot or it could have inhibited the officers' actions to have to take civilian safety into account at a dangerous time. (The man finally surrendered after a fourteen-hour standoff. No one was injured.)

In the second instance, a train rolled into a railroad yard in Tennessee with a tank car leaking deadly chlorine gas. Within a matter of hours, the gas had engulfed a surrounding neighborhood and continued to spread. Thousands were evacuated. Some were out of their homes for over five days. Once again, they had no choice as to whether they would leave or not. To stay would have meant death or serious illness and would have endangered the lives of the rescue workers who would have had to go in later and bring them out.

As for the stubborn people who decide not to evacuate in the face of hurricanes, they do so at their own risk. A friend who endured the 2004 hurricane season (Ivan, Charlie, and Frances) told me that the rescue workers left the last minute they could still safely get out of the area. My friend's neighbor stayed behind, and he was told to write his name on his forearm with a black permanent marker so they could identify his body when they returned, and that he should not expect any help if he was injured because he was on his own until the storm had passed.

Evacuation is usually not optional; it is mandatory. Once out, crossing back into a police-declared evacuation area is not allowed. It is therefore especially important that you have your plans in place before a need arises. If you have your neighbors and friends cooperating with you, it will be so much better in all aspects, emotionally and physically.

HAVE A MEETING—MAKE A PLAN

Who is going to make sure your children get out of the evacuated area if you're not home? Do your neighbors know where you keep your emergency kits? Do they even know you have emergency kits? Is there room in their car to take part of your family as well as their own? The following "Evacuation Topics for Discussion" planning pages will help you work through all the details of how your family (and your neighbor's) will be cared for. Some of the information will be the same as the Care-in-a-Crisis Plan worksheets. But some of the planning and decisions will be completely different. It is only natural that you'll want to fill out and discuss all these forms and questions at the same meeting since so much of the information is overlapping in scope.

Agreeing to be responsible for another person's family in a crisis is a decision not to be taken lightly. If you only have a few minutes to get out, some of those few minutes will have to be used to make certain your assigned family is taken care of. Before you evacuate, you'll need to ascertain whether the parents of the family are at home. If they're not, all of

a sudden your job just doubled. In addition to your own family, you must gather any children from your assigned family who are home alone and take them with you. Think through the ramifications of this and figure out how you'll do it. Is your car big enough for two families? Do you have access to two cars and potentially two drivers? I recognize you can never be positive how the future will play out; you may have five other drivers in your family and all or none of them will be home in an emergency. You just work through the possible scenarios as best you can, based on what you have. Perhaps your neighbor would want to leave a key to their car in your safekeeping in case of emergencies. If the parents are gone and a teenage sibling is watching the children at the time of the evacuation, another driver from your family could possibly drive their family car with their children in it to the evacuation center, if there's not room in one car for all of you. Think it through now.

This is one area where Care-in-a-Crisis disaster planning differs from Care-in-a-Crisis evacuation planning. In disaster planning you could feasibly watch over several families. In evacuation planning, your helpfulness is limited to the number of people you are physically able to relocate to an evacuation center.

You'll want to discuss with your assigned family the location of their 72-hour emergency kits. You'll need to take them with you during an evacuation if it is at all possible, even if you don't take the family itself. If they are not at home when the evacuation orders are issued, they will still need those supplies when they get to the shelter. You would be the only one who could provide them, since they would not be allowed back into the evacuated area to retrieve them.

If there is time, you will want to lock and care for your assigned family's home the same as you do for your own, including closing and locking doors and windows and turning off heaters or air conditioners, and so on. (See chapter 46, Evacuation Guidelines.) If there is not time, just grab the children who are home alone and the family emergency kits and shut the door on your way out.

You should leave a note posted in a prominent position (maybe taped to the front door or on the kitchen counter or similar highly visible place) stating that you have taken the children with you (or which of the children, if you only have some of them), and where you anticipate going. The parents probably will not see the note until the evacuation orders are lifted, but on the off chance the police or other officers come through the neighborhood, they might be able to pass the word on to worried parents.

> *Once you take someone's family to an evacuation center, you must keep them with you until you can reunite them with their parents.*

It's very important that once you take someone's family to an evacuation center, or wherever you have to go, that you keep them with you the entire time until you can reunite them with their parents. Both those parents and the children need to know that they can count on you to keep them safe until the crisis is over.

There are many, many issues you will want to discuss with your cooperating families. It's a big responsibility to take on the care of another family in a crisis. But on the other hand, it is big relief to know that someone will be there to help your family if you can't be. The important thing is to make sure you have a plan for your family. Being evacuated will be a frightening, stressful time. Being apart as a family during this time would be nearly unbearable unless you knew you have someone to count on to watch out for them.

EVACUATION TOPICS FOR DISCUSSION

Our assigned family is _____.
(Fill out the Family Information Worksheet, chapter 36, with necessary information about this family. Fill one out about your own family for the family you are assigned to.)

- What am I expected to do for my assigned family?
- What are their needs? Children, elderly, handicapped, and so on?
- Are there any special needs I must be aware of? (Critical medications, asthma inhalers, wheelchairs, and so on?)
- Children need to know I have their parents' permission to take them with me in an evacuation situation. Do I have signed permission slips?
- Does my car have sufficient room to transport my family as well as theirs? If not, what other options do we have?
- Where does my assigned family keep their 72-hour evacuation kits? Do I need a key to their home to access them if they are not at home at the time of an evacuation?
- The most likely place I will go in an evacuation. (Shelter, home of relatives, and so on.)
- The importance of staying together and not wandering off at a shelter.
- The steps I will take to let the parents of the assigned family know that I have their children and/or 72-hour kits.

CHAPTER FORTY-SIX

GUIDELINES TO AN EMERGENCY EVACUATION

If the time ever comes when you must evacuate your home, you'll know it because the authorized directions will be broadcast over the Emergency Alert System, or you'll be contacted by the police, National Guard, or Community Emergency Response Team (CERT) volunteers. When the authorities tell you to evacuate your home and go to another location temporarily, there will be specific things to do. Advance preparation and carefully thought-out plans (and alternate plans) will alleviate much of the confusion and panic that are sure to accompany a warning to get out.

MAPS, PLANS, AND PRACTICE SESSIONS

In some situations, you may need to evacuate your home within just a few minutes. You need to know how to get out fast. Part of preparedness should be an escape plan for your home. This consists of a detailed floor plan. Make a separate page for each floor of the home. Using a brightly colored marking pen, show the location of doorways, windows, and stairs. Then, using a different-colored marker, indicate where emergency kits, fire extinguisher, first aid kits, and other emergency essentials are located. Clearly show where utility shutoffs are. (Everyone in the household should learn how and when to turn off utilities completely. Keep the necessary wrenches near the gas and water shutoff valves.) Mark on the plan the paths to follow in order to get out of each room, the options being doors, halls, or windows. If you're rolling your eyes at the idea that you should need a map of your own home, you can stop now because, yes, you do. Remember, the purpose of detailed plans like these are to help you act calmly, not react blindly, when

the adrenaline is pumping and panic is bubbling just under the surface.

It's extremely important to have a safe-meeting place outside of your home where your family can gather safely in case of problems unique to your own home. This, ideally, is not on your property, but is still close by: a neighbor's porch or front lawn, for example. That way family members who meet there are out of danger but close enough to easily keep track of. For example: for years, our family's meeting place was our next-door neighbor's big front porch. Not only were family members to meet there in case of fire or other emergencies, they were to remain on the porch until everyone was accounted for. We made it a point that they were not to go inside the neighbor's house at all until everyone was accounted for. Our neighbor was the kindest lady and would no doubt want the children to come in to get warm if it was the middle of a winter night when our emergency occurred. But that would have defeated the purpose. They had to stay outside where we could see who was there and who was missing, even if they were cold and uncomfortable for a little while. When we were sure everyone was safe, then they could go inside. Make sure you write your safe meeting place on your escape plan.

It's a good idea to laminate this floor plan and securely fasten it where everyone is aware of it, like the inside of a centrally located closet door, or in the hall by the bedrooms. Place it at a level that even shorter household members can see. Make sure everyone knows how to act and what to do in each kind of emergency, and then practice doing the different things. Walk through turning off appliances and pointing out utility shutoff locations. Practice having younger children stay at the safe meeting place alone for a few minutes until a parent or responsible person comes. Involve your neighbors or other responsible individuals. Schedule evacuation drills at least twice a year. These practice drills could prove priceless if the real thing occurs. Being familiar with situations lessens panic. You are more likely to keep your wits about you if you have already practiced what you may sometime be forced to do. Practice sessions will also help you to see where you need to change your plans and make adjustments.

Before a disaster actually occurs, practice evacuating both in your automobile and on foot. Pay particular attention to the emergencies most likely to occur in your area. The questions in chapter 18, Emergency Preparedness: Getting Started, will help you focus. The details they reveal could make all the difference in the world to you as you map out an escape route and alternates. For example, a dry creek bed that normally appears harmless should stand out like a red warning flag. After several days of severe rain, it could become impassable. That could be a serious problem if it closes down a road you would normally take to evacuate your neighborhood.

Sometimes during an evacuation, buses are provided for those who need them, but lag time can interfere with this, and it may take a while to organize such transportation. As part of your Care-in-a-Crisis plans, organize transportation strategies with your neighbors as much as possible. If you live in a senior citizen retirement complex, student dorm, or similar facility where the majority of residents rely on outside transportation, find out what arrangements have been made for transportation in such an event by the management of the facility, or by the community. If no arrangements are in place, you may need to be the squeaky wheel that gets the oil. Campaign to get an emergency plan in place and take charge if no one else will. At least, maintain a list of names of those who live in your building or complex and set up a check-in site to account for everyone in an emergency (like a safe meeting place for a family, only for your building). This information would be invaluable for police or firefighters. Establish specific meeting places for anyone who would need transportation to an emergency shelter, block by block, for example, or every so many apartment buildings, in order to expedite the evacuation process. Review these steps in semiannual neighborhood drills.

Make sure your Neighborhood Care-in-a-Crisis plan (chapter 36) includes evacuation guidelines. Tell your cooperating families where your emergency kits are kept and find out from them where they keep theirs. If no one is at home when the evacuation orders come, grab their kits as well as your own, if you can. More importantly, if their children are home alone, take them with you to an evacuation shelter. You should have the phone number of their out-of-area contact person on your Care-in-a-Crisis paperwork. Contact that person immediately to let them know you have the children and where you will be. You should also leave a clear note in an obvious place at the neighbor's home indicating that you have the children with you, but since people are not allowed back into evacuated areas until the area has been declared safe, it's highly unlikely the parents will see the note until hours/days/weeks later.

To take the program one step further, plan to help your Care-in-a-Crisis families at the evacuation shelters!

SECURE YOUR HOME BEFORE YOU LEAVE

If there is time, and only if there is time, and if you have not received other instructions from local authorities, secure your home before you leave. If you are prepared with your kits and plans already, you probably will have time to do so.

- Turn off the heat/air conditioner.
- Turn off all gas appliances.
- Disconnect all electrical appliances except the refrigerator and freezer.
- Properly store perishables.
- Lock all windows and doors.
- Put plywood in place on your windows and glass doors if a hurricane is approaching.
- Park other vehicles in garages, carports, or driveways.
- Set your alarm system if you have one.

Remember, you should turn the gas off at the meter *only* if you suspect the in-house lines are damaged or if you are instructed to do so. When gas is turned off at the main meter into the house, it requires a professional to turn it back on. That can take several days, especially in a widespread disaster, when the utility crews will be working overtime just trying to get the main system up and running.

The National Guard and/or local police usually patrol evacuated areas in order to prevent looting.

FOLLOW INSTRUCTIONS

In a local or neighborhood evacuation, follow the instructions and advice of your local authorities. When you are told to evacuate, do so promptly! If you are instructed to move to a certain location, go there. Don't go anywhere else, at least until you have checked in and the authorities know you are safely out of the endangered area. In some instances, such as an impending flood or other predictable problem, you may have time to make shelter arrangements in advance with friends or relatives outside of the threatened area. If you have no place to stay, report to the local shelter.

TRAVEL WITH CARE

Usually when evacuated, you'll leave the area in your own car. This gives you the advantage of continued mobility and allows you to transport your supplies and household members. As a precaution, you should always keep the gas tank half-full. Gasoline pumps do not work if the electricity is off, or during a panic, you might not be able to get to them. Keep the following things in mind:

- In highly congested cities or large urban areas, traffic jams compound problems. (Another reason to make sure you have enough gas!) Try to maintain a level head and realize that progress may be slow.
- Leave as quickly as possible so you will not be stranded by flooded roads or fallen trees and wires.
- If certain routes are specified or recommended by the authorities, use them rather than taking shortcuts of your own.
- As you travel, keep listening to the radio's Emergency Alert System for updated information and instructions.
- If you drive a small car and are responsible for several people, consider investing in a suitable car-top carrier. If you

travel by motorcycle or bicycle, it would be practical to have racks and/or a small utility trailer to convey your needed items to a shelter location.

WHAT IF YOU HAVE TO WALK OUT?

Under some circumstances you may be forced to walk out of an evacuation area. For example, there could be a major gas leak and starting cars could create a spark that would trigger an explosion. Or, you could be a single-car household and someone else has the car at that time. Yet another situation would be that you normally rely on public transportation and, for whatever reason, it is not functioning. Or, the roads are broken up or impassable. Or, a tree could have fallen in front of your garage or on top of your car. There could be any number of reasons you may have to walk in an evacuation situation. You and your family should plan carefully for such an eventuality. Consider the ages, health, and strength of family members, the distance you might

At one of my workshops, a young, single mother reported that she had had to walk out of her neighborhood. She said, "They didn't give me any choice, and at the time, there was no one to help me. I strapped my littlest girl on my back, put my other child in the front of the stroller, set my makeshift kits on the back of the stroller, and away we went. I admit it wasn't the best but because I had the stroller we were able to get out." She further explained that because of difficult financial circumstances at the time, the only thing she had been able to use as kit containers were two rather dilapidated quilted diaper bags. And then smiling, she added, "But I tried. I hoped I'd never have to use them but when the police came and said I had to leave, I could, even though I was so scared."

have to walk, and the quantity of supplies you are planning to carry with you. Almost any type of conveyance will make the journey easier if you have to walk. Having something to work with would mean being able to take your supplies with you, whereas it may be physically impossible to carry much weight for any distance just with your hands.

You can carry supplies and children in a wagon, wheelbarrow, sturdy wheeled cart, buggy, or stroller. Other types of acceptable conveyances are metal marketing baskets, sturdy luggage totes, garden carts, and dollies or hand trucks. Keep rope or bungee cords with some of these options in order to secure your 72-hour-kit units to them. If it's necessary to push a person confined in a wheelchair, plan ahead and figure out how to wear a backpack as part of your kit, and then attach whatever else you will need to the wheelchair.

CHECK IN AT THE SHELTER AREA

As soon the shelter is set up and begins to function, check in. There will be someone registering individuals and families. This is very important, especially if you have someone else's children with you. It will save officials time as they try to verify who is missing, injured, or if there are fatalities. Search and rescue continues until all residents of a neighborhood are accounted for. It will also help the Red Cross, which has volunteers coordinating with relatives who live out of state and are worried whether or not their families are disaster victims. Continue to listen to the Emergency Alert System for advice and instructions periodically. As long as there is any need, updated information will be issued on: (1) where to obtain necessary medical care in the area, (2) where to go for emergency assistance for food, housing, clothing, and so on, (3) where to find counseling to help cope with the crisis, and so on.

RETURNING HOME IF DAMAGE IS INVOLVED

There are several important safety measures to follow upon returning to a home after an evacuation. Do not return home before those in authority say that it's safe. Shock, personal loss, and anxiety sometimes cloud reasoning and good judgment. Do not visit disaster areas. Your presence could hamper

rescue and other emergency operations.

The following safety precautions are adapted from "Disaster Operations" developed by the Civil Defense Preparedness Agency:

1. Do not enter buildings that obviously have been damaged or weakened by a disaster. They could collapse without warning.

2. Don't take lanterns, torches, lighted cigarettes, or any form of open flame into a disaster-damaged home or building. There may be leaking gas or flammable materials present. Use battery-powered flashlights, or lanterns. Check for leaking gas by smell. Do not use matches or candles. If you smell gas, open all of the windows. Turn off the main gas valve at the meter. Don't turn light switches on or off. This creates a spark, which can ignite gas. If gas is detected, leave the house immediately and notify the gas company or police. Because of the severity of such situations, do not reenter the house until an authority tells you it is safe. You have survived so far; don't be careless now.

3. Watch out for and stay away from fallen or damaged electrical wires, which may still be dangerous. Notify the power company or authorities.

4. If any electrical appliances are wet, first turn off the main power switch. Then unplug the wet appliance, dry it out, reconnect it, and then finally turn on the main power switch. Caution! Do not do any of these things if you are wet or standing in water. If fuses blow or breakers trip when the electricity is turned back on, turn the main switch off again and inspect for short circuits in home wiring, appliances, and equipment.

5. Wear shoes at all times until all the rubble is cleaned up.

6. Check food and water supplies before using them. Foods that require refrigeration may be spoiled if the power has been off for an extended time. Do not use food that has come in contact with floodwaters. It's safer to throw it out.

7. If there is property damage, check closets and storage shelf areas. Open doors carefully in case there are falling objects.

8. Immediately clean up spilled medicine, cleaning products, and other potentially harmful materials.

9. In dealing with a community disaster, don't drive unless necessary, and then drive with extreme caution.

10. Touch base with your out-of-the-area phone contact but refrain from tying up the phone lines with long calls as long as a crisis condition exists.

The clock is ticking. The alarm has already rung. Answer the wake-up call by preparing today for the uncertainties of tomorrow. Organize your evacuation kits now, and be ready to survive an emergency evacuation with dignity, confidence, and even some comfort. It's up to you.

CHAPTER FORTY-SEVEN

A FINAL NOTE

So it's up to you now. You now have all the information at your fingertips to design the personal preparedness umbrella that will best suit your needs and circumstances. It may be plaid or bright orange, patched or brand-new. Just take the time to make sure it works before the rainy day comes or the wind blows very hard. If you build it right, it will provide protection, confidence, and comfort, and will be strong enough to withstand life's gale-force winds. As I've said all along, "If you're prepared, you can cope." Being prepared doesn't make the crises disappear. It just makes them bearable. In other words, you might not be singing in the rain but with a working preparedness umbrella, you'll keep your head above water. I wish you the best. We're all in this together.

BUILDING PANTRY SOLUTIONS

1. SHELVES ABOVE THE WASHER AND DRYER

Required Materials

> 1 x 2 x ¾-inch pine furring strips cut to length
> for the frames
> ½- to ¾-inch shelving material
> 1½-inch wood screws

Mounting frames for the shelves should be cut to fit the available space.

Shelving material comes in various widths; you need only to select the width that fits your space and need. A 12-inch-wide shelf usually is ideal.

Build the frame to fit the length and width of the shelving material. Any shelf over 30 inches in length should have a center brace in the frame. Mount the frame to the wall using the wood screws.

Set the shelf on the frame and use two to three screws to hold the shelf to the frame.

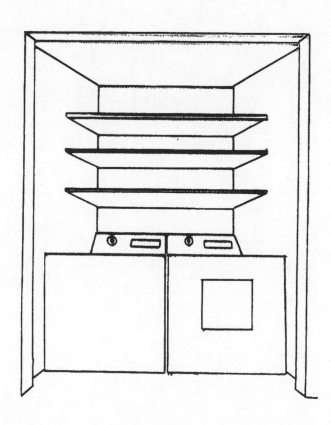

2. SHELVES IN A CLOSET

Required Materials

1 x 2 x ¾-inch pine furring strips cut to length for the mounting frames

½- to ¾-inch shelving material

1½-inch wood screws

Mounting frames for the shelves should be cut to fit the available space.

Shelving material comes in various widths you need only to select the width that fits your space and need. A 12-inch-wide shelf usually is ideal.

The number of shelves you could have would depend on the distance allowed between the shelves, which should vary according to what will be placed upon them.

For each shelf:

Cut one furring strip the width of the closet where the shelf will be mounted and attach to the rear wall.

Cut two furring strips to fit the width of the shelf you will be using and attach one to each sidewall level with the rear-mounted furring strip.

Mount the furring strips to the wall using the 1½-inch woodscrews. Try to put the screws into a wall stud if possible.

Set the shelf on the frame.

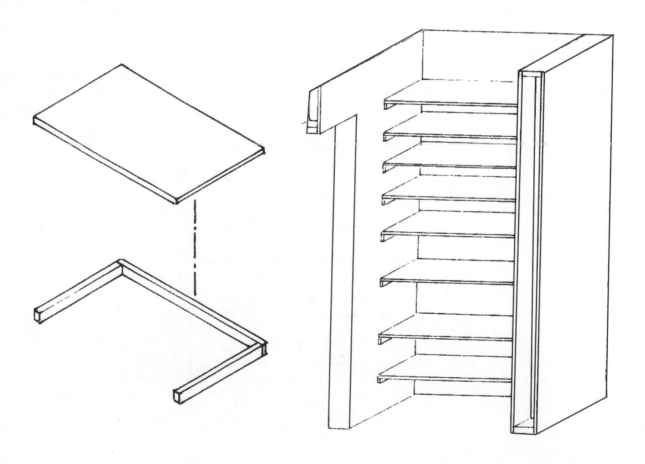

3. SHELVES ON BACKS OF DOORS

Required Materials

1 x 2 x ¾-inch pine furring strips

1 x 4-inch pine lumber for the sides of the frame cut to the length you desire

1 x 4-inch cut to the desired width of the frame

1 x 4-inch cut to fit within your frame

1½-inch #6 wood screws

1-inch finishing nails

Frames should be cut to fit your door. The side frame pieces should fit within the top and bottom frame pieces. Shelves should be cut to fit your frame and should be cut to fit within the shelf sides.

The number of shelves you could have would depend on the distance allowed between the shelves, which should vary according to what will be placed upon them.

For each shelf:

Cut two 1-by-4-inch side stiles the height you desire but will still fit on your door.

Cut the top and bottom of the frame so that the side stiles will fit in between them

Cut the 1 by 4 inches for the shelves to fit within the shelf frame.

Using the 1½-inch #6 screws, put the frame together and secure the shelves to the height you desire. Cut furring strips the width of the shelves.

Mount the furring strips to the frame approximately 2 inches above each shelf.

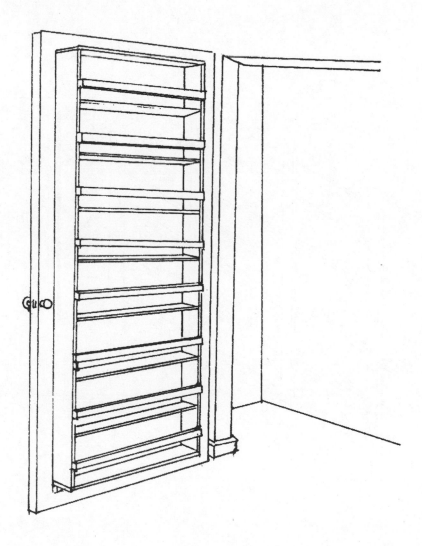

4. SHELVES ON THE WALL OF A ROOM

Required Materials

    1 x 2 x ¾-inch pine furring strips

    1 x ¾ x 12-inch pine or particleboard shelving material cut to your desired length

    1 x 3 x ¾-inch pine lumber

    1½-inch #6 wood screws

Shelves should be built to fit your wall and should be cut to fit within the shelf sides.

The number of shelves you could have would depend on the distance allowed between the shelves, which should vary according to what will be placed upon them.

For each shelf:

Prepare shelf frame by cutting two 1-by-2-inch furring strips to the length of your wall.

Cut end pieces and cross member frame pieces. A cross member should be placed every 24 inches. Cut the 1 by 3 inches for the front uprights of the shelves to a height of the top shelf, one for every 24 inches. One 1 by 3 inches could be attached across the top next to the ceiling as a stiffener.

Using the 1½-inch #6 screws, put the frame together and secure the shelves to the height you desire.

When mounting the shelves, try to locate a wall stud and screw the shelf frame to the studs.

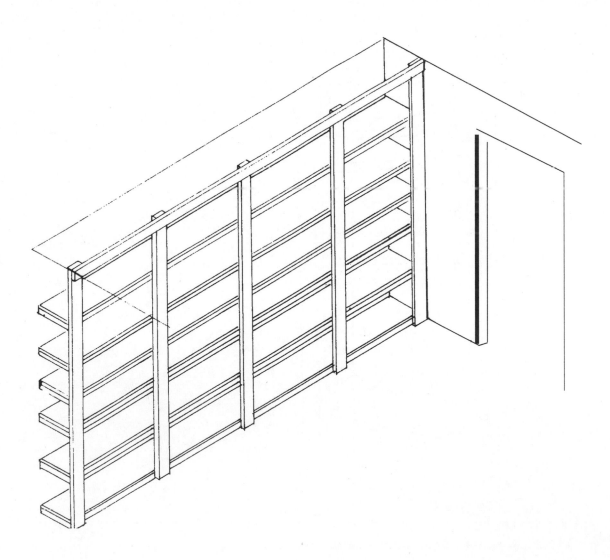

5. STORAGE ROOM SHELVES AND SHELVES AS A ROOM DIVIDER

Required Materials

1 x 2 x ¾-inch pine furring strips

1 x 3 x ¾-inch pine lumber

12 x ¾-inch pine or particleboard shelving material cut to your desired length 4-by-8-foot particleboard, pegboard or plywood

1½-inch #6 wood screws

Shelves should be built to fit your wall and should be cut to fit within the shelf sides.

The number of shelves you could have would depend on the distance allowed between the shelves, which should vary according to what will be placed upon them.

For each shelf:

Prepare shelf frame by cutting two 1-by-2-inch furring strips to the length of your wall.

Cut end pieces and cross member frame pieces. A cross member should be placed every 24 inches.

Using the 1½-inch #6 screws, put the frame together and secure the shelves to the height you desire. When mounting the shelves, try to locate a wall stud and screw the shelf frame to the studs.

Shelves should be mounted on the wall of the room on three sides. On the fourth wall, it will be a freestanding wall. The shelves will be built in the same as those above but the shelves will be fastened to 1 by 3 inches on both sides. On the bedroom side, particleboard, Peg Board, or plywood could be attached, then painted to simulate a finished wall. This whole wall could be removed at a later date without damaging the walls or floor.

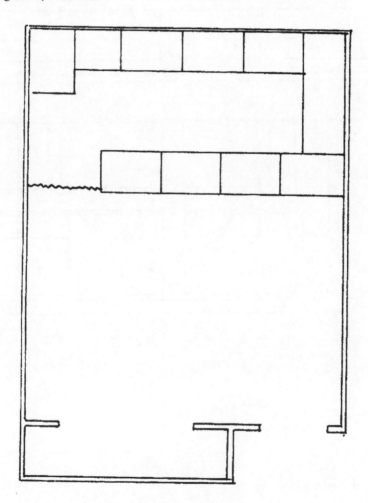

6. SHELVES UNDER A SINK

Required Materials

1 x 2 x ¾-inch pine furring strips cut to length for the mounting frames

½- to ¾-inch shelving material

½ x ¼-inch Round Stock cut to length

1½-inch wood screws

1-inch finishing nails

Mounting frames for the shelves should be cut to fit the available space.

Shelving material comes in various widths; you need only to select the width that fits your space and need. A 12-inch-wide shelf usually is ideal.

The number of shelves you could have would depend on the distance allowed between the shelves, which should vary according to what will be placed upon them.

For each shelf:

Cut furring strips the width and length of the closet where the shelf will be mounted.

Cut the ¼-inch-round stock (molding) to mount the base of the divider partition and secure with finishing nails.

Mount the furring strips to the wall using the 1½-inch woodscrews.

Set the shelf on the frame.

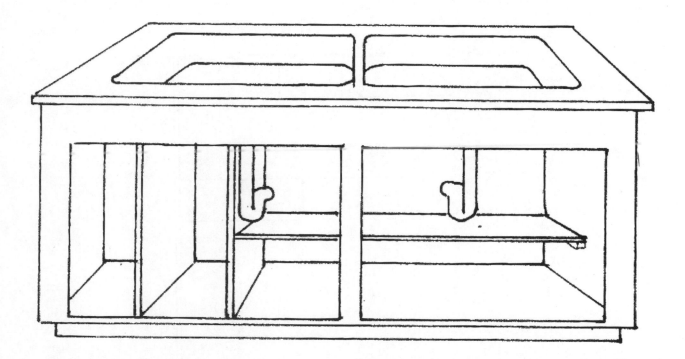

7. SHELVES IN THE STAIRWELL UNDER THE STAIRS

Required Materials

1 x 2 x ¾-inch pine furring strips

1 x ¾ x 12-inch pine or particleboard shelving material cut to your desired length

1½-inch #6 wood screws

Shelves should be built to fit your wall and should be cut to fit within the shelf sides. The number of shelves you could have would depend on the distance allowed between the shelves, which should vary according to what will be placed upon them.

For each shelf:

Prepare shelf frame by cutting two 1-by-2-inch furring strips to the length of your wall.

Cut end pieces and cross member frame pieces. A cross member should be placed every 24 inches.

Using the 1½-inch #6 screws, put the frame together and secure the shelves to the height you desire.

When mounting the shelves, try to locate a wall stud and screw the shelf frame to the studs.

MEALS SOLELY FROM FOODS IN YOUR PANTRY

If you are one who never, ever fixes meals at home, yet you'd still like to be prepared, you can simply store all the ingredients for easy meals in your pantry (multiplied by the number of days you want to eat). Here are two weeks' worth of recipes to get you started and to get you thinking about what else to add to your pantry.

1. VEGETABLE CAN SOUP

1 15-oz can Italian-style diced tomatoes
1 15-oz can zucchini with Italian-style tomato sauce
1 15-oz can green beans, drained
1 15-oz can whole potatoes, drained and chunked
1 14-oz can chicken broth

Combine all ingredients in a large pot. Bring to a boil, reduce heat, and simmer five minutes. Optional: add a can of chunk chicken, cooked pasta or rice, or canned beans. For each additional two cups of ingredients you add, add an additional can each of broth and tomatoes. Serves six to eight.

2. CHEESEBURGER PASTA

1 10-oz can beef chunks, undrained
1 can cheddar cheese soup
1 can tomato soup
1½ cups water
2 cups uncooked medium shell pasta

Mix all ingredients and bring to a boil. Cover and simmer ten minutes or until pasta is tender, stirring often. Serves four.

3. BEEF STEW

1 10-oz can beef chunks
1 can tomato soup
1 can French onion soup
1 soup can water
1 tablespoon Worcestershire sauce
1 15-oz can potatoes drained and chunked
1 15-oz can sliced carrots, drained

In a large skillet or pot, heat all ingredients to a boil. Reduce heat, cover and simmer ten minutes. Serves four.

4. CHICKEN WITH RICE AND BLACK-EYED PEAS

1 tablespoon vegetable oil
1 can (10–12 oz) chicken chunks
½ cup dried onions (or 1 medium onion chopped)
½ teaspoon minced garlic
1 14-oz can chicken broth
¼ teaspoon salt
¼ teaspoon dried oregano or thyme leaves
Dash ground red pepper (cayenne)
¾ cup uncooked long-grain rice
1 15-oz can corn (or 1 cup frozen corn)
1 15-oz can black-eyed peas, drained
Chopped parsley

In a large skillet over medium-high heat, heat chicken, broth, onion, garlic, Worcestershire sauce, salt, oregano, and red pepper. Bring to a boil. Reduce heat to medium-low. Stir in rice. Cover and cook ten minutes. Stir in corn and black-eyed peas. Cover and cook an additional ten to fifteen minutes or until liquid is absorbed, stirring occasionally. Sprinkle with parsley. This can also be made vegetarian by eliminating meat and replacing chicken broth with vegetable broth. Serves four.

5. SPAGHETTI

Use canned spaghetti sauce over cooked spaghetti noodles or make your own sauce:

2 8-oz cans tomato sauce
2 15-oz cans stewed tomatoes, chopped
1 cup water
½ teaspoon oregano
½ teaspoon basil
1 teaspoon salt
¼ teaspoon pepper
1–2 cloves garlic, crushed OR 1 teaspoon dry minced garlic OR ½ teaspoon garlic powder
¼ cup dehydrated onion OR ½ cup chopped onion
2 4-oz cans sliced mushrooms

Simmer everything for thirty minutes until thick. Serve over cooked and drained spaghetti noodles. Serves four.

6. ITALIAN TUNA SOUP

2 6-oz cans tuna, drained
1 onion chopped OR ½ cup dehydrated onion
½ teaspoon dry minced garlic
1 15-oz can Italian-style tomatoes, undrained
1 14-oz can chicken broth
1 15-oz can cannellini beans
1 15-oz can zucchini in Italian-style tomato sauce
4 cups water
1 teaspoon salt
½ teaspoon basil
½ teaspoon oregano
¼ teaspoon rosemary
Parsley for garnish

Drain tuna and set aside. (If using fresh onion and garlic, sauté in 2 tablespoons oil in a large saucepan until soft.) Simmer tomatoes, broth, onion, garlic, beans, water, salt, and spices uncovered for twenty-five minutes. Add tuna and zucchini and heat through. Sprinkle each serving with parsley before serving. Serves six to eight.

7. CHEESY SPAGHETTI NOODLE DINNER

½ cup dehydrated onion
1 4-oz can sliced mushrooms, undrained
4 cups water
8 oz uncooked spaghetti, broken in half
1 teaspoon salt
Dash pepper
1 8-oz jar pasteurized process cheese spread
1 12-oz can luncheon meat, diced

Bring water, salt, and pepper to a boil. Gradually add uncooked spaghetti so that water continues to boil. Cover and simmer, stirring occasionally, about seven minutes or until spaghetti is just tender enough to swirl. Do not overcook. Add cheese spread, mushrooms, and luncheon meat. Toss gently until cheese melts. Serve immediately. Serves six.

8. MEXICAN SUPPER CASSEROLE

¼ cup dehydrated onion
2 15-oz cans chili with beans
1 12-oz can whole kernel corn, drained
1 4½-oz can chopped olives
1 cup shredded processed cheese*
1 15-oz package corn muffin mix

In a large skillet mix onions, chili, corn, and olives; bring to boiling. Add cheese and stir to melt. Pour into 8-by-11-inch baking pan. Prepare muffin mix according to package directions. (If your package calls for eggs and you don't have any, try just increasing the liquid by 2 tablespoons per egg.) Spoon dough over top of casserole. Bake at 400⁰ for fifteen to twenty minutes. Serves eight.

9. MEXICAN BAKED BEANS

1½ cups cooked rice
1 14-oz can baked beans (not pork and beans)
1 15-oz can Mexican-style stewed tomatoes, undrained
1 7-oz can whole-kernel corn

Mix all ingredients in a large skillet. Add ½ cup water. Bring to a boil. Reduce heat to low, cover, and simmer ten to fifteen minutes. Serves six.

10. MEXICAN CASSEROLE

1 10½-oz can cream of chicken soup
½ 8-oz jar (½ cup) pasteurized processed cheese spread
½ cup milk (from dried, if necessary)
1 10-oz can chunk chicken breast, drained
¼ cup diced green chilies
1 tablespoon dehydrated (instant minced) onion
1 15-oz package corn muffin mix

Beat soup, cheese, and milk with electric beater until smooth. Stir in chicken, chilies, and onion. Pour into an 8-by-8-inch baking dish. Prepare corn muffin mix and spoon over the top. (If your mix calls for eggs and you don't have any, increase the liquid by 2 tablespoons per egg.) Bake at 400⁰ for eighteen to twenty minutes. Serves four.

11. EASY CORNED-BEEF HASH

1 7¼-oz package dry hash brown potatoes
1 12-oz can corned beef
½ 2-oz envelope dry onion soup mix
¼ cup oil

Cook hash brown potatoes according to package directions. Drain.

Add corned beef and dry onion soup mix. Mix gently. Heat oil in a large skillet. Add potato mixture and pat evenly to cover the pan. Cook over medium-low heat until lightly browned, about ten minutes. Cut into wedges and turn. Cook ten minutes longer, adding a little oil if necessary, until golden brown. Serves four.

12. CHILI-MAC

1 15-oz can chili with beans
1 8-oz can tomato sauce
1 8-oz macaroni noodles, cooked and drained
½ cup grated Parmesan cheese.

Mix and heat chili and tomato sauce. Add drained macaroni noodles and cheese. Toss to mix. Top with additional cheese if desired. Serves four.

13. TUNA RICE BAKE

1½ cups uncooked instant rice
2 cups (8 oz) shredded processed cheese*
2 6-oz cans tuna, drained
⅓ cup sliced pimiento-stuffed olives, optional
2 tablespoons parsley
2 tablespoons instant minced onion
2 teaspoons dried mustard
Dash pepper
1 12-oz can evaporated milk
½ cup water

Mix rice, 1½ cups cheese, tuna, olives, parsley, onion, mustard, and pepper in a 2-quart casserole dish. Stir in milk and water. Sprinkle remaining cheese on top. Cover and bake at 350⁰ degrees for forty-five minutes. Serves six.

*Processed cheese (like Velveeta) will keep unopened at least six months in your cupboard. Once the package is opened, it must be refrigerated and used promptly.

POSSIBLE GARDEN LAYOUTS FOR SMALL PLOTS OR PATIOS

The containers in this diagram could easily fit into a space 8 feet by 15 feet.

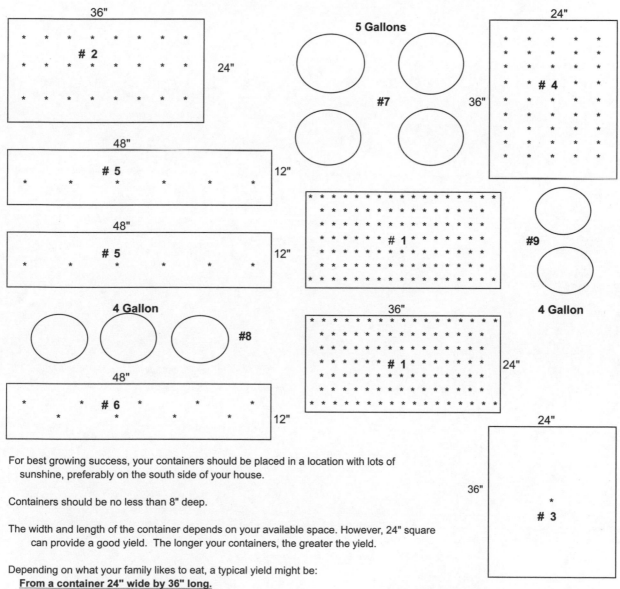

For best growing success, your containers should be placed in a location with lots of sunshine, preferably on the south side of your house.

Containers should be no less than 8" deep.

The width and length of the container depends on your available space. However, 24" square can provide a good yield. The longer your containers, the greater the yield.

Depending on what your family likes to eat, a typical yield might be:

From a container 24" wide by 36" long.
1   44 carrots and 36 green onions
2   Leaf Lettuce, Chard or spinach - 15 to 25 pickings
3   Zucchini - 5 per week for 8-10 weeks = 40 to 50
4   Beets, including the leaf greens - 72

From a container 12" wide by 48" long
5   Pole beans - 6 plants, or about 1 pound of beans per plant
6   Pole cucumbers - 4 per container - approx. 25 per plant

From a 5-gallon container
7   4 tomato plants - 80 to 100 tomatoes

From a 4-gallon container
8   3 bell pepper plants - 10 to 20 peppers
9   2 broccoli plants - 5 to 8 lbs. per plant

303

DIRECTIONS FOR BUILDING A STACK GARDEN

If you don't have a saw, don't be too concerned; all of the materials may be cut by the building-material store when you purchase your materials. The wood being used is the same lumber that is used to build fences; therefore, all of the wood is precut and ready to use. You will only have to cut the lumber to length. Most fencing materials come in six-foot lengths; therefore, if you want the planter boxes to be six feet in length, you would just have to have the end pieces cut for you. All lumber should be redwood, cedar, or some other lumber that is rot resistant when it is wet for long periods of time.

PARTS:

Two Stair Risers

Precut stair risers may be purchased from your local building materials store or you may cut your own. For cutting your own, the dimensions are on the plans.

Two Legs

The legs are cut from standard two-by-fours.

Three Planter Boxes

To complete the four planter boxes, you will need twelve pieces of wood all cut the same length. The two sideboards and bottom are all the same dimensions. Place the box bottom on a flat surface. Stand one of the sideboards against the bottom board. Make sure the ends are even. Drill pilot holes where the screws will be placed; using 1½-inch wood screws, attach the sideboard to the base. Wood screws should be placed approximately every six inches. Repeat the same operation on the other side.

Insert the end piece on the bottom board flush with the end of the bottom and sideboards. Drill holes. Then attach with 1½-inch wood screws on all three sides. Repeat the process for all planter boxes.

Stand the stair riser up so that it appears like a set of steps. Lean the stair risers against a wall or something similar until the boxes have been attached. Using 2½-inch wood screws, attach one of the legs to the upright stair riser so that it remains standing. Repeat the process with the other stair riser. With both stair risers in the standing position, place a planter box on one of the steps and attach with a 1½-inch screw through the base of the box into the step of the stair riser. Repeat the process on the other side. Place the remaining planter boxes on the other three steps, attaching them in the same manner. One last step: drill several ¾-inch holes in the bottoms of the boxes to allow for drainage.

You are now ready to fill the boxes with the compost or a planter mix of your choice and plant your seeds. Happy eating.

REQUIRED MATERIALS:

2 stair risers
8 end pieces (all the same size)
2 legs
12 boards for bottom and sides (all the same size)
1 box 2½-inch wood screws
1 box 1½-inch wood screws

TOOLS REQUIRED:

saw	drill
screwdriver	¾-inch drill bit
tape measure	3/32-inch drill bit

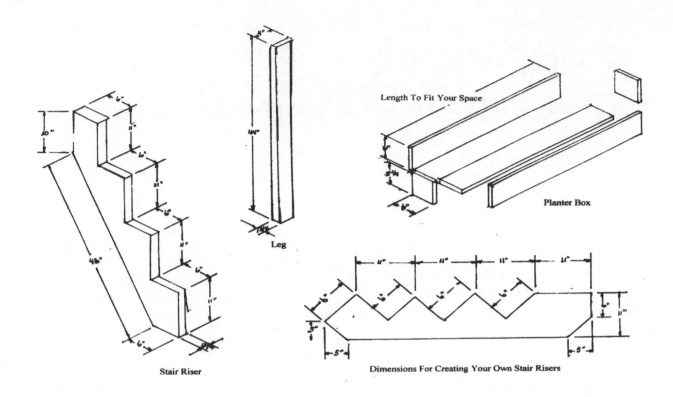

Leg

Length To Fit Your Space

Planter Box

Stair Riser

Dimensions For Creating Your Own Stair Risers

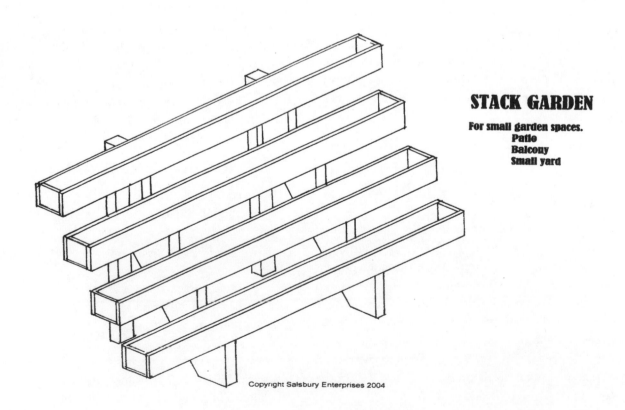

STACK GARDEN

For small garden spaces.
Patio
Balcony
Small yard

GETTING ALGAE OUT OF WATER BARRELS

To clean a large water barrel, empty out three-fourths of the water. Using a small funnel, add a full box of baking soda and a half-gallon of vinegar to the water. If you'll remember back to your elementary school science fair days, you know that mixing soda and vinegar causes a violent reaction (like lava from a volcano).

You're not going to get anything spectacular like a science fair volcano going on in your barrel (you have too much water and not enough soda and vinegar) but the two agents combined will cause a foaming action to take place. It will boil and bubble. Put the plugs back in the barrel, lay it on its side, and roll the barrel back and forth so that the mixture sloshes quite a bit.

If your algae problem is serious, you may need to let it sit a day or so, rolling and sloshing it frequently to try to get rid of it. I've even turned my barrels upside down to make sure I've gotten the inside top of the barrel also. When you're ready, drain the barrel on the lawn or driveway. Then fill the barrel one-fourth to one-half full of clean water (not so heavy you can't move it), and rinse well by rolling and sloshing. Drain and then repeat the rinsing process several times until the barrel is clean. Any residual soda or vinegar will dissipate in the water. Refill the container and replace the plugs.

You may also use just soda or just vinegar for cleaning out the barrels. Don't use soap to clean out your barrels. It is very difficult if not impossible to completely rinse out. Many times as you add more water to rinse out the barrel, the bubbles just seem to increase. After a dozen rinsings, you'll still be getting lather.

THE THERMOS: A COMMON YET UNIQUE PIECE OF EMERGENCY PREPAREDNESS EQUIPMENT

Commercially dehydrated foods are small, hard, dry, and brittle. Reconstituting them takes time, heat, and water—things you won't have a lot of in an emergency situation. By the same token, whole grains and dry beans also require time, heat, and water to make them edible. But lacking time, heat, or water, you can still use whole grains and legumes, if you have to, by employing a little creativity and imagination. Your common, everyday thermos bottle or jug is actually a unique piece of emergency preparedness equipment that can turn otherwise inappropriate storage foods into acceptable food for an emergency situation.

Using a thermos bottle or other insulated jug with a tight-fitting lid to soak or reconstitute these foods allows for more efficient fuel and water usage during crisis times. The thermoses retain their heat without continual fuel usage. For example, instead of simmering dehydrated apples on a camping stove for twenty minutes (the normally recommended method of reconstitution), you can heat water to almost boiling and pour it into a thermos jug over the apples, cap it tightly, and wait an hour. Check to see if it's ready; if not, replace the lid and soak a little longer. The results are the same, yet you have used substantially less fuel and less water, since none of it is lost to evaporation. If your thermos does not have an insulated lid, you can approximate the same insulation qualities by covering the lid with a dish-towel folded several times and topped with a saucepan lid or upside down bowl or saucer.

Thermoses or insulated jugs range in size anywhere from a one-cup child's lunch box size up to a two-gallon camping jug. A standard one-quart thermos bottle will only hold about one cup of dry wheat kernels, while a gallon-sized or bigger camping jug will hold four or five times that much. You may want to take a minute now, while water isn't preciously guarded, to measure the capacity of your thermoses. Write it on the bottom with a permanent marker or put the information in a file folder or safe place for later reference (not in a place so safe you can never find it again!).

EXPANSION ROOM IS A MUST

Knowing the capacity of your thermos is important because dehydrated foods or whole grains and beans expand to two or three times their original size after soaking or reconstitution. You *must* allow sufficient room for expansion! A general rule of thumb is two parts water to one part product. Whatever the capacity of the container, divide that number by three to determine how much dehydrated food or grain you can soak in it. If the bottle will hold 1½ cups of water, then you can safely put ½ cup of product in it and one cup of water. If it holds twelve cups of water when you measure it, it will accommodate four cups of product and eight cups of water for reconstitution purposes. Keep in mind that this is a *general* rule; beans, for example, can be an exception. Some types of beans can increase in volume three to four times, not just double. When using beans in a thermos, use fewer beans until you're familiar with how much they will expand.

Be sure to use sufficient water. Too much water is better than not enough water. If the water is insufficient, the product will get wet, absorb what water is available, and that will be all. It may not be enough to make the food edible. Then you'll have wasted the food, the water, and the time. If you use too much water, the product will absorb all it needs for full reconstitution, and you can simply drain off any unabsorbed liquid and use it as juice or stock for soups.

It goes without saying that using several thermoses at the same time will supply more options, particularly if you have a large family. If you decide to purchase one or two now for future use, I highly suggest choosing ones that have wide mouths. I'll tell you up front, it can take patience and time getting the cooked food out of your thermos if it is one of the small-mouthed varieties. You'll have to use a knife to help it out of the bottle. It will be inconvenient but remember, during an emergency situation, everything is going to be inconvenient. This is just one of the minor annoyances you may have to put up with in order to have warm, healthy food to eat.

To use your thermos for reconstitution or preparation purposes, measure your food product into the bottle or jug. Add the right amount of very hot, but not boiling water. Boiling water can cause plastic thermos bottles to melt and can shatter glass-lined bottles. Screw the lid on tightly and shake the jug gently to stir it up. Then wait. Dehydrated food should be completely reconstituted in an hour or so. Whole grains or cracked beans take longer, maybe eight hours or so. The smaller the chunks or kernels of food, the faster they will be done. Oatmeal or other flaked grains can be prepared in a much shorter time span than whole grains or beans. The thermos system is appropriate for pasta also; the preparation time is often no more than half an hour or so.

Here's a bonus idea for using your thermos and picnic jugs in emergency cooking situations: Heat as large a container of water as possible while your emergency stove is in use. Fill as many thermoses as you have with almost boiling water. Put the lids on tightly and set them aside. You would then be able to have hot water for hot drinks throughout the day or evening without using additional fuel.

Barbara's Thermos Soup

Thermos food preparation isn't limited to plain grain or a single variety of dehydrated food at a time. Try this recipe for thermos soup. It's delicious, easy to prepare, and, if started in the morning, is ready to eat for dinner. The only fuel required is what is needed to heat the water initially.

1–1½ cups grain: any kind, any combination (try basmati rice, cracked wheat, sweet brown rice and barley, or split peas, lentils and long-grain rice)

¼–½ cup dehydrated onions

¼ cup bacon bits from a jar, real or imitation

¼ cup dehydrated celery

¼ teaspoon each marjoram and thyme

2–3 bay leaves

1 tablespoon chicken soup base (or 3–4 bouillon cubes)

salt and pepper to taste

¼ cup dehydrated carrots*

¼ cup dehydrated green beans*

½ cup dehydrated potato dices*

½–¾ cup pasta* (prepare in another thermos and add last half hour)

Place all ingredients in a gallon-sized insulated jug. Pour very hot—but not boiling—water over the ingredients to fill the jug three-fourths full (approximately eight cups). Cap tightly and shake gently. Let it sit for eight hours or so and enjoy!

ADAPTING A BLANKET INTO A TEMPORARY BLANKET ROBE

You will need a blanket per person and several large safety pins. A twin-sized blanket will fit most people. A crib blanket will adapt more easily for a toddler.

Hold the blanket up to the person to determine how deep the fold-over needs to be. You don't want the finished robe to drag on the ground or trip the person wearing it. Since the fold-over is going to be the sleeves of the robe, it needs to be at least fifteen inches deep but it can be much more if it needs to be in order for the robe to not drag.

Lay the blanket on the floor with the folded-over piece on top. The fold-over should be along the lengthwise edge. Pin along the bottom edge of the folded-over piece, leaving an unpinned space about two feet wide in the center.

Take the edge of the fold-over in the unpinned center part and fold it up and inside one more time. Pin it in place with the pin on the outside of the blanket so it won't annoy your neck. This part becomes the collar. The second fold will angle the inside portion of the blanket towards the top.

If your original fold-over was very deep, you may need to shape a sleeve with safety pins. Calculate where the "armhole" will fit the intended wearer and pin a slanted edge in place. If your original fold-over was only fifteen inches or so deep to begin with, you don't need to add more pins.

Try it on. Slip your arms into the pockets created by the pinned fold-over and adjust the armhole pins for comfort. Rearrange the collar fold if you need to so it is comfortable also. Fold back the cuffs and pin them in place. Hold the front closed with more pins, or tie a large belt, bathrobe tie, or piece of rope around you.

You probably won't be receiving any best-dressed awards in this blanket robe but you'll stay warmer and still be able to move around, and that's what really matters.

MAKING NEWSPAPER LOGS

Use the following method to make newspaper logs, a good and inexpensive source of fuel. The supplies needed are:

- Newspaper
- Thin or fine wire (such as florist or craft wire), or strong cord—two 16-inch pieces per log
- A 4 to 5 gallon tub or large bucket
- Laundry detergent
- Water

1. You may wish to wear gardening gloves because the newsprint may irritate sensitive skin.

2. To begin, all the newspaper you'll be working with should be the width of a standard sheet of newspaper (not a double sheet). Open several sections of paper out (fourteen inches wide, twenty-six inches long) and make a stack three to four inches thick, ready to draw from as needed.

3. Have your sixteen-inch pieces of wire or cord cut and ready.

4. Stack several sections of newspaper on top of each other about two inches deep. These sections should be folded in the middle, just like the way they're laid on your porch or at a newspaper stand (fourteen by thirteen inches). Grasp the papers on the fold and begin rolling the whole stack tightly into a tube. It should end up about four inches wide. The more compactly you roll the paper, the heavier the finished log will be. The heavier the log, the longer it will burn.

5. Holding the tube of newspapers tightly, lay it on the edge of a fourteen- by twenty-inch newspaper section. Roll it up in the new section until about eight inches of paper are left.

6. Slip another section of newspaper into the space between the unrolled bit of paper and the rolled log. Continue rolling. Roll until about eight inches of paper from the newest section are left, and then slip another section in and keep rolling. Continue this process until you have a log about six inches in diameter.

7. Holding the log firmly so that it won't unroll (kneeling on it works), slip a piece of wire or cord under the newspaper log, wrap it around, and twist or tie it tightly. The ends of cut wire tend to be sharp, so be careful.

8. Tie another piece of wire or cord on the other end. It's done!

Some people choose to roll their newspapers around an eighteen-inch length of old broom handle or one-inch dowel. This is also an efficient way to make newspaper logs, though you'll probably have to twist and turn the broom when you're done in order to pull the handle out of the finished log. Commercial log rollers are also available that make nice, tight, heavy, long-burning newspaper logs.

You can improve your newspaper log by soaking it in a detergent solution and letting it dry. Soaking the log expands the fibers to let the oxygen pass through after the logs are completely dried out. The detergent causes them to burn better. Fill a plastic tub or bin with enough water to cover your logs. Add a tablespoon of regular laundry detergent to the water and swish it through the water so it mixes well. Make sure any lumps are dissolved. Place your logs in, a few at a time and roll them over several times until they are good and soaked. Set them on end on the sidewalk or patio or driveway to drain and dry. It may take several days for them to dry thoroughly, depending on how humid the air is.

Stack your newspaper logs just like regular wood. You must take more care, though, that they stay dry. Rain, sprinklers, or even too much heavy dew will cause them to eventually rot away.

Burn your newspaper logs just like regular wood also. If you've rolled them tightly, you'll need kindling or wadded up newspapers under the grate to get them started. But after they begin burning, they burn roughly as long as a dry log of the same size, less time if they were not rolled tightly.

HOW TO FILL AND USE AN OIL LAMP

ASSEMBLING YOUR OIL LAMP

Remove the glass chimney and unscrew the burner assembly. Pour in lamp oil. (*Never* use gasoline, alcohol, camping fuel, or anything else except lamp oil in an oil lamp.) Do not overfill. The lamp oil level should be at least half an inch below the reservoir lip. Thread the wick into the burner assembly. Screw the burner assembly back onto the base and allow the wick to become completely saturated with lamp oil.

LIGHTING YOUR OIL LAMP

Turn the wick up until it is just high enough over the brass lip to light easily, approximately one-fourth of an inch. After lighting, turn the wick back down to level with or barely below the brass lip. Replace the glass chimney on the burner so it fits tightly inside the chimney bracket. You then can adjust the wick slightly up or down to achieve the desired brightness. Generally, the higher the wick, the higher the flame and the brighter the light. Watch for smoking. The wick should never be extended above the combustion chamber (brass lip) because that will result in incomplete combustion and will cause smoke and soot deposits, as well as excessive heat. If you see smoke or soot, lower the wick until it stops.

To turn off the lamp, turn the wick down into the burner until the flame goes out. Don't turn it so far as to unthread the wick from the burner assembly completely.

PREVENT BREAKAGE

After an oil lamp has been burning for any substantial length of time, the chimney will be extremely hot. If you absolutely must move the lamp, do so very carefully by the base only. Better yet, set the lamp where you want it in the first place and don't move the lamp once you've lighted it. After turning it off for the night, let it sit for a few minutes to cool slightly and then you can move it to a secure out-of-the-way spot until it's needed again. Do *not* put the hot lamp or chimney on a cold tile counter—it could crack the lamp or the tile. Set the hot lamp on a pot holder or folded towel to cool.

FOR OPTIMUM BURNING

For optimum burning, the wick should be periodically trimmed to remove the burned edges and carbon deposits. Do this when the lamp is cold. Cut off the burned edges with scissors rather than just pinching them off with your fingers.

USING A FIRE EXTINGUISHER

In a fire, your first priority is not your home; it is your life. Use a fire extinguisher to fight a fire only if *all* of the following situations apply:

- The fire department has been called (dial 911).
- The fire is small and contained, and it is not spreading beyond it starting point
- You are not in any immediate danger, your path to an exit is absolutely clear, and you can fight the fire with your back to the exit (the fire is not between you and the exit).
- You can avoid breathing in smoke.
- Your fire extinguisher is close at hand.
- You know how to use a fire extinguisher.

If any of these conditions have not been met, you must not fight the fire yourself. Call for help and leave the area immediately!

1. If your personal safety is even remotely in question, leave immediately and close off the area. (Close doors but don't lock them.) Tell a firefighter any information you know about the fire.

2. If you decide to fight the fire, pull the pin on the fire extinguisher.

3. Stand back from the fire, depress the handle, and spray with broad back-and-forth sweeping motions.

4. Direct the spray at the base of the fire until the fire is completely out, or until the extinguisher is empty. You usually can't expect more than about ten seconds of extinguishing power from a fire extinguisher—possibly less.

5. Recharge or replace your fire extinguisher immediately after use! Don't go a single day without a working fire extinguisher in your house.

HOW TO SHUT OFF YOUR GAS IN AN EMERGENCY

- You need to know where your gas meter is before an emergency occurs.
- If it is dark, use only battery-powered flashlights or lanterns to help you find the meter.
- Have a wrench stored in a specific location where it will be available. Consider wiring it loosely to the meter.
- If you smell or hear gas escaping after an earthquake or any emergency, or if you notice a large consumption of gas being registered by the gas meter, turn off your gas at the meter as shown. The male shutoff valve is located next to the meter on the inlet pipe.
- Use a crescent wrench and give the protruding valve a quarter turn in either direction so that it runs perpendicular (crosswise) to the pipe. The line is now closed.
- Do not use matches, lighters, or open flame appliances; operate electrical switches anywhere in your home; or start a car in your garage or driveway until you are sure no gas leaks exist. Flames and sparks from electrical switches could ignite gas, causing an explosion.
- Turning off the gas after an emergency is not always necessary. You do not need to turn off the gas unless you have reason to suspect a leak or unless you are told to do so by authorities. Once the gas is turned off, it can only be turned back on by a professional. In an emergency, that could take a week or more.

You may copy this page of instructions. Laminate it and attach it to your gas meter with a wire.

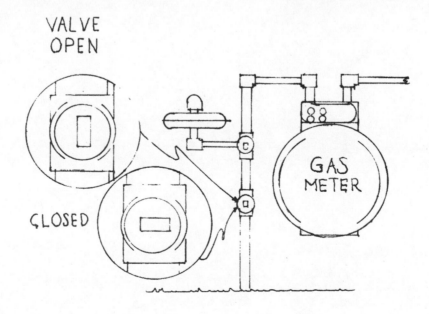

VALVE OPEN

CLOSED

GAS METER

WHAT TO DO WITH YOUR REFRIGERATOR AND FREEZER WHEN THE ELECTRICITY IS OUT

This information is courtesy of the University of Georgia Extension office. The following steps can be taken to save food in refrigerators and freezers whenever electricity is off.

REFRIGERATOR

Keep the door shut.

Plan meals and snacks and then open the refrigerator only long enough to get food out.

Refrigerated foods need to stay at or below 40°F. Once the temperature of the refrigerator increases so that foods are no longer in this safe range, the safest rule to follow is the two-hour rule: *Don't leave perishables above 40°F. for longer than two hours.*

- **Highly Perishable Foods.** Discard if they have been in the danger zone (40 to 140°F.) for more than two hours. Examples of highly perishable foods are: milk, eggs, meat and poultry, gravies, casseroles, vegetables, salads, and any food containing protein (lunch meat, hot dogs, bacon).
- **High-Acid Foods.** Will keep longer at temperatures above 40°F. but will lose quality and should be discarded if visible signs of spoilage are detected. If the temperature remains above 40°F. for more than twenty-four hours, it would be advisable to discard these foods as well. Examples of high acid foods are: fruits, commercially processed mayonnaise, pickles, jams and jellies, ketchup, mustard, or foods that are low in moisture like the hard cheeses such as cheddar. After twenty-four hours, pitch all food or transport to coolers packed with ice.

FREEZER

Keep the door shut. Foods will remain frozen for about two days if freezer is full, is in a cool area, and is well insulated.

Plan meals for the entire day. Seafood, poultry, and liver should be used before other meats. Then open the freezer only long enough to get food out once a day.

Some thawed foods can be refrozen. However, the texture will not be as good. Other foods may need to be discarded. Here are some guidelines.

THAWED FROZEN FOODS

- **Meat and Poultry.** Refreeze if (1) the temperature of the freezer is 40°F. or below, (2) meat or poultry is still partially frozen or contains ice crystals, and (3) the color and odor are good. Check each package. Rewrap if necessary. Throw out if packages are smelly or showing signs of spoilage.
- **Vegetables.** Refreeze if ice crystals are still in the foods, even though quality will suffer. If condition is poor and questionable, throw it out. If condition is good, boil twenty minutes and eat, or cook twenty minutes and refreeze, or can in pressure canner.
- **Fruits.** Refreeze if taste and smell are good, or use for cooking, baking, or jelly making.
- **Shellfish and Cooked Foods.** Refreeze if ice crystals are present or the freezer is still 40°F. or below. Smell is not a sign of

safe food in shellfish or cooked foods. If condition is poor or questionable, throw it out. If condition is good, boil or bake twenty minutes and eat.

- **Ice Cream.** Throw out if thawed.
- **Breads.** Refreeze.
- **Pies and Cakes or Other Baked Goods.** Refreeze plain cakes and fruit pies if the freezer is still 40°F. or below.

USING DRY ICE DURING A POWER FAILURE

If it seems likely that your freezer will not be operating properly within one or two days, dry ice may help keep some frozen food from spoiling.

- Obtain dry ice quickly.
- Wear gloves when handling dry ice. Do not touch it with your bare hands because it can cause burns.
- Allow two and a half to three pounds of ice per cubic foot of freezer space (More on each shelf). Twenty-five pounds of dry ice in a half-full eighteen-cubic-foot freezer should keep the food frozen two to three days. The same amount of dry ice in a full freezer should keep the food frozen three to four days.
- Place boards or heavy cardboard on top of the packages. Place dry ice on top of boards. In an upright freezer, place ice on each shelf.
- Cover the freezer with blankets but do not lock it or cover air vent openings.

Gas given off by the dry ice needs a place to escape.

SOURCES OF DRY ICE

- Available in many grocery stores.
- Check telephone yellow pages for a complete listing.

For additional information on keeping food safe during a power outage, check out this site from the Food Safety and Inspection Service of the U.S. Department of Agriculture: http://www.fsis.usda.gov/home/index.asp.

WHEN CANNED GOODS FREEZE

Canned foods stored in unheated areas may freeze during severe cold spells. These foods will be safe to eat if there is no sign of:

- Leakage from seams.
- Bulging ends on cans or jars.
- Cracks in jars.
- Broken seals on home-canned foods.
- No spurting liquid, mold, or off odor when opened.

The danger comes from food expanding in the container. The expansion can put stress on the container, which could break, allowing bacteria to seep in and make the food unsafe. If the damaged containers are discovered six to eight hours after freezing, it is safe to eat the contents. The temperature of the food and surrounding area would not drop sufficiently in this time to allow bacteria growth. However, do not expect accidentally frozen canned foods to have the same texture as when originally purchased or canned.

PREPARING FOR SPECIFIC NATURAL DISASTERS

This information is provided by the Federal Emergency Management Agency (FEMA). You can access additional tips and information at the agency's Website: http://www.fema.gov.

NATURAL DISASTERS

Some of the things you can do to prepare for the unexpected, such as making an emergency supply kit and developing a family communications plan, are the same for both a natural or man-made emergency. However, there are important differences among natural disasters that will impact the decisions you make and the actions you take. Some natural disasters are easily predicted, others happen without warning. Planning what to do in advance is an important part of being prepared.

Find out what natural disasters are most common in your area. You may be aware of some of your community's risks; others may surprise you. Historically, **flooding** is the nation's single most common natural disaster. Flooding can happen in every U.S. state and territory. **Earthquakes** are often thought of as a West Coast phenomenon, yet forty-five states and territories in the United States are at moderate to high risk from earthquakes and are located in every region of the country. Other disasters may be more common in certain areas. **Tornadoes** are nature's most violent storms and can happen anywhere. However, states located in "Tornado Alley," as well as areas in Pennsylvania, New York, Connecticut, and Florida are at the highest risk for tornado damage. **Hurricanes** are severe tropical storms that form in the southern Atlantic Ocean, Caribbean Sea, Gulf of Mexico, and in the eastern Pacific Ocean. Scientists can now predict hurricanes but people who live in coastal communities should plan what they will do if they are told to evacuate.

EARTHQUAKES

An earthquake is a sudden shaking of the earth caused by the breaking and shifting of rock beneath the earth's surface. Earthquakes can cause buildings and bridges to collapse, telephone and power lines to fall, and result in fires, explosions, and landslides. Earthquakes can also cause huge ocean waves, called tsunamis, which travel long distances over water until they crash into coastal areas.

The following information includes general guidelines for earthquake preparedness and safety. Because injury prevention techniques may vary from state to state, it is recommended that you contact your local emergency management office, health department, or American Red Cross chapter.

What to do before an earthquake

1. Know the terms associated with earthquakes.
   - **Earthquake**—A sudden slipping or movement of a portion of the earth's crust, accompanied and followed by a series of vibrations.
   - **Aftershock**—An earthquake of similar or lesser intensity that follows the main earthquake.
   - **Fault**—The earth's crust slips along a fault—an area of weakness where two sections of crust have separated. The crust may only move a few inches to a few feet in a severe earthquake.
   - **Epicenter**—The area of the earth's surface directly above the origin of an earthquake.

- **Seismic Waves**—Vibrations that travel outward from the center of the earthquake at speeds of several miles per second. These vibrations can shake some buildings so rapidly that they collapse.
- **Magnitude**—Indicates how much energy was released. This energy can be measured on a recording device and graphically displayed through lines on a Richter Scale. A magnitude of 7.0 on the Richter Scale would indicate a very strong earthquake. Each whole number on the scale represents an increase of about thirty times the energy released. Therefore, an earthquake measuring 6.0 is about thirty times more powerful than one measuring 5.0.

2. Look for items in your home that could become a hazard in an earthquake:

- Repair defective electrical wiring, leaky gas lines, and inflexible utility connections.
- Bolt down water heaters and gas appliances (have an automatic gas shutoff device installed that is triggered by an earthquake).
- Place large or heavy objects on lower shelves. Fasten shelves to walls. Brace high and top-heavy objects.
- Store bottled foods, glass, china, and other breakables on low shelves or in cabinets that can fasten shut.
- Anchor overhead lighting fixtures.
- Check and repair deep plaster cracks in ceilings and foundations. Get expert advice, especially if there are signs of structural defects.
- Be sure the residence is firmly anchored to its foundation.
- Install flexible pipe fittings to avoid gas or water leaks. Flexible fittings are more resistant to breakage.

3. Know where and how to shut off electricity, gas, and water at main switches and valves. Check with your local utilities for instructions.

4. Hold earthquake drills with your household:

- Locate safe spots in each room under a sturdy table or against an inside wall.

Reinforce this information by physically placing yourself and your household in these locations.

- Identify danger zones in each room—near windows where glass can shatter, bookcases or furniture that can fall over, or under ceiling fixtures that could fall down.

5. Review your insurance policies. Some damage may be covered even without specific earthquake insurance. Protect important home and business papers.

What to do during an earthquake

Stay inside until the shaking stops and it is safe to go outside. Most injuries during earthquakes occur when people are hit by falling objects when entering or exiting buildings.

1. Drop, cover, and hold on! Minimize your movements during an earthquake to a few steps to a nearby safe place. Stay indoors until the shaking has stopped and you are sure exiting is safe.

2. If you are *indoors*, take cover under a sturdy desk, table, or bench, or against an inside wall, and hold on. Stay away from glass, windows, outside doors or walls, and anything that could fall, such as lighting fixtures or furniture. If you are in bed, stay there, hold on, and protect your head with a pillow, unless you are under a heavy light fixture that could fall.

3. If there isn't a table or desk near you, cover your face and head with your arms and crouch in an inside corner of the building. Doorways should only be used for shelter if they are in close proximity to you and if you know that it is a strongly supported load-bearing doorway.

4. If you are *outdoors*, stay there. Move away from buildings, streetlights and utility wires.

5. If you live in an *apartment building* or other multihousehold structure with many levels, consider the following:

- Get under a desk and stay away from windows and outside walls.
- Stay in the building (many injuries occur as people flee a building and are struck by falling debris from above).
- Be aware that the electricity may go out and sprinkler systems may come on.
- *Do not* use the elevators.

6. If you're in a crowded indoor public location:
   - Stay where you are. Do not rush for the doorways.
   - Move away from tall shelves, cabinets, and bookcases containing objects that may fall.
   - Take cover and grab something to shield your head and face from falling debris and glass.
   - *Do not* use the elevators.

7. In a moving vehicle, stop as quickly as safety permits and stay in the vehicle. Avoid stopping near or under buildings, trees, overpasses, or utility wires. Then proceed cautiously, watching for road and bridge damage.

8. If you become trapped in debris:
   - Do not light a match.
   - Do not move about or kick up dust.
   - Cover your mouth with a handkerchief or clothing.
   - Tap on a pipe or wall so rescuers can locate you. Use a whistle if one is available. Shout only as a last resort—shouting can cause you to inhale dangerous amounts of dust.

9. Stay indoors until the shaking has stopped and you are sure exiting is safe.

What to do after an earthquake

1. Be prepared for aftershocks. These secondary shock waves are usually less violent than the main quake but can be strong enough to do additional damage to weakened structures.

2. Check for injuries. Do not attempt to move seriously injured persons unless they are in immediate danger of death or further injury. If you must move an unconscious person, first stabilize the neck and back, then call for help immediately.
   - If the victim is not breathing, carefully position the victim for artificial respiration, clear the airway, and start mouth-to-mouth resuscitation.
   - Maintain body temperature with blankets. Be sure the victim does not become overheated.
   - Never try to feed liquids to an unconscious person.

3. If the electricity goes out, use flashlights or battery-powered lanterns. Do not use candles, matches, or open flames indoors after the earthquake because of possible gas leaks.

4. Wear sturdy shoes in areas covered with fallen debris and broken glass.

5. Check your home for structural damage. If you have any doubts about safety, have your home inspected by a professional before entering.

6. Check chimneys for visible damage; however, have a professional inspect the chimney for internal damage before lighting a fire.

7. Clean up spilled medicines, bleaches, gasoline, and other flammable liquids. Evacuate the building if gasoline fumes are detected and the building is not well ventilated.

8. Visually inspect utility lines and appliances for damage.
   - If you smell gas or hear a hissing or blowing sound, open a window and leave. Shut off the main gas valve. Report the leak to the gas company from the nearest working phone or cell phone available. Stay out of the building. If you shut off the gas supply at the main valve, you will need a professional to turn it back on.
   - Switch off electrical power at the main fuse box or circuit breaker if electrical damage is suspected or known.
   - Shut off the water supply at the main valve if water pipes are damaged
   - Do not flush toilets until you know that sewage lines are intact.

9. Open cabinets cautiously. Beware of objects that can fall off shelves.

10. Use the phone only to report life-threatening emergencies.

11. Listen to news reports for the latest emergency information.

12. Stay off the streets. If you must go out, watch for fallen objects, downed electrical wires, and weakened walls, bridges, roads, and sidewalks.

EXTREME HEAT (HEAT WAVE)

Heat kills by pushing the human body beyond its limits. Under normal conditions, the body's internal thermostat produces perspiration that evaporates and cools the body. However, in extreme heat and high humidity, evaporation is slowed and the body must work extra hard to maintain a normal temperature.

Most heat disorders occur because the victim has been overexposed to heat or has overexercised for his age and physical condition. The elderly, young children, and those who are sick or overweight are more likely to succumb to extreme heat.

Conditions that can induce heat-related illnesses include stagnant atmospheric conditions and poor air quality. Consequently, people living in urban areas may be at greater risk from the effects of a prolonged heat wave than those living in rural areas. Also, asphalt and concrete store heat longer and gradually release heat at night, which can produce higher nighttime temperatures, known as the "urban heat island effect."

What to do before an extreme heat emergency

1. Know the terms associated with extreme heat:
   - **Heat wave**—prolonged period of excessive heat, often combined with excessive humidity.
   - **Heat index**—A number in degrees Fahrenheit (^{0}F.) that tells how hot it feels when relative humidity is added to the air temperature. Exposure to full sunshine can increase the heat index by fifteen degrees.
   - **Heat cramps**—Muscular pains and spasms due to heavy exertion. Although heat cramps are the least severe, they are often the first signal that the body is having trouble with the heat.
   - **Heat exhaustion**—Typically occurs when people exercise heavily or work in a hot, humid place where body fluids are lost through heavy sweating. Blood flow to the skin increases, causing blood flow to decrease to the vital organs. This results in a form of mild shock. If not treated, the victim's condition will worsen. Body temperature will keep rising and the victim may suffer heat stroke.
   - **Heat Stroke**—Heat stroke is life-threatening. The victim's temperature control system, which produces sweating to

cool the body, stops working. The body temperature can rise so high that brain damage and death may result if the body is not cooled quickly.
   - **Sun Stroke**—Another term for heat stroke.

2. Consider the following preparedness measures when faced with the possibility of extreme heat.
   - Install window air conditioners snugly; insulate if necessary.
   - Check air conditioning ducts for proper insulation.
   - Install temporary window reflectors (for use between windows and drapes), such as aluminum-foil-covered cardboard, to reflect heat back outside and be sure to weather-strip doors and sills to keep cool air in.
   - Cover windows that receive morning or afternoon sun with drapes, shades, awnings, or louvers. Outdoor awnings or louvers can reduce the heat that enters a home by up to 80 percent. Consider keeping storm windows up all year.

What to do during extreme heat or a heat wave emergency

1. Stay indoors as much as possible.
   - If air conditioning is not available, stay on the lowest floor out of the sunshine.
   - Circulating air can cool the body by increasing the rate of perspiration evaporation.

2. Eat well-balanced, light, and regular meals. Avoid using salt tablets unless directed to do so by a physician.

3. Drink plenty of water regularly, even if you do not feel thirsty.
   - Persons who have epilepsy or heart, kidney, or liver disease, are on fluid-restrictive diets, or have a problem with fluid retention should consult a doctor before increasing liquid intake.

4. Limit intake of alcoholic beverages.
   - Although beer and alcoholic beverages appear to satisfy thirst, they actually cause further body dehydration.

5. Never leave children or pets alone in closed vehicles.

6. Dress in loose-fitting clothes that cover as much skin as possible.

- Lightweight, light-colored clothing reflects heat and sunlight and helps maintain normal body temperature.

7. Protect face and head by wearing a wide-brimmed hat.

8. Avoid too much sunshine.

- Sunburn slows the skin's ability to cool itself. Use a sunscreen lotion with a high SPF (sun protection factor) rating (fifteen or greater).

9. Avoid strenuous work during the warmest part of the day. Use a buddy system when working in extreme heat and take frequent breaks.

10. Spend at least two hours per day in an air-conditioned place. If your home is not air conditioned, consider spending the warmest part of the day in public buildings such as libraries, schools, movie theaters, shopping malls, and other community facilities.

11. Check on family, friends, and neighbors who do not have air conditioning and who spend much of their time alone.

First aid for heat-induced illnesses

1. Sunburn

- **Symptoms:** Skin redness and pain, possible swelling, blisters, fever, headaches.
- **First Aid:** Take a shower, using soap, to remove oils that may block pores, preventing the body from cooling naturally. If blisters occur, apply dry, sterile dressings and get medical attention.

2. Heat cramps

- **Symptoms:** Painful spasms, usually in leg and abdominal muscles. Heavy sweating.
- **First Aid:** Get the victim out of the heat and to a cooler location. Lightly stretch and gently massage affected muscles to relieve spasm. Give sips of up to half a glass of cool water every fifteen minutes. Do not give liquids with caffeine or alcohol. If nauseous, discontinue liquids.

3. Heat exhaustion

- **Symptoms:** Heavy sweating; skin may be cool, pale, or flushed. Weak pulse.

Normal body temperature is possible but temperature will likely rise. Fainting or dizziness, nausea or vomiting, exhaustion and headaches are possible.

- **First Aid:** Get victim to lie down in a cool place. Loosen or remove clothing. Apply cool, wet cloths. Fan or move victim to air conditioned place. Give sips of water if victim is conscious. Be sure water is consumed slowly. Give half a glass of cool water every fiifteen minutes. If nausea occurs, discontinue. If vomiting occurs, seek immediate medical attention.

4. Heat stroke (sun stroke)

- **Symptoms:** High body temperature (105 plus). Hot, red, dry skin. Rapid, weak pulse and rapid, shallow breathing. Possible unconsciousness. Victim will likely not sweat unless victim was sweating from recent strenuous activity.
- **First Aid:** Heat stroke is a severe medical emergency. Call 911 or emergency medical services or get the victim to a hospital immediately. Delay can be fatal. Move victim to a cooler environment. Remove clothing. Try a cool bath, wet spongue, or wet sheet to reduce body temperature. Watch for breathing problems. Use extreme caution. Use fans and air conditioners.

FIRES

Each year more than 4,000 Americans die and more than 25,000 are injured in fires, many of which could be prevented. Direct property loss due to fires is estimated at $8.6 billion annually.

To protect yourself, it's important to understand the basic characteristics of fire. Fire spreads quickly; there is no time to gather valuables or make a phone call. In just two minutes a fire can become life-threatening. In five minutes a residence can be engulfed in flames.

Heat and smoke from fire can be more dangerous than the flames. Inhaling the superhot air can sear your lungs. Fire produces poisonous gases that make you disoriented and drowsy. Instead of being awakened by a fire, you may fall into a deeper sleep.

Asphyxiation is the leading cause of fire deaths, exceeding burns by a three-to-one ratio.

What to do before fire strikes

1. Install smoke alarms. Working smoke alarms decrease your chances of dying in a fire by half.

- Place smoke alarms on every level of your residence: outside bedrooms on the ceiling or high on the wall, at the top of open stairways or at the bottom of enclosed stairs and near (but not in) the kitchen.
- Test and clean smoke alarms once a month and replace batteries at least once a year.
- Replace smoke alarms once every ten years.

2. With your household, plan two escape routes from every room in the residence. Practice with your household escaping from each room.

- Make sure windows are not nailed or painted shut. Make sure security gratings on windows have a fire safety-opening feature so that they can be easily opened from the inside.
- Consider escape ladders if your home has more than one level and ensure that burglar bars and other antitheft mechanisms that block outside window entry are easily opened from inside.
- Teach household members to stay low to the floor (where the air is safer in a fire) when escaping from a fire.
- Pick a place outside your home for the household to meet after escaping from a fire.

3. Clean out storage areas. Don't let trash such as old newspapers and magazines accumulate.

4. Check the electrical wiring in your home.

- Inspect extension cords for frayed or exposed wires or loose plugs.
- Outlets should have cover plates and no exposed wiring.
- Make sure wiring does not run under rugs, over nails, or across high-traffic areas.
- Do not overload extension cords or outlets. If you need to plug in two or three

appliances, get a UL-approved unit with built-in circuit breakers to prevent sparks and short circuits.

- Make sure home insulation does not touch electrical wiring.
- Have an electrician check the electrical wiring in your home.

5. Never use gasoline, benzine, naptha, or similar liquids indoors.

- Store flammable liquids in approved containers in well-ventilated storage areas.
- Never smoke near flammable liquids.
- After use, safely discard all rags or materials soaked in flammable material.

6. Check heating sources. Many home fires are started by faulty furnaces or stoves, cracked or rusted furnace parts, or chimneys with creosote buildup. Have chimneys, woodstoves and all home heating systems inspected and cleaned annually by a certified specialist.

7. Insulate chimneys and place spark arresters on top. The chimney should be at least three feet higher than the roof. Remove branches hanging above and around the chimney.

8. Be careful when using alternative heating sources, such as wood, coal, and kerosene heaters and electrical space heaters.

- Check with your local fire department on the legality of using kerosene heaters in your community. Be sure to fill kerosene heaters outside after they have cooled.
- Place heaters at least three feet away from flammable materials. Make sure the floor and nearby walls are properly insulated.
- Use only the type of fuel designated for your unit and follow manufacturer's instructions.
- Store ashes in a metal container outside and away from the residence.
- Keep open flames away from walls, furniture, drapery, and flammable items. Keep a screen in front of the fireplace.
- Have chimneys and woodstoves inspected annually and cleaned if necessary.
- Use portable heaters only in well-ventilated rooms.

9. Keep matches and lighters up high, away from children, and if possible in a locked cabinet.

10. Do not smoke in bed, or when drowsy or medicated. Provide smokers with deep, sturdy ashtrays. Douse cigarette and cigar butts with water before disposal.

11. Safety experts recommend that you sleep with your door closed.

12. Know the locations of the gas valve and electric fuse or circuit breaker box and how to turn them off in an emergency. If you shut off your main gas line for any reason, allow only a gas company representative to turn it on again.

13. Install ABC-type fire extinguishers in the home and teach household members how to use them. (Type A—wood or paper fires only; Type B—flammable liquid or grease fires; Type C—electrical fires; Type ABC—rated for all fires and recommended for the home.)

14. Consider installing an automatic fire sprinkler system in your home.

15. Ask your local fire department to inspect your residence for fire safety and prevention.

16. Teach children how to report a fire and when to call 911.

17. To support insurance claims in case you do have a fire, conduct an inventory of your property and possessions and keep the list in a separate location. Photographs are also helpful.

What to do during a fire

1. Use water or a fire extinguisher to put out small fires. Do not try to put out a fire that is getting out of control. If you're not sure if you can control it, get everyone out of the residence and call the fire department from a neighbor's residence.

2. Never use water on an electrical fire. Use only a fire extinguisher approved for electrical fires.

3. Smother oil and grease fires in the kitchen with baking soda or salt, or put a lid over the flame if it is burning in a pan. Do not attempt to take the pan outside.

4. If your clothes catch on fire, stop, drop, and roll until the fire is extinguished. Running only makes the fire burn faster.

5. If you are escaping through a closed door, use the back of your hand to feel the top of the door, the doorknob, and the crack between the door and door frame before you open it. Never use the palm of your hand or fingers to test for heat—burning those areas could impair your ability to escape a fire (such as using ladders and crawling).

- If the door is cool, open slowly and ensure fire and/or smoke is not blocking your escape route. If your escape route is blocked, shut the door immediately and use an alternate escape route, such as a window. If clear, leave immediately through the door. Be prepared to crawl; smoke and heat rise. The air is clearer and cooler near the floor. If the door is warm or hot, do not open. Escape through a window. If you cannot escape, hang a white or light-colored sheet outside the window, alerting firefighters to your presence.

6. If you must exit through smoke, crawl low under the smoke to your exit—heavy smoke and poisonous gases collect first along the ceiling.

7. Close doors behind you as you escape to delay the spread of the fire.

8. Once you are safely out, stay out. Call 911.

What to do after a fire

1. Give first aid where needed. After calling 911 or your local emergency number, cool and cover burns to reduce chance of further injury or infection.

2. Do not enter a fire-damaged building unless authorities say it is okay.

3. If you must enter a fire-damaged building, be alert for heat and smoke. If you detect either, evacuate immediately.

4. Have an electrician check your household wiring before the current is turned on.

5. Do not attempt to reconnect any utilities yourself. Leave this to the fire department and other authorities.

6. Beware of structural damage. Roofs and floors may be weakened and need repair.

7. Contact your local disaster relief service, such as the American Red Cross or Salvation Army, if you need housing, food, or a place to stay.

8. Call your insurance agent.
- Make a list of damage and losses. Pictures are helpful.
- Keep records of cleanup and repair costs.

Receipts are important for both insurance and income tax claims.

- Do not throw away any damaged goods until an official inventory has been taken. Your insurance company takes all damages into consideration.

9. If you are a tenant, contact the landlord. It's the property owner's responsibility to prevent further loss or damage to the site.

10. Secure personal belongings or move them to another location.

11. Discard food, beverages, and medicines that have been exposed to heat, smoke, or soot. Refrigerators and freezers left closed hold their temperature for a short time. Do not attempt to refreeze food that has thawed.

12. If you have a safe or strongbox, do not try to open it. It can hold intense heat for several hours. If the door is opened before the box has cooled, the contents could burst into flames.

13. If a building inspector says the building is unsafe and you must leave your home:

- Ask local police to watch the property during your absence.
- Pack identification, medicines, glasses, jewelry, credit cards, checkbooks, insurance policies, and financial records if you can reach them safely.
- Notify friends, relatives, police and fire departments, your insurance agent, the mortgage company, utility companies, delivery services, employers, schools, and the post office of your whereabouts.

Wildland Fires

If you live on a remote hillside or in a valley, prairie, or forest where flammable vegetation is abundant, your residence could be vulnerable to wildland fire. These fires are usually triggered by lightning or accidents.

1. Fire facts about rural living:

- Once a fire starts outdoors in a rural area, it is often hard to control. Wildland firefighters are trained to protect natural resources, not homes and buildings.
- Many homes are located far from fire stations. The result is longer emergency response times. Within a matter of minutes, an entire home may be destroyed by fire.
- Limited water supply in rural areas can make fire suppression difficult.
- Homes may be secluded and surrounded by woods, dense brush, and combustible vegetation that fuel fires.

2. Ask fire authorities for information about wildland fires in your area. Request that they inspect your residence and property for hazards.

3. Be prepared and have a fire safety and evacuation plan:

- Practice fire escape and evacuation plans.
- Mark the entrance to your property with address signs that are clearly visible from the road.
- Know which local emergency services are available and have those numbers posted near telephones.
- Provide emergency vehicle access through roads and driveways at least twelve feet wide with adequate turn-around space.

4. Tips for making your property fire resistant:

- Keep lawns trimmed, leaves raked, and the roof and rain gutters free from debris such as dead limbs and leaves.
- Stack firewood at least thirty feet away from your home.
- Store flammable materials, liquids and solvents in metal containers outside the home at least thirty feet away from structures and wooden fences.
- Create defensible space by thinning trees and brush within thirty feet around your home. Beyond thirty feet, remove dead wood, debris, and low tree branches.
- Landscape your property with fire-resistant plants and vegetation to prevent fire from spreading quickly. For example, hardwood trees are more fire-resistant than pine, evergreen, eucalyptus, or fir trees.
- Make sure water sources, such as hydrants, ponds, swimming pools, and wells, are accessible to the fire department.

5. Protect your home:
- Use fire-resistant, protective roofing and materials like stone, brick, and metal to protect your home. Avoid using wood materials. They offer the least fire protection.
- Cover all exterior vents, attics, and eaves with metal mesh screens no larger than six millimeters or one-quarter inch to prevent debris from collecting and to help keep sparks out.
- Install multipaned windows, tempered safety glass or fireproof shutters to protect large windows from radiant heat.
- Use fire-resistant draperies for added window protection.
- Have chimneys, woodstoves, and all home heating systems inspected and cleaned annually by a certified specialist.
- Insulate chimneys and place spark arresters on top. Chimney should be at least three feet above the roof.
- Remove branches hanging above and around the chimney.

6. Follow local burning laws:
- Do not burn trash or other debris without proper knowledge of local burning laws, techniques, and the safest times of day and year to burn.
- Before burning debris in a wooded area, make sure you notify local authorities and obtain a burning permit.
- Use an approved incinerator with a safety lid or covering with holes no larger than three-quarters of an inch.
- Create at least a ten-foot clearing around the incinerator before burning debris.
- Have a fire extinguisher or garden hose on hand when burning debris.

7. If wildfire threatens your home and time permits, consider the following:

Inside
- Shut off gas at the meter. Turn off pilot lights.
- Open fireplace damper. Close fireplace screens.
- Close windows, vents, doors, blinds or noncombustible window coverings, and heavy drapes. Remove flammable drapes and curtains.
- Move flammable furniture into the center of the home, away from windows and sliding glass doors.
- Close all interior doors and windows to prevent drafts.
- Place valuables that will not be damaged by water in a pool or pond.
- Gather pets into one room. Make plans to care for your pets if you must evacuate.
- Back your car into the garage or park it in an open space facing the direction of escape. Shut doors and roll up windows. Leave the key in the ignition and the car doors unlocked. Close garage windows and doors but leave them unlocked. Disconnect automatic garage door openers.

Outside
- Seal attic and ground vents with precut plywood or commercial seals.
- Turn off propane tanks.
- Place combustible patio furniture inside.
- Connect garden hose to outside taps. Place lawn sprinklers on the roof and near above-ground fuel tanks. Wet the roof.
- Wet or remove shrubs within fifteen feet of the home.
- Gather fire tools such as a rake, ax, handsaw or chainsaw, bucket, and shovel.

If advised to evacuate, do so immediately. Choose a route away from the fire hazard. Watch for changes in the speed and direction of fire and smoke.

FLOODS

Floods are one of the most common hazards in the United States. However, all floods are not alike. Riverine floods develop slowly, sometimes over a period of days. Flash floods can develop quickly, sometimes in just a few minutes, without any visible signs of rain. Flash floods often have a dangerous wall of roaring water that carries a deadly cargo of rocks, mud, and other debris, and can sweep away most things in its path. Overland flooding occurs outside a defined river or stream, such as when a levee is breached, but still can be destructive. Flooding can also occur from a dam break, producing effects similar to flash floods.

Flood effects can be very local, impacting a neighborhood or community, or very large, affecting entire river basins and multiple states.

Be aware of flood hazards no matter where you live, but especially if you live in a low-lying area, near water, or downstream from a dam. Even very small streams, gullies, creeks, culverts, dry streambeds, or low-lying ground that appear harmless in dry weather can flood. Every state is at risk from this hazard.

What to do before a flood

1. Know the terms used to describe flooding:
    - **Flood Watch**—Flooding is possible. Stay tuned to NOAA Weather Radio or commercial radio or television for information. Watches are issued twelve to thirty-six hours in advance of a possible flooding event.
    - **Flash Flood Watch**—Flash flooding is possible. Be prepared to move to higher ground. A flash flood could occur without any warning. Listen to NOAA Weather Radio or commercial radio or television for additional information.
    - **Flood Warning**—Flooding is occurring or will occur soon. If advised to evacuate, do so immediately.
    - **Flash Flood Warning**—A flash flood is occurring. Seek higher ground on foot immediately.
2. Ask local officials whether your property is in a flood-prone or high-risk area. (Remember that floods often occur outside high-risk areas.) Ask about official flood warning signals and what to do when you hear them. Also ask how you can protect your home from flooding.
3. Identify dams in your area and determine whether they pose a hazard to you.
4. Purchase a NOAA Weather Radio with battery backup and a tone alert feature that automatically alerts you when a watch or warning is issued (tone alert not available in some areas). Purchase a battery-powered commercial radio and extra batteries.
5. Be prepared to evacuate. Learn your community's flood evacuation routes and where to find high ground.

6. Talk to your household about flooding. Plan a place to meet in case you are separated from one another in a disaster and cannot return home. Choose an out-of-town contact for everyone to call to say they are okay. In some emergencies, calling out-of-state is possible even when local phone lines are down.

7. Determine how you would care for household members who may live elsewhere but might need your help in a flood. Determine any special needs your neighbors might have.

8. Prepare to survive on your own for at least three days. Assemble a disaster supply kit. Keep a stock of food and extra drinking water.

9. Know how to shut off electricity, gas, and water at main switches and valves. Know where gas pilot lights are located and how the heating system works.

10. Consider purchasing flood insurance.
    - Flood losses are not covered under homeowner's insurance policies. Keep supplies on hand for an emergency. Remember a battery-operated NOAA Weather Radio with a tone alert feature and extra batteries.
    - FEMA manages the National Flood Insurance Program, which makes federally-backed flood insurance available in communities that agree to adopt and enforce floodplain management ordinances to reduce future flood damage.
    - Flood insurance is available in most communities through insurance agents.
    - There is a thirty-day waiting period before flood insurance goes into effect, so don't delay.
    - Flood insurance is available whether the building is in or out of the identified flood-prone area. Consider options for protecting your property.
    - Make a record of your personal property. Take photographs or videotapes of your belongings. Store these documents in a safe place.
    - Keep insurance policies, deeds, property records, and other important papers in a safe place away from your home.
    - Avoid building on a floodplain unless you elevate and reinforce your home.

- Elevate furnace, water heater, and electric panel to higher floors or the attic if they are susceptible to flooding.
- Install check valves in sewer traps to prevent floodwater from backing up into the drains of your home.
- Construct barriers such as levees, berms, and floodwalls to stop floodwater from entering the building.
- Seal walls in basements with waterproofing compounds to avoid seepage.
- Call your local building department or emergency management office for more information.

What to do during a flood

1. Be aware of flash flood. If there is any possibility of a flash flood, move immediately to higher ground. Do not wait for instructions to move.

2. Listen to radio or television stations for local information.

3. Be aware of streams, drainage channels, canyons, and other areas known to flood suddenly. Flash floods can occur in these areas with or without such typical warning signs as rain clouds or heavy rain.

4. If local authorities issue a flood watch, prepare to evacuate:

- Secure your home. If you have time, tie down or bring outdoor equipment and lawn furniture inside. Move essential items to the upper floors.
- If instructed, turn off utilities at the main switches or valves. Disconnect electrical appliances. Do not touch electrical equipment if you are wet or standing in water.
- Fill the bathtub with water in case water becomes contaminated or services cut off. Before filling the tub, sterilize it with a diluted bleach solution.

5. Do not walk through moving water. Six inches of moving water can knock you off your feet. If you must walk in a flooded area, walk where the water is not moving. Use a stick to check the firmness of the ground in front of you.

6. Do not drive into flooded areas. Six inches of water will reach the bottom of most passenger cars, causing loss of control and possible stalling. A foot of water will float many vehicles. Two feet of water will wash away almost all vehicles. If floodwaters rise around your car, abandon the car and move to higher ground, if you can do so safely. You and your vehicle can be quickly swept away as floodwaters rise.

What to do after a flood

1. Avoid floodwaters. The water may be contaminated by oil, gasoline, or raw sewage. The water may also be electrically charged from underground or downed power lines.

2. Avoid moving water. Moving water only six inches deep can sweep you off your feet.

3. Be aware of areas where floodwaters have receded. Roads may have weakened and could collapse under the weight of a car.

4. Stay away from downed power lines and report them to the power company.

5. Stay away from designated disaster areas unless authorities ask for volunteers.

6. Return home only when authorities indicate it is safe. Stay out of buildings if surrounded by floodwaters. Use extreme caution when entering buildings. There may be hidden damage, particularly in foundations.

7. Consider your family's health and safety needs:

- Wash hands frequently with soap and clean water if you come in contact with floodwaters.
- Throw away food that has come in contact with floodwaters.
- Listen for news reports to learn whether the community's water supply is safe to drink.
- Listen to news reports for information about where to get assistance for housing, clothing, and food.
- Seek necessary medical care at the nearest medical facility.

8. Service damaged septic tanks, cesspools, pits, and leaching systems as soon as possible. Damaged sewage systems are serious health hazards.

9. Contact your insurance agent. If your policy covers your situation, an adjuster will be assigned to visit your home. To prepare:

- Take photos of your belongings and your home or videotape them.

- Separate damaged and undamaged belongings.
- Locate your financial records.
- Keep detailed records of cleanup costs.

10. If your residence has been flooded, obtain a copy of "Repairing Your Flooded Home" from the local American Red Cross chapter.

HURRICANES

A hurricane is a type of tropical cyclone, the generic term for a low pressure system that generally forms in the tropics. The ingredients for a hurricane include a preexisting weather disturbance, warm tropical oceans, moisture, and relatively light winds aloft. A typical cyclone is accompanied by thunderstorms, and in the Northern Hemisphere, a counterclockwise circulation of winds near the earth's surface.

All Atlantic and Gulf of Mexico coastal areas are subject to hurricanes or tropical storms. Although rarely struck by hurricanes, parts of the southwest United States and the Pacific Coast experience heavy rains and floods each year from hurricanes spawned off Mexico. The Atlantic hurricane season lasts from June to November, with the peak season from mid-August to late October.

Hurricanes can cause catastrophic damage to coastlines and several hundred miles inland. Winds can exceed 155 miles per hour. Hurricanes and tropical storms can also spawn tornadoes and microbursts, create surges along the coast, and cause extensive damage due to inland flooding from trapped water.

Tornadoes most often occur in thunderstorms embedded in rain bands well away from the center of the hurricane; however, they also occur near the eye wall. Typically, tornadoes produced by tropical cyclones are relatively weak and short-lived but still pose a threat.

A storm surge is a huge dome of water pushed on-shore by hurricane and tropical storm winds. Storm surges can reach twenty-five feet high and be fifty to one hundred miles wide. Storm tide is a combination of the storm surge and the normal tide (a fifteen-foot storm surge combined with a two-foot normal high tide over the mean sea level creates a seventeen-foot storm tide). These phenomena cause severe erosion and extensive damage to coastal areas.

Despite improved warnings and a decrease in the loss of life, property damage continues to rise because an increasing number of people are living or vacationing near coastlines. Those in hurricane-prone areas need to be prepared for hurricanes and tropical storms.

Hurricanes are classified into five categories based on their wind speed, central pressure, and damage potential. Category Three and higher are considered major hurricanes, though Category One and Two are still extremely dangerous and warrant your full attention.

Inland/freshwater flooding from hurricanes

Hurricanes can produce widespread torrential rains. Floods are the deadly and destructive result. Excessive rain can also trigger landslides or mud slides, especially in mountainous regions. Flash flooding can occur due to the intense rainfall. Flooding on rivers and streams may persist for several days or more after the storm.

The speed of the storm and the geography beneath the storm are the primary factors regarding the amount of rain produced. Slow-moving storms and tropical storms moving into mountainous regions tend to produce more rain.

Between 1970 and 1999 more people lost their lives from freshwater flooding associated with land-falling tropical cyclones than from any other weather hazard related to tropical cyclones.

What to do before a hurricane

1. Learn the terms used by weather forecasters:
   - **Tropical Depression**—An organized system of clouds and thunderstorms with a defined surface circulation and maximum sustained winds of thirty-eight miles per hour (thirty-three knots) or less. Sustained winds are defined as one-minute average wind measured at about thirty-three feet (ten meters) above the surface.
   - **Tropical Storm**—An organized system of strong thunderstorms with a defined surface circulation and maximum sustained winds of thirty-nine to seventy-three miles per hour (thirty-four to sixty-three knots).
   - **Hurricane**—An intense tropical weather system of strong thunderstorms with

Saffir-Simpson Hurricane Scale			
Scale Number (Category)	Sustained Winds (MPH)	Damage	Storm Surge
1	74–95	Minimal: Unanchored mobile homes, vegetation, and signs.	4–5 feet
2	96–110	Moderate: All mobile homes, roofs, small crafts, flooding.	6–8 feet
3	111–130	Extensive: Small buildings, low-lying roads cut off.	9–12 feet
4	131–155	Extreme: Roofs destroyed, trees down, roads cut off, mobile homes destroyed. Beach homes flooded.	13–18 feet
5	155>	Catastrophic: Most buildings destroyed. Vegetation destroyed. Major roads cut off. Homes flooded.	>18 feet

a well-defined surface circulation and maximum sustained winds of seventy-four miles per hour (sixty-four knots) or higher.

- **Storm Surge**—A dome of water pushed on shore by hurricane and tropical storm winds.
- **Storm Tide**—A combination of storm surge and the normal tide (a fifteen-foot storm surge combined with a two-foot normal tide over the mean sea level creates a seventeen-foot storm tide.)

2. Know the difference between Watches and Warnings.

- **Hurricane/Tropical Storm Watch**—Hurricane/tropical storm conditions are possible in the specified area, usually within thirty-six hours.

- **Hurricane/Tropical Storm Warning**—Hurricane/tropical storm conditions are expected in the specified area, usually within twenty-four hours.
- **Short-Term Watches and Warnings**—These warnings provide detailed information on specific hurricane threats, such as flash floods and tornadoes.

3. Listen for local radio or television weather forecasts. Purchase a NOAA Weather Radio with battery backup and a tone alert feature that automatically alerts you when a watch or warning is issued (tone alert is not available in some areas). Purchase a battery-powered commercial radio and extra batteries as well because information on other events will be broadcast by the media.

4. Ask your local emergency management office about community evacuation plans relating to your

neighborhood. Learn evacuation routes. Determine where you would go and how you would get there if you needed to evacuate. Sometimes alternate routes are desirable.

5. Talk to your household about hurricane issues. Create a household disaster plan. Plan to meet at a place away from your residence in case you are separated. Choose an out-of-town contact for everyone to call to say they are safe.

6. Determine the needs of your household members who may live elsewhere but need your help in a hurricane. Consider the special needs of neighbors, such as people that are disabled or those with limited sight or vision problems.

7. Prepare to survive on your own for at least three days. Assemble a disaster supplies kit. Keep a stock of food and extra drinking water. See Section Five for more information.

8. Make plans to secure your property. Permanent storm shutters offer the best protection for windows. A second option is to board up windows with five-eighths-inch marine plywood, cut to fit and ready to install. Tape does not prevent windows from breaking.

9. Learn how to shut off utilities and where gas and water shutoffs are located. Do not actually shut off the gas for practice, to see how it works, or to show others. Only the gas company can safely turn it back on.

10. Have your home inspected for compliance with local building codes. Many of the roofs destroyed by hurricanes were not constructed or retrofitted according to building codes. Installing straps or additional clips to securely fasten your roof to the frame structure will substantially reduce roof damage.

11. Be sure trees and shrubs around your home are well trimmed. Dead limbs or trees could cause personal injury or property damage. Clear loose and clogged rain gutters and downspouts.

12. If you have a boat, determine where to secure it in an emergency.

13. Consider flood insurance. Purchase insurance well in advance—there is a thirty-day waiting period before flood insurance takes effect.

14. Make a record of your personal property. Take photographs or videotapes of the exterior and interior of your home, including personal belongings. Store these documents in a safe place, such as a safe-deposit box.

What to do during a hurricane threat

1. Listen to radio or television newscasts. If a hurricane watch is issued, you typically have twenty-four to thirty-six hours before the hurricane hits land.

2. Talk with household members. Make sure everyone knows where to meet and who to call in case you are separated. Consider the needs of relatives and neighbors with special needs.

3. Secure your home. Close storm shutters. Secure outdoor objects or bring them indoors. Moor your boat if time permits.

4. Gather several days' supply of water and food for each household member. Water systems may become contaminated or damaged. After sterilizing the bathtub and other containers with a diluted bleach solution of one part bleach to ten parts water, fill them with water to ensure a safe supply in case you are unable or told not to evacuate. Refer to Section Four for important information.

5. If you are evacuating, take your disaster supplies kit with you to the shelter. Remember that alcoholic beverages and weapons are prohibited within shelters. Also, pets are not allowed in a public shelter due to health reasons.

6. Prepare to evacuate. See Chapter 46, Guidelines to an Emergency Evacuation.

7. Evacuate to an inland location if:
- Local authorities announce an evacuation and you live in an evacuation zone.
- You live in a mobile home or temporary structure—they are particularly hazardous during hurricanes, no matter how well fastened to the ground.
- You live in a high-rise. Hurricane winds are stronger at higher elevations.
- You live on the coast, on a floodplain, or near a river or inland waterway.
- You feel you are in danger.

8. When authorities order an evacuation:
- Leave immediately.
- Follow evacuation routes announced by local officials.
- Stay away from coastal areas, riverbanks, and streams.
- Tell others where you are going.

9. If you are not required or are unable to evacuate, stay indoors during the hurricane and away from

windows and glass doors. Keep curtains and blinds closed. Do not be fooled if there is a lull: it could be the eye of the storm—the winds will pick up again.

- If not instructed to turn off, turn the refrigerator to its coldest setting and keep it closed.
- Turn off propane tanks.

10. In strong winds, follow these rules:

- Take refuge in a small interior room, closet, or hallway.
- Close all interior doors. Secure and brace external doors.
- In a two-story residence, go to an interior first-floor room, such as a bathroom or closet.
- In a multiple-story building, go to the first or second floors and stay in interior rooms away from windows.
- Lie on the floor under a table or other sturdy object.

11. Avoid using the phone except for serious emergencies. Local authorities need first priority on telephone lines.

What to do after a hurricane

1. Stay where you are if you are in a safe location until local authorities say it is safe to leave. If they evacuated the community, do not return to the area until authorities say it is safe to return.

2. Stay tuned to local radio or television stations for information about caring for your household, where to find medical help, how to apply for financial assistance, and so on.

3. Drive only when necessary. Streets will be filled with debris. Roads will have weakened and could collapse. Do not drive on flooded or barricaded roads or bridges. Roads are closed for your protection. As little as six inches of water may cause you to lose control of your vehicle—two feet of water will carry most cars away.

4. Do not drink or prepare food with tap water until notified by officials that it is safe to do so.

5. Consider your family's health and safety needs. Be aware of symptoms of stress and fatigue. Keep your household together and seek crisis counseling if you have need. See the "Mental Health and Crisis Counseling" section of the "Recovering from Disaster" chapter for more information.

6. Talk with your children about what has happened and how they can help during the recovery. Being involved will help them deal with the situation. Consider the needs of your neighbors. People often become isolated during hurricanes.

7. Stay away from disaster areas unless local authorities request volunteers. If you are needed, bring your own drinking water, food, and sleeping gear.

8. Stay away from riverbanks and streams until potential flooding has passed. Do not allow children to play in flooded areas. There is a high risk of injury or drowning in areas that may appear safe.

9. Stay away from moving water. Moving water only six inches deep can sweep you off your feet. Standing water may be electrically charged from underground or downed power lines.

10. Stay away from downed power lines and report them to the power company. Report broken gas, sewer or water mains to local officials.

11. Don't use candles or other open flames indoors. Use a flashlight to inspect damage.

12. Set up a manageable schedule to repair property.

13. Contact your insurance agent. An adjuster will be assigned to visit your home. To prepare:

- Take photos or videotapes of your damaged property.
- Separate damaged and undamaged belongings.
- Locate your financial records.
- Keep detailed records of cleanup costs.

14. Consider building a safe room or shelter to protect your household.

LANDSLIDES AND DEBRIS FLOWS (MUD SLIDES)

Landslides occur in all U.S. states and territories and occur when masses of rock, earth, or debris move down a slope. Landslides may be small or large and can move at slow or very high speeds. They are activated by rainstorms, earthquakes, volcanic eruptions, fires, and by human modification of the land.

Debris flows and mudflows are rivers of rock, earth, and other debris saturated with water. They develop when water rapidly accumulates in the ground, during heavy rainfall or rapid snowmelt, changing the earth into a flowing river of mud, or "slurry." They can flow rapidly down slopes or through channels and can strike with little or no warning at avalanche speeds. They can also travel several miles from their source, growing in size as they pick up trees, large boulders, cars, and other materials along the way.

Landslide, mudflow, and debris-flow problems are occasionally caused by land mismanagement. Improper land use practices on ground of questionable stability, particularly in mountain, canyon, and coastal regions, can create and accelerate serious landslide problems. Land use zoning, professional inspections, and proper design can minimize many landslide, mudflow, and debris flow problems.

What to do before a landslide or debris flow

1. Contact your local emergency management office or American Red Cross chapter for information on local landslide and debris flow hazards.

2. Get a ground assessment of your property.

   - County or state geological experts, local planning department, or departments of natural resources may have specific information on areas vulnerable to landslides. Consult an appropriate professional expert for advice on corrective measures you can take.

3. Minimize home hazards by having flexible pipe fittings installed to avoid gas or water leaks. Flexible fittings are more resistant to breakage. Only the gas company or professionals should install gas fittings.

4. Familiarize yourself with your surrounding area.

   - Small changes in your local landscape could alert you to the potential of greater future threat.
   - Observe the patterns of storm water drainage on slopes and especially the places where runoff water converges.
   - Watch for any sign of land movement, such as small slides, flows, or progressively leaning trees, on the hillsides near your home.

5. Be particularly observant of your surrounding area before and during intense storms that could heighten the possibility of landslides or debris flows. Many debris flow fatalities occur when people are sleeping.

6. Talk to your insurance agent. Debris flow may be covered by flood insurance policies from the National Flood Insurance Program (NFIP).

7. Learn to recognize landslide warning signs.

   - Doors or windows stick or jam for the first time.
   - New cracks appear in plaster, tile, brick, or foundations.
   - Outside walls, walks, or stairs begin pulling away from the building.
   - Slowly developing, widening cracks appear in the ground or on paved areas, such as streets or driveways.
   - Underground utility lines break.
   - Bulging ground appears at the base of a slope.
   - Water breaks through the ground surface in new locations.
   - Fences, retaining walls, utility poles, or trees tilt or move.
   - The ground slopes downward in one specific direction and may begin shifting in that direction under your feet.

What to do during a heightened threat of landslide or debris flow (such as an intense storm)

1. Listen to radio or television for warning of intense rainfall.

   - Be prepared to evacuate if instructed by local authorities or if you feel threatened.
   - Should you remain at home, move to a second story if possible to distance yourself from the direct path of debris flow and landslide debris.

2. Be alert when intense, short bursts of rain follow prolonged heavy rains or damp weather, which increase risks of debris flows.

3. Listen for any unusual sounds that might indicate moving debris, such as trees cracking or boulders knocking together. A trickle of flowing or falling mud or debris may precede larger landslides. Moving debris can flow quickly and sometimes without warning. You may hear a faint rumbling sound that increases in volume as a landslide nears.

4. If you are near a stream or channel, be alert for sudden increases or decreases in water flow and for a

change from clear to muddy water. Such changes may indicate landslide activity upstream. Be prepared to move quickly.

5. Be especially alert when driving. Embankments along roadsides are particularly susceptible to landslides. Watch for collapsed pavement, mud, fallen rocks, and other indications of possible debris flows.

6. Evacuate when ordered by local authorities or if you feel the need.

What to do during a landslide or debris flow

1. Quickly move away from the path of a landslide or debris flow.

2. Areas generally considered safe include:
- Areas that have not moved in the past.
- Relatively flat-lying areas away from drastic changes in slope.
- Areas at the top of or along ridges set back from the tops of slopes.

3. If escape is not possible, curl into a tight ball and protect your head.

What to do after a landslide or debris flow

1. Stay away from the slide area. There may be danger of additional slides.

2. Check for injured and trapped persons near the slide, without entering the direct slide area. Direct rescuers to their locations.

3. Help a neighbor who may require special assistance—large families, children, elderly people, and people with disabilities.

4. Listen to local radio or television stations for the latest emergency information.

5. Landslides and debris flows can provoke associated dangers, such as broken electrical, water, gas, and sewage lines, and disrupt roadways and railways.
- Look for and report broken utility lines to appropriate authorities. Reporting potential hazards will get the utilities turned off as quickly as possible, preventing further hazard and injury.
- If you smell gas or hear hissing, do not enter a building to turn off utilities. If you can turn the gas off outside the building at the meter, do so. However,

only the gas company or other qualified professionals can turn the gas back on.
- Check the building foundation, chimney, and surrounding land for damage. Damage to foundations, chimneys, or surrounding land may help you assess the safety of the area.

6. Watch for flooding, which may occur after a landslide or debris flow. Floods sometimes follow landslides and debris flows because they may both be started by the same event.

7. Replant damaged ground as soon as possible, since erosion caused by loss of ground cover can lead to flash flooding and additional landslides in the near future.

8. Seek the advice of a geotechnical expert for evaluating landslide hazards or designing corrective techniques to reduce landslide risk. A professional will be able to advise you of the best ways to prevent or reduce landslide risk without creating further hazard.

THUNDERSTORMS

Thunderstorms are very common and affect great numbers of people each year. Despite their small size in comparison to hurricanes and winter storms, all thunderstorms are dangerous. Every thunderstorm produces lightning. Other associated dangers of thunderstorms include tornadoes, strong winds, hail, and flash flooding. Flash flooding is responsible for more fatalities—more than 140 annually—than any other thunderstorm-associated hazard.

Some thunderstorms do not produce rain that reaches the ground. These are generically referred to as dry thunderstorms and are most prevalent in the western United States. Known to spawn wildfires, these storms occur when there is a large layer of dry air between the base of the cloud and the ground. The falling raindrops evaporate but lightning can still reach the ground.

What to do before thunderstorms approach

1. Know the terms used by weather forecasters:
- **Severe Thunderstorm Watch**—Tells you when and where severe thunderstorms are likely to occur. Watch the sky and stay tuned to radio or television to know when warnings are issued.

- **Severe Thunderstorm Warning**—Issued when severe weather has been reported by spotters or indicated by radar. Warnings indicate imminent danger to life and property to those in the path of the storm.

2. Know thunderstorm facts:
- Thunderstorms may occur singly, in clusters, or in lines.
- Some of the most severe weather occurs when a single thunderstorm affects one location for an extended time.
- Thunderstorms typically produce heavy rain for a brief period, anywhere from thirty minutes to an hour.
- Warm, humid conditions are favorable for thunderstorm development.
- A typical thunderstorm is fifteen miles in diameter and lasts an average of thirty minutes.
- Of the estimated 100,000 thunderstorms each year in the United States, about ten percent are classified as severe.
- A thunderstorm is classified as severe if it produces hail at least three-quarters of an inch in diameter, has winds of fifty-eight miles per hour or higher, or produces a tornado.

3. Know the calculation to determine how close you are to a thunderstorm:
- Count the number of seconds between a flash of lightning and the next clap of thunder. Divide this number by five to determine the distance to the lightning in miles.

4. Remove dead or rotting trees and branches that could fall and cause injury or damage during a severe thunderstorm.

5. When a thunderstorm approaches, secure outdoor objects that could blow away or cause damage. Shutter windows, if possible, and secure outside doors. If shutters are not available, close window blinds, shades, or curtains.

LIGHTNING

The ingredient that defines a thunderstorm is lightning. Since lightning creates thunder, a storm producing lightning is called a thunderstorm. Lightning occurs during all thunderstorms.

Lightning results from the buildup and discharge of electrical energy between positively and negatively charged areas.

The unpredictability of lightning increases the risk to individuals and property. In the United States, an average of 300 people are injured and eighty people are killed each year by lightning. Although most lightning victims survive, people struck by lightning often report a variety of long-term, debilitating symptoms, including memory loss, attention deficits, sleep disorders, numbness, dizziness, stiffness in joints, irritability, fatigue, weakness, muscle spasms, depression, and an inability to sit for a long period of time.

When thunderstorms threaten your area, get inside a home, building, or hard-top automobile (not a convertible) and stay away from metallic objects and fixtures.

1. If you are inside a home:
- Avoid showering or bathing. Plumbing and bathroom fixtures can conduct electricity.
- Avoid using a corded telephone, except for emergencies. Cordless and cellular telephones are safe to use.
- Unplug appliances and other electrical items such as computers and turn off air conditioners. Power surges from lightning can cause serious damage.
- Use your battery-operated NOAA Weather Radio for updates from local officials.

2. If outside, with no time to reach a safe location, follow these recommendations:
- In a forest, seek shelter in a low area under a thick growth of small trees.
- In open areas, go to a low place such as a ravine or valley. Be alert for flash floods.
- Do not stand under a natural lightning rod such as a tall, isolated tree in an open area.
- Do not stand on a hilltop, in an open field, on the beach, or in a boat on the water.
- Avoid isolated sheds or other small structures in open areas.
- Get away from open water. If you are boating or swimming, get to land and find shelter immediately.

- Get away from anything metal—tractors, farm equipment, motorcycles, golf carts, golf clubs, and bicycles.
- Stay away from wire fences, clotheslines, metal pipes, rails, and other metallic paths that could carry lightning to you from some distance away.
- If you feel your hair stand on end (which indicates that lightning is about to strike), squat low to the ground on the balls of your feet. Place your hands over your ears and your head between your knees. Make yourself the smallest target possible and minimize your contact with the ground. *Do not* lie flat on the ground.

3. Remember the following facts and safety tips about lightning.

Facts:

- Lightning often strikes outside of heavy rain and may occur as far as ten miles away from any rainfall.
- Lightning-strike victims carry no electrical charge and should be attended to immediately. If breathing has stopped, begin mouth-to-mouth resuscitation. If the heart has stopped, a trained person should administer CPR. If the victim has a pulse and is breathing, look for other possible injuries. Check for burns where the lightning entered and left the body. Be alert also for nervous system damage, broken bones, and loss of hearing or eyesight. Contact your local emergency management office or American Red Cross chapter for information on CPR and first aid classes.
- Heat lightning is actually lightning from a thunderstorm too far away for thunder to be heard. However, the storm may be moving in your direction!
- Most lightning deaths and injuries occur when people are caught outdoors in the summer months during the afternoon and evening.
- Many fires in the western United States and Alaska are started by lightning.

- Lightning can occur from cloud-to-cloud, within a cloud, cloud-to-ground, or cloud-to-air.
- Your chances of being struck by lightning are estimated to be one in 600,000 but could be made even less by following safety tips.

Safety Tips:

- Postpone outdoor activities if thunderstorms are likely.
- Remember the 30/30 lightning safety rule—Go indoors if, after seeing lighting, you cannot count to thirty before hearing thunder. Stay indoors for thirty minutes after hearing the last clap of thunder.
- Rubber-soled shoes and rubber tires provide *no* protection from lightning. However, the steel frame of a hard-topped vehicle provides increased protection if you are not touching metal. Although you may be injured if lightning strikes your car, you are much safer inside a vehicle than outside.

TORNADOES

Tornadoes are nature's most violent storms. Spawned from powerful thunderstorms, tornadoes can uproot trees, destroy buildings, and turn harmless objects into deadly missiles. They can devastate a neighborhood in seconds.

A tornado appears as a rotating, funnel-shaped cloud that extends to the ground, with whirling winds that can reach three-hundred miles per hour. Damage paths can be in excess of one mile wide and fifty miles long. Every state is at some risk from this hazard.

Tornado facts:

1. A tornado is a violently rotating column of air extending from a thunderstorm to the ground.

2. Tornadoes are capable of destroying homes and vehicles and can cause fatalities.

3. Tornadoes may strike quickly, with little or no warning.

4. Tornadoes may appear nearly transparent until dust and debris are picked up or a cloud forms in

the funnel. The average tornado moves southwest to northeast, but tornadoes have been known to move in any direction.

5. The average forward speed is thirty miles per hour but may vary from stationary to seventy miles per hour, with rotating winds that can reach three hundred miles per hour.

6. Tornadoes can accompany tropical storms and hurricanes as they move onto land.

7. Waterspouts are tornadoes that form over water.

8. Tornadoes are most frequently reported east of the Rocky Mountains during spring and summer months but they can occur in any state at any time of year.

9. In the southern states, peak tornado season is March through May, while peak months in the northern states are during the late spring and early summer.

10. Tornadoes are most likely to occur between 3 P.M. and 9 P.M. but can occur at any time of the day or night.

What to do before tornadoes threaten

1. Know the terms used to describe tornado threats:

- **Tornado Watch**—Tornadoes are possible. Remain alert for approaching storms. Watch the sky and stay tuned to radio or television to know when warnings are issued.
- **Tornado Warning**—A tornado has been sighted or indicated by weather radar. Take shelter immediately.

2. Ask your local emergency management office or American Red Cross chapter about the tornado threat in your area. Ask about community warning signals.

3. Purchase a NOAA Weather Radio with a battery backup and tone alert feature that automatically alerts you when a watch or warning is issued (tone alert not available in some areas). Purchase a battery-powered commercial radio and extra batteries as well.

4. Know the county or parish in which you live. Counties and parishes are used in watches and warnings to identify the location of tornadoes.

5. Determine places to seek shelter, such as a basement or storm cellar. If an underground shelter is not available, identify an interior room or hallway on the lowest floor.

6. Practice going to your shelter with your household.

7. Know the locations of designated shelters in places where you and your household spend time, such as public buildings, nursing homes, and shopping centers. Ask local officials whether a registered engineer or architect has inspected your children's schools for shelter space.

8. Ask your local emergency manager or American Red Cross chapter if there are any public safe rooms or shelters nearby.

9. Assemble a disaster supplies kit. Keep a stock of food and extra drinking water.

10. Make a record of your personal property. Take photographs or videotapes of the exterior and interior of your home, including personal belongings. Store these documents in a safe place, such as a safe-deposit box.

What to do during a tornado watch

1. Listen to NOAA Weather Radio or to commercial radio or television newscasts for the latest information.

2. Be alert for approaching storms. If you see any revolving funnel-shaped clouds, report them immediately by telephone to your local police department or sheriff's office.

3. Watch for tornado danger signs:
- Dark, often greenish sky
- Large hail
- A large, dark, low-lying cloud (particularly if rotating)
- Loud roar, similar to a freight train

Caution:
- Some tornadoes are clearly visible, while rain or nearby low-hanging clouds obscure others.
- Occasionally, tornadoes develop so rapidly that little, if any, advance warning is possible.
- Before a tornado hits, the wind may die down and the air may become very still.
- A cloud of debris can mark the location of a tornado even if a funnel is not visible.

- Tornadoes generally occur near the trailing edge of a thunderstorm. It is not uncommon to see clear, sunlit skies behind a tornado.

4. Avoid places with wide-span roofs such as auditoriums, cafeterias, large hallways, supermarkets, or shopping malls.

5. Be prepared to take shelter immediately. Gather household members and pets. Assemble supplies to take to the shelter such as flashlight, battery-powered radio, water, and first aid kit.

What to do during a tornado warning

When a tornado has been sighted, go to your shelter immediately.

1. In a residence or small building, move to a pre-designated shelter, such as a basement, storm cellar, or safe room or shelter."

2. If there is no basement, go to an interior room on the lower level (closets, interior hallways). Put as many walls as possible between you and the outside. Get under a sturdy table and use arms to protect head and neck. Stay there until the danger has passed.

3. Do not open windows. Use the time to seek shelter.

4. Stay away from windows, doors, and outside walls. Go to the center of the room. Stay away from corners because they attract debris.

5. In a school, nursing home, hospital, factory, or shopping center, go to predetermined shelter areas. Interior hallways on the lowest floor are usually safest. Stay away from windows and open spaces.

6. In a high-rise building, go to a small, interior room or hallway on the lowest floor possible.

7. Get out of vehicles, trailers, and mobile homes immediately and go to the lowest floor of a sturdy nearby building or a storm shelter. Mobile homes, even if tied down, offer little protection from tornadoes.

8. If caught outside with no shelter, lie flat in a nearby ditch or depression and cover your head with your hands. Be aware of potential for flooding.

9. Do not get under an overpass or bridge. You are safer in a low, flat location.

10. Never try to outrun a tornado in urban or congested areas in a car or truck; instead, leave the vehicle immediately for safe shelter. Tornadoes are erratic and move swiftly.

11. Watch out for flying debris. Flying debris from tornadoes causes most fatalities and injuries.

What to do after a tornado

1. Look out for broken glass and downed power lines.

2. Check for injuries. Do not attempt to move seriously injured persons unless they are in immediate danger of death or further injury. If you must move an unconscious person, first stabilize the neck and back, then call for help immediately.

- If the victim is not breathing, carefully position the victim for artificial respiration, clear the airway, and commence mouth-to-mouth resuscitation.
- Maintain body temperature with blankets. Be sure the victim does not become overheated.
- Never try to feed liquids to an unconscious person.

3. Use caution when entering a damaged building. Be sure that walls, ceiling, and roof are in place and that the structure rests firmly on the foundation. Wear sturdy work boots and gloves.

Wind Safe Room and Shelter

Extreme windstorms in many parts of the country pose a serious threat to buildings and their occupants.

Your residence may be built "to code," but that does not mean that it can withstand winds from extreme events like tornadoes or major hurricanes.

The purpose of a wind shelter or safe room is to provide a space where you and your household can seek refuge that provides a high level of protection. You can build a shelter in one of the several places in your home:

- In your basement
- Beneath a concrete slab-on-grade foundation or garage floor
- In an interior room on the first floor. Shelters built below ground level provide the greatest protection, but a shelter built in a first-floor interior room can also provide the necessary protection. Below-ground shelters must be designed to avoid accumulating water during the heavy rains that often accompany severe windstorms.

To protect its occupants, an in-house shelter must be built to withstand high winds and flying debris, even if the rest of the residence is severely damaged or destroyed. Therefore:

- The shelter must be adequately anchored to resist overturning and uplift.
- The walls, ceiling, and door of the shelter must withstand wind pressure and resist penetration by wind-borne objects and falling debris.
- The connections between all parts of the shelter must be strong enough to resist the wind.
- If sections of either interior or exterior residence walls are used as walls of the shelter, they must be separated from the structure of the residence, so that damage to the residence will not cause damage to the shelter.

If you are concerned about wind hazards where you live, especially if you live in high-risk areas, you should consider building a shelter. Publications are available from FEMA to assist in determining if you need a shelter and how to construct a shelter. Contact the FEMA distribution center for a copy of *Taking Shelter from the Storm* (L-233 for the brochure and FEMA-320 for the booklet with complete construction plans).

TSUNAMIS

Tsunamis (pronounced soo-ná-mees), also known as seismic sea waves (mistakenly called "tidal waves"), are a series of enormous waves created by an underwater disturbance such as an earthquake. A tsunami can move hundreds of miles per hour in the open ocean and smash into land with waves as high as one hundred feet or more, although most waves are less than eighteen feet high. From the area where the tsunami originates, waves travel outward in all directions much like the ripples caused by throwing a rock into a pond. In deep water the tsunami wave is not noticeable. Once the wave approaches the shore it builds in height. All tsunamis are potentially dangerous, even though they may not damage every coastline they strike. A tsunami can strike anywhere along most of the U.S. coastline. The most destructive tsunamis have occurred along the coasts of California, Oregon, Washington, Alaska, and Hawaii.

Tsunamis are most often generated by earthquake-induced movement of the ocean floor. Landslides, volcanic eruptions, and even meteorites can also generate tsunamis. If a major earthquake or landslide occurs close to shore, the first wave in a series could reach the beach in a few minutes, even before a warning is issued. Areas are at greater risk if less than twenty-five feet above sea level and within a mile of the shoreline. Drowning is the most common cause of death associated with a tsunami. Tsunami waves and the receding water are very destructive to structures in the run-up zone. Other hazards include flooding, contamination of drinking water, and fires from gas lines or ruptured tanks.

What to do before a tsunami

1. Know the terms used by the West Coast/Alaska Tsunami Warning Center (WC/ATWC—responsible for tsunami warnings for California, Oregon, Washington, British Columbia, and Alaska) and the Pacific Tsunami Warning Center (PTWC—responsible for tsunami warnings to international authorities, Hawaii, and the U.S. territories within the Pacific basin).

- **Advisory**—An earthquake has occurred in the Pacific basin, which might generate a tsunami. WC/ATWC and PTWC will issue hourly bulletins advising of the situation.
- **Watch**—A tsunami was or may have been generated but is at least two hours travel time to the area in watch status.
- **Warning**—A tsunami was or may have been generated, which could cause damage; therefore, people in the warned area are strongly advised to evacuate.

2. Listen to radio or television for more information and follow the instructions of your local authorities.

3. Immediate warning of tsunamis sometimes comes in the form of a noticeable recession in water away from the shoreline. This is nature's tsunami warning and it should be heeded by moving inland to higher ground immediately.

4. If you feel an earthquake in a coastal area, leave the beach or low-lying areas. Then turn on your radio to learn if there is a tsunami warning.

5. Know that a small tsunami at one beach can be a larger wave a few miles away. The topography of

the coastline and the ocean floor will influence the size of the wave.

6. A tsunami may generate more than one wave. Do not let the modest size of one wave allow you to forget how dangerous a tsunami is. The next wave may be bigger.

7. Prepare for possible evacuation. Learn evacuation routes. Determine where you would go and how you would get there if you needed to evacuate.

What to do during a tsunami

8. If you are advised to evacuate, do so immediately.

9. Stay away from the area until local authorities say it is safe. Do not be fooled into thinking that the danger is over after a single wave—a tsunami is not a single wave but a series of waves that can vary in size.

10. Do not go to the shoreline to watch for a tsunami. When you can see the wave, it is too late to escape.

What to do after a tsunami

1. Stay away from flooded and damaged areas until officials say it is safe to return.

2. Stay away from debris in the water; it may pose a safety hazard to boats and people.

VOLCANOES

A volcano is a vent through which molten rock escapes to the earth's surface. When pressure from gases within the molten rock becomes too great, an eruption occurs.

Some eruptions are relatively quiet, producing lava flows that creep across the land at two to ten miles per hour. Explosive eruptions can shoot columns of gases and rock fragments tens of miles into the atmosphere, spreading ash hundreds of miles downwind. Lateral blasts can flatten trees for miles. Hot, sometimes poisonous gases may flow down the sides of the volcano.

Lava flows are streams of molten rock that either pour from a vent quietly through lava tubes or by lava fountains. Because of their intense heat, lava flows are also great fire hazards. Lava flows destroy everything in their path, but most move slowly enough that people can move out of the way.

Fresh volcanic ash, made of pulverized rock, can be abrasive, acidic, gritty, glassy, and odorous. While not immediately dangerous to most adults, the combination of acidic gas and ash could cause lung damage to small infants, very old people, or those suffering from severe respiratory illnesses. Volcanic ash can also damage machinery, including engines and electrical equipment. Ash accumulations mixed with water become heavy and can collapse roofs.

Volcanic eruptions can be accompanied by other natural hazards: earthquakes, mudflows and flash floods, rock falls and landslides, acid rain, fire, and (under special conditions) tsunamis. Active volcanoes in the U.S. are found mainly in Hawaii, Alaska, and the Pacific Northwest.

What to do before an eruption

1. Make evacuation plans. If you live in a known volcanic hazard area, plan a route out and have a backup route in mind.

2. Develop a household disaster plan. In case household members are separated from one another during a volcanic eruption (a real possibility during the day when adults are at work and children are at school), have a plan for getting back together. Ask an out-of-town relative or friend to serve as the "household contact," because after a disaster, it's often easier to call long distance. Make sure everyone knows the name, address, and phone number of the contact person.

3. Assemble a disaster supplies kit.

4. Get a pair of goggles and a throw-away breathing mask for each member of the household in case of ashfall.

5. Do not visit an active volcano site unless officials designate a safe viewing area.

What to do during an eruption

1. If close to the volcano, evacuate immediately away from the volcano to avoid flying debris, hot gases, lateral blast, and lava flow.

2. Avoid areas downwind from the volcano to avoid volcanic ash.

3. Be aware of mudflows. The danger from a mudflow increases as you approach a stream channel and decreases as you move away from a stream channel toward higher ground. This danger increases with prolonged heavy rains. Mudflows can move faster than you can walk or run. Look upstream before crossing a bridge, and do not cross if the mudflow is approaching. Avoid river valleys and low-lying areas.

4. Stay indoors until the ash has settled unless there is danger of the roof collapsing.

5. During an ashfall, close doors, windows, and all ventilation in the house (chimney vents, furnaces, air conditioners, fans, and other vents).

6. Do not drive in heavy ashfall unless absolutely required. If you do drive in dense ashfall, keep speed down to thirty-five miles per hour or slower.

7. Remove heavy ash from flat or low-pitched roofs and rain gutters.

8. Volcanic ash is actually fine, glassy fragments and particles that can cause severe injury to breathing passages, eyes, and open wounds, and irritation to skin. Follow these precautions to keep yourself safe from ashfall:

- Wear long-sleeved shirts and long pants.
- Use goggles and wear eyeglasses instead of contact lenses.
- Use a dust mask or hold a damp cloth over your face to help breathing.
- Do not run car or truck engines. Driving can stir up volcanic ash that can clog engines and stall vehicles. Moving parts can be damaged from abrasion, including bearings, brakes, and transmissions.

What to do after the eruption

1. Stay away from ashfall areas if possible. If you are in an ashfall area, cover your mouth and nose with a mask, keep skin covered, and wear goggles to protect the eyes.

2. Clear roofs of ashfall because it can be very heavy and may cause buildings to collapse. Exercise great caution when working on a roof.

3. Do not drive through ashfall, which is easily stirred up and can clog engine air filters, causing vehicles to stall.

4. If you have a respiratory ailment, avoid contact with any amount of ash. Stay indoors until local health officials advise it is safe to go outside.

WINTER STORMS AND EXTREME COLD

Heavy snowfall and extreme cold can immobilize an entire region. Even areas that normally experience mild winters can be hit with a major snowstorm or extreme cold. The impacts include flooding, storm surges, closed highways, blocked roads, downed power lines and hypothermia.

You can protect yourself and your household from the many hazards of winter by planning ahead.

What to do before a winter storm threatens

1. Know the terms used by weather forecasters:
- **Freezing Rain**—Rain that freezes when it hits the ground, creating a coating of ice on roads, walkways, trees, and power lines.
- **Sleet**—Rain that turns to ice pellets before reaching the ground. Sleet also causes moisture on roads to freeze and become slippery.
- **Winter Storm Watch**—A winter storm is possible in your area.
- **Winter Storm Warning**—A winter storm is occurring or will soon occur in your area.
- **Blizzard Warning**—Sustained winds or frequent gusts to thirty-five miles per hour or greater and considerable amounts of falling or blowing snow (reducing visibility to less than a quarter mile) are expected to prevail for a period of three hours or longer.
- **Frost / Freeze Warning**—Below-freezing temperatures are expected.

2. Prepare to survive on your own for at least three days. Assemble a disaster supplies kit. Be sure to include winter specific items such as rock salt to melt ice on walkways, sand to improve traction, snow shovels, and other snow removal equipment. Keep a stock of food and extra drinking water.

3. Prepare for possible isolation in your home:
- Have sufficient heating fuel; regular fuel sources may be cut off.
- Have emergency heating equipment and fuel (a gas fireplace or a wood-burning stove or fireplace) so you can keep at least one room of your residence at a livable temperature. (Be sure the room is well ventilated.) If a thermostat controls your furnace and your electricity is cut off by a storm, you will need emergency heat.
- Kerosene heaters are another emergency heating option. Never use any fuel other than kerosene in a kerosene heater.

- Store a good supply of dry, seasoned wood for your fireplace or wood-burning stove.
- Keep fire extinguishers on hand and make sure your household knows how to use them.
- Never burn charcoal indoors.

4. Winterize your home to extend the life of your fuel supply.

- Insulate walls and attics.
- Caulk and weather-strip doors and windows.
- Install storm windows or cover windows with plastic.

5. Maintain several days' supply of medicines, water, and food that needs no cooking or refrigeration.

What to do during a winter storm

1. Listen to your radio, television, or NOAA Weather Radio for weather reports and emergency information.

2. Eat regularly and drink ample fluids but avoid caffeine and alcohol.

3. Dress for the season:

- Wear several layers of loose-fitting, lightweight, warm clothing rather than one layer of heavy clothing. The outer garments should be tightly woven and water-repellent.
- Mittens are warmer than gloves.
- Wear a hat; most body heat is lost through the top of the head.
- Cover your mouth with a scarf to protect your lungs.

4. Be careful when shoveling snow. Overexertion can bring on a heart attack—a major cause of death in the winter. If you must shovel snow, stretch before going outside and don't overexert yourself.

5. Watch for signs of frostbite: loss of feeling and white or pale appearance in extremities such as fingers, toes, earlobes, or the tip of the nose. If symptoms are detected, get medical help immediately.

6. Watch for signs of hypothermia: uncontrollable shivering, memory loss, disorientation, incoherence, slurred speech, drowsiness, and apparent exhaustion. If symptoms of hypothermia are detected, get the victim to a warm location, remove any wet clothing, warm the center of the body first, and give warm,

nonalcoholic beverages if the victim is conscious. Get medical help as soon as possible.

7. When at home:

- Conserve fuel if necessary by keeping your residence cooler than normal. Temporarily close off heat to some rooms.
- When using kerosene heaters, maintain ventilation to avoid buildup of toxic fumes. Refuel kerosene heaters outside and keep them at least three feet from flammable objects.

Winter Driving

About seventy percent of winter deaths related to snow and ice occur in automobiles. Consider public transportation if you must travel. If you travel by car, travel in the day, don't travel alone, and keep others informed of your schedule. Stay on main roads; avoid back-road shortcuts.

1. Winterize your car. This includes a battery check, antifreeze, wipers and windshield washer fluid, ignition system, thermostat, lights, flashing hazard lights, exhaust system, heater, brakes, defroster, oil level, and tires. Consider snow tires, snow tires with studs, or chains. Keep your car's gas tank full.

2. Carry a winter car kit of disaster supplies in the trunk of your car. The kit should include:

- Shovel
- Windshield scraper
- Battery-powered radio
- Flashlight
- Extra batteries
- Water
- Snack food
- Mittens
- Hat
- Blanket
- Tow chain or rope
- Tire chains
- Bag of road salt and sand
- Fluorescent distress flag
- Jumper/booster cables
- Road maps
- Emergency flares
- Cellular telephone or two-way radio, if available.

3. If a blizzard traps you in your car:

- Pull off the highway. Turn on hazard

lights and hang a distress flag from the radio aerial or window.

- Remain in your vehicle where rescuers are most likely to find you. Do not set out on foot unless you can see a building close by where you know you can take shelter. Be careful: distances are distorted by blowing snow. A building may seem close but be too far to walk to in deep snow.

- Run the engine and heater about ten minutes each hour to keep warm. When the engine is running, open a window slightly for ventilation. This will protect you from possible carbon monoxide poisoning. Periodically clear snow from the exhaust pipe.

- Exercise to maintain body heat but avoid overexertion. In extreme cold, use road maps, seat covers, and floor mats for insulation. Huddle with passengers and use your coat for a blanket.

- Take turns sleeping. One person should be awake at all times to look for rescue crews.

- Drink fluids to avoid dehydration.

- Be careful not to waste battery power. Balance electrical energy needs—the use of lights, heat, and radio—with supply.

- At night, turn on the inside light so work crews or rescuers can see you.

- If stranded in a remote area, stomp large block letters in an open area spelling out HELP or SOS and line with rocks or tree limbs to attract the attention of rescue personnel who may be surveying the area by airplane.

- Once the blizzard passes, you may need to leave the car and proceed on foot.

PREPARING FOR TERRORISM

The following information is courtesy of the U.S. Department of Homeland Security. You can find out what the department is doing to keep America safe, as well as access additional information at their Website, http://www.ready.gov.

BIOLOGICAL THREAT

Overview: A biological attack is the deliberate release of germs or other biological substances that can make you sick. Many agents must be inhaled, enter through a cut in the skin, or be eaten to make you sick. Some biological agents, such as anthrax, do not cause contagious diseases. Others, like the smallpox virus, can result in diseases you can catch from other people.

If There Is a Biological Threat

Unlike an explosion, a biological attack may or may not be immediately obvious. While it is possible that you will see signs of a biological attack, as was sometimes the case with the anthrax mailings of 2000, it is perhaps more likely that local health-care workers will report a pattern of unusual illness, or there will be a wave of sick people seeking emergency medical attention. You will probably learn of the danger through an emergency radio or TV broadcast or some other signal used in your community. You might get a telephone call or emergency response workers may come to your door.

In the event of a biological attack, public health officials may not immediately be able to provide information on what you should do. It will take time to determine exactly what the illness is, how it should be treated, and who is in danger. However, you should watch TV, listen to the radio, or check the Internet for official news, including the following:

- Are you in the group or area authorities consider to be in danger?
- What are the signs and symptoms of the disease?
- Are medications or vaccines being distributed?
- Where? Who should get them?
- Where should you seek emergency medical care if you become sick?

During A Declared Biological Emergency:

1. If a family member becomes sick, it is important to be suspicious.

2. Do not assume, however, that you should go to a hospital emergency room, or that any illness is the result of the biological attack. Symptoms of many common illnesses may overlap.

3. Use common sense, practice good hygiene and cleanliness to avoid spreading germs, and seek medical advice.

4. Consider if you are in the group or area authorities believe to be in danger.

5. If your symptoms match those described and you are in the group considered at risk, immediately seek emergency medical attention.

If You Are Potentially Exposed:

1. Follow instructions of doctors and other public health officials.

2. If the disease is contagious, expect to receive medical evaluation and treatment. You may be advised to stay away from others, or even deliberately quarantined.

3. For noncontagious diseases, expect to receive medical evaluation and treatment.

If You Become Aware of an Unusual or Suspicious Substance Nearby:

1. Quickly get away.

2. Protect yourself. Be prepared to improvise with what you have on hand to protect your mouth, nose, eyes, and cuts in your skin. Cover your mouth and nose with layers of fabric that can filter the air but still allow breathing. Examples include two to three layers of cotton, such as a T-shirt, handkerchief, or towel. Otherwise, several layers of tissue or paper towels may help. Any dense-weave cotton fabric can help filter contaminants in an emergency. It is very important that most of the air you breathe comes through the mask or cloth, not around it. Do whatever you can to make the best fit possible for children. There are also a variety of face masks readily available in hardware stores that are rated based on how small a particle they can filter in an industrial setting. Simple cloth facemasks can filter some of the airborne junk or germs you might breathe into your body but will probably not protect you from chemical gases. Still, something over your mouth and nose in an emergency is better than nothing.

3. Wash with soap and water.

4. Contact authorities.

5. Watch TV, listen to the radio, or check the Internet for official news and information, including what the signs and symptoms of the disease are, if medications or vaccinations are being distributed, and where you should seek medical attention if you become sick. While antibiotics are often an appropriate treatment for the diseases associated with biological weapons, the specific drug must match the illness to be effective. One antibiotic, for example, may be appropriate for treating anthrax exposure but inappropriate for treating smallpox. All antibiotics can cause side effects, including serious reactions. Plan to speak with your health care provider in advance about what makes sense for your family.

6. If you become sick, seek emergency medical attention. At the time of a declared biological emergency, if a family member becomes sick, it is important to be suspicious. Do not automatically assume, however, that you should go to an emergency room or that any illness is the result of the biological attack. Symptoms of many common illnesses may overlap. Use common sense, practice good hygiene and cleanliness to avoid spreading germs, and seek medical advice.

CHEMICAL THREAT

A chemical attack is the deliberate release of a toxic gas, liquid, or solid that can poison people and the environment.

Possible Signs of Chemical Threat

- Many people suffering from watery eyes, twitching, choking, having trouble breathing, or losing coordination.
- Many sick or dead birds, fish, or small animals are also cause for suspicion.

If You See Signs of Chemical Attack: Find Clean Air Quickly

- Quickly try to define the impacted area or where the chemical is coming from, if possible.
- Take immediate action to get away.
- If the chemical is inside a building where you are, get out of the building without passing through the contaminated area, if possible.
- If you can't get out of the building or find clean air without passing through the area where you see signs of a chemical attack, it may be better to move as far away as possible and shelter in place.
- If you are outside, quickly decide on the fastest way to find clean air. Consider if you can get out of the area or if you should go inside the closest building and shelter-in-place.

If You Think You Have Been Exposed to a Chemical

If your eyes are watering, your skin is stinging, and you are having trouble breathing, you may have been exposed to a chemical.

- If you think you may have been exposed to a chemical, strip immediately and wash.
- Look for a hose, fountain, or any source of water, and wash with soap if possible, being sure not to scrub the chemical into your skin.
- Seek emergency medical attention.

EXPLOSIONS

If There Is an Explosion

- Take shelter behind your desk or a sturdy table.
- Exit the building ASAP.
- Do not use elevators.
- Check for fire and other hazards.
- Take your emergency supply kit if time allows.

If There Is a Fire

- Exit the building ASAP.
- Crawl low if there is smoke.
- Use a wet cloth, if possible, to cover your nose and mouth.
- Use the back of your hand to feel the upper, lower, and middle parts of closed doors.
- If the door is not hot, brace yourself against it and open slowly.
- If the door is hot, do not open it. Look for another way out.
- Do not use elevators.
- If you catch fire, do not run. Stop, drop, and roll to put out the fire.
- If you are at home, go to a previously designated meeting place.
- Account for your family members and carefully supervise small children.
- Never go back into a burning building.

If You Are Trapped in Debris

- If possible, use a flashlight to signal your location to rescuers.
- Avoid unnecessary movement so that you don't kick up dust.
- Cover your nose and mouth with anything you have on hand. (Dense-weave cotton fabric can act as a good filter. Try to breathe through the fabric.)
- Tap on a pipe or wall so that rescuers can hear where you are.
- If possible, use a whistle to signal rescuers.
- Shout only as a last resort. Shouting can cause a person to inhale dangerous amounts of dust.

NUCLEAR BLAST

A nuclear blast is an explosion with intense light and heat, a damaging pressure wave, and widespread radioactive material that can contaminate the air, water, and ground surfaces for miles around. During a nuclear incident, it is important to avoid radioactive material, if possible. While experts may predict at this time that a nuclear attack is less likely than other types, terrorism by its nature is unpredictable.

If There Is a Nuclear Blast: If There Is Advanced Warning of an Attack

Take cover immediately, as far below ground as possible, though any shield or shelter will help protect you from the immediate effects of the blast and the pressure wave.

If There Is No Warning

1. Quickly assess the situation.

2. Consider if you can get out of the area, or if it would be better to go inside a building to limit the amount of radioactive material you are exposed to.

3. If you take shelter, go as far belowground as possible, close windows and doors and turn off air conditioners, heaters, or other ventilation systems. Stay where you are, watch TV, listen to the radio, or check the Internet for official news as it becomes available.

4. To limit the amount of radiation you are exposed to, think about *shielding, distance,* and *time*:

- **Shielding:** If you have a thick shield between yourself and the radioactive materials, more of the radiation will be absorbed by the shield, and you will be exposed to less.
- **Distance:** The farther away you are from the blast and the fallout, the lower your exposure.
- **Time:** Minimizing time spent exposed will also reduce your risk.

Use available information to assess the situation. If there is a significant radiation threat, health-care authorities may or may not advise you to take potassium iodide. Potassium iodide is the same stuff added to your table salt to make it iodized. It may or may not protect your thyroid gland, which is particularly vulnerable, from radioactive iodine exposure. Consider keeping potassium iodide in your emergency kit and learn what the appropriate doses are for each of your family members. Plan to speak with your health care provider in advance about what makes sense for your family.

Radiation Threat

A radiation threat, commonly referred to as a dirty bomb or radiological dispersion device (RDD), is the use of common explosives to spread radioactive materials over a targeted area. It is not a nuclear blast. The force of the explosion and radioactive contamination will be more localized. While the blast will be immediately obvious, the presence of radiation will not be clearly defined until trained personnel with specialized equipment are on the scene. As with any radiation, you want to try to limit exposure. It is important to avoid breathing radiological dust that may be released in the air.

If There Is a Radiation Threat or Dirty Bomb

1. If you are outside and there is an explosion, or if authorities warn of a radiation release nearby, cover your nose and mouth and quickly go inside a building that has not been damaged. If you are already inside, check to see if your building has been damaged. If your building is stable, stay where you are.

Close windows and doors; turn off air conditioners, heaters, or other ventilation systems.

2. If you are inside and there is an explosion near where you are, or you are warned of a radiation release inside, cover your nose and mouth and go outside immediately. Look for a building or other shelter that has not been damaged and quickly get inside.

Once you are inside, close windows and doors; turn off air conditioners, heaters, or other ventilation systems.

3. If you think you have been exposed to radiation, take off your clothes and wash as soon as possible.

4. Stay where you are, watch TV, listen to the radio, or check the Internet for official news as it becomes available.

5. Remember: To limit the amount of radiation you are exposed to, think about *shielding, distance,* and *time.*

- **Shielding:** If you have a thick shield between yourself and the radioactive materials more of the radiation will be absorbed by the shield, and you will be exposed to less.
- **Distance:** The farther away you are away from the blast and the fallout, the lower your exposure.
- **Time:** Minimizing time spent exposed will also reduce your risk.

As with any emergency, local authorities may not be able to immediately provide information on what is happening and what you should do. However, you should watch TV, listen to the radio, or check the Internet often for official news and information as it becomes available.

SHELTERING IN PLACE

Sheltering in place is when you make a shelter out of the place you are in. In case of terrorist activities, leaving your area might take too long or put you in harm's way. In such cases, it's safer to stay indoors than to go outside.

PREPARING TO SHELTER IN PLACE

Choose a room in your house, apartment, or business to use as a shelter. The best room would be a room with as few windows and doors as possible. A large room with a water supply is best, something like a master bedroom that is connected to a bathroom. For a chemical attack, this room should be as high in the building as possible to avoid vapors (gases) that sink. This is different than the sheltering techniques for severe storms, when the shelter should be low in the home.

Have the following items on hand (ideally in the shelter room, to save time):

- Food and bottled water: a gallon of water per person in plastic bottles, as well as ready-to-eat foods that will keep without refrigeration. If bottled water isn't available at the time, the water in a toilet tank (not the bowl) is suitable for drinking.
- First aid kit.
- Flashlight, battery-powered radio, and extra batteries for both.
- Duct tape and scissors.
- Towels and plastic sheeting.
- A working telephone.

HOW WILL I KNOW IF I NEED TO SHELTER IN PLACE?

You will hear from the local police, emergency coordinators, or government officials on the radio and television if you need to take shelter. In case of a severe or code red terror alert, listen to the radio or television to know right away if a shelter-in-place alert is announced for your area. If you are away from your home when a chemical event occurs, follow the instructions of emergency coordinators to find the nearest shelter. If your children are at school, they will be sheltered there. Unless you are specifically instructed to do so, do not try to get to the school to bring your children home.

WHAT DO I DO?

If a shelter-at-home alert is announced, act quickly and follow the instructions of your local emergency coordinators. Every situation can be different and local emergency coordinators might have special instructions for you to follow. In general, do the following:

- Get inside as quickly as possible.
- If there is time, shut and lock all outside doors and windows. Locking them may provide a tighter seal against chemicals. Turn off the air conditioner or heater and all fans. Close the fireplace damper and any other place that air can come in from the outside.
- Go into the shelter-in-place room and shut the door. Take pets with you, if possible.

- Tape plastic over any windows in the room. Use duct tape around the windows and doors, and make an unbroken seal. Use the tape over any vents into the room and seal any electrical outlets or other openings. Sinks and toilet drain traps should have water in them, which acts as a seal. (You can use the sink and toilet as you normally would.) Push a wet towel up against the door and the floor to seal it. If it is necessary to drink water, drink your stored water, not water from the tap.

- Turn on the radio. Keep a telephone close at hand but don't use it unless there is a serious emergency. (This keeps the phone lines open for police and emergency personnel use.)

Sheltering this way will keep you safer than if you are outdoors. Most likely, you will not be in your shelter for more than a few hours. Listen to your radios for announcements indicating that it is safe to leave your shelters. For more information, contact your state and local health departments, or the Centers for Disease Control.

IMPORTANT PAPERS TO INCLUDE IN YOUR 72-HOUR EMERGENCY KIT

Keep the originals in a safe place. Make three copies of each. Give one copy each to two different people in other parts of the state or country. Keep one copy in your 72-hour emergency kit.

1. Legal
   a. Marriage certificate
   b. Birth certificate
   c. Vehicle registration/title
2. Will
   a. Power of attorney
   b. Guardianship
   c. Property value
   d. Personal property
3. Financial
   a. Income for both spouses
   b. Assets
   c. Stocks/bonds
4. Insurance
   a. Life: agent and policy number
   b. Auto: agent and policy number
   c. Home: agent and policy number
   d. Medical: agent and policy number
5. Immunizations
   a. Records
   b. Medicine
6. Monthly expenses
   a. Budget
   b. Bills
   c. Outstanding debts
7. Tax returns
   a. Last four years
8. Bank deposits
   a. Safe-deposit box information
   b. Checking
   c. Savings
9. Records
   a. Diplomas
   b. Military
   c. School certificates
10. Important miscellaneous
    a. Recent pictures of children
    b. Fingerprints of children

This information was compiled by the Salt Lake County Fire Department of Emergency Services, 440 South 300 East, Salt Lake City, Utah 84111. (You might not want all of this in your evacuation kit. Decide what is most important to have access to should your information at home be inaccessible, and put only those in your kit. See chapter 43 for suggestions.)

INDEX

G

H

I

J

K

L

M

N

ABOUT THE AUTHOR

Best-selling author Barbara Salsbury, a nationally recognized personal preparedness expert, is one of America's leading authorities on self-reliance. For more than twenty-five years, she has been teaching, researching, and developing practical preparedness solutions based on experience and in-depth research.

She has been an emergency preparedness consultant for several cities, including San Francisco. Currently she is a personal preparedness consultant for the city of Sandy, Utah.

Barbara is the author of two national newsletters and the producer of three videos. Her eight books include *Just in Case, Just Add Water, Beating the High Cost of Eating,* and *It's Time to Plan, Not Panic.*

She has lectured extensively and conducted many workshops and seminars for civic, professional, and church groups, including Education Week at Brigham Young University. She has had several weekly TV programs on consumer affairs courses and has been a regular on a national cable television program as a consumer specialist. She is a veteran of the national television and radio talk show circuit.

Barbara is active in church and community. She and her husband, Larry, live in Sandy, Utah. They have two children and seven grandchildren.